The American Discovery of Ancient Egypt

The American

Discovery of Ancient Egypt

Nancy Thomas

With essays by

Gerry D. Scott, III
Bruce G. Trigger

LOS ANGELES COUNTY MUSEUM OF ART
AMERICAN RESEARCH CENTER IN EGYPT
Distributed by HARRY N. ABRAMS, INC., PUBLISHERS

Published by the
Los Angeles County Museum of Art
5905 Wilshire Boulevard
Los Angeles, California 90036

Distributed worldwide by
Harry N. Abrams, Inc.
100 Fifth Avenue
New York, New York 10011

Library of Congress Catalog Card Number:
95-078317

ISBN: 0-8109-6312-4 (cloth)
ISBN: 0-87587-174-7 (paper)

*Printed in Hong Kong through
Global Interprint*

This book was published in conjunction
with the exhibition *The American Discovery
of Ancient Egypt*.

Exhibition Itinerary

LOS ANGELES COUNTY MUSEUM OF ART
November 5, 1995–January 21, 1996

THE SAINT LOUIS ART MUSEUM
February 29–May 27, 1996

THE INDIANAPOLIS MUSEUM OF ART
July 13–September 29, 1996

This exhibition was co-organized by the
Los Angeles County Museum of Art and the
American Research Center in Egypt.
Exclusive sponsorship for this exhibition has
been provided through a generous grant from
The May Department Stores Company and
its Robinsons-May division in Los Angeles,
its Famous-Barr and Lord & Taylor divisions
in St. Louis, and its L.S. Ayres stores in
Indianapolis. Additional funds were provided
by Gily AG, the National Endowment for
the Arts, and the National Endowment
for the Humanities.

COVER: Photograph by A. Bougault,
c. 1910; courtesy Stephen White

TITLE PAGE: W. S. Webb (holding flag) and
friends at Giza, April 26, 1899

ABOVE: Giza Plateau, with the Sphinx in
the foreground and the pyramid of Menkaure
in the background; BELOW: Cat. no. 36;
RIGHT: Cat. no. 27

Contents

Forewords

Writing in 1923, Egyptologist Arthur C. Mace of the Metropolitan Museum of Art expressed bewilderment (and more than a hint of amusement) at the public and media attention then being focused on the unearthing of the intact tomb of Tutankhamun by British archaeologists:

Lord Carnarvon's and Howard Carter's discovery of the tomb of Tutankhamun has aroused an interest, not merely in this particular find, but in archaeology generally, that to the excavator is almost embarrassing. Ordinarily he spends his time quietly and unobtrusively enough, half the year burrowing mole-like in the ground, and the other half writing dull papers for scientific journals, and suddenly he finds himself in the full glare of the limelight, with newspaper reporters lying in wait for him at every corner, and snapshotters recording his every movement. . . . Whence has the ordinary every-day citizen derived this sudden enthusiasm for the funeral furniture of a long-dead Pharaoh?

Earlier this year ancient Egypt was once again front-page news, following the discovery of the tomb of the sons of Ramesses II—possibly the largest and most elaborate tomb ever found in Egypt—by American excavators in the famed Valley of the Kings. Clearly popular interest in ancient Egypt and its artifacts remains strong, yet few members of the public are aware of the contributions that American scholars, often working "quietly and unobtrusively," have made throughout this century to our knowledge of this complex culture.

To highlight these accomplishments, *The American Discovery of Ancient Egypt* lucidly interweaves the activities of American Egyptologists with the lengthy chronology of Egyptian cultural development. Viewers will see the development of Egyptian art over four millennia: the abstract figurines of the Predynastic Period; sturdy monuments of the Old Kingdom "pyramid builders"; dramatic sculpture and artifacts of the great monarchs of the New Kingdom, including those of the female pharaoh Hatshepsut; and Roman and Ptolemaic period objects that reveal an overlay of Eastern Mediterranean culture. American Egyptologists also studied Egypt's southern neighbor, the culturally rich area of Nubia (modern Sudan), and made exceptional contributions to the understanding of this region. For the first time in an exhibition of Egyptian art, monuments from Nubia will be shown in a parallel manner.

The preeminent figures of American Egyptology—James Henry Breasted, George A. Reisner, and Herbert E. Winlock—along with less-heralded individuals such as Dows Dunham and Clarence S. Fisher, quickly emerge from these pages and from the exhibition. The abundant holdings of excavated Egyptian objects in American museums, outstanding examples of which are represented in this exhibition, are the result of expeditions conducted by the first and second generation of Egyptologists, active in this country from the turn of the century to 1960. And, as exemplified by the dramatic discovery of the Ramesside royal tomb, American work in Egypt continues. Many of the current projects reflect a new emphasis on the preservation of ancient cultures through the salvage of sites threatened by modern encroachment, the utilization of multidisciplinary archaeology, and site maintenance and conservation. Recent American projects in Egypt are listed at the end of this catalogue and are discussed more fully in ten essays in a companion volume.

The Los Angeles County Museum of Art is very pleased to present *The American Discovery of Ancient Egypt*, which was organized by Nancy Thomas, the museum's curator of ancient and Islamic art. She was assisted by cocurator Gerry D. Scott, III, of the San Antonio Museum of Art, David O'Connor of New York University, and Peter Lacovara of the Museum of Fine Arts, Boston. Although the museum has selections from its Egyptian collection on permanent display in the galleries, the present exhibition marks our first major showing of ancient Egyptian art since *The Treasures of Tutankhamun* was seen in Los Angeles in 1978–79. As the success of that exhibition proved, there is keen interest in ancient Egypt in our community, and *The American Discovery of Ancient Egypt* provides an unparalleled opportunity to retrace the history of this sophisticated civilization through objects from the finest and most comprehensive American collections.

We are grateful to the institutions that so generously lent these objects. We also extend our gratitude to the co-organizer of this exhibition, the American Research Center in Egypt, represented by Executive Director Terence Walz, and to the members of the Supreme Council of Antiquities of Egypt, who continue to make American fieldwork in Egypt possible. On behalf of the directors of the museums participating with us in this exhibition, James Burke of the Saint Louis Art Museum and Bret Waller of the Indianapolis Museum of Art, I thank our staffs and supporters who have helped bring this project to fruition.

WILLIAM A. MINGST
President, Board of Trustees, Los Angeles County Museum of Art

he fascination exerted by ancient Egypt starts at an early age for Americans. We all have a memory of the first stirrings of awe. Was it the vastness of the pyramids and their perfect shape, the mysteriously preserved mummies, the strange and wonderful system of writing, or the annual inundation symbolizing nature's renewal of life? And, shortly thereafter, the first trip to the museum and the beginning of an undeclared but lasting pact with the Egyptian people and their extraordinarily lively and interesting civilization. Books, cinema, and trips to Egypt—for those lucky enough to take them—merely confirm those childhood discoveries. By understanding Egypt, we come to comprehend the mysteries of evolving civilizations, including our own.

American institutions have played an important role in our "discovery" of ancient Egypt, yet Americans visiting their national museums or Egypt itself are not always aware of it. How many travelers, when gazing dumbfoundedly at the great pyramids of Giza, realize that an American archaeologist helped shape the world's understanding of their history? Of those who know of Queen Hatshepsut, the Egyptian monarch who took power in ancient Thebes, how many associate the work carried out at her great funerary complex with American scholars? The organizing of *The American Discovery of Ancient Egypt* grew out of a desire to underline those contributions and to make specific the achievement of American scholars in extending popular appreciation of the glories of ancient Egypt.

In this catalogue you will read much about the work of great institutions such as the Brooklyn Museum, the Metropolitan Museum of Art, the Oriental Institute of the University of Chicago, the University of Pennsylvania Museum of Archaeology and Anthropology, and the Museum of Fine Arts, Boston. We are immensely indebted to them all for making this exhibition possible. Many smaller institutions have shared in the discovery of ancient Egypt, and their special contributions are mentioned in the pages of the catalogue as well. This exhibition and catalogue are, in fact, a remarkable collective effort, and it is because the American Research Center in Egypt (ARCE) acts as a facilitator of research and excavation in Egypt that we are a co-organizer.

Exhibition-goers and catalogue readers will learn a great deal about two outstanding American figures in ancient Egyptian studies, James Henry Breasted and George A. Reisner, the former closely associated with the University of Chicago, and the latter affiliated first with the University of California, Berkeley, and later with Boston's Museum of Fine Arts and Harvard University. Their long years of endeavor changed the face of American archaeology in Egypt. Many other eminent scholars made substantial contributions to Egyptology, and one of the joys of bringing this exhibition together is to pay tribute to their accomplishments.

The American Discovery of Ancient Egypt is a collaborative effort by museum professionals and leading university scholars and directors of excavations. The idea was originally suggested by Bruce Ludwig, a member of the ARCE board of governors and a supporter of the Los Angeles County Museum of Art. The project was embraced warmheartedly by the curators of Egyptian art also sitting on the ARCE board, who since have extended unstinting help to exhibition organizer Nancy Thomas, curator of ancient and Islamic art at the Los Angeles County Museum of Art. She has been ably assisted by Gerry D. Scott, III, curator of ancient art at the San Antonio Museum of Art; David O'Connor, now at the Institute of Fine Arts, New York University, and formerly of the University of Pennsylvania Museum of Archaeology and Anthropology; and Peter Lacovara of the Museum of Fine Arts, Boston. In 1992 ARCE sponsored a symposium in New York on the theme of the exhibition, thanks to a grant from the National Endowment for the Humanities. We gratefully acknowledge the generous support received from The May Department Stores Company, Gily AG, the National Endowment for the Arts, and the National Endowment for the Humanities, and we extend our profound gratitude to lenders of objects on display in the exhibition.

The American Discovery of Ancient Egypt occurs at a remarkable moment in the history of the American Research Center in Egypt. For years the outpost of archaeological and academic research by Americans in Egypt, ARCE has recently begun to play a new and vital role in the conservation of Egyptian antiquities, thanks to a major grant from the Agency for International Development and the generosity of the American people. Once before, ARCE was involved in an international conservation effort in Egypt, the Nubian Salvage Campaign of the 1960s. Today the remarkable monuments of the world's oldest civilization confront steady environmental degradation due to a deadly combination of factors. Recognizing that the monuments are part of the world's cultural heritage, the United States and other nations are providing Egyptians with assistance in their ongoing conservation and preservation efforts.

Last, but by no means least, mention must be made of the welcome and help extended unstintingly by the government and peoples of Egypt, without whose cooperation American institutions could not work in Egypt; the Supreme Council of Antiquities and its chairman, Adel Halim Nour ed-Din; and the diplomatic representatives of Egypt in the United States.

Do enjoy this unique cultural experience, and take pride in the scholarly cooperation between our peoples and our countries.

TERENCE WALZ
Executive Director, American Research Center in Egypt

America "discovered" ancient Egypt through the outstanding achievements of its first and second generation of Egyptologists, renowned scholars such as James Henry Breasted, George A. Reisner, Harold H. Nelson, Herbert E. Winlock, Charles E. Wilbour, and John A. Wilson. They have been followed in more recent times by scholars and researchers whose enormous contributions have equaled and in some cases surpassed those of other non-Egyptian pioneers of Egyptology.

More than forty American museums, universities, institutions, and societies have participated in this effort. They include, among others, the American Research Center in Egypt, the Oriental Institute of the University of Chicago, and the University of Pennsylvania Museum of Archaeology and Anthropology. Each is participating in special ways in scientific research and field activities along the Nile Valley, in the Egyptian deserts, and in Upper and Lower Nubia. At the same time scores of museums all over America exhibit artifacts from Egypt, arrange exhibitions and symposia, send archaeological missions to Egypt, and engage in Egyptological research. Among them one can single out the Brooklyn Museum, the Metropolitan Museum of Art, and the Museum of Fine Arts, Boston.

Americans are covering all varieties of activities in their discovery of Egypt: excavations, epigraphic work, documentation, mapping, restoration, and conservation. They are bringing to this endeavor modern technology and nondestructive scientific applications. They are also sponsoring research, educational programs, scholarly publications, conferences, academic meetings, and exhibitions that focus on the specific contributions made by Egypt. Many North American institutes have undertaken interesting and useful Egyptological projects—one thinks of the University of Toronto's Akhenaten Temple Project and the work of the Getty Conservation Institute at the tomb of Nefertari. Finally, America has participated in the rescue of the great Nubian monuments at Abu Simbel, Philae, and other sites by offering financial, scientific, and archaeological aid.

I am sure that the American discovery of ancient Egypt will continue, and I hope too for the success of this interesting exhibition.

GAMAL MOKHTAR
First Undersecretary of State, Egyptian Ministry of Culture
Former Chairman, Egyptian Antiquities Organization

Chronology of Ancient Egypt

Predynastic Period

6100–2920 B.C.

Badarian (6100–3800 B.C.)

Naqada I, Amratian (3800–3600 B.C.)

Naqada II, Early Gerzean (3600–3400 B.C.)

Naqada III, Late Gerzean (3400–3100 B.C.)

Dynasty 0, Late Predynastic (3100–2920 B.C.)

The Predynastic cultures of ancient Egypt (so called because they preceded the establishment of the united ancient Egyptian state under a series of monarchs who are grouped into successive dynasties) were essentially prehistoric in the strict sense that they left no written records of their achievements. Nevertheless archaeologists have discovered that these cultures, the most important of which are called Naqada I, II, and III (formerly Amratian, Early Gerzean, and Late Gerzean), witnessed the emergence of village life in the Nile Valley. This period was marked by the development of social stratification and the domestication of plants and animals, which created a settled, agrarian mode of life. As the Predynastic Period advanced, there was increased specialization of labor, and rulers, craftsmen, and religious practitioners were allowed to perform their particular functions while being sustained by the agricultural bounty produced through the labor of others. A class system eventually emerged in the early Egyptian state, with a hierarchy of god-kings, officials, priests, scribes, craftsmen, soldiers, and peasants. Burial practices indicate that the inhabitants of the Nile Valley already maintained a belief in an afterlife in which the needs and occupations of the deceased were similar to those of the living. Grave goods, seemingly in keeping with the deceased's social and economic station, were interred with the corpse.

Early Dynastic Period

2920–2649 B.C.

1st Dynasty (2920–2770 B.C.)

2d Dynasty (2770–2649 B.C.)

Around 3000 B.C. a series of energetic warrior kings consolidated their hold on Upper (southern) Egypt and extended their domination into Lower (northern) Egypt. The victorious monarchs seem to have utilized the Nile as a unifying feature of the traditional "two lands" of Upper and Lower

Mud-brick funerary enclosure of King Khasekhemwy of the 2d Dynasty, north Abydos.

11

Old Kingdom private tombs at Giza, with the pyramid of King Khafre in the distance.

Egypt. The river served as an avenue of communication, commerce, and transportation as well as an agricultural resource whose bounty could be greatly enhanced through effective state-sponsored irrigation. Although the sacred city of Abydos remained the royal burial spot (eventually becoming the legendary resting place of the god of the resurrection, Osiris), the great necropolis at Saqqara was developed during this period to serve the inhabitants of the newly established capital, Memphis (near modern Cairo). It is probable that the Egyptians practiced a form of mass burial upon the death of the earliest kings, but this soon passed into obsolescence. Those who served the royal court directly, however, continued to favor an eventual burial near the monarch they had attended in life. During this period of cultural experimentation, Egyptian religious, artistic, and cultural norms became fixed along broad lines. Despite apparent internal warfare near the close of the period, the Egyptian centralized state remained strong.

Old Kingdom

2649–2134 B.C.

3d Dynasty (2649–2575 B.C.)

4th Dynasty (2575–2465 B.C.)

5th Dynasty (2465–2323 B.C.)

6th Dynasty (2323–2150 B.C.)

7th–8th Dynasty (2150–2134 B.C.)

The Old Kingdom produced two of the most important monuments to have survived from ancient Egypt, the Great Pyramid and the Sphinx. This period saw the first great flowering of the civilization of ancient Egypt and the emergence of sophisticated architecture, distinctive visual art, and an incipient literature. The forms of artistic expression developed during the Old Kingdom became the "classical" ideal that guided later phases of ancient Egyptian cultural history. Kings were generally buried in pyramid-shaped tombs, and the mastaba tombs of the royal court and dependents were grouped around the pyramid complex to form a necropolis, or "city of the dead." The solar god Re gained ascendancy, and Osiris, associated with death and the afterlife, began to attain increased importance toward the end of the period. The era closed with the collapse of the centralized state, probably the result of a combination of circumstances, including disastrous climate patterns, decreased royal revenues, and a weakened monarchy.

First Intermediate Period

2134–2040 B.C.

9th–10th Dynasty (2134–2040 B.C.)

Preunification 11th Dynasty (2134–2040 B.C.)

When the Old Kingdom succumbed, the unified state drifted apart. Regional governors assumed nearly autonomous powers within their districts, and internecine warfare, presumably over diminished resources, proliferated. Eventually two major alliances emerged, one based in the north, at Herakleopolis (9th–10th Dynasty), and the other centered in the south, at Thebes (11th Dynasty).

Middle Kingdom

2040–1640 B.C.

Postunification 11th Dynasty (2040–1991 B.C.)

12th Dynasty (1991–1783 B.C.)

13th Dynasty (1783–1640 B.C.)

14th Dynasty (partially contemporaneous
with 13th Dynasty, ending c. 1640 B.C.)

The south seems to have provided the initial impetus to reunite Egypt and establish the period of stability now termed the Middle Kingdom. Some scholars, however, have detected a possible revisionist or apologist tone in literary texts produced at this time, which may suggest that the Herakleopolitans played a more important role than was once believed. In any event the 11th Dynasty king Nebhepetre Mentuhotep must have secured a substantial victory that allowed him to claim the kingship of Upper and Lower Egypt, and he left as his monument a funerary temple at Deir el-Bahri, whose scant remains are still impressive. After the reign of two subsequent kings the 11th Dynasty was succeeded by the 12th, whose first king, Amenemhat I, established a northern capital of a united Egypt at a city he named Itjtawy, "seizer of the two lands," not far from the Old Kingdom capital of Memphis. The period produced some of the most memorable compositions in the surviving corpus of ancient Egyptian literature, and the ancient Egyptians themselves maintained the style of language then in use as the classical form of written communication for the rest of their history. The period is also notable for its foreign relations and for Egyptian colonial expansion into Nubia. The Middle Kingdom ended with a series of ephemeral kings, who may have lost the loyalty of their retainers.

Mortuary temples of Nebhepetre Mentuhotep II, founder of the Middle Kingdom (left), and Hatshepsut, the 18th Dynasty pharaoh (right), at Deir el-Bahri, c. 1912.

Second Intermediate Period

1640–1532 B.C.

15th–16th Dynasty, Hyksos (1640–1532 B.C.)

17th Dynasty, Theban (1640–1550 B.C.)

Like the First Intermediate Period, the Second Intermediate Period was a time of internal discord and strife. Moreover, a new element was present—foreign intervention—with a massive incursion of invaders from western Asia in the north and a considerable Nubian presence in the south. Dynasties of major and minor west Asian kings (the Hyksos) claimed the monarchy, but this was contested by the rulers of Thebes, who maintained a small, independent state in the south.

Colossal statuary of Ramesses II at Luxor Temple.

New Kingdom

1550–1070 B.C.

18th Dynasty, Tuthmoside (1550–1307 B.C.)

19th Dynasty, 1st Ramesside (1307–1196 B.C.)

20th Dynasty, 2d Ramesside (1196–1070 B.C.)

Third Intermediate Period

1070–664 B.C.

21st Dynasty, Tanite (1070–945 B.C.)

22d–23d Dynasty, Bubastite (945–712 B.C.)

24th Dynasty, pre-Saite (724–712 B.C.)

25th Dynasty, Kushite (712–664 B.C.)

Late Period

664–332 B.C.

26th Dynasty, Saite (664–525 B.C.)

27th Dynasty, Persian (525–404 B.C.)

28th Dynasty (404–399 B.C.)

29th Dynasty (399–380 B.C.)

30th Dynasty (380–343 B.C.)

31st Dynasty, Persian (343–332 B.C.)

Throughout the New Kingdom, Egypt carried the bitter memory of foreign domination. The warrior pharaohs of the illustrious 18th Dynasty decided that the best defense against foreign domination lay in an effective offense, and they campaigned actively against their enemies both to the east and to the south. Eventually their military campaigns created the world's first imperial state. Egyptian hegemony stretched from the Tigris and Euphrates Rivers in Mesopotamia to the fourth cataract of the Nile in Nubia. The New Kingdom is notable not only for its military exploits but also for its sophisticated art and literature. During this period some of ancient Egypt's greatest monarchs held sway, and the land enjoyed a prosperity unequaled in previous generations. Still the country was weakened by King Akhenaten's temporary religious reforms, dynastic squabbles, and a migration of a group known as the Sea Peoples, and the New Kingdom's authority diminished amid economic decline, rampant tomb robbing, workmen's strikes, and external threats. Before its close, however, the era had seen the reigns of the female ruler Hatshepsut; the conqueror Tuthmosis III; the iconoclast Akhenaten; Tutankhamun, whose funerary treasure has captured the modern imagination; and Ramesses II, Percy Bysshe Shelley's Ozymandias.

As had happened in the past, Egypt split apart along the old lines of north and south, Upper and Lower Egypt, at the close of the New Kingdom. At first a rather weak dynasty of kings controlled Lower Egypt, while a priestly dynasty held sway over Upper Egypt from Thebes. The period ultimately witnessed Egypt's domination by foreign powers, initially a series of Libyan kings, then a Nubian dynasty, which, after a century of rule, was overthrown by invading Assyrian armies bent on sacking the land of Egypt.

The final flowering of ancient Egyptian civilization occurred in the Late Period, under the last native Egyptian dynasties. The Saite monarchs seem to have come to the kingship with an active desire to restore Egypt's former grandeur, and to some extent they succeeded. Certainly the arts flourished during their tenure. The dynasty also witnessed the establishment of a Greek trading colony at Naukratis and increased Hellenic influence, which would become more pervasive. The Saite dynasty fell to the Persians, who incorporated Egypt into their vast empire on two occasions, interrupted by a time of native rule. The second Persian domination sent the last native pharaoh of Egypt, Nectanebo II, into exile, but the Persian Empire, which then stretched from Egypt to India, soon fell to Alexander the Great.

Ptolemaic Period

332–30 B.C.

Conquest of Alexander the Great (332 B.C.)

Macedonian dynasty (332–304 B.C.)

Ptolemaic dynasty (304–30 B.C.)

In 332 B.C. Alexander the Great was crowned pharaoh, and prior to leaving Egypt that year, he overhauled the land's internal administration, reorganized the army, and founded a new city, Alexandria, which still bears his name. He died suddenly in 323 B.C., and his successor, Philip III Arrhidaeus, dispatched the general Ptolemy Lagus to serve as governor of Egypt, now an important province of the Macedonian Empire. When that vast empire began to dissolve into smaller states ruled by Alexander's other principal generals, Ptolemy Lagus consolidated his hold over Egypt and proclaimed himself king in 304 B.C. The dynasty he founded, the Ptolemaic, flourished until 30 B.C., when the last, and certainly the best known, of the line, Cleopatra VII, committed suicide with her lover Marc

The Ptolemaic and Roman period temple at Kom Ombo.

Antony. Under Ptolemaic rule Greek influence on ancient Egyptian life greatly increased, but the Ptolemies were also careful to observe native Egyptian traditions and to preserve Egyptian institutions. The art of the period shows limited influence from the Hellenistic world, perhaps because of the intrinsically religious nature of ancient Egyptian art and the respectful conservatism shown by the Ptolemies in matters of Egyptian religious practice.

Roman Period

30 B.C.–A.D. 395

Roman conquest (30 B.C.)

Roman emperors (30 B.C.–A.D. 395)

With the defeat of Antony and Cleopatra by Octavian at the battle of Actium in 30 B.C., Egypt became part of the Roman Empire as the personal estate of the emperor. As a result, Egypt also became an integral part of the greater Mediterranean world and was even more influenced by Hellenistic culture and taste. Although a degree of ancient pharaonic tradition survived during the first three centuries of Roman rule, most of the art produced during this period bears little resemblance to that of Dynastic Egypt. Rather, its subject matter was drawn primarily from the classical tradition. When the Roman Empire was later divided into two administrative segments, east and west, Egypt fell to the eastern empire, later known as Byzantium. The era saw the establishment of Christianity as the state religion, which it remained until Egypt was conquered in A.D. 641 by the Arabs, who were largely successful in converting the inhabitants to Islam.

Chronology of Ancient Nubia

Prehistoric Nubia

6000–3100 B.C.

The occupants of northern Nubia in prehistoric times were nomadic cattle herders. A more sophisticated culture, termed Khartoum Mesolithic, developed in settlements in the south. This culture created the earliest known ceramics in North Africa. The later Khartoum Neolithic culture (5000–3100 B.C.) began producing human figurines, slate palettes, and black-topped red pottery.

A-Group

3100–2800 B.C.

At the beginning of the historic period (c. 3100 B.C.), the Nubian state was centered in Lower (northern) Nubia. Rich grave goods of the A-Group culture rivaled comparable burials in Egypt and included gold jewelry, carefully crafted ceramics, and stone vessels. The Egyptians conquered the A-Group and ruled Lower Nubia as a colony, while Nubian lands south of the third cataract remained independent. Although the term *B-Group* was assigned to a successive phase of Nubian culture, cultural remains from the B-Group may not be distinctive enough from those of the A-Group and C-Group to warrant this designation.

The northern boundary of Nubia, marked by the first cataract of the Nile, south of Aswan.

C-Group

2250–1500 B.C.

Remains of this culture are centered in Lower Nubia. Flourishing during a period roughly paralleling the Egyptian Middle Kingdom (2040–1640 B.C.) and Second Intermediate Period (1640–1532 B.C.), C-Group Nubians traded and maintained friendly relations with their Egyptian neighbors. The C-Group culture is characterized by cattle raising, agriculture, and the production of fine artistic pottery.

Pan-Grave Culture

2200–1700 B.C.

The Pan-Grave culture existed about the same time as the C-Group culture. Named for its shallow, round graves, which somewhat resemble frying pans, this culture may have originated from the nomadic tribes of the desert east of the Nile.

Remains of the western section of the mud-brick temple complex known as the Lower Defuffa, Kerma.

Kerma Culture
2000–1500 B.C.

Based in Upper Nubia, south of the third cataract of the Nile, and roughly contemporaneous with the emergence of the C-Group culture in Lower Nubia, the Kerma culture flourished at a time when the power of Egypt was declining and the influence of the Nubian kingdom of Kush was expanding. It is known as the Kerma culture because the remains of its capital lie within the modern Sudanese town of Kerma. Royal burials from this period reveal the wealth and complexity of the culture, with royal individuals interred on inlaid beds, adorned with gold jewelry, accompanied by animal and sometimes human sacrifices, and buried beneath high mounds of earth.

Napatan Period
Kingdom of Kush, c. 750–270 B.C.

Egypt again became weak as the power of the Kushite kings increased. Around 712 B.C. Piye conquered Egypt and became king of both Egypt and Nubia, initiating the 25th Dynasty. Napatan cultural traditions reflect the strong influence of Egyptian customs, with royal tombs bearing superstructures with steep stone pyramids and containing Egyptian-influenced funerary equipment, such as canopic jars and multiple tomb figurines (shawabtis). This period of rule lasted about sixty years, ending when the Assyrians invaded Egypt in about 660 B.C., driving the Kushite kings back into the heartland of Nubia.

Royal Pyramid at Gebel Barkal, the primary religious center of Nubia during the Napatan period.

Meroitic Period
Kingdom of Kush, c. 270 B.C.–A.D. 350

By about 270 B.C. the kingdom of Kush had moved even farther south, to the area between the fifth and sixth cataracts of the Nile, with its capital at Meroe. The Meroitic kings continued to be buried in pyramid tombs and to build temples to Nubian and Egyptian gods in a hybrid Egyptian-Roman-African style. Grave goods, particularly ceramics and jewelry, represent this cross-fertilization and include many objects imported from the Mediterranean world. Meroe slowly declined during the third century A.D., and local traditions died out entirely with the active introduction of Christianity by missionaries during the sixth century A.D.

Relief of the royal funerary chapel and pyramid N20 in the southern cemetery at Meroe.

17

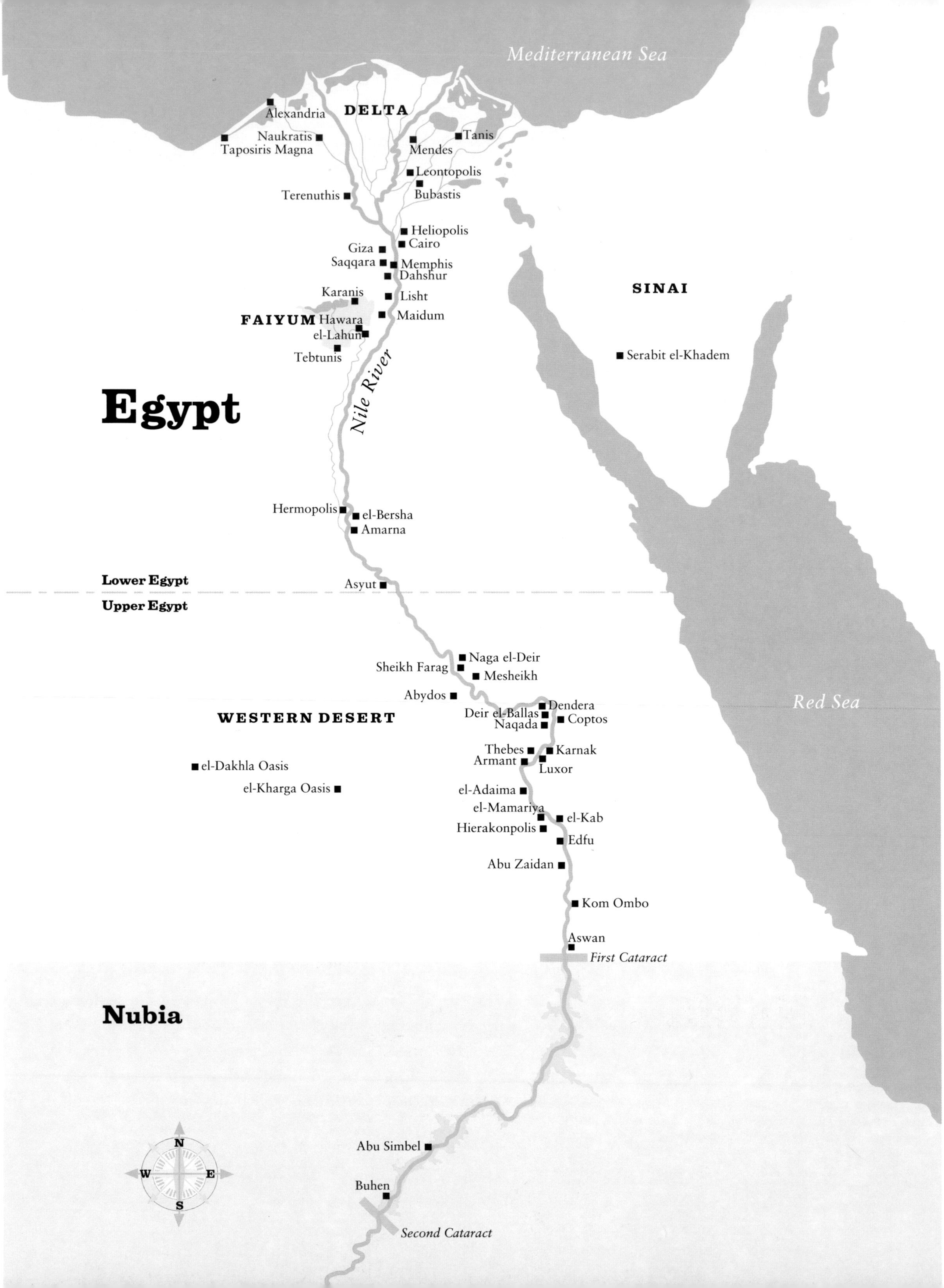

Egypt

Mediterranean Sea

DELTA

Alexandria
Naukratis
Taposiris Magna
Tanis
Mendes
Leontopolis
Terenuthis
Bubastis

Heliopolis
Cairo
Giza
Saqqara
Memphis
Dahshur
Karanis
Lisht
FAIYUM
Hawara
el-Lahun
Maidum
Tebtunis

SINAI

Serabit el-Khadem

Nile River

Hermopolis
el-Bersha
Amarna

Lower Egypt

Asyut

Upper Egypt

Naga el-Deir
Sheikh Farag
Mesheikh
Abydos

WESTERN DESERT

Deir el-Ballas
Dendera
Naqada
Coptos

Thebes
Karnak
Armant
Luxor

el-Dakhla Oasis

el-Kharga Oasis

el-Adaima
el-Mamariya
el-Kab
Hierakonpolis
Edfu

Abu Zaidan

Red Sea

Kom Ombo

Aswan
First Cataract

Nubia

N
W E
S

Abu Simbel

Buhen

Second Cataract

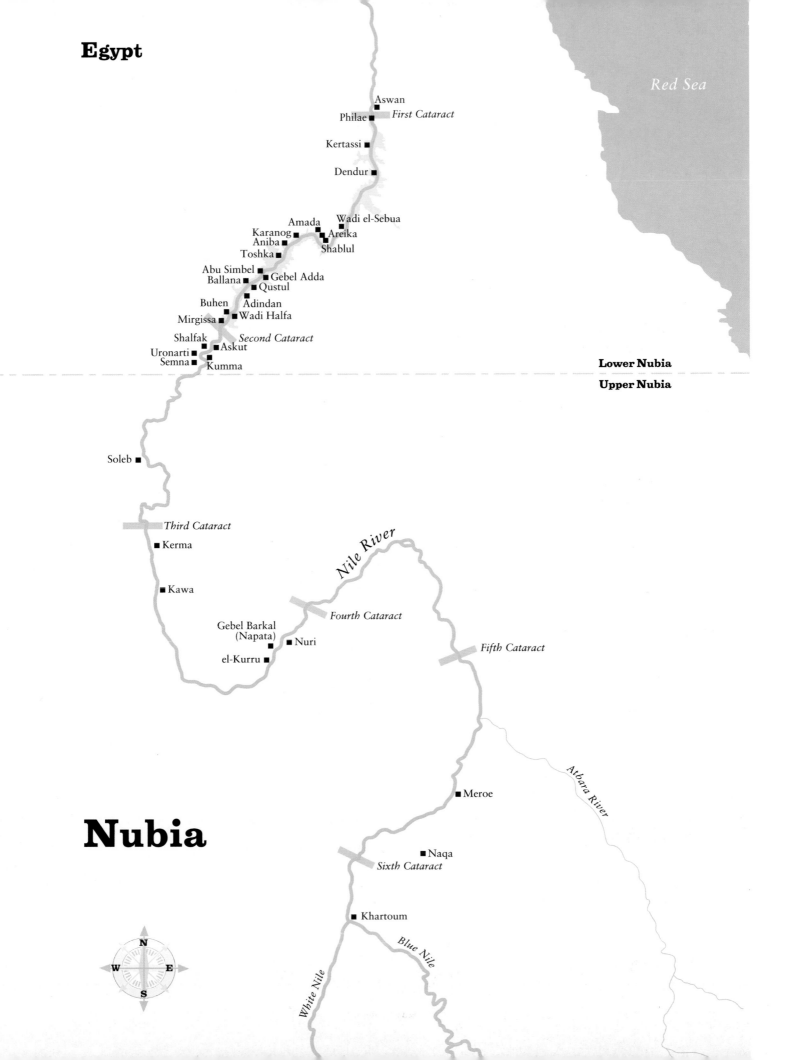

Egypt

Red Sea

Aswan
Philae ■   First Cataract
Kertassi ■
Dendur ■

Wadi el-Sebua
Amada ■
Karanog ■   Areika ■
Aniba ■   Shablul
Toshka ■
Abu Simbel ■
Ballana ■   Gebel Adda ■
            Qustul ■
Buhen ■   Adindan ■
Mirgissa ■   Wadi Halfa ■
Shalfak ■   Second Cataract
Uronarti ■   Askut ■
Semna ■
        Kumma ■

Lower Nubia

Upper Nubia

Soleb ■

Third Cataract
Kerma ■

Kawa ■

Gebel Barkal
(Napata) ■   Nuri ■
el-Kurru ■

Nile River

Fourth Cataract

Fifth Cataract

Atbara River

Meroe ■

Nubia

■ Naqa

Sixth Cataract

■ Khartoum

White Nile   *Blue Nile*

N
W   E
S

Egyptology, Ancient Egypt, and the American Imagination

Bruce G. Trigger

The study of ancient civilizations does not proceed in a purely empirical and objective fashion. The questions scholars ask and the answers they are predisposed to accept are influenced to a considerable degree by the beliefs that guide their daily lives.[1] Yet, while John Wilson has published an admirable narrative history of American Egyptology,[2] there has been no examination of how popular conceptions about Egypt's ancient civilization have shaped Egyptological scholarship and, in turn, have been affected by it.[3]

As a preliminary step toward filling this need, I will survey some of the popular concepts that have molded the study of ancient Egypt in the United States during the past two hundred years and will examine how increasing scientific knowledge has influenced the public's perception of ancient Egypt. I will consider, in order of their origin, various concepts about ancient Egypt that were formulated at different periods and lasted for varying lengths of time. Some of these views replaced older ones, while others have persisted, often in debased forms, to the present.[4]

Primordial Visions

An extraordinary fascination with ancient Egypt was evident in both the popular culture and the intellectual life of the United States at least a century before there were any professional Egyptologists. The number of travel books on Egypt published in the United States, amounting to more than thirty volumes, steadily increased between 1800 and 1830.[5] At the same time American travelers were bringing home Egyptian mummies and artifacts. A mummy was on display in the Library Society of Charleston, South Carolina, already in the late eighteenth century, and by the 1820s others could be seen in the Massachusetts General Hospital in Boston and Peale's Museum and Gallery of Fine Art in Baltimore. Ships' captains were donating Egyptian artifacts to the East India Marine Society in Salem, Massachusetts, as early as 1803, and twenty years later Lieutenant Thomas Tanner presented the

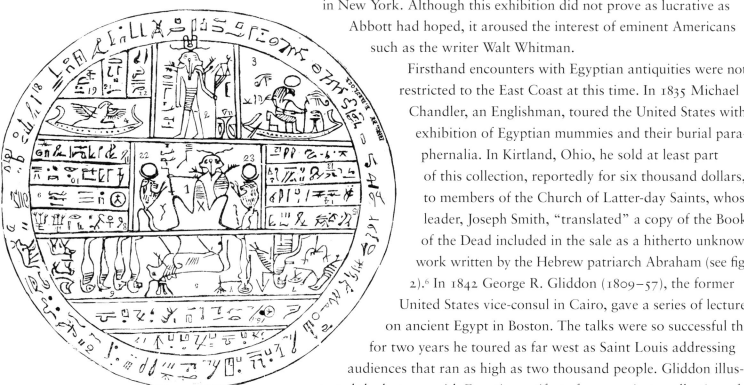

museum with a collection of objects he had purchased from the Italian excavator Giovanni Belzoni (1778–1823). In 1853 and 1854 Henry Abbott (1812–59), a British physician who had practiced in Cairo, exhibited his large collection of Egyptian antiquities, including a mummified bull, at the Stuyvesant Institute in New York. Although this exhibition did not prove as lucrative as Abbott had hoped, it aroused the interest of eminent Americans such as the writer Walt Whitman.

Firsthand encounters with Egyptian antiquities were not restricted to the East Coast at this time. In 1835 Michael Chandler, an Englishman, toured the United States with an exhibition of Egyptian mummies and their burial para- phernalia. In Kirtland, Ohio, he sold at least part of this collection, reportedly for six thousand dollars, to members of the Church of Latter-day Saints, whose leader, Joseph Smith, "translated" a copy of the Book of the Dead included in the sale as a hitherto unknown work written by the Hebrew patriarch Abraham (see fig. 2).[6] In 1842 George R. Gliddon (1809–57), the former United States vice-consul in Cairo, gave a series of lectures on ancient Egypt in Boston. The talks were so successful that for two years he toured as far west as Saint Louis addressing audiences that ran as high as two thousand people. Gliddon illus- trated the lectures with Egyptian artifacts from a private collection of 680 objects that Colonel Mendes Cohen (c. 1790–1847), a resident of Baltimore, had brought back to America in 1835. Gliddon's pamphlet *Ancient Egypt* (1843) sold more than twenty-four thousand copies.[7]

Nor was a more scholarly interest in ancient Egypt lacking at this time. In the first year of its existence, 1802, the American Academy of the Arts in New York elected Napoleon Bonaparte and Dominique-Vivant Denon as hon- orary members in recognition of their efforts to promote the scientific study of Egypt. An abridged translation of Denon's *Voyage dans la basse et haute Egypte* (Travels in Lower and Upper Egypt) was published in the United States in 1803, and more complete translations were available before 1810. By 1823 the *North American Review* was publishing articles describing archaeological research in Egypt, and in 1829 it printed the first of a number of discussions relating to Jean-François Champollion's decipherment of ancient Egyptian. The *American Quarterly Review* devoted more than forty pages to a study of ancient Egyptian architecture that year, and in 1848 Louisa Caroline Tuthill published an even longer treatment of this subject in her pioneering *History of Architecture*.[8]

Ancient Egypt was clearly not unknown or lacking in interest to Americans in the early nineteenth century.

At least four sets of ideas that were already of considerable antiquity shaped Americans' perceptions of ancient Egypt at this time. First and foremost, ancient Egypt was known to most Americans through the Bible, and to more educated ones also through the writings of ancient Greek and Roman authors such as Herodotus, Diodorus Siculus, and Strabo. Many Americans of the period knew their Bibles so well that the lands and peoples they described were a living presence, and biblical patriarchs and prophets provided models for their daily actions. Ancient Egypt was part of this familiar world, but rather peripheral. In biblical accounts Palestine, not Egypt, was the focus of world history. Whether Egypt was portrayed as a welcome refuge from famine or a realm of oppression and misery for the Hebrews, it was always a place where God worked out relations with his chosen people, and the Egyptians were merely instruments of his will. Scarcely any pharaoh is mentioned by name in the Bible, and none emerges as more than a stereotyped figure. This distanced view was reinforced by Greek and Roman writers who portrayed Egypt as an alien and exotic land, much as Western European visitors did India in the eighteenth and nineteenth centuries.

While the stereotypes of ancient Egypt that were established in the Judeo-Christian tradition were mixed, the predominant picture, derived from the Book of Exodus, was negative. Egypt was portrayed as a land of slavery, tyranny, and oppression. It was a pagan and idolatrous civilization, a view strongly reinforced by classical writers' descriptions of Egyptian cults, including some that had become popular in Rome. The story of Potiphar's wife, who tried unsuccessfully to seduce Joseph, also suggested that ancient Egypt had been a sexually promiscuous society. Roman propaganda directed against Cleopatra VII supported this notion by portraying this skillful politician as a femme fatale. To the many Americans who closely read their Bibles, ancient Egypt was a civilization of awesome power and exotic splendor but also the antithesis of what was judged godly in the Judeo-Christian tradition.

This image has persisted to the present, although intimate familiarity with the Bible has declined since the nineteenth century. In the 1950s and early 1960s old stereotypes were recycled in mammoth Hollywood spectacles such as *The Egyptian* (1954), *Land of the Pharaohs* (1955), *The Ten Commandments* (1956; see fig. 1), and *Cleopatra* (1963; see fig. 3).[9] *The Ten Commandments*, which explicitly contrasted Egyptian tyranny and Hebrew love of freedom, resonated powerfully with the cold-war rhetoric and Arab-Israeli conflicts of the late 1950s. These films reworked ancient Judeo-Christian images of Egypt to appeal to the prejudices of a more secular society.

Ancient Egypt was long believed to have been a source of wisdom and occult knowledge, an assumption based primarily on a statement in the New Testament Book of Acts that in his youth the Hebrew prophet Moses had been "instructed in all the wisdom of the Egyptians" (7:22). This claim seemed to be corroborated by the assertions of Greek scholars, most notably Plato, that they, or the Greeks as a whole, had derived much of their philosophical knowledge from the Egyptians.

The notion of Egypt as a primordial source of arcane wisdom was further reinforced in the fifteenth century by the rediscovery of Horapollon's *Hieroglyphica*, written in the fifth century A.D., which suggested that the ancient Egyptians had expressed their wisdom emblematically in their writing. The same century saw the rediscovery of a series of Neoplatonic treatises attributed to Hermes Trismegistos, the Egyptian god Thoth. These Hermetic writings led various Renaissance scholars to speculate that, long prior to Moses, the Egyptians had possessed a pristine revelation of divine wisdom, much of which later was forgotten by the Hebrews and the Greeks and Romans. Hermetic thinking included a belief in divine power animating the natural world, the interconnectedness of everything, the presence of the All in even the smallest created thing, and the pervasiveness of irrational and unseen forces throughout the universe. Hermeticism therefore had a close affinity with alchemy, magic, and symbolism. Hermetic speculations were treated indulgently during the Renaissance, when Pope Alexander VI claimed descent from the Egyptian god Osiris, but during the Counter-Reformation hardening attitudes led to the execution in 1600 of the Italian mystic Giordano Bruno, partly for claiming that Egyptian religious concepts were older and therefore less corrupted than Christian ones.[10]

The great antiquity of the Hermetic texts was definitively refuted in 1614 by Isaac Casaubon, who demonstrated linguistically that they could not antedate the Christian era. Yet the idea of the lost wisdom of the ancient Egyptians continued to be championed during the seventeenth century by the Jesuit priest Athanasius Kircher. In the claim that all modern ideas had been anticipated or surpassed by those of the ancient Egyptians, he saw, while carefully remaining within the bounds of Catholic orthodoxy, a means to combat the spread of mechanistic philosophy and modern science, both of which he believed were major threats to Christianity.[11]

Hermetic concepts became part of the European intellectual underground through their adoption by Rosicrucian and Freemasonic circles. In this way the idea of Egypt as a source of ancient wisdom continued to exert considerable influence into the early nineteenth century. John Irwin has demonstrated the considerable degree to which major American writers such as Ralph Waldo Emerson, Herman Melville, Edgar Allan Poe, Henry David Thoreau, and Walt Whitman construed the material world and fortuitous happenings in it as a hieroglyphic text expressing God's will.[12] "Hieroglyphic Bibles," in which religious concepts were expressed emblematically, were among the most popular children's books in America at the beginning of the nineteenth century.[13]

One of the most entertaining secular expressions of the concept of ancient Egyptian wisdom is Poe's famous short story "Some Words with a Mummy," published in 1845. In this work a condescending Egyptian mummy, restored to life by electrical shocks, refutes all of his American interlocutors' claims of modern-day superiority by demonstrating the preeminence of the government, religion, and scientific knowledge of the ancient Egyptians. An Egyptologist present at this seance, a Mr. Gliddon, deciphers the mummy's name as Allamistakeo. This sobriquet seems to embody Poe's own attitude toward Champollion's decipherment, which had exploded the idea, cherished by romantics, that hieroglyphs were emblems. In 1850 George Gliddon actually presided at the unwrapping of a mummy, whose sex he erroneously identified on the basis of the name on its coffin.[14]

Among the more recent artistic reflections of the theme of Egypt as a source of arcane wisdom is Karl Freund's much-underrated 1933 movie *The Mummy* and Norman Mailer's novel *Ancient Evenings* (1983). In both works secret knowledge, which in the case of *The Mummy* was derived from the Book of Thoth, is used to defy death itself.

In addition to being renowned for their wisdom, the ancient Egyptians were celebrated in the early American republic for their skill as builders. Their massive construction works featured prominently in the biblical account of their oppression of the Hebrews, and Greek and Roman authors recorded admiring descriptions of major Egyptian tombs and temples. Even before the Napoleonic invasion of Egypt

in 1798, the pyramids at Giza were renowned as the most massive structures erected in human history.

On the basis of this acclaim it was widely speculated that the Hebrews might have acquired their architectural skills from the Egyptians. The idea that Solomon's temple had been constructed using such knowledge provided the Freemasons, who claimed that their order had been founded by the builders of the temple, with another, emotionally powerful link to ancient Egypt.[15] In the late eighteenth century Freemasonry was actively promoting the Enlightenment ideals of liberalism and human brotherhood, and many of the founders of the American republic, including Benjamin Franklin, Thomas Jefferson, and George Washington, were members of the order. An unfinished Egyptian pyramid, capped by the All-seeing Eye, was incorporated into the Great Seal of the United States, approved by Congress in 1782 (see fig. 4).[16] In this fashion ancient Egypt was symbolically linked to the wisdom of the Enlightenment, which in turn had played a role in shaping the new government of the United States.

During the Renaissance Egyptian elements that had been incorporated into the Roman architectural tradition, such as sphinxes, obelisks, and pyramids, once again became part of architecture's vernacular. A growing number of Egyptian motifs were included in the rococo decoration of the eighteenth century. Toward the end of that century French architects such as Etienne-Louis Boullée and Antoine-Chrysostôme Quatremère de Quincy began to draw inspiration from Egyptian architectural forms, which they praised for their simplicity and geometrical purity as well as for their grandiose, solemn, and sublime (awe-inspiring) qualities.[17]

More specific efforts to base architectural designs on Egyptian models followed the publication of the archaeological findings of the Napoleonic expedition to Egypt in Denon's *Voyage* and later in the *Description de l'Egypte* (Description of Egypt, 1809–28). In the early nineteenth century the United States became the center of Egyptian revival architecture, its most successful exponent being the Philadelphia architect John Haviland (see fig. 5).[18] Egyptian revival, which, like the Gothic style, went through a horizontal phase followed by a perpendicular one, was used to design public structures such as courthouses, prisons, churches, synagogues, libraries, medical colleges, cemetery gates, reservoirs, railway stations, and suspension bridges (see figs. 6–8). These buildings were admired for their solemnity, strength, and economy of construction. Unlike those of their ancient prototypes, the walls of such buildings were left plain, which reduced construction costs. Richard Carrott has suggested that this solid and venerable style also endowed new technologies not entirely accepted by the public, such as waterworks and railways, with an aura of reliability.[19]

While Egyptian revival architecture never became as popular as Greek, Roman, or Gothic revival, it was recognized in the United States as a significant style. Nevertheless, sectarians objected to its use in religious contexts. Even though the Christian motto "The Dead Shall Be Raised" was boldly carved across the top of the Egyptian Gate of the Grove Street Cemetery in New Haven, Connecticut (fig. 8), it and similar structures were criticized for being modeled on pagan prototypes. Egyptian revival architecture succumbed in the 1860s as part of a general decline of romanticism in art and literature.

Egyptian mummies were also perceived to be the products of a valiant, if misguided, struggle to arrest human decay. In the early nineteenth century the impression of ancient Egyptian changelessness acquired an important new dimension as a result of scientific study. Naturalists who had accompanied Napoleon's expedition to Egypt had sent back to France a large number of mummified animals

FIGURE 9
James Henry Breasted
and family at the
Amada temple during
the Nubian expedition
of 1906.

as well as samples of ancient cereals recovered from tombs. These proved to be identical to modern forms. French biologists ethnocentrically suggested that a providential "Nature" must have inspired the ancient Egyptians to embalm "with so much care the brutes which were the object of their stupid adoration" as a means of ensuring that important scientific knowledge would be preserved for modern scholars.[20]

In a like manner the Philadelphia physician Samuel Morton (1799–1851) utilized a collection of ancient Egyptian skulls supplied by Gliddon, as well as ancient Egyptian representations of themselves and of neighboring peoples, to argue that human races had not altered physically since close to the time of creation, around 4000 B.C. The Alabama physician Josiah Nott (1804–73) and Gliddon used this evidence to popularize the theory of polygenesis, which claimed that the various human races had been created independently of one another and in essentially their modern form, within the framework of a biblical chronology.[21] Just as in the seventeenth century Kircher had employed ancient Egyptian data to oppose a new confidence in scientific and technological progress, so individuals in the nineteenth century relied on evidence from ancient Egypt to oppose a growing interest in biological evolution. Ancient Egypt was seen not only as a civilization that had opposed change but also as a source of ideas that could be used to fight doctrines of change in the natural sciences.

Egyptology in America

Philanthropists and municipal governments founded public museums across the United States in the middle and late nineteenth century as they sought to emulate European cultural achievements. Egyptian artifacts were highly prized parts of such collections, and curatorial positions in major museums facilitated the professional development of Egyptology. Museums initially depended on donations from private collectors, but by the end of the nineteenth century many institutions were making financial contributions to excavations carried out by two British organizations, the Egypt Exploration Fund and W. M. Flinders Petrie's British School of Archaeology. In return they received a share of each season's finds. Eventually American individuals and institutions started to conduct major excavations in Egypt. Among the pioneers were Phoebe Apperson Hearst (1842–1919), who in 1899 began financing the University of California expeditions to Egypt, and the Rhode Island businessman Theodore Munroe Davis (1837–1915), who between 1903 and 1912 sponsored a series of highly successful excavations in the Valley of the Kings.[22]

Egyptology became a university discipline in the United States with the arrival of James Henry Breasted (1865–1935) at the University of Chicago in 1895. In 1905 he began a systematic study of ancient Egyptian inscriptions in the Sudan (see fig. 9), and in 1924, at sites such as Medinet Habu and Karnak, he initiated the Epigraphic Survey, which has since set an international standard for copying ancient Egyptian reliefs and inscriptions. In 1899 George Andrew Reisner (1867–1942), who was appointed professor of Egyptology at Harvard University in 1914, began a long series of archaeological excavations in Egypt and the Sudan. Characterized by an exacting methodology, Reisner's work set standards for fieldwork in Egypt which have been surpassed only in recent times.[23] Although both Breasted and Reisner were born in the Midwest, they were trained in Germany; hence it is not surprising that they, and other German-trained Egyptologists, introduced to American Egyptology the humanistic ideals that guided research in German universities.

The German research tradition, inspired by the eighteenth-century philosopher Johann Herder, was committed to interpreting human behavior as a reflection of cultural patterns, which were considered to be expressions of the unique spiritual values of different human groups. Such an approach emphasized the need to determine what individual cultures meant to those whose lives were governed by them. Like their German counterparts, American Egyptologists tended to stress philological studies, which were seen as essential for understanding civilizations on their own terms, and art history, which was regarded as the best means for comprehending each civilization's spiritual qualities. Both approaches were believed to require special skills that could be acquired only through prolonged training. Despite Adolf Erman's *Ägypten und ägyptisches Leben in Altertum* (*Life in Ancient Egypt*, 1885), far less attention was paid to understanding daily life in ancient Egypt. This work, it was believed, could be accomplished without specialized training.

American professional Egyptologists were eager to escape from their longstanding connections with biblical studies and to make Egyptology an independent discipline. This became possible as funding was obtained that did not rely directly on public interest in the Bible. It was also facilitated by the development of a more critical approach to biblical studies, as exemplified by the work of the German scholar Julius Wellenhausen in the 1880s. Yet it was difficult to alter public expectations. Breasted's writings were never more popular than when he portrayed Akhenaten as a Christian, and more specifically as a Protestant, before his time, and when he suggested historical connections between New Kingdom and Old Testament wisdom literature. Egyptian archaeology also remained largely the study of temples and tombs, reinforcing the popular image of the ancient Egyptians as preoccupied with theology and death.

Yet the intellectual milieu in which professional American Egyptology developed was very different from the romanticism that had prevailed in the early nineteenth century. The idea that civilizations were fully formed at their beginning and thereafter had remained essentially static had been replaced by an evolutionary view of human history. This approach had begun with the Enlightenment in the eighteenth century but was given a powerful new impetus following the publication of Charles Darwin's *Origin of Species* in 1859 and the triumph of evolutionary biology.[24] As long as it did not openly criticize religious beliefs, cultural evolutionism was popular in America, a nation that took pride in being a leader in technological and social progress.

Champollion's decipherment of ancient Egyptian, which exploded the belief that ancient Egyptian writings were a repository of lost wisdom, also prepared the way for the adoption of an evolutionary perspective in Egyptology.[25] Although many prominent American writers refused to abandon the idea that hieroglyphs were emblems, Champollion's decipherment was generally welcomed by American scholars as a major contribution to knowledge.[26] Beginning in the early 1830s, these scholars were prepared to view Egypt as a civilization that was earlier, and therefore in many respects less developed, than those of ancient Greece and Rome.

As Egyptian archaeology and historical records became better understood, it became evident that change and development had occurred throughout the course of ancient Egyptian history. This was especially so after archaeologists early in the twentieth century learned more about the Predynastic and Early Dynastic Periods. The principal American contribution to an evolutionary approach in Egyptology was Breasted's *Development of Religion and Thought in Ancient Egypt* (1912), which traced the growth of religious and philosophical concepts from prehistoric times to the Late Period. In Breasted's view this involved a transition from primitive totemism to something closely approaching monotheism. Other important evolutionary studies included Reisner's *The Development of the Egyptian Tomb down to the Accession of Cheops* (1936).

FIGURE 10
Herbert E. Winlock's
excavation of the temple
of Nebhepetre Men-
tuhotep, Deir el-Bahri,
1922.

Despite their acceptance of an evolutionary perspective, most Egyptologists found little use for a comparative anthropological approach as a basis for understanding ancient Egyptian civilization. They were inhibited from doing so by their conviction, derived from traditional German humanism, that the ancient Egyptians had played a unique and major role in the development of Western civilization. They continued to believe that, even if the Egyptian way of life had differed strikingly from their own in many respects, all human beings possessed a similar nature. Thus they remained convinced that they could understand ancient Egyptian behavior using common sense alone. These ideas were not seriously disturbed by Henri Frankfort's efforts, in the 1940s, to analyze Egyptian patterns of thought as examples of a radically different, nonmodern form of "mythopoeic" or "primitive" reasoning, as defined by the French philosopher Lucien Lévy-Bruhl.[27]

Qualified evolutionism has provided the framework within which American Egyptology continues to operate. Its dominant interests and major contributions have been in the areas of philology, art history, and, to a lesser extent, political history. Although Herbert E. Winlock (1884–1950; see fig. 10) of the Metropolitan Museum of Art exhibited a marked interest in studying everyday life in ancient Egypt, much less attention has been paid to social and economic history and to the ecological concerns that have dominated anthropological archaeology since the 1960s. Most studies of ancient Egyptian ecology have been undertaken by geographers and anthropologists.[28]

In recent years the greatest external challenge to Egyptology has come from the theory, originally proposed in the mid-1950s by the Senegalese physicist Cheikh Anta Diop, that ancient Egypt constituted the first black civilization.[29] Diop's diffusionist views, which were formulated prior to the substantial development of Iron Age archaeology in sub-Saharan Africa, seriously underestimated the cultural creativity characteristic of life in all parts of Africa throughout the continent's history.

Yet his ideas have helped to expose lingering racial biases that attributed the development of Egyptian civilization to ideas and peoples supposedly from the north and counteracted claims concerning the alleged "inertia" of Egypt's original African inhabitants. Viewing ancient Egypt as an African nation has made it of interest to a wider spectrum of Americans than ever before.

While the white racist rhetoric that permeated most early twentieth-century writings about the development of Egyptian civilization has long been abandoned, ideas formulated at the time have continued to influence thinking about the origins and nature of Egyptian civilization and the role it has played throughout history.[30] Prior to the development of modern racism in Europe in the nineteenth century, scholars had been willing to entertain classical speculations that Egyptian civilization might have arisen in the Sudan.[31] By the early twentieth century, as a result of growing racial prejudice, Egyptologists were not inclined to consider the possibility that Egyptian civilization might have evolved without major stimuli from the north.

Modern claims that ancient Egypt was a black civilization are no farther from the mark than the older belief, embodied in H. M. Herget's 1941 paintings in *National Geographic Magazine*, that ancient Egyptians were a light-colored, not even very suntanned, people.[32] Herget's paintings, which were reinforced by Hollywood movies of the 1950s, shaped an entire generation's perceptions of ancient Egypt.

The Current Situation

Where does Egyptology stand in relation to American society today? As a result of mass tourism, books, and educational television, the average American probably knows more about ancient Egypt and about Egyptological research than at any time in the past. Many bizarre ideas about ancient Egypt, such as the belief that its culture was derived from an even more advanced earlier civilization and that the pyramids were built using a more advanced technology than any known today, continue to attract followers. Lucrative fads, based on the belief in pyramid power and in the efficacy of various amulets, are being actively promoted. Yet, on the whole, the gap between the public view and the Egyptological understanding of ancient Egypt appears to be narrowing. The closing of this gap is one of the main benefits to Egyptology of high educational levels, increasing leisure, and growing attention from mass media in the United States.

At the same time the technological gap between ancient Egypt and the modern world is widening rapidly. If Ramesses II, like Allamistakeo, had been able to return to life any time before 1850, he might have been intrigued by technological innovations, such as windmills, and perhaps troubled by many of the political and religious changes that had taken place since the thirteenth century B.C., but he would have encountered very little that his experience of life in ancient Egypt would not have equipped him to understand. Exposure to today's world, however, with its electricity, automobiles, airplanes, telephones, electronic media, and modern architecture, probably would convince him that he had awakened in some realm of the gods rather than on earth. The world has been so altered by technological change in the past 150 years that the basic concepts that have guided human understanding for millennia would no longer suffice.

The gap that we imagine opening for Ramesses II has in reality opened in the other direction for Egyptologists. The pyramids at Giza may remain the most massive structures in the world, but in recent years they have been dwarfed, physically and psychologically, by the modern city of Cairo, whose daily functioning is a marvel of technology and individual resourcefulness that far outstrips anything of which the ancient Egyptians were capable. It is, moreover, a creation that has as its very essence change rather than stability. This gap between modern expectations and ancient realities was initially signaled in the 1950s, when Hollywood producers, in order to impress viewers, created sets representing ancient Egyptian buildings that were considerably larger and more elaborate than the originals.

This greater distancing of ancient Egypt is ultimately in the best interests of Egyptology. Even when evolutionism exerted a powerful influence on Western thought, Egyptologists so greatly admired the ancient Egyptians' cultural achievements that they minimized the differences between ancient Egypt and the modern world. Today, in a powerful expression of this uniformitarian view, the scholar Martin Bernal is encouraging Egyptologists to discard the last vestiges of evolutionism and regard the ancient Egyptians as our spiritual ancestors.[33]

I do not suggest that the ancient Egyptians' practical knowledge, or that of any other people, was fundamentally different from our own.[34] They clearly did not believe, any more than we do, that spells or incantations were necessary to make water run downhill or that prayer could routinely make it run uphill. But it is clear that their views about how the universe worked were very different from our own. They did not distinguish, as Western civilization has done since the late first millennium B.C., between nature, society, and the supernatural. What we understand as the natural world they perceived as suffused with supernatural power that had both consciousness and will, and hence they believed humans could interact socially rather than merely instrumentally with natural forces. The problem confronting ancient Egyptians was how to determine what the natural and supernatural powers willed. This led them to explore the relations that ordered the universe by means of omens, puns, and metaphors. They used forms of argument that in our society are encountered more commonly in literature than in science. This aspect of ancient Egyptian civilization must be understood on its own terms before Egyptologists can begin to comprehend all but the most commonplace aspects of ancient Egyptian behavior.

The increasing differentiation between Egyptologists and the object of their study as a result of rapidly accelerating technological change is reinforced by postmodernist trends in the humanities and social sciences. The relativistic nature of human thought and the differences between cultures are primary concerns of postmodernism, as is the assumed incapacity of one human being, especially a member of a different culture, to understand another. This is expressed in textual terms by the assertion that every decoding is another encoding.[35]

Carried to an extreme, postmodernism leads to a crippling relativism and subjectivism that can destroy any hope not only of objective communication between individuals or cultures but also of ever being able to understand the past other than as we or our society wish it to have been. Ironically postmodernism also offers the possibility of a more objective understanding of alien societies, including ancient Egypt. Frankfort erred in suggesting that the ancient Egyptians were so enmeshed in mythopoeic thought that they were incapable of practical reason and possibly also in his specific analysis of Egyptian kingship. But his *Kingship and the Gods* (1948) did point the way to an understanding of Egyptian religious beliefs on their own terms and hence to a better understanding of Egyptian behavior based on these beliefs.

In recent years American Egyptologists such as David O'Connor have taken the lead in the study of the intellectual structures underlying ancient Egyptian behavior as they are expressed, for example, in the layout of New Kingdom urban centers, the distribution of motifs in temples and tombs, the symbolic significance of differently colored stones used to make statuary, and even something as esoteric as the theological and astronomical significance of New Kingdom spoons.[36] Such work not only draws Egyptologists closer to recent trends in other humanistic studies but also makes possible a major advance in their understanding of ancient Egyptian civilization.

While the interplay between popular beliefs and scholarship is never simple or direct, a study of the changing relations between Egyptology and American society indicates that over the past century a set of beliefs about ancient Egypt which at first was dominated by a heterogeneous collection of unexamined and often contradictory assumptions has given way to a more detailed and accurate understanding of what ancient Egypt was really like. Error and folly are not precluded, and much remains to be learned about the social and political organization and the beliefs of ancient Egyptians, as well as about their everyday life. Yet more evidence points to irreversible gains in knowledge than to a merely cyclical flux in popular and professional concepts.

Notes

This essay, written while the author held sabbatical leave from McGill University, has benefited from Barbara Lawson's comments.

1 Bruce G. Trigger, "Archaeology and the Image of the American Indian," *American Antiquity* 45 (1980): 662–76; R. R. Wilk, "The Ancient Maya and the Political Present," *Journal of Anthropological Research* 41 (1985): 307–26; T. C. Patterson, "The Last Sixty Years: Toward a Social History of Americanist Archeology in the United States," *American Anthropologist* 88 (1986): 7–26.

2 John A. Wilson, *Signs and Wonders upon Pharaoh: A History of American Egyptology* (Chicago: University of Chicago Press, 1964).

3 A brilliant model for such an investigation is Benjamin Keen, *The Aztec Image in Western Thought* (New Brunswick, N.J.: Rutgers University Press, 1971).

4 A general account of the development of archaeological thought is found in Bruce G. Trigger, *A History of Archaeological Thought* (Cambridge: Cambridge University Press, 1989).

5 For accounts of early American interest in Egypt and Egyptian antiquities, see Wilson, *Signs and Wonders*, 35–39; Richard G. Carrott, *The Egyptian Revival: Its Sources, Monuments, and Meaning, 1808–1858* (Berkeley and Los Angeles: University of California Press, 1978), 47–50; John T. Irwin, *American Hieroglyphs: The Symbol of the Egyptian Hieroglyphics in the American Renaissance* (New Haven: Yale University Press, 1980), 3–4.

6 On Joseph Smith, see Fawn M. Brodie, *No Man Knows My History: The Life of Joseph Smith, the Mormon Prophet* (New York: Knopf, 1945), 170–75.

7 George R. Gliddon, *Ancient Egypt: Her Monuments, Hieroglyphics, History and Archaeology, and Other Subjects Connected with Hieroglyphical Literature* (New York: Winchester, 1843).

8 Carrott, *Egyptian Revival*, 50–52.

9 Ancient Egypt was the subject of American films long before the 1950s: versions of *Cleopatra* were produced in 1917 and 1934; Cecil B. DeMille's first version of *The Ten Commandments*, in 1923; and *The Mummy*, in 1933.

10 See James S. Curl, *The Egyptian Revival: An Introductory Study of a Recurring Theme in the History of Taste* (London: Allen and Unwin, 1982); Paolo Rossi, *The Dark Abyss of Time: The History of the Earth and the History of Nations from Hooke to Vico* (Chicago: University of Chicago Press, 1984); Maurice Pope, *The Story of Decipherment from Egyptian Hieroglyphic to Linear B* (London: Thames and Hudson, 1975); Frances A. Yates, *Giordano Bruno and the Hermetic Tradition* (London: Routledge and Kegan Paul, 1964).

11 Rossi, *The Dark Abyss*, 123.

12 Irwin, *American Hieroglyphs*.

13 Ibid., 30–31.

14 Wilson, *Signs and Wonders*, 41.

15 Carrott, *Egyptian Revival*, 108, 110.

16 Wilson, *Signs and Wonders*, 37.

17 Curl, *Egyptian Revival*, 89–95.

18 Carrott, *Egyptian Revival*, 66–68.

19 Ibid., 102–4.

20 Charles Lyell, *Principles of Geology*, vol. 2 (1832; reprint, Chicago: University of Chicago Press, 1991), 29.

21 William R. Stanton, *The Leopard's Spots: Scientific Attitudes toward Race in America, 1815–59* (Chicago: University of Chicago Press, 1960).

22 Wilson, *Signs and Wonders*, 115–23, 144.

23 Ibid., 124–58. Through Alfred V. Kidder, who studied briefly under Reisner at Harvard University, Reisner also played a major role in upgrading the standards for scientific excavation in the United States; see Douglas R. Givens, *Alfred Vincent Kidder and the Development of Americanist Archaeology* (Albuquerque: University of New Mexico Press, 1992), 25, 51.

24 Marvin Harris, *The Rise of Anthropological Theory* (New York: Crowell, 1968), 142–216.

25 The less exalted view of ancient Egypt's intellectual achievements was not, contrary to Martin Bernal's claim, the consequence of Wilhelm von Humboldt's decision, taken in 1809, that the Prussian educational system should glorify classical Greece at the expense of earlier civilizations; see Bernal, *Black Athena: The Afroasiatic Roots of Classical Civilization*, vol. 1, *The Fabrication of Ancient Greece 1785–1985* (London: Free Association Books, 1987), 283–88.

26 Irwin, *American Hieroglyphs*, 4–10.

27 Henri Frankfort, *Kingship and the Gods: A Study of Ancient Near Eastern Religion as the Integration of Society and Nature* (Chicago: University of Chicago Press, 1948); Lucien Lévy-Bruhl, *La mentalité primitive* (Paris: Alcan, 1922). For a more recent and moderate discussion of this subject, see Christopher R. Hallpike, *The Foundations of Primitive Thought* (Oxford: Oxford University Press, 1979).

28 E.g., Karl W. Butzer, *Early Hydraulic Civilization in Egypt: A Study in Cultural Ecology* (Chicago: University of Chicago Press, 1976).

29 Cheikh Anta Diop, *The African Origin of Civilization: Myth or Reality* (Westport, Conn.: Lawrence Hill, 1974).

30 For discussions of these limitations with respect to Egyptian-Sudanese relations, see Robert G. Morkot, "Nubia in the New Kingdom: The Limits of Egyptian Control," in *Egypt and Africa: Nubia from Prehistory to Islam*, ed. W. V. Davies (London: British Museum Press in association with the Egypt Exploration Society, 1991), 294–301.

31 Diodorus Siculus, *Bibliotheca historica* 3:3.

32 William C. Hayes, "Daily Life in Ancient Egypt," *National Geographic Magazine* 80 (1941): 419–515. Compare with Bruce G. Trigger, "Nubian, Negro, Black, Nilotic?" in *Africa in Antiquity: The Arts of Ancient Nubia and the Sudan*, vol. 1, *The Essays*, exh. cat. (Brooklyn: Brooklyn Museum, 1978), 26–35.

33 Bernal, *Black Athena*, vol. 1, 272–80; vol. 2, *The Archaeological and Documentary Evidence* (1991), 309–10.

34 For a discussion of the concepts of practical and cultural reason, see Marshall D. Sahlins, *Culture and Practical Reason* (Chicago: University of Chicago Press, 1976).

35 Margaret A. Rose, *The Post-Modern and the Post-Industrial: A Modern Analysis* (Cambridge: Cambridge University Press, 1991). For examples of post-modernist trends in archaeology, see Michael Shanks and Christopher Tilley, *Social Theory and Archaeology* (Cambridge, U.K.: Polity Press, 1987); Christopher Tilley, *Reading Material Culture: Structuralism, Hermeneutics, and Post-Structuralism* (Oxford: Blackwell, 1990); Ian Hodder, *Reading the Past: Current Approaches to Interpretation in Archaeology*, 2d ed. (Cambridge: Cambridge University Press, 1991). For a critical review of this movement, see Robert W. Preucel, ed., *Processual and Postprocessual Archaeologies: Multiple Ways of Knowing the Past* (Carbondale, Ill.: Center for Archaeological Investigations, 1991).

36 David O'Connor, "City and Palace in New Kingdom Egypt," *Cahier de recherches de l'Institut de papyrologie et d'égyptologie de Lille* 11 (1989): 73–87. This approach seems to be spreading rapidly among Egyptologists; see, for example, Arielle P. Kozloff and Betsy M. Bryan, *Egypt's Dazzling Sun: Amenhotep III and His World*, exh. cat. (Cleveland: Cleveland Museum of Art, 1992).

Go Down into Egypt: The Dawn of American Egyptology

Gerry D. Scott, III

The rugged individualism that is often cited as a distinctly American trait characterized the approach taken by Americans to the study of ancient Egypt until the beginning of the twentieth century. Americans did not, at first, play a major role in the decipherment of hieroglyphs, nor did they undertake vast scientific and epigraphic expeditions, as did their European colleagues. Rather, the dawn of American Egyptology is a chronicle of adventurous travel, novel approaches to earning a living or turning a profit, intensely passionate study of antiquity, simple scientific curiosity, religious zeal, and aesthetic admiration, each in keeping with the character and proclivities of the individuals concerned.

American contact with ancient Egypt can be traced to the colonial period. The English traveler and antiquarian George Sandys (1578–1644; see fig. 12) probably provides the first link between the two lands, for he spent time both in Egypt and in the colony of Virginia during the early seventeenth century. The youngest son of the archbishop of York, Sandys was educated at Oxford and set out on an extensive tour of Europe and the Near East in 1610. During his travels he visited Egypt, climbing the Great Pyramid and exploring its interior. In the account of his journey published in 1615, Sandys correctly stated that the pyramids were the burial spots of kings and not the granaries of the biblical Joseph, as medieval tradition had maintained.[1] Sandys also rejected the erroneous notion that these monuments were constructed by Hebrew slaves.

The Scottish author and traveler Alexander Gordon (c. 1692–c. 1754) makes another early connection between America and Egypt during the colonial period. Gordon received his master's degree from the University of Aberdeen and in 1741 served as secretary to an organization called the Egyptian Society. His published works in the field of Egyptology include *An Essay towards Explaining the Hieroglyphical Figures on the Coffin of the Ancient Mummy belonging to Captain William Lethieullier* (1737) and *An Essay towards Illustrating the History,*

FIGURE 11
View of Alexandria with "Cleopatra's Needle," which was moved to Central Park, New York, in 1881. Photograph by Félix Bonfils, c. 1878.

FIGURE 12
Engraved portrait of
George Sandys by
Hallett Hyatt, after a
painting by Cornelius
Janssen.

Chronology, and Mythology of the Ancient Egyptians (1741). About this time Gordon traveled to South Carolina, where he served the colonial governor as secretary and where he died about 1754.[2]

The first American in Egypt appears to have been John Ledyard (1751–89), who, bored with his missionary studies at Dartmouth, instead went to sea, eventually sailing the South Pacific with Captain James Cook's expedition of 1776–80. In 1785 Ledyard met Thomas Jefferson in Paris, where Jefferson was serving as United States ambassador to France. Following a difficult journey to Siberia, Ledyard renewed his acquaintance with Jefferson in 1788, when he again visited Paris, this time on his way to explore the Nile and the Niger for Sir Joseph Banks and the African Association of London. Jefferson asked Ledyard to keep him abreast of the latter's discoveries, and three of Ledyard's letters to Jefferson survive in the collection of the New-York Historical Society. Ledyard saw Pompey's Pillar and Cleopatra's Needle (now in Central Park, New York; see fig. 11) in Alexandria; was unimpressed with his view of the Nile, which he compared unfavorably to the Connecticut River; and complained of conditions in Cairo. Unfortunately, before Ledyard could journey beyond Cairo, he fell ill and died there, but not before bringing his Yankee background to the examination of Egyptian antiquities. On being shown an Egyptian mummy, he noted that the "mummy beads" on it were reminiscent of American Indian "wampum-work."[3]

A decade after Ledyard's death, Napoleon Bonaparte's Egyptian campaign opened the land of Egypt to the West and provided the means through which the modern discipline of Egyptology was born. Although Napoleon's challenge to Great Britain's colonial supremacy in the East was foiled by the Royal Navy under Horatio Nelson, the small army of scholars, scientists, artists, and savants who accompanied the expedition succeeded brilliantly in exposing Egypt's ancient past to modern scholarship.

In addition to the Royal Navy and the British army, Napoleon's troops had to deal with soldiers under the command of Mohammed Ali, who had been sent to drive the French from Egypt and to bring the land back under the control of the Ottoman Empire. An effective politician and military commander, Mohammed Ali was acknowledged as pasha of Egypt in 1806 and had become the unchallenged master of the country by 1811. At least three American adventurers sought service with him. One, George Bethune English (1787–1828), who had graduated from Harvard in 1807 and had served as a lieutenant in the United States Marine Corps with the Mediterranean squadron, was appointed a general of artillery in the

Egyptian army. He accompanied an Egyptian expedition to Dongola and Senaar in 1820 and published an account of his experience.[4] With this publication English became the first American to record a trip up the Nile. He also noted that he had with him "two soldiers, one Khalil Aga, an American of New York, and the other Achmed Aga, Swiss by birth but American by naturalization."[5]

Another American in Egypt at this time was Luther Bradish (1783–1863), who traveled as far as the second cataract of the Nile in 1821. He played a minor role in the rivalry between the consuls general of Great Britain and France, Henry Salt and Bernardino Drovetti, respectively, in their efforts to amass outstanding collections of Egyptian antiquities. On his journey Bradish carved his name on the temple of Dendur, where it can still be seen, even though the Nubian temple now stands in the Egyptian galleries of the Metropolitan Museum of Art, New York.[6]

FIGURE 13
View of Karnak temple, 1862. Photograph by Francis Bedford; courtesy of Michael Wilson.

The two most important American travelers of this era, however, were John Lowell Jr. (1799–1836) of Lowell, Massachusetts, and Colonel Mendes Cohen (see fig. 14) of Baltimore. Both formed significant collections of Egyptian antiquities which subsequently became part of institutional collections in the United States.

Lowell was a successful businessman who embarked on a world tour following the death of his wife and two daughters from scarlet fever. After visiting Europe, Lowell arrived in Egypt in 1834 and remained there until the following year. While in Luxor he collected a number of Egyptian antiquities, including portions of the granite shrine of Amun at Karnak (see fig. 13). He traveled up the Nile as far as Meroe and Khartoum, and then set out for India, where he took ill and ultimately succumbed.[7] In 1875, five years after the founding of the Museum of Fine Arts, Boston, Lowell's heirs presented some of his most important objects to the museum.

Cohen, of Portuguese descent, settled in Baltimore and served in the War of 1812. Like Lowell, he was successful financially and determined to travel abroad, first to Europe, then to the Near East. In 1832 he made a voyage up the Nile, traveling as far as the second cataract. Cohen's boat on this journey had the distinction of being the first vessel on the Nile to fly the Stars and Stripes. Although Cohen declined to purchase the Egyptian collection formed by Francis Barthou, an American expatriate living in Egypt,[8] he did purchase objects in Egypt and acquired additional antiquities from the 1835 sale of Henry Salt's third and final collection of Egyptian artifacts. George R. Gliddon used Cohen's collection, numbering nearly seven hundred objects, to illustrate his popular lectures on ancient Egypt. In 1884 Cohen's heirs presented the lot to Johns Hopkins University, where it forms the foundation of the university's Egyptian collection.[9]

Two non-American collectors whose efforts ultimately benefited two American museums were the Englishman Henry Abbott (1812–59; see fig. 15) and the Scot Robert Hay (1799–1863). Abbott had once served in the Royal Navy as a ship's surgeon and acquired the courtesy title doctor, although he seems never to have received an actual medical degree, and he later entered the service of Mohammed Ali as physician to the Egyptian fleet. In Egypt Abbott formed an extensive collection of antiquities, numbering in excess of eleven hundred objects. He brought his collection to New York in 1853 and placed it on public exhibition at the Stuyvesant Institute on Broadway (see fig. 16). Like others before him, he hoped that paid

FIGURE 15
Portrait of Henry
Abbott by Thomas
Hicks, c. 1852–53.

FIGURE 16
Advertisement for exhi-
bition of the Henry
Abbott collection.

admissions would support him, but in this he was disappointed. He returned to Egypt the following year, abandoning the collection to his creditors. In 1860, following Abbott's death, it was purchased for the New-York Historical Society, where it remained until its transfer to the Brooklyn Museum in 1937.[10] Abbott's collection, the first major collection of Egyptian art and artifacts on regular public view in the United States, now forms a cornerstone of the Brooklyn Museum's illustrious holdings.

Hay had also served with the Royal Navy, but he abandoned his midshipman's berth in 1824 at Malta, where he met Frederic Catherwood and Henry Parke, both of whom had recently left Egypt. Inspired by this meeting, Hay arrived in Egypt in November 1824. Over the next fourteen years he made several extended visits to Egypt, often in the company of accomplished artists. Hay published only a small portion of his own drawings, plans, notes, and copies, but they remain a valuable research asset of the British Museum and the British Library. Hay also acquired an extensive collection of Egyptian antiquities, part of which entered the British Museum. The rest were donated to the Museum of Fine Arts, Boston, by the Reverend C. Granville Way in 1872.[11]

The Lowell, Cohen, Abbott, and Hay collections were not, however, the first Egyptian antiquities on view in the United States. American museums can trace their educational mission and history to the eighteenth century, when several colleges formed collections, or "cabinets of curiosities," modeled on European predecessors.[12] The first museum in America that was not directly associated with a college or private individual was the Library Society of Charleston, South

Carolina, founded in 1748. In addition to other possible Egyptian artifacts, this collection is reported to have displayed an Egyptian mummy.[13]

Both commercial and naval seafarers of New England, Commodore Matthew Calbraith Perry among them (see fig. 17 and cat. no. 4), acquired a number of Egyptian objects that found their way into different American museum collections. The East India Marine Society, founded in 1799 in Salem, Massachusetts, became the repository for several small Egyptian collections acquired by maritime men, including a mummified ibis presented by a Captain Apthorp in 1803, a carved wooden bird donated by Captain Nathaniel Page in 1813, and a group of six wooden shawabti figures of King Seti I, the gift of Lieutenant Thomas Tanner. Tanner had purchased the shawabti figures from the great Italian explorer Giovanni Belzoni "at the Catacombs of Thebes in 1822."[14] Five years earlier Belzoni had discovered the tomb of Seti I, which remained known as Belzoni's Tomb until the present century.

The greatest early American museums were those created by the Peale family. The patriarch, Charles Willson Peale (1741–1827), was an eminent American artist who had studied under Benjamin West. Peale's interests, however, went far beyond painting, and he established in Philadelphia the first American museum probably worthy of the name. Housed on the second floor of Independence Hall during the late eighteenth and early nineteenth centuries, the museum boasted a mastodon skeleton, George Washington's stuffed pheasants, various artifacts collected by Lewis and Clark on their exploratory journey through the newly acquired Louisiana Purchase, and an Egyptian mummy. Peale's sons Rembrandt and Rubens also established museums in New York City and Baltimore, and each could boast the mummified remains of an ancient Egyptian.[15]

Like Abbott's display, the Peale family museums depended solely upon admissions to survive, and in the long run none remained solvent. The collections were eventually dispersed at auctions and sheriff's sales to satisfy debts, and the mummies became the possessions of entertainment impresario P. T. Barnum. Placed on display in Barnum's American Museum in New York City, they were destroyed in a catastrophic fire that raged through the museum building in 1865.[16]

Among the most intriguing figures from this early period of American interest in Egypt is George R. Gliddon. Gliddon had served as United States vice-consul in Egypt, and upon his return to America he lectured widely on ancient Egypt, often utilizing objects from the Cohen collection as illustrations (see cat. nos. 2, 3). In 1843–44 he lectured at the Lowell Institute, recently established through a bequest made by John Lowell, Jr., whom Gliddon had met in Egypt. Gliddon deserves more than passing mention for, in addition to bringing ancient Egypt to American audiences from Boston to Saint Louis, he was a pioneer in attempting to draw both scholarly and popular attention to the importance of preserving Egypt's ancient monuments before they were lost to future generations.[17]

Apparently Gliddon sometimes unwrapped Egyptian mummies during his public lectures, but he was not the first American to do so. In 1821 John Collins Warren (1778–1856), first professor of anatomy and surgery at Harvard, unrolled and described a Ptolemaic mummy that had been donated to the Massachusetts General Hospital by merchant A. O. van Lennep of Smyrna, Turkey.[18] Smyrna, it would seem, was an important stop on the American route to or from Egypt at the time, for Philip Rhinelander Jr. (1815–39), who had traveled up the Nile as far as Philae in 1839, shipped his collection of Egyptian antiquities to Smyrna, from which they were to be sent to the United States.[19]

Among the last of this long line of casual, but important, early American visitors to Egypt is Henry James Anderson (1799–1875). Following a familiar pattern, after the death of his wife in 1843 he traveled to Europe first, and then on to Egypt, Nubia, and Abyssinia. In 1848 he served as both geologist and medical doctor for the U.S. Navy expedition to the Dead Sea under Lieutenant William Francis Lynch. In 1864, after returning to New York, Anderson donated a portion of the Egyptian antiquities he had collected to the New-York Historical Society. His heirs later gave the remaining Egyptian materials in his collection to the society. Like the Abbott collection, these objects are now housed in the Brooklyn Museum.[20]

The closing decades of the nineteenth century saw both continuity and change in the approach of Americans to ancient Egypt. There were still travelers like James Bayard Taylor (1825–78), who published an account of his tour of Egypt and the Sudan for the benefit of his countrymen addicted to travel literature, as well as expatriates like Edwin Smith (1822–1906), who went to Egypt to make his fortune. Smith is a difficult, but intriguing, figure. He could read the ancient Egyptian language in both the hieroglyphic and hieratic scripts and was regarded by many as a competent Egyptologist. He resided in Luxor from 1858 to 1876 and earned his living by selling antiquities and lending money. According to several accounts, however, he also was not above selling and even creating fakes to make ends meet.[21] Despite all his efforts, both fair and foul, Smith was never able to make a success of his various enterprises in Egypt, and he ultimately returned to America. Following his death his daughter presented his prize possession, an important ancient Egyptian medical text now known as the Edwin Smith Surgical Papyrus, to the New-York Historical Society. Today it is in the collection of the New York Academy of Medicine.

Another American who lived in Egypt and sold antiquities to tourists was the Reverend Chauncey Murch (1856–1907). A Presbyterian missionary, Murch formed a large collection of antiquities, mainly at Luxor. He enhanced his meager

salary by acting as both agent-broker and dealer to European and American travelers, often selling things from his personal holdings. What remained of his
collection was eventually acquired by the British Museum, the Metropolitan
Museum of Art, the Detroit Institute of Arts, and the Art Institute of Chicago.[22]
Other American missionaries in Egypt at the time included a Doctor Alexander,
who, in addition to heading up the American College at Asyut, assisted visitors in
acquiring antiquities from that region, and Gulian Lansing, a Hebrew scholar who
could read hieroglyphs. Lansing wrote an article on the possible incorporation of
Egyptian words into the Old Testament, which Charles Edwin Wilbour (see below)
felt was a credible and potentially important study.[23] Lansing also served as an
agent-broker from time to time. The Papyrus Lansing in the British Museum was
so named in recognition of his assistance in acquiring it.

Despite these numerous American contacts with Egypt, Americans who
wished to receive formal instruction in Egyptology still had to travel abroad.
William N. Groff (1857–1901) studied Egyptology in Paris under the great French
scholar Gaston Maspero (1846–1916) and subsequently lived in Cairo from 1891
to 1899. Maspero published Groff's collected scholarly papers in 1908.[24] Another
American pupil of Maspero's, William Berman Sedgwick Berend (1855–84), was
a banker by profession but published successfully in the field of Egyptology.[25]

Maspero's great American student, however, was Charles Edwin Wilbour
(1833–96; see fig. 18). A journalist and businessman, Wilbour studied Egyptology
in both Paris and Berlin. Judged by British orientalist the Reverend Archibald H.
Sayce to be "the best Egyptologist living,"[26] Wilbour had a keen command of the
ancient Egyptian language, a fine memory for detail, the patience to be a meticulous copyist, and superior powers of observation and analysis. He also had a
well-developed sense of humor. All these qualities are evident in his letters from
Egypt, published posthumously.[27] In a style uniquely American, he remarked in
one letter on a monument of King Tuthmosis III which was reused by a much later
pharaoh, Shabako: "This is the story everywhere in Egypt and the world. Nothing
is new. Everything is hash from yesterday's roast; we included."[28]

For several years, during Maspero's first stint as director of the Egyptian
Antiquities Service, Wilbour was a guest on the official steamer of the service. During
these voyages Wilbour freely shared his scholarly discoveries with his French colleagues, and the majority of his insights were ultimately published by these and other
companions. Hence the often-implied criticism that Wilbour contributed little to the
field is certainly too harsh.[29] In addition he formed an important collection of antiquities (see cat. nos. 7, 9, 10), which his heirs donated to the Brooklyn Museum. Further,
endowments provided by the same heirs at Brown University and the Brooklyn
Museum have greatly contributed to the advancement of American Egyptology.

Another member of this first group of Americans to pursue Egyptology systematically is William Henry Goodyear (1846–1923), a graduate of Yale University who went on to study Egyptology at Heidelberg and Berlin. He served on the curatorial staffs of the Metropolitan Museum of Art and the Brooklyn Museum and was one of the founders of the American Anthropological Association.[30]

Charles E. Moldenke (1860–1933), a graduate of Columbia University, studied Egyptology in Germany and hoped to teach the subject at his alma mater. Unfortunately no American university was yet ready for a chair in Egyptology (James Henry Breasted held the first professorship in the subject in the United States, at the University of Chicago from 1905). Moldenke did, however, reportedly acquire a modest collection of Egyptian antiquities and published several articles, including an overview of American collections of Egyptian art and artifacts as they then existed.[31]

In the late nineteenth century American collections of Egyptian antiquities kept pace with the growth of American industrial wealth. Louis Palma di Cesnola, first director of the Metropolitan Museum of Art, acquired Egyptian antiquities for his museum from Maspero and from Emil Brugsch, also on the staff of the Egyptian Antiquities Service.[32] Another Brugsch customer was Anthony J. Drexel, Jr., who thus acquired an important Egyptian collection for the newly founded Drexel Institute of Philadelphia. That collection has been largely dispersed.[33]

In terms of collectors and dealers, it is surely worth noting that one of the primary sources of objects at about this time was an American, Ralph Harrup Blanchard (d. 1936). Blanchard maintained a shop at the entrance to the old Shepheard's Hotel in Cairo.[34]

United States naval officers continued to exercise a presence in the field of Egyptology during the late nineteenth century. One, Lieutenant Commander Henry Honeychurch Gorringe (1841–85), oversaw the removal from Egypt and erection in New York of the obelisk that now graces Central Park. Gorringe, like so many of his contemporaries, also acquired a collection of Egyptian antiquities.[35] Another naval officer, Edward Yorke McCauley (1827–94), retired from the navy as a rear admiral and published several Egyptological studies.[36]

As the century closed, so too did this rather tentative stage of development for American Egyptology. Characterized by individual initiative and motivation, lacking both continuity and long-term goals, the era nonetheless had nurtured an incipient American interest in ancient Egypt and set the stage for a most promising future. Collecting efforts by early aficionados formed the nuclei of many of the

nation's great holdings of ancient Egyptian art and archaeology, and several distinguished university programs in Egyptology that now exist had their genesis during this period.

One development that greatly influenced the future direction of American Egyptology was the founding of the Egypt Exploration Fund (now the Egypt Exploration Society) in England in 1882. This research organization sponsored archaeological excavations in Egypt and oversaw the rapid publication of the results. Money for the fund's projects was raised by subscription from museums, universities, and individuals. When excavations were concluded at a fund site (sometimes even at each season's end), the Egyptian Antiquities Service and the fund made an initial division of the recovered material. The fund then distributed its share among its subscribers. For fledgling American museum collections the advantages of acquiring antiquities in this manner were obvious. The institutions not only were supporting scholarly research, they were also receiving objects of a known provenance, authenticity, and historical significance.[37]

Shortly after the advent of American participation in the Egypt Exploration Fund and another British organization, the Egyptian Research Account, a significant number of museums and universities began to undertake their own systematic archaeological and epigraphic research in the Nile Valley. This tradition continues today.

In closing this account, it is fitting to examine briefly the career of Theodore Munroe Davis (see fig. 20), an American businessman who financed serious archaeological investigation in Egypt between 1903 and 1912. In many respects Davis is a transitional figure in the history of American Egyptology.[38] In his activities he gives a sense of having one foot in the past—that of the adventurous traveler forming a private collection for personal satisfaction—and the future—that of systematic archaeological investigation, with an eye toward solving the problems, especially historical, of Egypt's long past. In addition to his investigation of many minor Theban tombs, Davis and his archaeologists discovered the tombs of Queen Hatshepsut; Kings Tuthmosis IV, Siptah, and Horemheb; and the nobles Yuaa and Thuiu, parents of Queen Tiye. Some of the objects discovered in these important tombs are on display at the Museum of Fine Arts, Boston, and the Metropolitan Museum of Art. These American institutions also house the majority of Davis's private collection of Egyptian antiquities. Davis divided his finds with the Egyptian government, and the majority of the objects he discovered remained in their native land, housed in the Cairo Museum, a practice that set the tone for future American excavations.

Notes

For abbreviations used in the notes, see the list of abbreviations on p. 76.

1 For Sandys, see Warren R. Dawson and Eric P. Uphill, *Who Was Who in Egyptology*, 2d rev. ed. (London: Egypt Exploration Society, 1972), 259–60.

2 For Gordon, see ibid., 119; Erik Iverson, *The Myth of Egypt and Its Hieroglyphs in European Tradition* (Princeton: Princeton University Press, 1993), 119.

3 For Ledyard, see John A. Wilson, *Signs and Wonders upon Pharaoh: A History of American Egyptology* (Chicago: University of Chicago Press, 1964), 12–13, 198, 223–24; Andrew Oliver Jr., *Beyond the Shores of Tripoli: American Archaeology in the Eastern Mediterranean, 1789–1879* (Cambridge: Fogg Art Museum, Harvard University, 1979).

4 English's exploits are listed in Wilson, *Signs and Wonders*, 22–23, 219; Dawson and Uphill, *Who Was Who*, 98; Oliver, *Beyond the Shores*, n.p. English's account is entitled *A Narrative of the Expedition to Dongola and Senaar* (London, 1822; Boston, 1823).

5 Quoted in Oliver, *Beyond the Shores*, n.p.

6 For Bradish, see ibid.; Wilson, *Signs and Wonders*, 23, 25, 215; Dawson and Uphill, *Who Was Who*, 37–38.

7 Lowell is discussed in Wilson, *Signs and Wonders*, 39; Dawson and Uphill, *Who Was Who*, 184–85; Oliver, *Beyond the Shores*, n.p.; John McDonald, "The Egyptian Trip of John Lowell, Jr.," *BES* 6 (1984): 69–79. For some principal objects he collected, see Bernard V. Bothmer, "Ptolemaic Reliefs I: A Granite Block of Philip Arrhidaeus," *BMFA* 50 (1952): 19–27.

8 Barthou's name receives various spellings, see, e.g., Wilson, *Signs and Wonders*, 23 (Captain Barthow), and Oliver, *Beyond the Shores*, n.p.

9 Cohen is discussed in Wilson, *Signs and Wonders*, 38, 41, 217; Dawson and Uphill, *Who Was Who*, 67; Oliver, *Beyond the Shores*, n.p.; Ellen Reeder Williams, *The Archaeological Collections of the Johns Hopkins University* (Baltimore: Johns Hopkins University Press, 1984), 3–4; Betsy M. Bryan, "An Early Eighteenth Dynasty Group Statue from the Asasif in the Johns Hopkins Collection," *BES* 10 (1989–90): 25.

10 For Abbott, see Wilson, *Signs and Wonders*, 35, 39, 213; Dawson and Uphill, *Who Was Who*, 1; Richard A. Fazzini et al., *Ancient Egyptian Art in the Brooklyn Museum* (Brooklyn: Brooklyn Museum; New York: Thames and Hudson, 1989), viii.

11 For the major British travelers in Egypt at this time, including Hay, see Jason Thompson, *Sir Gardner Wilkinson and His Circle* (Austin: University of Texas Press, 1992). For Hay, see also Wilson, *Signs and Wonders*, 32, 222; Fred G. Bratton, *A History of Egyptian Archaeology* (New York: Thomas Y. Crowell, 1968), 60–61; Dawson and Uphill, *Who Was Who*, 135. For recent publications of some of the Hay objects in Boston, see *Egypt's Golden Age: The Art of Living in the New Kingdom, 1558–1085 B.C.*, exh. cat. (Boston: MFA, 1982); Sue D'Auria, Peter Lacovara, and Catharine Roehrig, *Mummies and Magic: The Funerary Arts of Ancient Egypt*, exh. cat. (Boston: MFA, 1988).

12 A brief account of early museum collections in America is given in Gerry D. Scott, III, "An Artist, a Showman, a Scientist and the Development of the Natural History Museum in America," *Discovery* 21 (1988): 8.

13 B. Narendra, archivist, Peabody Museum of Natural History, Yale University, conversation with author.

14 Belzoni is a popular and much-discussed character. He is mentioned often, e.g., in Peter A. Clayton, *The Rediscovery of Ancient Egypt* (New York: Thames and Hudson, 1982); and Jean Vercoutter, *The Search for Ancient Egypt* (New York: Abrams, 1992), both with additional bibliography. For a brief biographical sketch, see Dawson and Uphill, *Who Was Who*, 23–24. For Lieutenant Tanner and his fellow sailors, see Emma Swan Hall, "Some Ancient Egyptian Sculpture in American Museums," *Apollo* 88 (July 1968): 4.

15 For the Peale family and their museums, see Charles Coleman Sellers, *Charles Willson Peale* (New York: Scribner, 1969); Edgar P. Richardson et al., *Charles Willson Peale and His World* (New York: Abrams, 1982).

16 A succinct account of Peale and Barnum as "museum men" is in Scott, "An Artist, a Showman."

17 George R. Gliddon, *An Appeal to the Antiquaries of Europe on the Destruction of the Monuments of Egypt* (London, 1841).

18 For Warren, see Dawson and Uphill, *Who Was Who*, 298–99.

19 See Oliver, *Beyond the Shores*, n.p.

20 For Anderson, see ibid.; Wilson, *Signs and Wonders*, 38.

21 A lively account is quoted in Wilson, *Signs and Wonders*, 53–54.

22 For Murch, see ibid. 78–79, 203, 226; Dawson and Uphill, *Who Was Who*, 209–10.

23 Charles Edwin Wilbour, *Travels in Egypt (December 1880 to May 1891): Letters of Charles Edwin Wilbour*, ed. Jean Capart (Brooklyn: Brooklyn Museum, 1936), 441.

24 For Groff, see Wilson, *Signs and Wonders*, 79, 222; Dawson and Uphill, *Who Was Who*, 128.

25 For Berend, see Wilson, *Signs and Wonders*, 79, 214; Dawson and Uphill, *Who Was Who*, 25.

26 Wilson, *Signs and Wonders*, 105.

27 Wilbour, *Travels in Egypt*.

28 Ibid., 246.

29 The implication comes through even in Wilson, *Signs and Wonders*, 92, 105–8.

30 For Goodyear, see ibid., 79, 221; Dawson and Uphill, *Who Was Who*, 31.

31 For Moldenke, see Wilson, *Signs and Wonders*, 80.

32 Wilbour may well have influenced Cesnola's purchases, see Wilbour, *Travels in Egypt*, 349.

33 Some objects from the Drexel collection are now in the Minneapolis Institute of Arts and the Harer Family Trust Collection, see Gerry D. Scott, III, *Temple, Tomb, and Dwelling: Egyptian Antiquities from the Harer Family Trust Collection* (San Bernardino, Calif.: California State University, 1992), ix–x.

34 For Blanchard, see Dawson and Uphill, *Who Was Who*, 31.

35 Gorringe published an account of his activities, *Egyptian Obelisks* (New York, 1882); see also Wilson, *Signs and Wonders*, 59–60, 202, 221; Dawson and Uphill, *Who Was Who*, 120; Oliver, *Beyond the Shores*, n.p.

36 For McCauley, see Dawson and Uphill, *Who Was Who*, 188.

37 For the Egypt Exploration Fund, see T. G. H. James, ed., *Excavating in Egypt: The Egypt Exploration Fund, 1882–1982* (Chicago: University of Chicago Press, 1982).

38 Davis is discussed in Wilson, *Signs and Wonders*, 115–23, 128, 162, 205, 218; Dawson and Uphill, *Who Was Who*, 78–79. For a more recent study, see John A. Larson, "Theodore M. Davis: Pioneer to the Past," parts 1 and 2, *KMT* 1 (Spring 1990): 48–53, 60–61; (Summer 1990): 43–46.

American Institutional Fieldwork in Egypt, 1899–1960

Nancy Thomas

A round the turn of the twentieth century American museums and universities undertook archaeological fieldwork in Egypt in a first wave of activity that lasted, with some exceptions, into the early 1930s. During this time American expeditions, "taken together, were more elaborate in their equipment, more ambitious in their objectives, and more generously financed, than any archaeological expeditions sent by any country to any area."[1] From the beginning, fieldwork in Egypt was expensive, limiting the number of participants to seven institutions, along with their academic partners. Apart from actual excavations, much of the history of American Egyptology concerns the development of personal careers, strategies for obtaining concessions to sites, and a constant struggle for funding. As with many disciplines, the field's early era is rife with anecdotal stories, such as the near disaster for James Henry Breasted (see fig. 21) when he almost discarded a casually written but long-awaited pledge from his patron John D. Rockefeller Jr.[2]

The success of the British Egypt Exploration Society (founded in 1882, and until 1919 called the Egypt Exploration Fund, or EEF) in both excavating Egyptian sites and obtaining artifacts for supporting institutions, along with direct American participation in the EEF, spurred American institutions to proceed with their own fieldwork beginning in the late 1890s. The funders of most American institutional projects were in pursuit of Egyptian collections, but this interest was often paralleled by a desire to make advances within the field and to substantiate events of ancient history. The following account, organized chronologically from the onset of the systematic collecting of Egyptian objects, sketches the activities of each institutional participant and reveals varying motivations, strategies, and foci. The work of each institution took on a distinctive character. For example, both the University of Chicago and the Metropolitan Museum of Art made early commitments to the recording and preservation of Egyptian monuments in addition to undertaking excavation projects. Other museums, such as the Brooklyn Museum, entered into

FIGURE 21
James Henry Breasted and team surveying the temple of Ramesses II at Abu Simbel during the University of Chicago's first epigraphic survey, 1905–6.

fieldwork projects quite early (1906–8) but also focused on purchasing works of art, connoisseurship, exhibitions, and art historical studies. Institutions with academic affiliations, such as the universities of Pennsylvania, California (Berkeley), and Michigan, concentrated less on the display and acquisition of Egyptian objects than on the building of academic departments.

The Museum of Fine Arts, Boston

The Museum of Fine Arts, Boston, which incorporated in 1870, received its first major gift of Egyptian objects in 1872 from Bostonian C. Granville Way. Way's father had purchased part of the collection of Scottish antiquarian Robert Hay, most of whose Egyptian objects were sold to the British Museum in 1865.[3] Soon after, in 1875, Francis Cabot Lowell presented the museum with significant objects collected in Egypt by his brother John Lowell Jr. during the 1830s.[4] In addition to artifacts (see cat. no. 77), the gift included Lowell's extensive diaries and the sketches and watercolors of the Scottish artist Charles Gleyre, whom Lowell hired to document Egypt during his travels.

From 1885 to 1909 the museum received Egyptian objects in exchange for its financial support of British excavations under the auspices of the EEF (see cat. no. 27). In 1902 Albert M. Lythgoe (1868–1934), a Harvard-educated Egyptologist who had studied with Alfred Wiedemann at the University of Bonn, became the first curator of a newly established department of Egyptian art.[5] Lythgoe was soon sent to Egypt to purchase objects for the museum's collections and to gain additional field experience with George Andrew Reisner, who was then heading an expedition for the University of California. (Lythgoe had previously worked with Reisner at Deir el-Ballas and Naga el-Deir, and in 1906 he became curator of the Egyptian department at the Metropolitan Museum of Art.)

Born in Indianapolis in 1867, Reisner (see fig. 22) first studied law at Harvard but completed his graduate studies in Semitic languages and history and finished postgraduate work in Germany under the acknowledged leaders of Egyptian philology in the 1890s, Adolf Erman and Kurt Sethe.[6] When private financial support for Reisner's University of California expedition ended in 1905, the Museum of Fine Arts and Harvard University assumed sponsorship of the project, which was to continue for nearly forty years as the Harvard-Boston expedition. During the following three decades (the expedition stopped digging in 1937, but Reisner continued working until his death in 1942), Reisner refined his system of conscientious fieldwork. Basic to his technique was thorough recording of finds, attention to site stratigraphy, the production of sophisticated multilevel plans, and extensive field photography. The Harvard-Boston expeditions generated more than sixty thousand glass-plate negatives and hundreds of object registers and excavation

FIGURE 22
George A. Reisner, 1938.

FIGURE 23
Aerial view of the Giza plateau, showing the Western Cemetery at the right of the Great Pyramid of Khufu.

FIGURE 24
Excavations at Menkaure Valley Temple, 1910.

diaries recording daily observations (currently stored in the Egyptian department of the Museum of Fine Arts). As evidenced by a recent exhibition at the Phoebe A. Hearst Museum of Anthropology at the University of California, Berkeley,[7] Reisner was the first archaeologist to successfully use photographic documentation as a standard component of fieldwork.[8]

In 1902, after Reisner complained of unprofessional excavation in the area of the Giza Plateau, the Egyptian Antiquities Service considered concession applications for the site from Ernesto Schiaparelli of the Turin Museum expedition; Ludwig Borchardt, representing Georg Steindorff of the Sieglin Expedition of the University of Leipzig; and Reisner.[9] The three parties were told to divide, by mutual consent, the potentially rich cemetery to the west of the Great Pyramid of Khufu. In a dramatic draw of lots Reisner won a concession to excavate the northern strip of the Western Cemetery as well as the Menkaure pyramid, the smallest of the three royal pyramids, with its adjacent mortuary complex (see figs. 23, 24). He ended up with excavation rights to two-thirds of the Western Cemetery when, in 1905, the Italian excavators relinquished their portion to the American expedition.

From 1903 to 1937 Reisner supervised the excavation of more than 429 Old Kingdom mastaba tombs at Giza, ranging in date from the 4th to 6th Dynasties (2575–2150 B.C.).[10] Among the most significant finds were the spectacular examples of royal statuary from the valley temple of Menkaure[11] (see cat. no. 39) and the intact tomb of King Khufu's mother, Queen Hetepheres, wife of Sneferu.[12] The meticulous excavation techniques employed by Reisner and the Harvard-Boston team marked a clear advance over the recording methods introduced by British Egyptologist W. M. Flinders Petrie (1853–1942), and Reisner also produced comprehensive publications such as *The Development of the Egyptian Tomb down to the Accession of Cheops* (1936),[13] which stood in marked contrast to the hastily published excavation reports of Petrie or the more methodical data-oriented publications of German (Hermann Junker, working 1912–29, with the exception of the World War I years)[14] and Egyptian colleagues (Selim Hassan, working 1929–37).[15]

In addition to discoveries at Giza, Reisner's Harvard-Boston excavations uncovered extensive remains from the First Intermediate Period and Middle Kingdom at Naga el-Deir[16] and Deir el-Bersha, including extremely fine burial goods from the tomb of a local monarch, Djehutynakht.[17] Other projects included excavations at Kafr Ghattati,[18] Zawiyet el-Aryan,[19] and Coptos.

In 1906 Reisner was invited by the Egyptian government to conduct an archaeological survey of northern Nubia, in the area that was to be covered by the lake forming behind the first Aswan Dam, completed in 1902. From 1913 to 1932 expeditions headed by Reisner worked their way southward through Nubia, excavating major sites such as the royal necropolis at Kerma, the tombs of a wealthy Nubian dynasty that flourished above the third cataract of the Nile during a period contemporaneous with the Second Intermediate Period in Egypt (1640–1532 B.C.). Reisner's Nubian expeditions also explored a series of five massive mud-brick forts (Uronarti, Shalfak, Mirgissa, Semna, and Kumma) guarding the frontier of Egypt at the second cataract.

Beginning in 1916 Reisner excavated the royal cemeteries of the 25th Dynasty located in Nubia at el-Kurru and Nuri. Remarkably, on the first day of work, he discovered the tomb chambers of the royal pyramids, soon leading to finds that would clarify the sequence of the 25th Dynasty kings (see cat. nos. 97–101). Despite plundering by thieves, more than a thousand stone shawabtis (funerary figurines; see cat. no. 100 and fig. 25) were discovered in the tomb chamber of King Taharqa at Nuri. Reisner also initiated work at the fourth cataract at the Great Temple at Gebel Barkal, the stronghold of the Nubian dynasty that gained political control of Egypt around 712 B.C. The southernmost excavations, conducted in the area between the fifth cataract and Khartoum, focused on three extensive cemeteries at Meroe, ranging in date from the 26th Dynasty (664–525 B.C.) to the mid-fourth century A.D.

Following Reisner's death at Harvard Camp in 1942, Dows Dunham (1890–1984) became curator of the Egyptian department of the Museum of Fine Arts, Boston, and was assisted by William Stevenson Smith (1907–69) and Suzanne E. Chapman (1904–90). Reisner had held the post since 1910, although he was very seldom in Boston. Dunham, who had worked with Reisner in the field from 1914 to 1928, resigned the position in 1955 to concentrate more fully on the publication of Reisner's work in the Sudan.[20] Egyptologist and art historian Smith, known especially for his publications *Ancient Egypt as Represented in the Museum of Fine Arts, Boston* (1942), *A History of Egyptian Sculpture and Painting in the Old Kingdom* (1946), and the extensive *Art and Architecture of Ancient Egypt* (1958),[21] served as curator of the department from 1955 to 1969. Rather than initiate new excavations, he focused on the vast amount of material acquired by the museum. Chapman, a skilled archaeological illustrator, served as special assistant to several museum departments for more than forty years, producing highly accurate and detailed drawings and contributing to conservation and installation projects.[22]

The University of Pennsylvania Museum of Archaeology and Anthropology

In 1890, three years after its founding, the University Museum of the University of Pennsylvania appointed Sara Yorke Stevenson (1847–1921) as its first curator of the Egyptian section.[23] Although Stevenson made an ambitious trip to Egypt in 1898 to organize the museum's first Egyptian field project, excavations did not begin until 1906–7, under the direction of David Randall-MacIver (1873–1945). In the meantime Stevenson ensured that the museum's holdings of excavated Egyptian objects would grow substantially by contributing to the EEF. She maintained cordial relations with the fund's primary excavator, the highly successful but temperamental Flinders Petrie. As a major contributor among the eighteen American institutions[24] subscribing to the EEF between 1890 and 1907, and to a lesser degree from 1913 to 1915 and in 1924, the University Museum received objects from the royal cemeteries at Abydos (see cat. nos. 31, 32) and from sites such as Hierakonpolis (see cat. no. 27), Dendera, Sedment, Maidum, and Memphis.

Petrie's field techniques and excavation strategies in Egypt strongly
influenced the work of successive
American excavations, including those
of Randall-MacIver, who worked with
him at Dendera, Abydos, and other
sites from 1897 to 1900.[25] The expeditions of both Petrie and Reisner were
training grounds for American field
Egyptologists, but it was Petrie who
first introduced systematic archaeological fieldwork in Egypt, beginning with his
initial excavation for the EEF at Tanis in 1884. Surprisingly Petrie had no formal
education, but he had received considerable training in British prehistory and
archaeology from his father, William Petrie, a civil engineer and surveyor, with
whom he surveyed Stonehenge in 1872. Childhood reading stimulated his interest
in Egypt, and he traveled to Egypt to survey the pyramids of the Giza Plateau in
1880–82.[26] Taking advantage of his association with the EEF, Petrie conducted a
rapid succession of excavations and introduced a comprehensive approach to the
study of excavated objects in which he wove (as he described in 1885) "a history
out of scattered evidence using all material of inscriptions, objects, positions, and
probabilities."[27] Based on the relative chronologies established for ceramics by the
German archaeologist Adolf Furtwängler, Petrie developed a technique he termed
"sequence dating," which could be used to systematically identify Predynastic
material. The orderly classification of a wide range of excavation finds—including
pottery and evidence of ancient life apart from royal and elite activities—was
increasingly to become the standard for future generations of excavators.

The University Museum's field projects were sponsored by Eckley Brinton
Coxe Jr., president of the museum's board of trustees. From 1907 to 1911 Randall-
MacIver proceeded with an ambitious program for excavation in Lower Nubia
(between the first and second cataracts). Following Stevenson's resignation in
1905, he was appointed as the museum's first professional Egyptologist. During
a period when other prominent Egyptologists, such as Junker, Reisner, and
British philologist Francis L. Griffith, were eager to excavate in the region, Randall-
MacIver and his assistant, British archaeologist Charles Leonard Woolley (1880–
1960; see fig. 26), were the first to record the distinctive characteristics of early
Nubian C-Group culture at Areika and Aniba, the Middle and New Kingdom
Egyptian military installations at Buhen (see cat. nos. 65, 82), and the virtually
unknown Meroitic culture of Nubia as evidenced at Shablul and Karanog (see
cat. no. 123).

Clarence S. Fisher (1876–1941; see fig. 27), who trained as an architect at the University of Pennsylvania, served the University Museum as Egyptian curator and field director from 1914 to 1925. His major achievements included the retrieval of the architectural plan of a remarkably well preserved royal palace of the 19th Dynasty king Merneptah at Memphis (see cat. nos. 87–89) and the excavation of a major provincial cemetery at Dendera in southern Egypt. Fisher had worked in the Near East from 1897 to 1900 with the museum's Nippur expedition, which provided him with experience at a multilevel urban site. He had also worked as expedition architect for Reisner during his 1908–10 seasons in Egypt and at Samaria (in ex-Palestine). With this training, Fisher initiated a project at Memphis, an enormous and complex site that had served as a major royal center for several millennia. An exacting excavator whose careful field recording techniques were directly influenced by Reisner, Fisher is hardly recognized, for his significant excavations remain unpublished.

The University Museum's fieldwork resumed in 1929 under British Egyptologist Alan Rowe (1891–1968), who had worked with Fisher at Beth Shan and was supervisor of the Reisner excavations at Giza in 1925 at the time of the dramatic discovery of the intact tomb of Hetepheres. Rowe sought to establish Snefru as the royal builder of the pyramid at Maidum by excavating the pyramid, its associated funerary temple, and the adjoining cemeteries. His work was interrupted by the Great Depression in 1931, yet his unpublished excavation reports are an important record of the Maidum necropolis, the earliest royal cemetery complex of the Old Kingdom.

From 1905 onward Coxe underwrote much of the expense of both the University Museum's Egyptian expeditions and its curatorial department. Upon his death in 1916 he bequeathed an endowment that maintained the department without supplement through the 1950s. During the 1930s and 1940s Coxe excavation funds were used to engage curators who could catalogue the extant Egyptian collections. English Egyptologist Battiscomb Gunn (1883–1950) served as Egyptian curator from 1931 to 1934, and German scholar Hermann Ranke (1878–1953) published the first collection catalogue while he was associated with the museum in the years before and during World War II.[28] Also displaced from Germany by the Nazi regime, Rudolf Anthes (1896–1985) was curator of the Egyptian section from 1950 to 1963. During 1955–56 he undertook an ambitious excavation of a portion of

Memphis, including the small temple of Ramesses II, which resulted in a clear stratigraphic view of this highly complex site.[29] Anthes proposed to expand his initial survey into a major fieldwork project, but changing priorities led the museum to focus instead on excavations simultaneously under way at Gordion, Tikal, and Hasanlu which combined scientific results with the recovery of visually striking artifacts. Anthes was assisted with his curatorial duties and in the field by Henry G. Fischer (b. 1923), the first recipient of a Ph.D. in Egyptology from the University of Pennsylvania.

FIGURE 29
Phoebe Apperson Hearst (back row, second from left) and party at Giza, c. 1900.

The Phoebe A. Hearst Museum of Anthropology, University of California, Berkeley

The Phoebe Apperson Hearst Museum of Anthropology (formerly the Robert H. Lowie Museum of Anthropology), a remarkable repository of more than 17,700 excavated Egyptian objects, is named for its primary benefactor (see fig. 29). George Hearst, her husband, had made his fortune in the American mining boom of the mid-nineteenth century; her son was William Randolph Hearst, the newspaper magnate. Phoebe Hearst supported the University of California's Egyptian fieldwork projects for more than six years and had the foresight to contribute funding for subsequent publications.[30]

In 1899 Hearst offered excavation funding to Reisner, then fresh from two years' service with the International Catalogue Commission at the Cairo Museum.[31] Soon after, he received permission from the Egyptian Antiquities Service (then headed by French papyrologist Gaston Maspero) to excavate in the area of "Coptos-Shurafa-Der," about twenty miles north of modern Luxor. Reisner, who had no experience as an excavator, described how Hearst had "agreed that I should have three years to develop scientific methods of excavating and recording. During this time, I would work on unimportant sites and would not be expected to produce important antiquities."[32] He engaged two assistants, British Egyptologist Frederick W. Green (1869–1949), who had been successful the previous season working with James Quibell at Hierakonpolis, and another unseasoned Harvard graduate, Albert M. Lythgoe. In letters and expense reports to Hearst written between 1899 and 1905, Reisner provided a telling view of Egyptian expedition camp life.[33] In September 1899 Quibell helped him survey potential sites and structure the initial excavation. Beginning in late 1899, they investigated two Predynastic sites, a flint camp and a heavily plundered cemetery at Shurafa.

During early 1900 the expedition team moved to nearby Deir el-Ballas (see fig. 30), where they uncovered a large royal palace, a settlement, and a series of cemeteries dating to the late Second Intermediate Period and early 18th Dynasty (see cat. no. 72).[34] In May 1900 Reisner was informed that el-Ahaiwah, a site sixty miles upriver, was being looted, and he received permission to start an additional excavation there. He focused for four months on a Predynastic cemetery, a New Kingdom town and necropolis, and a Middle to New Kingdom fortress. In 1901 he shifted to another site in the same area which was being denigrated by tomb robbers, the extensive cemetery of Naga el-Deir (see cat. nos. 34–35, 48–49). Having improved excavation and recording techniques during the previous projects, Reisner could comment: "I now felt that we had learned enough to attempt such a site."[35] His confidence must have been shared by the Antiquities Service, as Maspero granted him a concession to the entire site. The systematic survey and clearance of a series of cemeteries from 1901 to 1904 revealed tombs ranging in date from the Predynastic Period to the twentieth century A.D. In November 1901, following the first few months' work at Naga el-Deir, British Egyptologist Arthur C. Mace (1874–1928) joined Reisner and Lythgoe on the project and later contributed to the multivolume publication of the site.[36]

Another participant at Naga el-Deir was Australian anatomist and anthropologist Grafton Elliot Smith (1871–1937), a professor of anatomy at the Cairo University School of Medicine from 1900 to 1909. Smith is respected for his evaluation of human remains and mummies, which led to a clearer understanding of the mummification process, although his diffusionist theories naming Egypt as the place of origin for most of humankind's customs and beliefs were later discredited.[37]

Shifting his focus to Giza in early 1903, Reisner sent Mace to open the concession at the site. The University of California sponsored Reisner's work there for two more years, until 1905, when the project became a joint venture of Harvard University and the Museum of Fine Arts, Boston.

During the early years at Giza separate royal cemeteries for Kings Khufu, Khafre, and Menkaure were identified, and as Reisner noted, the excavators accumulated a "mass of material on the development of the mastaba, the masonry, the art, and the burial customs of this period."[38] Reisner published the reports of the University of California excavation, and he incorporated additional information into later publications such as *A History of the Giza Necropolis* (vol. 1, 1942; vol. 2 with W. S. Smith, 1955) and *The Development of the Egyptian Tomb down to the Accession of Cheops* (1936). American Egyptologist Henry Frederick Lutz (1886–1973) continued the cataloguing of objects with two volumes, *Egyptian Tomb Steles and Offering Stones* (1927) and *Egyptian Statues and Statuettes* (1930).[39] Lutz, who had received his doctorate in Semitics from Yale University

FIGURE 30
Excavation camp at
Deir el-Ballas, 1901.

in 1916, served as the sole faculty member in the fields of Egyptology, Assyriology, and Semitics at the University of California, Berkeley, from 1921 until his retirement in 1954. The appointment of Klaus Baer (1930–87) to the department of Egyptology at the University of California in 1959 (he returned to his home institution, the University of Chicago, in 1965) marked the beginning of a more active program of academic instruction in the field.

Phoebe Hearst also sponsored a somewhat less ambitious project during the 1899–1900 season, an expedition by two British papyrologists, Bernard P. Grenfell (1869–1926) and Arthur S. Hunt (1871–1934), to Tebtunis, in the Faiyum region of Egypt. As a result, the university acquired many papyrus documents, in addition to sculpture and funerary equipment, from the Ptolemaic and Roman periods. Reisner added another rare medical papyrus, a collection of remedial incantations, which he purchased near Deir el-Ballas in 1901 and named in honor of his sponsor.[40]

The Brooklyn Museum

The Brooklyn Museum, like other American institutions, received some of its first Egyptian objects via subscription to the EEF.[41] Beginning in 1902, these gifts endowed Brooklyn with an unusually strong representation of the Amarna period (see cat. nos. 11, 13–14) and also with objects from Deir el-Bahri, Kahun, el-Lahun, and Amara West and Sesebi in the Sudan.

The French Egyptologist Henri de Morgan (1854–1909) undertook the first excavations directly sponsored by the Brooklyn Museum in two seasons, 1906–7 and 1907–8. De Morgan worked closely with his brother, Jacques de Morgan, who had served from 1892 to 1897 as director of the Egyptian Antiquities Service and had made important discoveries at Dahshur, Naqada, and Saqqara. Their experience with Predynastic and Early Dynastic material was particularly appropriate to the wealth of early cemeteries in the Brooklyn concession, which stretched from Esna in the north to Edfu in the south, and was extended farther southward to Gebel el-Silsila during the second season of work. Henri de Morgan excavated and recorded tombs at el-Adaima, el-Mamariya, Kom el-Ahmar, el-Qara, Abu Zaidan, and el-Masaid (see cat. nos. 18–22, 25–26), from which he retrieved many significant objects now in the Brooklyn Museum. He failed to number burial objects or to use photographic documentation, however, which made identification of objects problematic for subsequent museum cataloguers Walter Federn (working 1942–45) and Winifred Needler (working 1970–83). Nevertheless Needler published the second season of de Morgan's field reports and a comprehensive catalogue of the Brooklyn collection of Predynastic and Early Dynastic objects.[42]

In 1916 the children of pioneering American Egyptologist Charles Edwin Wilbour began to donate objects from their father's collection to the Brooklyn

Museum. A successful journalist and printer, Wilbour turned to Egyptology later in life, spending a portion of each year in Egypt studying the monuments and making accurate copies of inscriptions. Although he authored only one brief article on his recordings,[43] he contributed to the discipline of Egyptology by supplying colleagues with transcribed material. In letters written to his family during his travels from 1880 to 1891, Wilbour recorded a lively, informed view of his interaction with colleagues in Egypt.[44]

Wilbour's personal Egyptological accomplishments are overshadowed by the research strength and autonomy that Wilbour endowments have provided to the Egyptian department of the Brooklyn Museum since 1916. In addition to his substantial collection of objects, given in three parcels (the latest in 1947), his library became the core of the Charles Edwin Wilbour Memorial Library of Egyptology (see fig. 31), one of the most complete reference sources in the world. Wilbour funds have been used for the acquisition of objects, the establishment and support of curatorial positions, and the continued growth and staffing of the library. They also have made possible gallery installations, special exhibitions, and conservation of objects.

Accomplished Belgian Egyptologist Jean Capart (1877–1947) was part-time curator of Brooklyn's Egyptian collection from 1932 to 1938. Assisted by Edwin Taggart, he organized the museum's first major installation of Egyptian art, exhibiting the Wilbour collection and other objects in the first of what are now thirteen galleries devoted to such displays. In 1937 the New-York Historical Society lent more than two thousand objects to the museum, which purchased the collection outright in 1948.[45]

Serving as Wilbour librarian and later as associate curator from 1936 to 1956, Elizabeth Riefstahl (1889–1986) made major contributions to the breadth of the museum's bibliographic acquisitions. At the same time she became a professional Egyptologist and during World War II maintained the department for the absent curator.[46]

John D. Cooney (1905–82; see fig. 32) succeeded Capart as department head from 1938 to 1963, and like his predecessor, he focused on the art historical side of Egyptological studies. Richard Fazzini noted in a recent catalogue of the Brooklyn collection that "under Cooney, the Department began to acquire individual objects of high aesthetic value on a consistent basis, in keeping with the philosophy that quality was more important than quantity."[47] The high level of acquisition activity that Cooney achieved during just five years, from 1951 to 1956, is documented by a catalogue accompanying a 1956–57 exhibition of 130 newly accessioned works of art.[48] In 1941 Cooney organized the exhibition *Pagan and Christian Egypt: Egyptian Art from the First to the Tenth Century A.D.*,[49] and he initiated a series of focused topical exhibitions. Widely recognized for his success in building the Brooklyn Egyptian collections, Cooney became curator of ancient art at the Cleveland Museum of Art in 1963.

Born and trained in Germany, art historian and Egyptologist Bernard V. Bothmer (1912–93) joined the Brooklyn staff in 1956. In 1960 he curated the ground-breaking exhibition *Egyptian Sculpture of the Late Period, 700 B.C. to A.D. 100*, and he maintained a strong research interest in Egyptian sculpture throughout his life. He assembled the Corpus of Late Egyptian Sculpture at the Brooklyn Museum, a significant archive of notes and photographs. An influential teacher of Egyptian art history, he became a full professor at the Institute of Fine Arts at New York University upon his retirement from the museum in 1978.

The Metropolitan Museum of Art, New York

The Metropolitan began subscribing to the EEF in 1895, but not until 1906 did the museum's trustees vote to establish a department of Egyptian art.[50] Reisner's fieldwork projects of

FIGURE 33
Metropolitan Museum curator Albert M. Lythgoe, left, with J. P. Morgan, center, and other travelers at el-Kharga Oasis, 1908.

1905–6 had generated a wealth of additions to the collection of the Museum of Fine Arts, Boston, and this may have affected the decision of the Metropolitan's trustees. Board president J. Pierpont Morgan (serving 1904–13) hired Albert M. Lythgoe (see fig. 33), then Reisner's lead fieldwork supervisor, as the department's first curator.

As Lythgoe later wrote in the preface to the department's first publication, *The Tomb of Senebtisi at Lisht* (1916), the Metropolitan's expedition had a dual purpose from the onset: "The programme adopted for the expedition comprised (1) the investigation, through excavation, of sites representing the successive periods of Egyptian history and civilization; and (2) the formation of a series of records of the constructive and decorative features of Egyptian monuments, through photographs, architectural drawings, and copies in color."[51]

Metropolitan excavations conducted between 1906 and 1936 focused on the sites of Lisht, the el-Kharga Oasis, Wadi Natrun, Hierakonpolis, and Thebes. Lythgoe began his fieldwork in 1906–7 at Lisht, a site excavated but not exhausted by an expedition of the French Institute of Oriental Archaeology in 1894–95.[52] He assembled a team consisting of Arthur C. Mace,[53] who had worked with both Petrie and Reisner, and a young American scholar, Herbert E. Winlock. Winlock continued to excavate extensively and became the director of the expedition; he later served as curator of the Department of Egyptian Art (1929–39) and director

of the Metropolitan Museum (1932–39). Fourteen seasons of work at Lisht focused on the pyramids of two kings, Amenemhat I and his son Senwosret I, and the surrounding tombs of high officials of the court, dating from the late Old Kingdom to the Roman period.

At el-Kharga, the largest of the oases in the Western Desert, Metropolitan teams spent portions of eleven seasons at the well-preserved temple of Hibis, dedicated to Amun and dating to the Persian period, and the nearby cemeteries of el-Baqawat and el-Deir. In 1910 the Metropolitan was granted a concession at Thebes, which became the excavators' primary focus through 1937.

Working as assistant curator under Lythgoe, Caroline Ransom Williams (d. 1952) focused on the cataloguing of the Metropolitan collections from 1910 to 1916. She had studied with Erman in Berlin and received a Ph.D. under Breasted from the University of Chicago.

From the inception of the museum's Egyptian department, Morgan was a major patron, funding fieldwork projects and advancing funds as needed to Lythgoe in the field. He underwrote a comfortable field house constructed in the Asasif area of the Theban Plain (see fig. 35), which was briefly called Morgan House but later renamed Metropolitan House when it was learned that the generous patron had "merely advanced the money as a loan and then paid himself back from museum funds."[54] Edward S. Harkness, a Cleveland philanthropist and a cousin to Lythgoe by marriage, became a Metropolitan trustee in 1912 and was another important benefactor of the department.

Known as the Graphic Section, the recording branch of the Metropolitan's expedition worked in Egypt from 1907 to 1937 (see fig. 36). Charles K. Wilkinson, who joined the section in 1920, later described its mission: "One might wonder why the Museum, in its golden age of discovering and acquiring ancient Egyptian objects, was also committed to making copies of wall paintings. The individual responsible for that policy was Lythgoe, a man whose modesty concealed rare administrative ability and a passion for thoroughness .... What Lythgoe wanted were permanent, accurate copies of the originals, exact in line, color, and when possible, in full scale, for study and exhibition at the Museum and for publication."[55] Norman de Garis Davies (1865–1941), an English Egyptologist and highly accomplished copyist who had first worked with Petrie, headed the Graphic Section for almost thirty years, working from 1907 to 1917 and again from 1919 to 1937. Along with his equally talented wife, Anna (Nina) Macpherson Davies (1881–1965), and other copyists—Lancelot Crane, Norman

Hardy, Hugh R. Hopgood, E. Harold Jones, Walter J. Palmer-Jones, Francis Unwin, and Wilkinson—Davies focused primarily on the recording of private tomb paintings at Thebes. Ambrose Lansing (1891–1959), an American born in Cairo, joined the expedition as an excavator from 1911 to 1922. He also worked in New York overseeing the collection and became department head in 1939. Lansing is particularly associated with work in the Theban tombs of the Asasif and at the Malqata palace of Amenhotep III.

Englishman Harry Burton (1879–1940), photographer of the Graphic Section from 1914 until his death, used large-format glass negatives to record Theban tomb interiors and other monuments in exquisite detail (see p. 149).[56] From a conservation standpoint it was fortunate that Burton preferred the more traditional glass-plate negative over the film negative available at the time, as his images remain extremely well preserved and stable. More than 12,300 glass plates in the Metropolitan archives document the expedition's work from 1914 to 1937, and more than six hundred photographs record Egyptian objects from Cairo and Italy.[57] Lythgoe, recognizing the urgent need for documentation of the highly important intact tomb of Tutankhamun, sent Burton, along with Mace, expedition architect Walter Hauser, and draftsman Lindsey Hall, to work for Lord Carnarvon and Howard Carter following the discovery of the tomb in 1922 (see fig. 34). Working from 1922 to 1933, Burton captured the pristine state of the tomb and its contents in nearly fourteen hundred photographs.[58]

In 1921 Burton experimented with the use of motion picture film to document excavations in Egypt, but his footage evidenced a need for more sophisticated lighting and panning techniques. In 1924, in preparation for the filming of the interior of Tutankhamun's tomb, Burton received instruction in filmmaking at several Hollywood studios. After two weeks, however, he determined that the movie industry's huge portable generators and strong lights would not be suitable for filming fragile objects, but he did incorporate certain aspects of his study into later footage, now in the Metropolitan Museum film archives.

FIGURE 36
The staff of the Metropolitan Museum expedition, 1925.
Back row, left to right: Herbert E. Winlock, Walter Hauser, Albert Lythgoe, Harry Burton, Charles K. Wilkinson, Norman de Garis Davies; *center row:* Helen Winlock, Nina de Garis Davies, Lucy Lythgoe, Minnie Burton, Miss Willis (governess); *front row:* Walter Cline, Barbara Winlock, Frances Winlock, Governour Peek.

By 1919 Winlock, with the approval of Lythgoe, had largely assumed the directorship of the Egyptian expedition. Working in Thebes the next year, Winlock made a remarkable discovery, an overlooked tomb chamber of Meketre, a high official of the 11th Dynasty king Nebhepetre Mentuhotep II, which contained superbly preserved and detailed models of the activities of daily life. Winlock also continued the excavations of Swiss Egyptologist Edouard Naville at Deir el-Bahri, which had been started with EEF funding in 1893–96. For twenty years Winlock focused on clearing sites in and around the Hatshepsut and Nebhepetre Mentuhotep II temples (see cat. no. 53) and on private Middle Kingdom cemeteries, at times employing up to seven hundred Egyptian workmen to move thousand of tons of sand and rubble from the sites. During the 1922–23 and 1927–29 seasons his crews unearthed fragments of numerous broken statues of Hatshepsut that had once been a part of the mortuary temple but were discarded in pits along the causeway (see fig. 37 and cat. no. 75). Among Winlock's numerous discoveries, which illuminated royal and private life in Thebes from the Middle Kingdom period onward, are the Heqanakht papyri; monuments of Senenmut, a powerful figure from the court of Hatshepsut (see cat. nos. 78, 79); and a private burial cache from the Third Intermediate Period (see cat. no. 91).

Winlock's success in the field was, in the end, his undoing, as he was called back to New York to become director of the Metropolitan Museum in 1932. As John Wilson noted: "Although he hated to leave the field, he accepted the new post with such dedication that he suffered a stroke in 1939 and had to retire from administration. Carefully husbanding his strength over his remaining eleven years of life, he produced six books."[59] His *Models of Daily Life in Ancient Egypt from the Tomb of Meket-Re at Thebes* was posthumously published in 1955.

Fieldwork projects for the Metropolitan ended after the 1936–37 season, largely because of the weak U.S. economy. During the 1940s and 1950s attention shifted from fieldwork to cataloguing and publishing the collections. William C. Hayes (1903–63), who had worked with the Metropolitan expedition from 1927 to 1936, became assistant curator in 1936 and curator in 1952. He authored, among numerous other publications, a collection guide and history of Egyptian art, *The Scepter of Egypt: A Background for the Study of Egyptian Antiquities in the Metropolitan Museum of Art*, published in two volumes in 1953 and 1959. Hayes's work on a detailed history of Egypt was cut short by his death in 1963; the first few chapters appeared posthumously as *Most Ancient Egypt* (1964).

FIGURE 37
The Metropolitan team reassembling fragmented statues of Hatshepsut at Deir el-Bahri, 1929.

Nora Scott (1905–94), who had worked in Egypt for only one season (with the Egypt Exploration Society at Armant in 1929–30), was an active member of the Metropolitan staff from 1931 to 1972. She spent much of her time processing results from the museum's expeditions, organizing records, photographic documentation, and objects; she also pursued personal research interests such as private 11th Dynasty Theban tombs, ancient Egyptian daily life, jewelry, and scarabs. Ludlow Bull (1886–1954), who had studied at the University of Chicago, became associate curator of the department during the 1940s. Charlotte Clark (1897?–1985), who served as a special assistant to Winlock, and Dorothy Phillips (1906–77) were assistant curators during the 1940s. William Kelly Simpson (b. 1928) joined the Metropolitan staff in 1948 and left to become Yale's first professor of Egyptology in 1958. Henry G. Fischer began as a Metropolitan staff member in 1957 and later spearheaded the museum's participation in the Nubian campaign of the 1960s.

The Oriental Institute, University of Chicago

James Henry Breasted, founder of the Oriental Institute, began his professional career as a pharmacist. Switching first to theology and then to Egyptology, he completed his Ph.D. studies in Berlin with Erman from 1891 to 1894.[60] Following a honeymoon in Egypt, spent copying and translating inscriptions from extant monuments, Breasted returned to Chicago to become an assistant professor of Egyptology and the assistant director of the Haskell Oriental Museum. In 1905 he was appointed professor of Egyptology and oriental history, the first chair in Egyptology in the United States. Following his work on an ambitious German philological project, the Berlin Dictionary (the first comprehensive dictionary of ancient Egyptian), and after compiling hieroglyphic inscriptions from European museum objects, Breasted resolved to publish a corpus of historical inscriptions in English. *Ancient Records of Egypt*, consisting of more than ten thousand manuscript pages, was published in five volumes in 1906 and remains a useful resource today.[61] In 1905–7 he led an expedition that produced photographs and facsimiles of hieroglyphic inscriptions in situ at Nile Valley sites from Meroe (150 miles northeast of Khartoum) north to Aswan.

In 1919, with funding from oil magnate John D. Rockefeller Jr., Breasted founded the Oriental Institute, a research institute of the University of Chicago devoted to the archaeology, philology, and history of the ancient Near East. Over many decades Rockefeller contributed more than $20 million in support of the University of Chicago, the Oriental Institute, Chicago House, and numerous publications, making him the most generous American patron of Egyptology.[62]

As described by Breasted, the purpose of the institute was to "contribute to the understanding of human life by furnishing a fuller knowledge of the process and

stages of the long development by which we have become what we are. This purpose involves us in the task of recovering a great group of lost civilizations in the Near East, which contributed the fundamentals of civilization to the Western World."[63] Focusing on the cultures of Egypt, Mesopotamia, Iran, Syria, Palestine, and Anatolia, research activities of the Oriental Institute have been conducted in three general areas: archaeological, epigraphic, and architectural field expeditions; philological and historical research, usually conducted in Chicago at the institute; and the interpretation and presentation of recovered objects housed at the institute's museum.

In 1894, during his first trip to Egypt, Breasted was appalled at the ongoing damage to ancient sites, which he was able to estimate by comparing standing monuments with records made earlier in the century. In 1924 he established the Epigraphic Survey of the Oriental Institute, which for seventy seasons has documented the monuments of Thebes through the production of precise facsimiles of carved reliefs, painted scenes, and inscriptions. Since 1929 the survey has published all or portions of sites such as the mortuary temple complex of Ramesses III at Medinet Habu, Karnak temple, the temples of Mut and Khonsu, Luxor temple, and the 18th Dynasty private tomb of Kheruef in the Asasif area of Thebes.

Under the auspices of the Oriental Institute, German architectural historian Uvo Hölscher (1878–1963) supervised eleven years of intensive archaeological work at the mortuary temple complex of Ramesses III at Medinet Habu. This enormous site (with an enclosure wall of 314 by 210 meters) is complex in both its original plan and its layers of occupation, which span more than three millennia (see fig. 39). Assisted by Harold H. Nelson (1878–1954), field director of the Epigraphic Survey from 1924 to 1947, and Rudolf Anthes, Hölscher completely cleared the complex. Publication of the site of Medinet Habu, with highly detailed plans and reconstruction drawings and accompanying oversize folios, set a new and superior standard for architectural recording of an extensive site.[64]

The institute sponsored other important field projects. From 1926 to 1933 the Englishmen Kenneth S. Sandford and William J. Arkell conducted a survey of prehistoric sites in Egypt and the Sudan. Prentice Duell (1894–1960) led an expedition to Saqqara from 1931 to 1937. His work resulted in a two-volume documentation of the wall scenes from the Old Kingdom private tomb of Mereruka, beautifully illustrated with oversize plates but lacking commentary or translation of inscriptions.[65]

Later field directors of the Epigraphic Survey included Richard Parker (serving 1948–49), who went on to found the Egyptology department at Brown

University;[66] George Hughes (1949–58 and 1959–64);[67] and John A. Wilson (acting 1958–59).

Since Breasted's arrival at Chicago in 1895 the university has remained a training ground for Egyptologists, particularly in the area of philology. Accomplished scholars associated with the university include Miriam Lichtheim (b. 1914), who later served as lecturer and bibliographer at the University of California, and Helene Kantor (1919–93), who placed Egyptian studies within the wider frame of the ancient Near East.[68] Dutch Egyptologist Henri Frankfort (1897–1954) served as research professor of Oriental archaeology from 1932 through the late 1940s, while simultaneously holding a position at the University of Amsterdam. He produced numerous books and articles, including *Ancient Egyptian Religion: An Interpretation* and *Kingship and the Gods*, both published in 1948.[69]

Chicago graduate John A. Wilson emerged as a major figure in Egyptology, succeeding Breasted as director of the Oriental Institute from 1936 to 1946 and authoring works such as *The Burden of Egypt: An Interpretation of Ancient Egyptian Culture* (1951) and *Signs and Wonders upon Pharaoh: A History of American Egyptology* (1964).[70] In addition, in 1964 Wilson served as director of the UNESCO Consultative Committee to the United Arab Republic for the Salvage of the Nubian Monuments.

Beginning with the publication of *Ancient Records of Egypt* in 1906–7, the institute has maintained a tradition of producing research tools for the study of Near Eastern cultures. The first volume documenting the Coffin Texts project, initiated by Breasted in 1922, was published in 1935.[71] A demotic dictionary (documenting the late stage of Egyptian language, in use from 650 B.C. to the third century A.D.), currently in progress under the direction of Janet Johnson, is scheduled for publication during the 1990s.

The Oriental Institute Museum, founded along with the institute in 1919, contains more than thirty thousand Egyptian objects acquired by both archaeological excavation and purchase. Breasted purchased the core of the collection in Egypt between 1894 and 1935, and significant additions of excavated finds were made via EEF and, later, British School of Archaeology in Egypt subscriptions. The excavation of Medinet Habu between 1926 and 1932 added extensive New Kingdom and later màterials to the collection, particularly in the areas of ancient Egyptian daily life, popular religion, and funerary practices. Remarkably, lost excavation field records documenting the Medinet Habu finds were located in Germany in 1994 and reunited with the collection.[72]

Kelsey Museum of Archaeology, University of Michigan, Ann Arbor

The University of Michigan sponsored expeditions to three Greco-Roman period sites in Egypt between 1924 and 1945. Karanis (Kom Aushim), located at the northeastern edge of the Faiyum, a broad ancient and modern agricultural district lying fifty miles southwest of Cairo, was the primary focus of the projects, with hundreds of houses, seventeen granaries, and two temples excavated during eleven seasons of work (see fig. 40). Dimai (Soknopaiou Nesos), north of the Birket Qarun, the lake of the Faiyum, was examined during 1931 and yielded customs seals, receipts, and Greek inscriptions. A single season in 1935 at Terenuthis (Kom Abu Billo), on the western edge of the Delta, resulted in the recovery of hundreds of funerary stelae from the late third and early fourth centuries A.D.

The excavations were initiated by Francis W. Kelsey (1858–1927), who had traveled to Egypt in 1920 to acquire Greco-Roman papyrus documents for the university. His interest was engendered by the discoveries of Bernard P. Grenfell and Arthur S. Hunt (whose work for the Hearst Museum is discussed above), who had found a "hitherto unknown work, Logia Iesu (The Sayings of Our Lord),"[73] which had associations with the Christian Bible. Elaine K. Gazda and Andrea M. Berlin, writing about the excavations at Karanis, described Kelsey's motivations: "At Oxyrhynchus, in the company of B. P. Grenfell, he observed the material remains of Graeco-Roman sites in the process of destruction at the hands of the *sebbakhin* (fertilizer gatherers). Upon inquiring what arrangements had been made to record and interpret the archaeology of the sites, he was told that not only was no effort being expended to document the archaeological record but that previous work in Egypt had almost totally neglected the cultural background of the Graeco-Roman period in favor of that of the Dynastic era."[74] Hoping to correct this situation, Kelsey procured funding from Horace H. Rackham, and the first expedition proceeded in 1924. Enoch E. Peterson (1891–1978) directed the work

FIGURE 40
Remains of houses
and granaries at
Karanis, excavated
by the Kelsey Museum
of Archaeology,
University of Michigan.

at Karanis from 1926 to 1935 and produced unpublished excavation reports on the architecture and topography of the site.

The more than forty-four thousand objects recovered from the site of Karanis, a rural agricultural village occupied from the mid-third century B.C. to the end of the fifth century A.D., provide a unique view of provincial life during this period (see cat. nos. 113–19). Of particular interest are the many papyrus documents, remarkably well preserved by the dry climate of Egypt. They include biblical fragments; religious writings; public and private documents; private letters; and astronomical, astrological, mathematical, and magical texts (see cat. no. 114). The importance of the contextual aspect of the discovery of these documents was recognized at the time of their excavation, and the findspot for each document was recorded, which was not the case with the papyri collected by Grenfell and Hunt for other institutions. Botanical and zoological remains documented by the Michigan expeditions were later published by Arthur E. R. Boak.[75]

The finds from Karanis have been published by philologists and art historians such as Donald B. Harden, Elinor Husselman, Lillian M. Wilson, and Herbert C. Youtie[76] and continue to provide material for doctoral dissertations, exhibitions, and ongoing research by the staff of the Kelsey Museum and the University of Michigan Papyrus Collection.

Other American Egyptological Activities prior to 1960

Most American institutions that sponsored major projects in Egypt between 1899 and 1960 first experienced the benefits of fieldwork as subscribers to the EEF. Other sizable U.S. institutions chose not to fund their own fieldwork, but they did become EEF subscribers and thus repositories of EEF finds. These included the Walters Art Gallery, Baltimore; the Art Institute of Chicago; the Cincinnati Art Museum; the Cleveland Museum of Art; the Detroit Institute of Arts; the University Art Museum, Princeton; and the Smithsonian Institution, Washington, D.C.

Other institutions most often acquired Egyptian objects at the impetus of a museum director, curatorial staff, or donors. For example, serious collecting of Egyptian art began at the Detroit Institute of Arts during the 1920s under the directorship of German art historian William Valentiner. In addition to purchasing objects on the European art market, Valentiner hired Howard Carter to serve as an agent for the museum in purchasing works of art in Egypt.[77] During the late 1940s and 1950s the Cleveland Museum of Art began to acquire major Egyptian objects and benefited from the appointment of Sherman Lee as curator of oriental and ancient art in 1952. The Los Angeles County Museum of Art (at that time known as the Los Angeles County Museum of History, Science, and Art) received numerous donations from William Randolph Hearst, particularly during the years 1946 to 1950, when James Henry Breasted Jr. (son of the notable Chicago Egyptologist) served as museum director.

Additional American academic centers active in the study of Egypt included Harvard, Yale, Princeton, New York University, Bryn Mawr College, Brown, and the University of Toronto, with some initiating smaller fieldwork projects. Harvard University sponsored excavations in 1927, 1930, and 1935 in the Sinai at Serabit el-Khadem, the site of a Middle Kingdom temple of Hathor and extensive turquoise mines that were active between the 12th and 20th Dynasties.[78] Although Yale did not conduct fieldwork until the Nubian campaign of the 1960s, the university, through the Yale University Art Gallery and the Peabody Museum of Natural History, contributed to the scholarly development of the discipline throughout this century. Ludlow Bull taught Egyptology at Yale and worked to build the collection of the University Art Gallery. William Kelly Simpson (Ph.D., Yale, 1954) worked in the field and became active in the Egyptian departments of several institutions;

from 1969 to 1988 he headed the department at the Museum of Fine Arts, Boston. Founded in 1948 with the hiring of Richard Parker (1905–93), the department of Egyptology at Brown University remains the only academic department in an American university dedicated solely to the teaching of Egyptology.

Several collections benefited from the displacement of German scholars by the Nazi regime and World War II. Georg Steindorff (1861–1951), for example, studied the collection of the Walters Art Gallery, compiling a twelve-volume manuscript and publishing a catalogue of the museum's Egyptian sculpture in 1946. He also made an extensive study of a late Old Kingdom royal portrait in the Freer Gallery of Art, Washington, D.C.[79]

Other, lesser-known scholars explored various areas of Egyptology during the period from the turn of the twentieth century to the 1960s. Robb de Peyster Tytus (1876–1913) excavated with British Egyptologist Percy E. Newberry at the palace of Amenhotep III at Thebes from 1899 to 1902 but is best remembered for the Metropolitan Museum publication series on Theban tombs which was funded posthumously in his name by his mother.[80] James Teackle Dennis (1865–1918), educated at Johns Hopkins University, worked with Naville at Deir el-Bahri in 1905–6 (see cat. no. 52).[81] Independent scholar Elizabeth Thomas (1907–86) completed graduate work at the Oriental Institute and served as a cryptologist during World War II. Thomas traveled extensively in Egypt, published numerous Egyptological articles, and authored *The Royal Necropolis of Thebes* (1966).[82]

University professors teaching in related fields were influential figures in Egyptology. Papyrologist Campbell Bonner (1876–1954) was professor of Greek at the University of Michigan from 1912 to 1946,[83] Egyptologist-Semiticist Aaron Ember (1878–1926) was professor at the University of Baltimore during the 1920s,[84] and architectural historian Earl Baldwin Smith (1888–1956), who taught at Princeton from 1916 to 1954, wrote *Egyptian Architecture as Cultural Expression* (1938).[85]

Founding of the American Research Center in Egypt

American institutions specializing in Egyptian studies took a major step toward the organization of their efforts in Egypt in 1948 with the founding of the American Research Center in Egypt (ARCE). ARCE's founders—including Dows Dunham, Joseph Lindon Smith, William Stevenson Smith, and Edward W. Forbes, a trustee of the Museum of Fine Arts, Boston—perceived the need to maintain an American archaeological presence in Egypt following the cessation in 1947 of the long-running Harvard-Boston expedition.[86] An umbrella organization for both individual and organizational research projects in Egypt, ARCE maintains headquarters in the United States (currently in New York) and in Cairo. ARCE provides technical and administrative support to North American expedition teams conducting fieldwork in Egypt. Staff members in Cairo negotiate concession permits, translate related documents, assist with accounting and financial needs, and supply equipment. In addition the Cairo office is a communication and social center for both expatriates and scholars working in Egypt and sponsors lecture programs, excursions, and study trips. In the United States ARCE serves as the primary organization for American scholars concerned with the study of pharaonic Egypt. (The scope of the organization's interests, however, spreads beyond the ancient world to the study of medieval and modern Egypt.) In addition to publishing a quarterly newsletter and the annual *Journal of the American Research Center in Egypt*, ARCE sponsors a conference at which several hundred members convene each year to present papers and communicate with colleagues. Over the past four decades ARCE has provided organizational support to all the institutions mentioned in the preceding pages. ARCE has also sponsored more than four hundred individual scholars since the initiation of a competitive fellowship program in 1957.

FOR ALL THE INSTITUTIONS DESCRIBED ABOVE, funding was the principal factor in the cessation or reduction of Egyptological fieldwork. The severe economic downturns of the late 1920s and the Great Depression of the 1930s eroded financial support for expeditions, including those that continued—

projects of the Oriental Institute, the Metropolitan Museum of Art, and the Harvard-Boston expedition. Sponsorship for fieldwork also declined after the Egyptian government reduced the number of objects that an expedition could claim following a successful excavation season. This change in policy was due largely to the dramatic discovery of the intact tomb of Tutankhamun in 1922. Many excavators, however, continued to return from Egypt with newly recovered objects until stricter regulations were implemented in 1936.[87]

Foreign visitors were allowed restricted travel within Egypt after World War II, but from then until the early 1960s very few American excavations were undertaken, although the Oriental Institute continued the Epigraphic Survey. John Wilson described the political climate of the times: "Anti-foreign feeling culminated in the agony of 'Black Saturday,' January 16, 1952, when an angry mob burned the best-known Western establishments in Cairo. There followed the peaceful coup of July 23, when (King) Faruq was forced to abdicate and a military regime took over."[88] Political unrest must have discouraged foreign archaeological projects in Egypt, although French, German, and British teams resumed work in 1953.[89] One of the few American projects initiated during this period was a joint University of Pennsylvania-Egyptian Antiquities Organization excavation at Mit Rahina (ancient Memphis), under the direction of Rudolf Anthes, which ended after two seasons due to lack of funding.

As early as 1956 Egyptologists recognized that archaeological sites and at least thirty temples were threatened by the pending submersion of more than three hundred miles of the Nile Valley beneath the waters of the Aswan High Dam.[90] In 1959 the Egyptian and Sudanese governments, in conjunction with UNESCO, issued an appeal to scholars to document the lands to be flooded. Only then did a resurgence of projects occur, in both Egypt and Nubia. By 1995 more than forty-five American institutions had conducted fieldwork projects in Egypt (see pp. 249–55). Other individuals and organizations have contributed to knowledge of the field through varied activities, including special exhibitions, museum permanent collection catalogues, research projects, and scholarly publications. Some of these recent activities are cited in the object entries that follow this essay, and others are discussed in the companion volume to this catalogue, *The American Discovery of Ancient Egypt: Essays.*

Notes

6 Ibid., 244–45; see also George A. Reisner, autobiographical ms., Department of Ancient Egyptian, Nubian, and Near Eastern Art, MFA, Boston, 1–2.

7 The exhibition was on view from 29 October 1993 to 1 August 1994; see Joan Knudsen and Patricia Podzorski, "Focus on Egypt's Past," *KMT* 5 (Spring 1994): 62–69, 87. See also Peter Der Manuelian, ed., "George Andrew Reisner on Archaeological Photography," *JARCE* 29 (1992): 1–34.

8 Reisner had several notable successors in the use of archaeological field photography; see, for example, the photos by Harry Burton. Much of Reisner's field photography was executed by Egyptian members of his staff.

9 Reisner, autobiographical ms., 4–5.

10 George A. Reisner, *A History of the Giza Necropolis*, vol. 1 (Cambridge: Harvard University Press, 1942); George A. Reisner and William S. Smith, *A History of the Giza Necropolis*, vol. 2 (Cambridge: Harvard University Press, 1955); George A. Reisner, "A History of the Giza Necropolis 1.2," ms., Department of Ancient Egyptian, Nubian, and Near Eastern Art, MFA, Boston.

11 George A. Reisner, *Mycerinus: The Temples of the Third Pyramid at Giza* (Cambridge: Harvard University Press, 1931).

12 Dunham, *The Egyptian Department*, 51–63. Contents of the tomb of Hetepheres were carefully recorded over a two-year period, under extremely difficult conditions.

13 George A. Reisner, *The Development of the Egyptian Tomb down to the Accession of Cheops* (Cambridge: Harvard University Press, 1936). Reisner also produced a manual for archaeological fieldwork, which is currently being prepared for publication by Peter Lacovara of the Museum of Fine Arts, Boston.

14 Hermann Junker, *Giza*, 12 vols. (Vienna and Leipzig: Holder-Pichler-Tempsky, 1929–55).

15 Selim Hassan, *Excavations at Giza*, 10 vols. (Oxford: Faculty of Arts of the Egyptian University; Cairo: Government Press, 1932–60).

16 George A. Reisner, *A Provincial Cemetery of the Pyramid Age: Naga ed-Dêr*, pt. 3, University of California Publications, Egyptian Archaeology 6 (Liepzig: J. C. Hinrichs, 1932).

17 Peter Lacovara et al., "Tomb of Djehutynakht," in *Mummies and Magic*, 109–18.

18 Drew R. Engles, "An Early Dynastic Cemetery at Kafr Ghattati," *JARCE* 27 (1990): 71–87.

19 Dows Dunham, *Zawiyet el-Aryan: The Cemeteries adjacent to the Layer Pyramid* (Boston: MFA, 1978).

20 Dunham's publications include *Naga-ed-Der Stelae of the First Intermediate Period* (London: Oxford University Press for the MFA, Boston, 1937); *The Royal Cemeteries of Kush*, 5 vols. (Cambridge: Harvard University Press, 1950–63); *The Egyptian Department* (1958); *Second Cataract Forts* (with J. Janssen), 2 vols. (Boston: MFA, 1960); *Recollections of an Egyptologist* (Boston: MFA, 1972); *The Mastaba of Queen Mersyankh III* (with William K. Simpson; Boston: MFA, 1974); *Zawiyet el-Aryan* (1978).

21 William S. Smith, *Ancient Egypt as Represented in the Museum of Fine Arts, Boston* (Boston: MFA, 1942); idem, *A History of Egyptian Sculpture and Painting in the Old Kingdom* (London: Oxford University Press, 1946); idem; *The Art and Architecture of Ancient Egypt* (Baltimore: Penguin Books, 1958).

22 For details of Chapman's career, see *In Tribute to Suzanne E. Chapman* (Boston: MFA, 1970).

23 For a brief history of the University Museum's involvement with Egyptology, see *The University Museum in Egypt*, special issue of *Expedition* 21 (Winter 1979): 4–63.

24 Ibid., 17; for the history of the EES and a list of American contributors, see also T. G. H. James, ed., *Excavating in Egypt: The Egypt Exploration Society, 1882–1982* (Chicago: University of Chicago Press, 1982), 187.

25 W. M. Flinders Petrie, *Seventy Years in Archaeology* (New York: Henry Holt, 1932), 180–87.

26 Ibid., 21–38.

27 Ibid., 113.

28 Hermann Ranke, "The Egyptian Collection of the University Museum," *University of Pennsylvania Museum Bulletin* 15 (November 1950).

29 Rudolf Anthes, *Mit Rahineh, 1955* (Philadelphia: University Museum, University of Pennsylvania, 1959). See also Henry G. Fischer, "Rudolf Anthes, 1896–1985," *JARCE* 22 (1985): 1–3.

30 For an affectionate biography of Phoebe Hearst commissioned by her son and a description of her philanthropic activities and travels to Egypt, see Winifred Black Bonfils, *The Life and Personality of Phoebe Apperson Hearst* (San Francisco: Privately printed, 1928), 86–89.

31 Reisner authored three volumes of the Catalogue général des antiquités égyptiennes du Musée du Caire (IFAO): *Amulets* (1907), *Models of Ships and Boats* (1913), and *Canopics* (1967).

32 Reisner, ms., 3.

33 For an accounting of trip expenses for 8–20 September 1899, see George A. Reisner, "Letters of George A. Reisner [to Mrs. Hearst]," Bancroft Library, University of California, Berkeley, 13–16.

34 Peter Lacovara, "State and Settlement: Deir el-Ballas and the Development, Structure and Function of the New Kingdom Royal City" (Ph.D. diss., University of Chicago, 1993), 11–12. See also idem, "The Hearst Excavations at Deir el-Ballas: The Eighteenth Dynasty Town," in *Studies in Ancient Egypt, the Aegean, and the Sudan: Essays in Honor of Dows Dunham*, ed. William K. Simpson and W. M. Davis (Boston: MFA, 1981), 120–24.

35 Reisner, autobiographical ms., 5.

36 George A. Reisner, *The Early Dynastic Cemeteries of Naga-ed-Der*, University of California Publications in Egyptian Archaeology 2 (Leipzig: J. C. Hinrichs, 1980); idem, *A Provincial Cemetery of the Pyramid Age*.

37 Dawson and Uphill, *Who Was Who*, 273–74.

38 Reisner, *Early Dynastic Cemeteries of Naga-ed-Der*.

39 Henry Frederick Lutz, *Egyptian Tomb Steles and Offering Stones of the Museum of Anthropology and Ethnology of the University of California*, University of California Publications, Egyptian Archaeology 4 (Leipzig: J. C. Hinrichs, 1927); idem, *Egyptian Statues and Statuettes in the Museum of Anthropology of the University of California*, University of California Publications, Egyptian Archaeology 5 (Leipzig: J. C. Hinrichs, 1930).

40 George A. Reisner, *The Hearst Medical Papyrus: Hieratic Text in Seventeen Facsimile Plates in Collotype*, University of California Publications, Egyptian Archaeology 1 (Leipzig: J. C. Hinrichs, 1905).

41 For a history of the Egyptian department of the Brooklyn Museum, see Richard A. Fazzini, "The Brooklyn Museum's Egyptian Collection," in Richard Fazzini et al., *Ancient Egyptian Art in the Brooklyn Museum* (Brooklyn: Brooklyn Museum, 1989), vii–x.

42 Winifred Needler, "Two Important Predynastic Graves from Henri de Morgan's Excavations," *Bulletin de l'Association internationale pour l'étude de la préhistoire égyptienne* 1 (1980): 1–15; idem, *Predynastic and Archaic Egypt in the Brooklyn Museum*, Wilbour Monographs 9 (Brooklyn: Brooklyn Museum, 1984). See also Ronald J. Williams, "Winifred Needler (1904–1987)," *JARCE* 25 (1988): 1.

43 Charles Edwin Wilbour, "Canalizing the Cataract," *Recueil de travaux relatifs à la philologie et à l'archéologie égyptiennes et assyriennes* 13 (1890): 202–3.

44 Charles Edwin Wilbour, *Travels in Egypt (December 1880 to May 1891): Letters of Charles Edwin Wilbour*, ed. Jean Capart (Brooklyn: Brooklyn Museum, 1936).

45 In addition to the well-known Henry Abbott collection, this group included objects given by Dr. Henry J. Anderson in 1864 and 1877, some objects given by Mrs. A. Minturn in 1890, and more than four hundred works from the Edwin Smith collection, donated in 1907.

46 Long interested in Egyptian glass and faience, Riefstahl published the pamphlet "Glass and Glazes from Ancient Egypt" (Brooklyn Museum, 1948) and, during her extended career as associate curator emeritus, *Ancient Egyptian Glass and Glazes* (Brooklyn: Brooklyn Museum, 1968). See also Robert S. Bianchi, "Elizabeth T. Riefstahl (1889–1986)," *JARCE* 24 (1987): 1.

47 Fazzini et al., *Ancient Egyptian Art*, viii.

48 *Five Years of Collecting Egyptian Art, 1951–1956* (Brooklyn: Brooklyn Museum, 1956).

49 John Cooney, *Pagan and Christian Egypt: Egyptian Art from the First to the Tenth Century A.D.* (Brooklyn: Brooklyn Museum, 1941).

50 For a history of the Metropolitan Museum and its Egyptian department, see Calvin Tomkins, *Merchants and Masterpieces: The Story of the Metropolitan Museum of Art* (New York: E. P. Dutton, 1970), 135–48.

51 Albert M. Lythgoe, preface to Arthur C. Mace and Herbert E. Winlock, *The Tomb of Senebtisi at Lisht*, MMA Egyptian Expedition 1 (New York: MMA, 1916), vii.

52 Dieter Arnold, *The Pyramid of Senwosret I*, MMA Egyptian Expedition 22 (New York: MMA, 1988), 15.

53 For a recent biography of Mace, see Christopher C. Lee, *...The Grand Piano Came by Camel: Arthur C. Mace, the Neglected Egyptologist* (Edinburgh and London: Mainstream Publishing, 1992).

54 Tomkins, *Merchants and Masterpieces*, 138.

55 Charles K. Wilkinson and Marsha Hill, *Egyptian Wall Paintings: The Metropolitan Museum of Art's Collection of Facsimiles* (New York: MMA, 1983), 10.

56 For information on Burton's career, see Marsha Hill, "The Life and Work of Harry Burton," in Erik Hornung, *The Tomb of Pharaoh Seti I* (Zurich: Artemis, 1991), 27–30.

57 Inventory by Marsha Hill, assistant curator and archivist, Egyptian Department, MMA, New York (conversation with author, 28 July 1994).

58 More than fourteen hundred of Burton's negatives are in the archives of the MMA's Egyptian department. A parallel set of nearly one thousand negatives is at the Griffith Institute, Ashmolean Museum, Oxford.

59 John A. Wilson, *Signs and Wonders upon Pharaoh: A History of American Egyptology* (Chicago: University of Chicago Press, 1964), 192.

60 For a biography written by Breasted's son, see Breasted, *Pioneer to the Past*.

61 James H. Breasted, *Ancient Records of Egypt*, 5 vols. (Chicago: University of Chicago Press, 1906–7; reprint, New York: Russell and Russell, 1962).

62 This figure has been revised downward from the $400 million cited in Dawson and Uphill, *Who Was Who*, 251, based on research provided by Irving L. Diamond, Wilmette, Illinois (letter to author, 2 February 1995).

63 James H. Breasted, "General Circular No. 2," Oriental Institute of the University of Chicago (August 1928), reproduced in William M. Sumner, "The Oriental Institute, Director's Introduction," in *Publications of The Oriental Institute, 1906–1991*, ed. Thomas A. Holland (Chicago: Oriental Institute, University of Chicago, 1991), ix.

64 Uvö Holscher, *The Excavation of Medinet Habu*, 5 vols., OIP 21, 41, 54, 55, 66 (Chicago: University of Chicago Press, 1934–54).

65 The Sakkarah Expedition, *The Mastaba of Mereruka*, 2 vols., OIP 31, 39 (Chicago: University of Chicago Press, 1938).

66 For a memorial to Richard Parker, see John Larson, "Richard Anthony Parker, 1905–1993," in *The Oriental Institute 1992–1993 Annual Report* (Chicago: Oriental Institute, University of Chicago, 1993), 8–9.

67 See Janet H. Johnson, "George R. Hughes, January 12, 1907–December 21, 1992," in *The Oriental Institute 1991–1992 Annual Report* (Chicago: Oriental Institute, University of Chicago, 1993), 13–15.

68 Abbas Alizadeh, "Helene J. Kantor, July 15, 1919–January 13, 1993," in ibid., 16–18.

69 For Frankfort's biography and publications, see Dawson and Uphill, *Who Was Who*, 108–9.

70 Elizabeth B. Hauser et al., "Bibliography of John Albert Wilson (September 12, 1899–August 30, 1976)," in Charles E. Jones, *Oriental Institute Research Archives Acquisition List, August–September 1990*, suppl., 4 October 1990, 1–20.

71 Adriaan de Buck, *The Egyptian Coffin Texts*, 7 vols., OIP 34, 49, 64, 67, 73, 81, 87 (Chicago: University of Chicago Press, 1935–61).

72 For the rediscovery of Medinet Habu excavation records in 1993–94, see John N. Wilford, "Long Lost Field Notes Help Decode Treasure," *New York Times*, 21 September 1993; idem, "Long Lost Notebooks of Egyptian Expedition," *New York Times*, 10 May 1994, Science section. See also Mary Ruth You, "For the Record," *University of Chicago Magazine* (October 1993): 16–17; idem, "Readers of the Lost Archives," *University of Chicago Magazine* (August 1994): 28–31; Emily Teeter, *News and Notes* (Oriental Institute), no. 140 (Winter 1994): 7–9.

73 Elaine K. Gazda, ed., *Karanis: An Egyptian Town in Roman Times*, exh. cat. (Ann Arbor: Kelsey Museum of Archaeology, University of Michigan, 1983), 2.

74 Ibid.

75 Arthur E. R. Boak, ed., *Karanis: The Temples, Coin Hoards, Botanical and Zoological Reports: Seasons 1924–31*, University of Michigan Studies, Humanistic Series 30 (Ann Arbor: University of Michigan, 1933).

76 Ibid.; see bibliography, 46–49.

77 William H. Peck, "The Discoverer of the Tomb of Tutankhamun and the Detroit Institute of Arts," *JSSEA* 10, no. 2 (1981): 65–67.

78 Kirsopp Lake et al., "The Serabit Expedition of 1930," *Harvard Theological Review* 25 (1932): 95–203. See also Richard F. S. Starr and Romain F. Butin, *Excavations and Protosinaitic Inscriptions at Serabit el Khadem*, Studies and Documents 6, ed. Kirsopp Lake and Silva Lake (London: Christophers, 1936).

79 Georg Steindorff, *Catalogue of the Egyptian Sculpture in the Walters Art Gallery* (Baltimore: Walters Art Gallery, 1946); idem, *A Royal Head from Ancient Egypt*, Freer Gallery of Art Occasional Papers 5 (Washington, D.C.: Freer Gallery of Art, 1951).

80 Dawson and Uphill, *Who Was Who*, 291.

81 Ibid., 83.

82 See Rita E. Freed, "Elizabeth Thomas (1907–1986)," *JARCE* 24 (1987): 1–2.

83 Ibid., 33.

84 Ibid., 96–97.

85 Ibid., 273.

86 Dunham, *Recollections of an Egyptologist*, 47. See also Dow, "The Founding of an American Research Center," 10–19.

87 Cyril Aldred, "El-Amarna," in James, *Excavating in Egypt*, 98.

88 Wilson, *Signs and Wonders*, 195.

89 Jean Leclant, "Fouilles et travaux en Egypte," *Orientalia*, n.s., 24, fasc. 3 (1955): 296–317. This useful annual compilation of archaeological fieldwork projects in Egypt (by various authors) begins with *Orientalia*, n.s., 17 (1948).

90 Jean Leclant, "Fouilles et travaux en Egypte, 1954–1955," *Orientalia*, n.s., 25, fasc. 3 (1956): 251.

Abbreviations

AJA   *American Journal of Archaeology*

ASAE   *Annales du Service des antiquités de l'Egypte*

BES   *Bulletin of the Egyptological Seminar*

BIFAO   *Bulletin de l'Institut français d'archéologie orientale du Caire*

BMB   *The Brooklyn Museum Bulletin*

BMFA   *Bulletin of the Museum of Fine Arts (Boston)*

BMMA   *Bulletin of the Metropolitan Museum of Art*

BSFE   *Bulletin de la Société française d'égyptologie*

CdE   *Chronique d'Egypte*

CG   Catalogue général des antiquités égyptiennes du Musée du Caire

IFAO   Institut français d'archéologie orientale du Caire

JARCE   *Journal of the American Research Center in Egypt*

JEA   *Journal of Egyptian Archaeology*

JNES   *Journal of Near Eastern Studies*

JSSEA   *Journal of the Society for the Study of Egyptian Antiquities*

KUSH   *Kush: Journal of the Sudan Antiquities Service*

LÄ   *Lexikon der Ägyptologie*, 6 vols., ed. H. W. Helck and W. Westendorf (Wiesbaden: Harrassowitz, 1975–86).

MDAIK   *Mitteilungen des Deutschen archäologischen Instituts, Abteilung Kairo*

MFA   Museum of Fine Arts, Boston

MMA   Metropolitan Museum of Art

NARCE   *Newsletter of the American Research Center in Egypt*

OIC   Oriental Institute Communications

OINE   Oriental Institute Nubian Expedition

OIP   Oriental Institute Publications

PAHMA   Phoebe A. Hearst Museum of Anthropology

PM   B. Porter and R. Moss, *Topographical Bibliography of Ancient Egyptian Hieroglyphic Texts, Reliefs, and Paintings*, 7 vols. (Oxford: Griffith Institute, Ashmolean Museum, 1934–81). The second, revised edition is cited for vols. 1 (pts. 1, 2), 2, and 3 (fascs. 1–3).

RdE   *Revue d'égyptologie*

SAK   *Studien zur altägyptischen Kultur*

ZÄS   *Zeitschrift für ägyptische Sprache und Altertumskunde*

Note to the Reader

DATES

The dates given for the major periods of Egyptian history, dynasties, and reigns of individual rulers are based upon those used in John Baines and Jaromír Málek, *Atlas of Ancient Egypt* (New York: Facts on File, 1994). A somewhat revised version of this chronology can be found in the article "Egypt," in the *Encyclopaedia Britannica*, 15th ed. (beginning with the 1988 printing).

PLACE NAMES

The orthography of place names also follows the usage in Baines and Málek, *Atlas of Ancient Egypt*. Frequently used modern names for ancient sites are provided in parentheses, such as Mit Rahina for Memphis or Tell Umm el-Breigat for Tebtunis.

SPELLING OF EGYPTIAN NAMES

The spelling of royal and private Egyptian personal names in this catalogue is based upon Bruce G. Trigger et al., *Ancient Egypt: A Social History* (Cambridge: Cambridge University Press, 1983). Exceptions have been made for key historical figures based on institutional preference (for example, the Metropolitan Museum of Art's use of "Senwosret," rather than "Senusret," for the second king of the 12th Dynasty). Other exceptions have been made to allow for more consistent spellings of the names of two Egyptian gods—Amun and Re—whose names are incorporated into many Egyptian royal and private names, such as Tutankhamun and Menkaure.

TRANSLATIONS

Square brackets used within translation of Egyptian texts indicate lost portions of the text that have been restored, while parentheses indicate words added by the translator to clarify meaning.

DIMENSIONS

Measurements of objects are given in centimeters and inches and appear in the following order: height, width, depth.

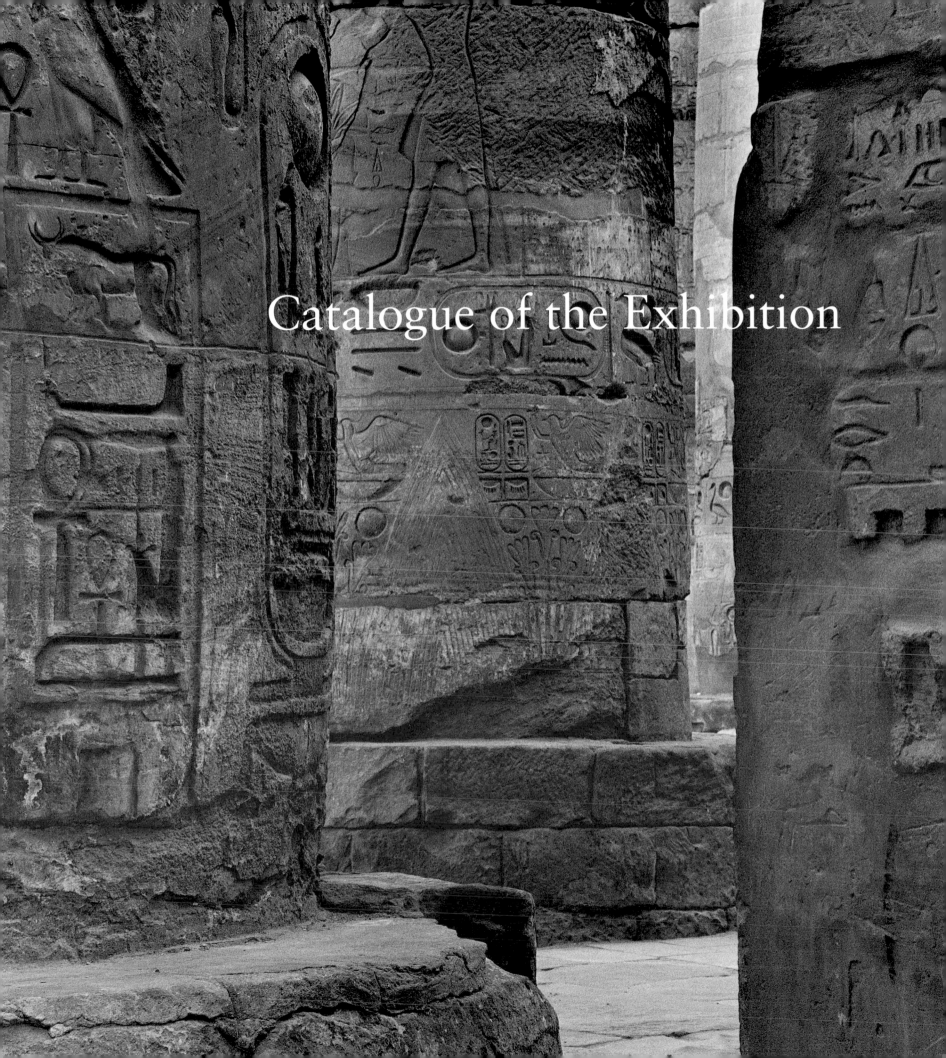

Catalogue of the Exhibition

T his introductory section contains objects acquired by some of America's early collectors and travelers in Egypt. Unlike those discussed in subsequent catalogue entries, these objects are not presented in chronological sequence according to their date of creation. Instead, they are ordered roughly by date of acquisition and serve as a preface to the first period of American field archaeology in Egypt. As such, they mark the transition from random collecting to the purchase of artifacts by more informed buyers, such as Henry Abbott and, to a greater degree, Charles Edwin Wilbour.

This section and the following catalogue entries are supplemented by significant additions made to American museums by subscription to the British-run Egypt Exploration Fund. The acquisition of objects through American support of British expeditions—particularly the 1884–1924 excavations headed by W. M. Flinders Petrie—stimulated public and institutional interest in the launching of the first American expeditions to Egypt.

1 Ma'at

Probably from Thebes
25th Dynasty (c. 712–664 B.C.)
Diorite
17.5 x 7.5 x 9 cm (6⅞ x 3 x 3½ in.)
H (with base): 27.2 cm (10¾ in.)
The Detroit Institute of Arts, gift of
Mr. and Mrs. H. L. Wadsworth, 68.37

When this statue was a given to the Detroit Institute of Arts, an accompanying document detailed its modern history from the time it was first purchased in 1820 in Egypt. As such the statue is a useful example of the mania for collecting Egyptian objects early in the nineteenth century.

Of particular interest is the nineteenth-century black marble base, whose raised, gilded lettering reads: "Antient [sic] statue brought from Thebes in upper Egypt by W.N.—A.D. 1820." The initials W. N. refer to William Nelson (1757–1835), brother of Admiral Lord Horatio Nelson. William, who was made Earl Nelson of Trafalgar in recognition of his brother's service to Britain, is known to have traveled in Egypt in 1820. According to the document, signed by Frederic William Cowley on November 26, 1895, the statue was found "buried in a tomb" at Thebes. At the death of William Nelson it

passed to Lady Collingwood, described as a relative of Nelson's, but probably the wife of Baron Cuthbert Collingwood, naval officer and longtime friend of the admiral. When the Collingwood estate was dispersed, the statue was purchased by George Harper, Esq., of Ashford, Kent, who sold it to Cowley.

The figure is a three-dimensional realization of the typical hieroglyphic representation of Ma'at, the goddess of truth and universal order. The body and limbs are extremely stylized, and only Ma'at's identifying ostrich feather, which may have been formed separately, is lacking. The small size of this piece suggests that it was a votive offering. Without the base it could have been held in one hand, and it is in scale with such offerings of Ma'at depicted in relief. The medium of so-called Chephren gray diorite, whose rarity precluded its use for little more than royal statues, suggests that this was an important dedicatory object for ritual purposes.

Dating a stylized and uninscribed object such as this is particularly challenging. Standards of proportion are of little help, and the rarity of the type makes it difficult to find well-documented examples. The date of this object is tentatively put in the 25th Dynasty on the basis of a comparison with details of the standing statue of the Divine Consort of Amun, Amunirdis, in the Egyptian Museum, Cairo (JE 3420, CG 565).[1] WP

BIBLIOGRAPHY William H. Peck, "The Present State of Egyptian Art in Detroit," *Connoisseur* 175 (December 1970): 271, fig. 6.

NOTES
1. Mohamed Saleh and Hourig Sourouzian, *Official Catalogue: The Egyptian Museum, Cairo* (Mainz: Philipp von Zabern, 1987), no. 244.

2 Female Figure

Middle Kingdom, 11th to 12th
Dynasty (c. 2040–1783 B.C.)
Wood, stone inlays
H: 33 cm (13 in.)
The Johns Hopkins University,
Archaeological Collection, 9213

Although individual objects and small groups of Egyptian antiquities were first brought to the United States by New England mariners, the earliest major Egyptian collection formed by an American was that of Colonel Mendes Cohen of Baltimore. Following Cohen's death, his collection was presented by his heirs to Johns Hopkins University, where it forms the cornerstone of the university's Archaeological Collection.[1]

This delicate statuette of a woman was one of Cohen's many acquisitions. It is typical of Egyptian wooden statuettes in its technique: the head and body were worked as one piece, while the arms and front of the feet (each group of five toes being treated as a single unit) were carved separately and attached. The right arm is now missing.

The figure wears a long, carefully striated wig that is parted in the center and swept behind the ears to frame the attractive face. Its lively appearance is heightened by the use of stone inlays for the eyes. A traditional, close-fitting sheath reveals the form of the body beneath it. The proportions are slender and somewhat elongated, as is common for such figures from the late Old Kingdom through the Middle Kingdom. Traces of pigment remain on the surface, reminding the viewer that the statuette was once brightly painted to heighten its sense of naturalism and animation. The remains of a painted bracelet appear at the left wrist.

Burials of the socially prominent during the First Intermediate Period and the Middle Kingdom often included wooden statuettes. In some instances they seem to have served the function fulfilled by Old Kingdom wall reliefs, which depicted the various agricultural, craft, and domestic activities on the ideal gentleman's estate of the era in order to maintain them in the afterlife for the eternal benefit of the tomb owner.[2] Other statuettes probably are servant figures or were intended to attend the deceased in some manner in the afterlife. Some statuettes must also have portrayed the tomb owner or members of the deceased's family. To judge from the quality of the execution of this single figure, it was most likely either a well-made servant figure or a representation of the deceased. GS

BIBLIOGRAPHY John A. Wilson, *Signs and Wonders upon Pharaoh* (Chicago: University of Chicago Press, 1964), pl. 12a; Ellen Reeder Williams, *The Archaeological Collections of the Johns Hopkins University* (Baltimore: Johns Hopkins University Press, 1984), 18.

NOTES
1. For more on Cohen, see Warren R. Dawson and Eric P. Uphill, *Who Was Who in Egyptology* (London: Egypt Exploration Fund, 1972), 67; Wilson, *Signs and Wonders*, 38, 41, 217; Betsy M. Bryan, "An Early Eighteenth Dynasty Group Statue from the Asasif in the Johns Hopkins Collection," *BES* 10 (1989–90): 25.
2. The best of these are no doubt those discovered by the Metropolitan Museum of Art in the tomb of Meketre, now divided between Cairo and New York. For a discussion of the New York models, see William C. Hayes, *The Scepter of Egypt*, vol. 1, *From the Earliest Times to the End of the Middle Kingdom* (New York: MMA, 1953), 262–71.

3 Pair Statue of Ruiu and Baki

Probably from Asasif, burial no. 729
New Kingdom, 18th Dynasty, reign
of Hatshepsut (c. 1473–1458 B.C.)
Granodiorite
35 x 18 x 22.2 cm (13¾ x 7⅛ x 8¾ in.)[1]
The Johns Hopkins University,
Archaeological Collection, 9212

Donated to the Johns Hopkins University by the heirs of Mendes Cohen (see cat. no. 2), this pair statue was originally part of the vast collections of Henry Salt (1780–1827), British painter and consul general to Egypt. Salt formed three major Egyptian collections: the first was sold to the British Museum and Sir John Soane, the second to King Charles X of France, and the third was auctioned in London in 1835.[2] Cohen purchased the present statue at the London sale.[3] It might have been acquired for Salt by Giovanni d'Athanasi, who worked at Thebes for the British consul general between 1819 and 1827.[4]

The statue and its texts have been well studied by Betsy M. Bryan,[5] and the present entry reflects many of her discoveries. Among the first things to strike the viewer is the statue's condition, particularly its cracked surface. While this sort of damage is often attributed to fire, recent research indicates that long-term but intermittent exposure to water produces similar results.[6]

Dating to the early 18th Dynasty, this pair statue is the visual descendant of a private statue type introduced during the Old Kingdom. The female and male owners, seated side by side, are identified by inscriptions that appear in single vertical columns down the front of their garments. Further texts identifying the pair and giving their filiation appear on the back slab, which has been cut to resemble a round-topped stela. The woman, Ruiu, and the man, Baki, are related, perhaps as husband and wife, but this is not specifically stated. Atypically Ruiu holds the place of primary importance on the statue's right side. She is also slightly taller than her male companion, another indication of her status. Within the conventions of ancient Egyptian art, size was directly proportional to importance. Interestingly the couple also exchange a mutual, supportive embrace. Their garments and hairstyles are characteristic of the fashion of the early 18th Dynasty,[7] and their facial features resemble those of Hatshepsut, during whose reign the sculpture likely was carved.

Two other family members are included, carved in elemental sunk relief. A female figure, identified as Amenhotep, appears on the front side of the seat, to Ruiu's right. A similar male figure to Baki's left is identified as Amenemhat.

Private statues of this type were usually employed as tomb sculpture during the New Kingdom, and Bryan has convincingly demonstrated the relationship of the present statue to a tomb discovered by the Metropolitan Museum of Art.[8] She has further linked this pair statue with monuments of other family members. GS

BIBLIOGRAPHY Ellen Reeder Williams, *The Archaeological Collections of the Johns Hopkins University* (Baltimore: Johns Hopkins University Press, 1984), 19, no. 5; Betsy M. Bryan, "An Early Eighteenth Dynasty Group Statue from the Asasif in the Collection of the Johns Hopkins University Archaeological Collection," *BES* 10 (1989–90): 25–38; Gerry D. Scott, III, *Dynasties: The Egyptian Royal Image in the New Kingdom*, exh. brochure (San Antonio: San Antonio Museum of Art, 1995), no. 8; idem, "Dynasties: The Egyptian Royal Image in the New Kingdom," *Varia Aegyptiaca* 10 (April 1995): 19, no. 8.

NOTES
1. Williams and Bryan (see Bibliography) give slightly different dimensions for this sculpture.
2. For Salt, see Warren R. Dawson and Eric P. Uphill, *Who Was Who in Egyptology* (London: Egypt Exploration Fund, 1972), 258.
3. Bryan, "An Early Eighteenth Dynasty Group Statue," 25.
4. For d'Athanasi, see Dawson and Uphill, *Who Was Who*, 13.
5. Bryan, "An Early Eighteenth Dynasty Group Statue."
6. See ibid., 27–28.
7. As noted by Bryan, ibid., 26.
8. Ibid., 30–32, 37.

4   Idi

6th Dynasty, c. 2200 B.C.
Limestone
H: 39 cm (15⅜ in.)
The Metropolitan Museum of Art,
Rogers Fund, 1937, 37.2.2

Idi's statuette is carefully and crisply cut,
although carved in a fissured limestone. His
huge eyes and mouth are strikingly defined
and further emphasized by the harsh modeling that breaks up the smooth surfaces of the
face. His low-set head juts forward slightly,
and his torso narrows excessively at the waist.
His arms and torso show minimal modeling,
but for the softness of the breasts and the delicate line of the lower edge of the rib cage.
His knees and shin ridges are schematically
sharp, and the attenuated toes and oval nails
are like those of wooden statuary.

Idi's pose is traditional, but the stylistic
treatment of the figure is evidence of the
recently identified and described "second
style."[1] As the naturalistic style so successful
in the 4th Dynasty gradually became dull and
repetitive, the second style emerged. Characterized by an animated, manneristic emphasis
on the features and articulations of the body,
the style seems to have appeared first in the
Saqqara cemeteries and spread from there.

Beside each foot are inscribed Idi's titles:
"count," "sole acquaintance," "overseer of the
two workshops," and "overseer of priests."
A quartzite statue in the University of Missouri
Museum of Art and Archaeology, Columbia
(60.46), and a false door in the Egyptian
Museum, Cairo (CG 1457), probably both
belonged to an Idi who was a vizier and was
buried at Abydos.[2] This sculpture might represent the same vizier of the late 6th Dynasty,
though its provenance is unknown.

The statue was a gift from the Khedive
Said Pasha to Commodore Matthew Calbraith Perry in 1854 on the latter's return
voyage to the United States after forcefully
convincing Japan's feudal rulers to conclude
trading treaties with the West. MH

BIBLIOGRAPHY William C. Hayes, "Two Egyptian
Statuettes," *BMMA* 33 (April 1938): 107–8; William
S. Smith, *History of Egyptian Sculpture and Painting
in the Old Kingdom* (Boston: MFA, 1946), 88;
William C. Hayes, *The Scepter of Egypt*, vol. 1, *From
the Earliest Times to the End of the Middle Kingdom*
(New York: MMA, 1953), 112; Henry G. Fischer,
"A Provincial Statue of the Egyptian Sixth Dynasty,"
AJA 66 (1962): 65–69; Cyril Aldred, "Some Royal
Portraits of the Middle Kingdom in Ancient Egypt,"
MMA Journal 3 (1970): 29; Edna R. Russmann, "A
Second Style in Egyptian Sculpture of the Old King-
dom," *MDAIK* 51 (forthcoming).

NOTES
1. See Russmann, "A Second Style," and her earlier
work referred to there.
2. See Fischer, "A Provincial Statue."

5 Shabti of Sati

18th Dynasty, reign of Amenhotep III
(c. 1391–1353 B.C.)
Polychrome faience
H: 25 cm (9⅞ in.)
The Brooklyn Museum,
Charles Edwin Wilbour Fund, 37.123E

Among the most numerous of all ancient Egyptian antiquities, funerary figurines—variously known as shabtis, shawabtis, or ushebtis, depending on the date of the particular example—were manufactured continuously from the early Middle Kingdom through the Ptolemaic period. They became essential components of a burial. Beginning in the 17th Dynasty, they were inscribed with chapter 6 of the Book of the Dead, which contained a spell instructing the figurine to perform various agricultural tasks for the deceased in the underworld. In the 18th Dynasty the production of funerary figurines reached its highest level of accomplishment. Whereas stone had been the traditional material, new media such as faience, glazed stone, metal, and even glass were used. Heretofore, perhaps just one or a few figurines were deposited in each burial, but during the reign of Amenhotep II (1427–1401 B.C.), the numbers increased dramatically. Amenhotep II was interred with about 90 figurines. Tuthmosis IV (r. 1401–1391 B.C.) owned 30, and Tutankhamun (r. 1333–1323 B.C.) was the proud possessor of 417.

In the reign of Tuthmosis IV the decoration of funerary figurines underwent a profoundly important development. As an elaboration on the agricultural tasks specified in the magical spell from the Book of the Dead, figurines were outfitted with either hoes and bags or baskets. The implements were painted or modeled directly on the figurines or fashioned separately in miniature. The position of the bag or basket, when painted or modeled on the figurine, is one of the most significant criteria for dating figurines. In the reign of Tuthmosis IV the bags or baskets were positioned on the front of the figurines at waist level. By the reign of Tutankhamun they had moved to the back.[1]

Carefully wrought in brilliant polychrome faience, the shabti of Sati and its companion in the Brooklyn Museum (37.124E) are splendid examples of 18th Dynasty craftsmanship. Indeed they are among the finest Egyptian funerary figurines ever made.[2] The extraordinary modeling and the position of the bags or baskets on the front suggest a date in the reign of Amenhotep III. Henry Abbott purchased this shabti at Saqqara, but it was not necessarily found there.[3] DS

BIBLIOGRAPHY Donald B. Spanel, *Through Ancient Eyes: Egyptian Portraiture,* exh. cat. (Birmingham, Ala.: Birmingham Museum of Art, 1988), 86–89, no. 23; Richard A. Fazzini et al., *Ancient Egyptian Art in the Brooklyn Museum* (Brooklyn: Brooklyn Museum, 1989), no. 47; Arielle P. Kozloff and Betsy M. Bryan, *Egypt's Dazzling Sun: Amenhotep III and His World,* exh. cat. (Cleveland: Cleveland Museum of Art, 1992), 328–29, no. 70.

NOTES
1. See Donald B. Spanel, "Two Unusual Eighteenth-Dynasty Shabtis in the Brooklyn Museum," *BES* 10 (1989–90): 145–67.
2. Rivaled only by the shabti of the priest of Amun, Ptahmose, who lived during the reign of Amenhotep III; see Mohamed Saleh and Hourig Sourouzian, *Official Catalogue: The Egyptian Museum, Cairo* (Mainz: Philipp von Zabern, 1987), no. 150.
3. A few comparable polychrome figurines have been excavated at Saqqara; see Spanel, *Through Ancient Eyes,* 89, n. 4.

6 Ostracon with Cat and Mouse

Thebes[1]
New Kingdom, 20th Dynasty
(1196–1070 B.C.)
Limestone
8.9 x 16.9 x 1.1 cm (3½ x 6⅝ x ½ in.)
The Brooklyn Museum, Charles
Edwin Wilbour Fund, 37.51E

The Egyptians used ostraca—fragments of pottery vessels and limestone flakes—in place of expensive papyrus for drawings and sketches. On this fragment a lean cat presents a bolt of cloth with one hand, and a fan and plucked goose with the other, to a plump mouse enthroned as a noblewoman. The gigantic mouse, wearing a lotus blossom on its forehead, holds a glass and a flower.[2]

In its reversal of natural roles the scene might be a satirical comment on the social decline of the late 20th Dynasty or an illustration to a lost fable. Whatever the case, it conveys the freedom and spontaneity of a sketch.

Papyri with similar subject matter were popular in the late Ramesside period. This scene, although it appears to be complete, might have been a sketch for a larger composition on papyrus.[3] BM

BIBLIOGRAPHY Richard A. Fazzini, *Images for Eternity: Egyptian Art from Berkeley and Brooklyn*, exh. cat. (San Francisco: Fine Arts Museums of San Francisco; Brooklyn: Brooklyn Museum, 1975), no. 84; Günter Dreyer, in *Ägyptische Kunst aus dem Brooklyn Museum*, exh. cat. (Berlin: Ägyptisches Museum, 1978), no. 56; Richard A. Fazzini et al., *Ancient Egyptian Art in the Brooklyn Museum* (Brooklyn: Brooklyn Museum, 1989), no. 62.

NOTES
1. According to the ostracon's first owner, Henry Abbott, the piece might be from Deir el-Medina, the village of artisans in western Thebes.
2. Some think the flower is a fish skeleton; see Dreyer, *Ägyptische Kunst*, no. 56.
3. Emma Brunner-Traut, *Egyptian Artists' Sketches: Figured Ostraka from the Gayer-Anderson Collection in the Fitzwilliam Museum, Cambridge*, Uitgaven van het Nederlands Historisch-Archeologisch Institut te Istanbul 45 (Leiden: Nederlands Historisch-Archaeologisch Institut te Istanbul, 1979), 11–18; idem, *Die altägyptische Scherbenbilder (Bildostraka) der Deutschen Museen und Sammlungen* (Wiesbaden: Franz Steiner, 1956), 96, pl. XXXIV; idem, *Altägyptische Tiergeschichte und Fabel* (Darmstadt: Wissenschaftliche Buchgesellschaft, 1980), 7–8; B. Peterson, "Zeichnungen aus einer Totenstadt: Bildostraka aus Theben-West, ihr Fundplatze, Themata und Zweckbereiche," *Medelhavsmuseet Bulletin* 7–8 (1973): 49.

7 Torso and Head of Mentuemhet

Late Period, late 25th to early 26th Dynasty, c. 680–650 B.C.
Black granite
Head: 13.5 x 19.2 cm (5⅜ x 7½ in.)
Torso: 14 x 16 cm (5½ x 6¼ in.)
Head: Field Museum of Natural History, 31723
Torso: The Brooklyn Museum, gift of the estate of Charles Edwin Wilbour, 16.580.186

As befits a sculpture of one of ancient Egypt's most renowned private individuals, this statue, which consists of two temporarily reunited fragments, has an illustrious modern history. Charles Edwin Wilbour, one of America's first Egyptologists, purchased the torso in Egypt; his estate bequeathed it to the Brooklyn Museum in 1916. Thirty-eight years later, John D. Cooney, then curator of the Brooklyn Museum's Egyptian collection, recognized the link between the torso and the head of Mentuemhet in the Field Museum of Natural History in Chicago, which had been acquired in Egypt by Edward E. Ayer.[1]

Mentuemhet's elevated position in ancient Egyptian history rests on at least three achievements.[2] Although he held the rather modest civil and religious titles "mayor of Thebes" and "fourth prophet of Amun," he was, as the governor of Upper Egypt, the most important political figure in southern Egypt after the Kushite kings withdrew to Nubia in the waning years of the 25th Dynasty. Psamtik I, an early ruler of the 26th Dynasty, negotiated with Mentuemhet to assume control over Upper Egypt. In the Asasif district of the Theban necropolis,

Mentuemhet built one of the largest of all Egyptian private tombs. He commissioned more than a dozen sculptures, a feat of self-promotion rarely equaled by a nonroyal Egyptian individual after the New Kingdom.[3]

For the most part the heads of Mentuemhet's many sculptures are missing, and the facial similarities among the few that remain are not immediately apparent. The reason for the variety is not clear. Perhaps Mentuemhet had himself represented in different aspects or at different ages.[4] The Chicago head is less archaizing than the numerous widely scattered reliefs from Mentuemhet's tomb,[5] but it nonetheless shows the legacy of past artistic styles. The elongated eyes, elegantly tapered, plastic eyebrows, and so-called echeloned wig (or wig *à revers*) are characteristic of New Kingdom sculpture. The waves in the wig, although certainly attested in the New Kingdom, are found much earlier in the reign of Senwosret II and then throughout the rest of the 12th Dynasty.[6]

The torso has several interesting details. Mentuemhet wears a leopard skin and a Hathor or Bat amulet; both attributes are paralleled in a similar fragmentary sculpture of Mentuemhet in Munich.[7] Images of cow-headed goddesses were popular in the western necropolis at Thebes, and at least three other of Mentuemhet's sculptures have this amulet.[8] Although the leopard skin appears much earlier as the attire of princes, high priests, and officiants in the "opening of the mouth" ceremony, by the 25th Dynasty it had acquired other, more general purposes and was appropriate garb for Mentuemhet as a priest of Amun-Re.[9] The hand on the back of Mentuemhet's left shoulder indicates that the sculpture was part of a group composition. Because women did not often stand to the right of men in Egyptian sculpture, the missing person most likely was either

Mentuemhet's son, Nesptah, or a god. For example, in a group statue in the Egyptian Museum, Cairo, Nesptah accompanies his father, and both wear the leopard skin,[10] but the men neither embrace nor touch. DS

BIBLIOGRAPHY John D. Cooney, "Souvenirs of a Great Egyptian," *Brooklyn Museum Bulletin* 18, no. 4 (1957): 13–18; Bernard V. Bothmer, *Egyptian Sculpture of the Late Period, 700 B.C. to 100 A.D.* (Brooklyn: Brooklyn Museum, 1960), 14–16, nos. 13a–b, pls. 12–13, figs. 29–31.

NOTES
1. For an entertaining account of Cooney's discovery, see "Souvenirs of a Great Egyptian," 15.
2. The definitive monograph on Mentuemhet is Jean Leclant's *Montuemhat, quatrième prophète d'Amon, prince de la ville,* Bibliothèque d'étude 35 (Cairo: IFAO, 1961).
3. For Mentuemhet's sculptures, see Jürgen von Beckerath, "Ein Torso des Mentemhēt in München," *ZÄS* 87 (1962): 2, n. 2.
4. See Donald B. Spanel, *Through Ancient Eyes: Egyptian Portraiture,* exh. cat. (Birmingham, Ala.: Birmingham Museum of Art, 1988), 22–23, n. 55.
5. For Mentuemhet's reliefs, see Edna R. Russmann, "Relief Decoration in the Tomb of Mentuemhat (TT 34)," *JARCE* 31 (1994): 1–20; idem, "The Motif of Bound Papyrus Plants and the Decorative Program in Mentuemhat's First Court (Further Remarks on the Decoration of the Tomb of Mentuemhat, 1)," *JARCE* 32 (in press); Peter Der Manuelian, "A Fragment of Relief from the Tomb of Mentuemhat Attributed to the Fifth Dynasty," *JSSEA* 12 (1982): 185–88; idem, "An Essay in Reconstruction: Two Registers from the Tomb of Montuemhat at Thebes (no. 34)," *MDAIK* 39 (1984): 131–50; idem, "Two Fragments of Relief and a New Model for the Tomb of Mentemhēt," *JEA* 71 (1985): 98–121.
6. Spanel, *Through Ancient Eyes,* 68, n. 3.
7. Staatliche Sammlung ägyptischer Kunst ÄS 127; see von Beckerath, "Ein Torso des Mentemhēt," 1–8.
8. See Bothmer, *Egyptian Sculpture of the Late Period,* 15.
9. Ibid., 4–7.
10. Cairo, Egyptian Museum CG 42241; see Georges Legrain, *Statues et statuettes des rois et des particuliers,* vol. 3, *Nos. 42192–42250,* CG (Cairo: IFAO, 1914), 92–94, pl. 48.

8 Relief Depiction of Mentuemhet

Asasif, TT 34
Late Period, late 25th to early 26th
Dynasty, c. 680–650 B.C.
Limestone
54.5 x 27 cm (21½ x 10⅝ in.)
Yale University, Peabody Museum
of Natural History,
Barringer Collection, 6098

Yale University was among the first educational institutions in the United States to form a collection of Egyptian antiquities. Although the university had previously acquired some miscellaneous Egyptian artifacts, the collection was established in earnest in 1888, when Yale's Peabody Museum of Natural History received the sizable Egyptian collection of Judge Victor Clay Barringer through the efforts of his attorney, William Walter Phelps, a Yale graduate of the class of 1860. Barringer had been appointed to the Court of Appeals of the Mixed Tribunals in Alexandria, Egypt, by President Ulysses S. Grant. According to surviving records, Barringer's collection was formed, in part, with the assistance of the German Egyptologist Emile Brugsch.[1]

This relief, which probably once decorated a doorjamb in the large tomb of the official Mentuemhet at Thebes, probably entered the collection through Brugsch, who had worked at Thebes for the Egyptian Antiquities Service. One of the most important officials of the Late Period, Mentuemhet survived the withdrawal of the 25th Dynasty to its Nubian homeland, the invasion of Egypt and the sack of Thebes by the Assyrians, and the triumph of the native Egyptian 26th Dynasty. A discerning patron of the arts, he decorated his massive tomb in the Theban necropolis with relief sculpture that emulated the artistic styles and compositions of earlier periods, including the Old, Middle, and New Kingdoms.

The present work is strongly evocative of the classic elegance associated with the finest examples of Old Kingdom and Middle Kingdom relief sculpture, work that was already ancient to the Egyptians of Mentuemhet's day. He is shown seated and once held a staff in his far hand and an official's scepter in the other. At the shoulder is one paw of his priestly leopard skin, each of its five claws

View of court, tomb of Mentuemhet.

carefully indicated. In addition Mentuemhet wears a full wig, broad collar, narrow sash, epaulet, and distinctive amulet. Above his head are the remains of a hieroglyphic inscription that once recorded his title and name, "The great mayor of Thebes, Mentuemhet, justified."[2] GS

BIBLIOGRAPHY Gerry D. Scott, III, *The Past Rediscovered: Everyday Life in Ancient Egypt*, exh. cat. (New Haven: Peabody Museum of Natural History, Yale University, 1983), cover; idem, "The Past Rediscovered," *Discovery* 17, no. 1 (1983–84): 10–12; idem, *Ancient Egyptian Art at Yale* (New Haven: Yale University Art Gallery, 1986), 140–41, no. 77.

NOTES
1. For the Barringer collection and its acquisition by Yale University, see Scott, "The Past Rediscovered," 11–12, and idem, *Ancient Egyptian Art at Yale*, 11–12. Both Barringer and Phelps were known to Wilbour; see Jean Capart, ed., *Travels in Egypt (December 1880 to May 1891): Letters of Charles Edwin Wilbour* (Brooklyn: Brooklyn Museum, 1936), 138, 140, 183, 338, 387, 408, 539.
2. An extremely close parallel, perhaps from the opposite doorjamb in the tomb, is now in the collection of the San Antonio Museum of Art (91.129.1). Another close parallel is illustrated in Jean Leclant, *Montouemhat, quatrième prophète d'Amon, prince de la ville*, Bibliothèque d'étude 35 (Cairo: IFAO, 1961), pl. LXIII.

9 Hawk-Headed Crocodile

Ptolemaic or Roman period,
c. 304 B.C.–A.D. 395
Limestone
H: 11.8 cm (4⅝ in.); L: 21.5 cm
(8½ in.); W: 6.3 cm (2½ in.)
The Brooklyn Museum,
gift of the estate of
Charles Edwin Wilbour, 16.86

This interesting sculpture represents a hybrid form of the god Sobek. It is difficult to define its identity more narrowly, however, because Sobek was quite congenial to association with other deities, especially during the Ptolemaic and Roman periods. As early as the Middle Kingdom Sobek was closely linked with the solar god Re. In one of the Ramesseum papyri, which date to the 13th Dynasty, Sobek is identified with a bull, ram, and lion.[1]

During the Ptolemaic and Roman periods the deity Soknopaios, a hellenized configuration of Sobek, was worshiped as a hawk-headed crocodile at Soknopaiou Nesos in the Faiyum.[2] Sobek had cults in many other local forms throughout the Faiyum and elsewhere in Egypt. In some of these localities Sobek and other gods assumed the shape of a hawk-headed crocodile, as in the case of Khonsu-Shu at the small temple at el-Qal'a, near Coptos, which was built by the emperor Augustus. In this context Khonsu-Shu is associated with Harpocrates, a form of Horus.[3] It seems likely that the present sculpture is also associated with Horus, although its full identity remains unknown.

Likewise, the purpose of the two holes on the side of the base and on the top of the head is not clear. Perhaps the sculpture was part of a larger composition, such as a group statue, or was attached to a base and served as an ex-voto (temple offering). DS

BIBLIOGRAPHY Javier M. Paysás, "Un ex-voto a Sobek en la coleccion Ogdon," *Aegyptus Antiqua* 6–7 (1993): 27–32.

NOTES
1. Edward Brovarski, "Sobek," *LÄ*, vol. 5, cols. 995, 1001, 1013; Maarten J. Raven, "A Criocephalous Crocodile," *Oudheidkundige Mededelingen uit het Rijksmuseum van Oudheden te Leiden* 73 (1993): 43–53.
2. Karl-Theodor Zauzich, "Soknopaios," *LÄ*, vol. 5, col. 1075; J. Grafton Milne, *A History of Egypt*, vol. 5, *Under Roman Rule*, 3d ed. (London: Methuen, 1924), 185–86.
3. Raven, "A Criocephalous Crocodile," 46, fig. 4, and 49; for another hawk-headed crocodile, see Hermann Kees, "Kulttopographische und mythologische Beiträge," *ZÄS* 64 (1929): 109–12.

10 The "Wilbour Plaque"

Amarna(?)
18th Dynasty, reign of Akhenaten
(c. 1353–1335 B.C.) or shortly thereafter
Limestone, pigment
15.7 x 22.1 x 4.2 cm (6⅛ x 8¾ x 1⅝ in.)
The Brooklyn Museum,
gift of the estate of
Charles Edwin Wilbour, 16.48

In the last years of Akhenaten's reign the angular, exaggerated style of early Amarna art was gradually superseded by graceful, curvilinear forms. This new style became the official model for all late Amarna royal images and continued into the reign of Tutankhaton (Tutankhamun).[1]

One of the best-known examples of this style is the Wilbour Plaque, named for the American collector Charles Edwin Wilbour, who purchased it in 1881 near Amarna.[2] On the left, in a sunk-relief representation, a king wears the baglike *khat* headdress;[3] opposite him a queen wears a cap crown.[4] These royal faces were never part of complete figures, and the piece was not a fragment of a larger scene. Egyptologists have interpreted the plaque as an artisan's model or trial piece that was attached to the wall of a sculptor's studio by the hole near the top edge.

Art historians have long debated the identity of the two faces. Biri Fay has convincingly demonstrated that the queen must be Nefertiti.[5] The king's identity is more elusive. If the faces were carved contemporaneously, Nefertiti would logically be paired with her husband, and the plaque's king would be Akhenaten, depicted at the very end of his eighteen-year reign. Perhaps the best parallel for the king's face, however, can be found on a relief in the Luxor Temple depicting Tutankhamun.[6] Since the plaque almost certainly comes from Amarna, the king's face might date to the short interval before Tutankhaton vacated Amarna, returned the royal residence to Thebes, and assumed the name Tutankhamun. JR

BIBLIOGRAPHY Cyril Aldred, *Akhenaten and Nefertiti,* exh. cat. (Brooklyn: Brooklyn Museum; New York: Viking Press, 1973), 190–91, no. 121 (with selected bibliography up to 1973); Richard A. Fazzini, *Images for Eternity: Egyptian Art from Berkeley and Brooklyn,* exh. cat. (San Francisco: Fine Arts Museums of San Francisco; Brooklyn: Brooklyn Museum, 1975), 81, 136, no. 63; Cyril Aldred, *Egyptian Art in the Days of the Pharaohs, 3100–320 B.C.* (New York and Toronto: Oxford University Press, 1980), 173, fig. 139; Richard A. Fazzini, in *Ancient Egyptian Art in the Brooklyn Museum* (Brooklyn: Brooklyn Museum, 1989), no. 51.

NOTES
1. For the best general discussion of the later Amarna style, see Aldred, *Akhenaten and Nefertiti,* 58–66.
2. Jean Capart, ed., *Travels in Egypt (December 1880 to May 1891): Letters of Charles Edwin Wilbour* (Brooklyn: Brooklyn Museum, 1936), 95–96, illus. opp. 104.
3. For this headdress, see Marianne Eaton-Krauss, "The *Khat* Headdress to the End of the Amarna Period," *SAK* 5 (1977): 21–39.
4. For this head covering, see Julia Sampson, "Amarna Crowns and Wigs: Unpublished Pieces from Statues and Inlays in the Petrie Collection at University College, London," *JEA* 59 (1973): 48; Earl L. Ertman, "The Cap-Crown of Nefertiti: Its Function and Probable Origin," *JARCE* 13 (1976): 63–67; A. Rammant-Peeters, "Les couronnes de Nefertiti à El-Amarna," *Orientalia Lovaniensia Periodica* 16 (1985): 37.
5. Biri Fay, "Nefertiti Times Three," in *Jahrbuch preussischer Kulturbesitz* (Berlin: Staatliche Museen, 1987), 359–76.
6. PM, vol. 2, 315 (87), III, 1; see Christiane Desroches-Noblecourt, *Tutankhamen: Life and Death of a Pharaoh* (New York: New York Graphic Society, 1963), 279, fig. 180.

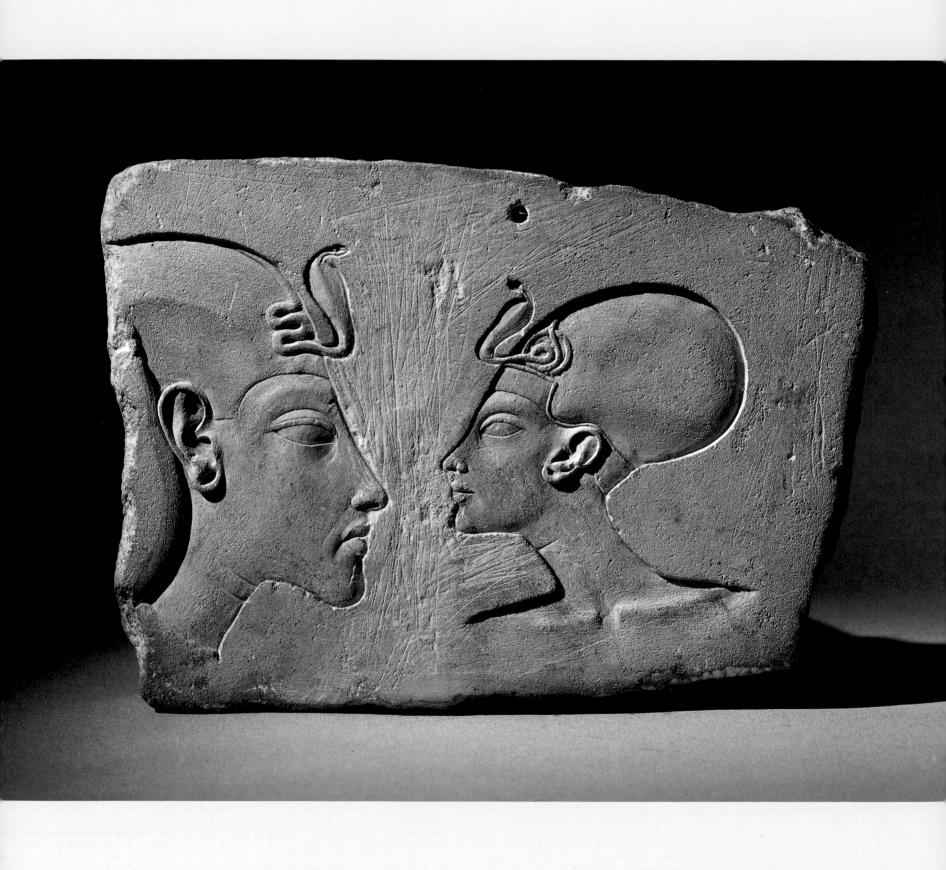

11 Statuette of a King ·

Amarna, house Q44.1, room 8
18th Dynasty, reign of Akhenaten
(c. 1353–1335 B.C.)
Limestone, pigment, gilding
21.9 x 4.8 x 4.4 cm (8⅝ x 1⅞ x 1¾ in.)
The Brooklyn Museum, gift of the
Egypt Exploration Society, 29.34

The king stands, feet together[1] and arms by his sides, against an uninscribed back pillar. He wears the Blue Crown with a uraeus, a broad collar, and a pleated kilt, with the belt and apron tied below his exposed belly. His deep-red flesh tones contrast with the blue and gold of the crown, collar, and apron. The painted white eyes have black pupils. The feet and base were restored from the ankles down in modern times.

In the absence of an inscription, the statuette must be dated on stylistic grounds. The drooping lips, long jaw, and sagging breasts and belly identify the king as Akhenaten. His facial features have been softened to conform to the later Amarna style.[2]

This figurine of the king is one of a number found in the private houses at Amarna.[3] The figures seem to have been worshiped, in much the same manner as traditional deities, in household shrines in observance of the cult of the royal family.

Following the king's demise, the head of the statuette appears to have been deliberately broken off with a single, straight cut.[4] It subsequently was carefully repaired in antiquity. BM

BIBLIOGRAPHY T. Whittemore, "A Statuette of Akhenaten for America," *The Brooklyn Museum Quarterly* 12, no. 2 (1925): 59–65; *Egyptian Art in the Brooklyn Museum Collection* (Brooklyn: Brooklyn Museum, 1952), no. 34; J. Vandier, *Manuel d'archéologie égyptienne*, vol. 3, *Les grandes époques: La statuaire* (Paris: Picard, 1958), 336–38, 348–49, pl. CX, 4; Cyril Aldred, *New Kingdom Art in Ancient Egypt during the Eighteenth Dynasty*, 2d rev. ed. (London: A. Tiranti, 1961), 82, pl. 137; B. Peterson, "Two Royal Heads from Amarna: Studies in the Art of the Amarna Age," *Medelshavmuseet Bulletin* 4 (1964): 19; Cyril Aldred, *Akhenaten and Nefertiti*, exh. cat. (Brooklyn: Brooklyn Museum; New York: Viking Press, 1973), 168, no. 96; Richard A. Fazzini, *Images for Eternity: Egyptian Art from Berkeley and Brooklyn*, exh. cat. (San Francisco: Fine Arts Museums of San Francisco; Brooklyn: Brooklyn Museum, 1975), 82, no. 64.

NOTES
1. This pose is characteristic of female statues; see Vandier, *Manuel d'archéologie égyptienne*, vol. 3, 337.
2. Aldred, *Akhenaten and Nefertiti*, 168.
3. Three similar figures are in the Ägyptisches Museum, Berlin (no. 21836); the Musées royaux d'art et d'histoire, Brussels (E.6730); and the Ashmolean Museum, Oxford (no. 1924.162). The latter two come from private houses.
4. The figurine in Brussels also had been "decapitated"; see Aldred, *Akhenaten and Nefertiti*, 130.

12 Fragment of a Manger with Ibex

Amarna, North Palace
18th Dynasty, reign of Akhenaten,
c. 1349–1335 B.C.
Limestone, pigment
25.4 x 54 x 17.5 cm
(10 x 21¼ x 6⅞ in.)
The Toledo Museum of Art, 25.744

Excavated by the British Egypt Exploration Society in 1923, this relief was given to the Toledo Museum of Art in 1925, in return for its financial support of EES expeditions. The manger was found in the so-called North Palace, possibly an additional royal residence at the short-lived capital of Akhenaten at Amarna. Following excavations at Amarna by W. M. Flinders Petrie in 1891–92 and by Ludwig Borchardt for the Deutsche Orient-Gesellschaft, from 1907 to 1914 (uncovering the sculpture studio of Tuthmosis and the well-known bust of Nefertiti), the EES was granted a concession for the site from 1921 to 1936. The expedition worked under a series of directors, including T. Eric Peet; Charles Leonard Woolley (later renowned for his discoveries at Ur); Francis Newton, who died "on camp" in 1924; Henri Frankfort; and John Pendlebury.[1]

During the 1923–24 season the Northern Palace was cleared, revealing a series of courts, halls, administrative offices, a throne room, gardens, aviaries, and animal quarters. The innovative yet highly fragile wall paintings of the area were recorded in facsimile by Charles Wilkinson and Norman and Nina de Garis Davies, on loan to the project from the Metropolitan Museum of Art, and published in 1929.[2] The remains of fourteen limestone animal mangers were discovered, each decorated with figures of oxen, antelopes, or ibex and, in one example, with a keeper. The reliefs were originally painted, as evidenced by traces of pigment: black on ibex backs and horns and green on the fodder. Boldly carved in sunk relief, the relief shows the naturalistic detail characteristic of the Amarna style. NT

BIBLIOGRAPHY F. G. Newton, "Excavations at El'Amarnah, 1923–24," *JEA* 10 (1924): 289–98, pl. 30(2); PM, vol. 4 (1934), 193; M. Hammed and H. Fr. Werkmeister, "Haus und Garten im alten Ägypten," *ZÄS* 80 (1955): 107; Kurt T. Luckner, "The Art of Egypt, Part II," *Toledo Museum News*, n.s., 14 (Fall 1971): 65; Cyril Aldred, *Akhenaten and Nefertiti*, exh. cat. (Brooklyn: Brooklyn Museum; New York: Viking, 1973), 212, no. 151; *The Toledo Museum of Art: A Guide to the Collections* (Toledo: Toledo Museum of Art, 1976), 6; Susan K. Doll, "Manger," in *Egypt's Golden Age: The Art of Living in the New Kingdom, 1558–1085 B.C.*, exh. cat. (Boston: MFA, 1982), 48.

NOTES
1. Cyril Aldred, "El-Amarna," in *Excavating in Egypt: The Egypt Exploration Society, 1882–1982*, ed. T. G. H. James (Chicago: University of Chicago Press, 1982), 89–106.
2. Henri Frankfort, ed., *The Mural Paintings of Tell El-'Amarneh* (London: Egypt Exploration Society, 1929).

13   The Aten and a Symbol of a Goddess or Queen(?)

Amarna

18th Dynasty, c. years 5–9
of the reign of Akhenaten
(c. 1349–1345 B.C.)

Limestone

23 x 34 x 15.1 cm (9 x 13⅜ x 6 in.)

The Brooklyn Museum, gift of the
Egypt Exploration Society, 36.886

The dating of this relief is based on two facts: work on the city of Akhetaten (now Amarna), the main cult center of the solar deity Aten, did not begin until year 5 of Akhenaten's reign, and the entrance to the temple or temple-like building depicted on the relief carries a form of the names of the solar deity that was no longer used by about year 9 of Akhenaten's reign.[1] In the relief the Aten disk, from which rays of light descend, is adorned with a uraeus and a pendant ankh. The building in whose entrance the disk appears is probably the same structure represented to the right by a lintel and column, whose capital is in the form of a Hathor-headed sistrum (rattle) surmounted by a naos (shrine).

English archaeologist John Pendlebury (1904–41) directed the Egypt Exploration Society's work at Amarna in 1935–36, when this relief was found on the approach from the west to the bridge/gateway spanning the Royal Road and linking the King's House, or Hut-Aten palace, with the so-called Great Palace.[2] Unfortunately the relief's findspot does not clearly establish its original provenance or the identity of the structure depicted.

Column capitals with the head of the goddess Hathor normally indicate a building dedicated to Hathor or another goddess.[3] Hathor and some other goddesses are known from the context of the workmen's village and chapels at Amarna,[4] but that does not explain this possibly unique depiction of Hathor capitals on what appears to be state building at Akhetaten. Hathor was not totally absent from the earlier state art of Amenhotep IV-Akhenaten at Karnak, however, and a recent study has argued that the king's chief queen, Nefertiti, played the mythological role of Hathor-Ma'at, with the king taking the part of Re in guaranteeing the ongoing regeneration of the ordered universe.[5] If so, might this relief be an early Amarna depiction of a building associated with Nefertiti? RF

BIBLIOGRAPHY John D. S. Pendlebury et al., *The City of Akhenaten*, pt. 3, *The Central City and the Official Quarters: The Excavations at Tell el-Amarna during the Seasons 1926–1927 and 1931–1936*, Egypt Exploration Society, 44th Memoir (London: Egypt Exploration Society, 1951), vol. 1, 69, vol. 2, pl. LXX, 8; T. G. H. James, *Corpus of Hieroglyphic Inscriptions in the Brooklyn Museum*, vol. 1, *From Dynasty I to the End of Dynasty XVIII*, Wilbour Monographs 6 (Brooklyn: Brooklyn Museum, 1974), 132, no. 298, pl. LXXV; Richard Fazzini, "Continuity and Change: The New Egyptian Installations in Brooklyn," *KMT* 4 (Winter 1993–94): 75–76; idem, "The Reinstallation of the Brooklyn Museum's Egyptian Collection," *Minerva* 5, no. 1 (1994): 41–43.

NOTES
1. The earlier form of the names was "Re-Horakhty, he who rejoices in the horizon in his name 'Light' [shu] which is in/from the sun-disk [Aten]." The later form of the names eliminated Horakhty (Horus of the two horizons) and shu (also the name of a god) and read "Live Re, ruler of the two horizons, rejoicing in the horizon in his name 'Re, the father, who has come as the sun-disk.'"
2. Pendlebury et al., *The City of Akhenaten*, vol. 1, 69, where other finds from this area are also listed, and vol. 2, pl. LXX(8). For this area, see also pls. I, II, XIIIA, XIV, XXIV. For more recent discussions of these parts of the central city of Amarna, see Barry Kemp, "The Window of Appearance at El-Amarna and the Basic Structure of This City," *JEA* 62 (1976): 81–99; David O'Connor, "City and Palace in New Kingdom Egypt," *Cahiers de recherches de l'Institut de papyrologie et d'égyptologie de Lille* 11 (1989): 82–85; idem, "Mirror of the Cosmos: The Palace of Merenptah," in *Fragments of a Shattered Visage: The Proceedings of the Annual Symposium on Ramesses the Great*, ed. E. Bleiberg and R. Freed, Monographs of the Institute of Egyptian Art and Archaeology 1 (Memphis: Memphis State University, 1991), 178–81.
3. E.g., Gerhardt Haeny, "Hathor-Kapitell," *LÄ*, vol. 1 (1975), col. 1039.
4. E.g., T. Eric Peet et al., *The City of Akhenaten*, pt. 1, *Excavations of 1921 and 1922 at El-'Amarneh*, Egypt Exploration Society, 38th Memoir (London: Egypt Exploration Society, 1923), 66, 100, 105, pls. XX(1), LIV(94); Ann Bomann, *The Private Chapel in Ancient Egypt: A Study of the Chapels in the Workmen's Village at El Amarna...*(London and New York: Kegan Paul International, 1991), 60–62, 65, 67–68. I owe some of these references to Michael Mallinson, an architect involved in the current English work at Amarna.
5. Claude Traunecker, "Aménophis IV et Néfertiti: Le couple royal d'après les talatates du IXe pylône de Karnak," *BSFE* 107 (1986).

14 Inlay of Profile Face

Amarna, *per-hai* of great temple
or palace
18th Dynasty, reign of Akhenaten
or Smenkhkare (c. 1353–1333 B.C.)
Quartzite
12.1 x 11.8 x 4.3 cm
(4¾ x 4⅝ x 1⅞ in.)
The Brooklyn Museum, gift of the
Egypt Exploration Society, 33.685

Discovered at Amarna in 1932 by the British archaeologist John Pendlebury, this fine inlay probably decorated the capital of a column in a large building, either a royal palace or a great temple.[1] It was found toward the western end of the building within a structure known as the *per-hai* (literally "house of rejoicing"), which had two sets of eight columns flanking the central aisle that spanned the east-west axis.[2]

The identity of the person depicted has not been established with certainty; the three candidates are Akhenaten, Nefertiti, and Smenkhkare. The eyebrow and eye would have been filled with a colored stone, faience, or glass. The graceful features suggest a date late in Akhenaten's reign (1353–1335 B.C.) or in that of Smenkhkare (1335–1333 B.C.),

and indeed the *per-hai* was not built until after the ninth year of Akhenaten's eighteen-year reign.[3] DS

BIBLIOGRAPHY Donald B. Spanel, *Through Ancient Eyes: Egyptian Portraiture*, exh. cat. (Birmingham, Ala.: Birmingham Museum of Art, 1988), 95–96, no. 27 (with bibliography).

NOTES
1. For the nature of this building, see David O'Connor, "City and Palace in New Kingdom Egypt," *Cahiers de recherches de l'Institut de papyrologie et d'égyptologie de Lille* 11 (1989): 85 (reference from Richard Fazzini).
2. John D. S. Pendlebury et al., *The City of Akhenaten*, pt. 3, *The Central City and the Official Quarters: The Excavations at Tell el-Amarna during the Seasons 1926–1927 and 1931–1936*, Egypt Exploration Society, 44th Memoir (London: Egypt Exploration Society, 1951), vol. 1, 12–16; for a reconstruction of the *per-hai*, see vol. 2, pls. 3–6.
3. Ibid., vol. 1, 13.

15 Hathor Fetish Capital

Bubastis, temple of Bastet,
hall of Osorkon II
19th Dynasty, reign of Ramesses II
(c. 1290–1224 B.C.)
Red granite
170 x 137 x 108 cm
(66⅞ x 53⅞ x 42½ in.)
Museum of Fine Arts, Boston, gift of
the Egypt Exploration Fund, 89.555

At Bubastis, in the portion of the great temple of Bastet called the festival hall of Osorkon II, Edouard Naville found two sets of four Bat-sistrum capitals (a Bat-sistrum is a musical rattle surmounted by the head of the goddess Bat).[1] The capital in the Museum of Fine Arts, Boston, is from the larger set.[2] The face is framed by an elaborate wig with an upcurled hairstyle and hair bands at chin level on both front tresses; diagonal markings indicate braided locks. Upon the head is a rectangular cornice bearing a frieze of uraei crowned by sun disks.

The capitals were originally painted, as Naville describes the red color that still adhered to the lips when the blocks were first lifted from the ground. The Boston capital was found face down, and this side was in perfect condition. Of the four capitals in this group, two represent the north and two the south. The Boston capital has the northern iconography, identified by the two uraei wearing red crowns, which flank the face. On the sides of the capital, centered between the tails of the uraei, is a papyrus plant in raised relief. Below the uraei are the cartouches of Osorkon II (r. 924–909 B.C.).

Colossal columns in the Bastet temple area represented giant sistra before the deity housed within. The images on the capitals, however, were not representations of Hathor to be adored. When used in conjunction with Hathor, the sistrum image served her in a subordinate role and must be considered as her insignia or fetish, having the same status as the *menat* necklace, a cult object carried by worshipers of Hathor. The image should not, however, be regarded as the face of the goddess herself.[3]

These capitals have been dated by Naville, Labib Habachi, Gustave Jéquier, Alexander Badawy, William S. Smith, and others to the 12th Dynasty;[4] some narrow the date to the reign of Senwosret III (1878–1841? B.C.). This dating would make these by far the earliest known Bat-sistrum columns.[5] Naville gave the first, if qualified, attribution to the Middle Kingdom based on the proximity of an architrave and doorjamb of Senwosret III which he felt were architecturally related.[6] Several features do not correspond to a 12th Dynasty date, however.[7] The capital does not resemble, for instance, contemporary 12th Dynasty Bat-naos-sistra. A sistrum from the reign of Senwosret III has not yet appeared with a wig. Not until the reign of Amenemhat III (1844–1797 B.C.) does the Bat image on the sistrum wear a wig. Numerous hypotheses elucidate the origin of this style within Egypt[8] or the Near East, but this hairstyle is not related to Hathor prior to the time it was adopted for the Bat face.[9]

The earliest example of a woman wearing the "Hathoric" hairstyle occurs in the reign of Senwosret I (1971–1926 B.C.), when it adorned two nonroyal women who flank a high official, Senweseretankh, in a group statue.[10] Many other nonroyal women wear this style throughout the 12th Dynasty.[11] In the reign of Senwosret II (1897–1878 B.C.) the coiffure is first seen on a queen, Nofret, whose statues from Tanis are adorned with this style.[12] From her reign and throughout the 12th Dynasty, this is the coiffure most commonly seen on royal women.[13] The elaborate diagonal crossed marks on the wig of the capital do not correspond to any of the numerous 12th Dynasty hairstyles. At this time the markings are either horizontal or vertical lines, typified by those seen on Queen Nofret.[14]

The evidence points to a date no earlier than the 19th Dynasty for the capitals, which have far more in common with the style of the sistra of this date than with those of the Middle Kingdom.[15] The 19th Dynasty date is in keeping with the pharaohs who constructed and or rebuilt portions of the festival hall, namely, Ramesses II (r. 1290–1224 B.C.), Osorkon I (r. 989–978 B.C.), and Osorkon II (r. 924–909).[16] Dedication inscriptions of Osorkon I are engraved on the bottom of the Bat-sistrum capitals, where they abut the column, a hidden and unusual spot.[17] In addition the cartouches of Osorkon II are etched into the sides of the Boston capital. Therefore, it is possible[18] that the capitals were created in the reign of Ramesses II, rebuilt and rededicated by Osorkon I, and later reinscribed with the cartouches of Osorkon II, who replaced Ramesses' cartouches with his own in the 22d Dynasty.[19]

JH

BIBLIOGRAPHY Henry G. Fischer, "The Cult of the Goddess Bat," *JARCE* 1 (1962): 7–24; Christiane Ziegler, "Sistrum," in *LÄ*, vol. 5, cols. 959–63; Geraldine Pinch, *Votive Offerings to Hathor* (Oxford: Griffith Institute, Ashmolean Museum, 1993).

NOTES

1. The other set of four Bat-sistrum capitals is smaller and simpler than the first group. They have no uraei on their cornices and have plain sides.

2. Edouard Naville, *Bubastis* (London, 1891), 11. The other three of this group are in the Musée du Louvre, Paris; the British Museum, London; and the Ägyptisches Museum, Berlin.

3. Ziegler, "Sistrum," col. 960, notes that in the temple of Dendera, the sistrum with naos was considered an incarnation itself of the goddess.

4. Naville, *Bubastis*, 11–13; Labib Habachi, *Tell Basta*, ASAE Supplement 22 (Cairo: IFAO, 1957), 62, 110, 111; Gustave Jéquier, *Manuel d'archéologie égyptienne*, vol. 3 (Paris: A. et J. Picard, 1924), 184; Alexander Badawy, *A History of Egyptian Architecture: The First Intermediate Period, the Middle Kingdom, and the Second Intermediate Period* (Berkeley and Los Angeles: University of California Press, 1966), 88; William S. Smith, *The Art and Architecture of Ancient Egypt* (Harmondsworth: Penguin Books, 1958), XXXX.

5. Even when the naos is not included on flat cornice-topped capitals such as these, it is clear that the naos-sistrum was intended; see Pinch, *Votive Offerings*, 155.

6. Naville, *Bubastis*, 11–13 ("This attribution may be questionable particularly as regards the Hathor and palm-leaf columns" [idem, 13]).

7. Joyce Haynes, "Bat Capital in the MFA, Boston," in *For His Ka: Festschrift in Honor of W. K. Simpson* (forthcoming).

8. Smith (*Art and Architecture*, 27) suggests that the hairstyle of the two seated limestone figures from Hierakonpolis (pl. I) anticipates the Hathoric wig, as the two front locks are large and marked by horizontal lines. I disagree that a royal prototype should exist. At least in the 18th Dynasty less prominent women were the first to be seen with new hairstyles (Joyce Haynes, "The Development of Women's Hairstyles in Dynasty XVIII," *JSSEA* 8 [1977]: 18ff.). For example, in tomb paintings and reliefs, women who were not given positions of honor were those to wear the newest and most elaborate fashions. The wife of the deceased usually wears a somewhat more conservative style, especially early in the 18th Dynasty, and the mother of the deceased is almost invariably portrayed with the traditional tripartite hairstyle. This general trend, if applied to all classes of women, would suggest that queens as well as goddesses would be the last to be depicted with a new fashion.

9. Similar hairstyles with upturned ends were worn by several Near Eastern goddesses from the late third millennium B.C. onward. Some scholars have argued for a Mesopotamian origin; see J. B. Pritchard, *Palestinian Figurines in Relation to Certain Goddesses Known through Literature* (New Haven: Yale University Press, 1943), 40–41; Emma Brunner-Traut, *Die altägyptischen Scherbenbilder (Bildostraka) der Deutschen Museen und Sammlungen* (Wiesbaden: Franz Steiner, 1956), 27.

10. Jacques Vandier, *Manuel d'archéologie égyptienne*, vol. 3 (Paris: A. et J. Picard, 1978), 257, pl. XC, 3, 4.

11. For other nonroyal women wearing this wig in the 12th Dynasty, see Steffen Wenig, *The Woman in Egyptian Art,* trans. B. Fischer (New York: McGraw-Hill, 1969), pl. 27b; Percy E. Newberry, *El Bersheh I* (London: Egypt Exploration Fund, 1892–93), pl. XXVI; Vandier, *Manuel*, vol. 3, pls. LXXVI-6, LXXXI-7, LXXXIV-1, 3, 5, LXXXV-2, LXXXIX-4, XC-6.

12. Smith, *Art and Architecture*, pl. 67; Janine Bourriau, *Pharaohs and Mortals* (Cambridge: Cambridge University Press, 1988), 26. A bust of a queen with this hairstyle is dated to the reign of Senwosret I or Senwosret II. If the earlier date holds, it would be the earliest royal example of this hairstyle.

13. Vandier (*Manuel*, vol. 3, 254) states that all queens except examples in Berlin (Ägyptisches Museum 14475) and New York (MMA 08.202.7) wear the "Hathoric" style in the 12th Dynasty.

14. Considering the number of Hathoric styles that exist in the 12th Dynasty, it is significant that none matches the Bubastis capital style. The treatment of the tresses does correlate with that on a sidelock of the child sun god on a statue dating to the reign of Ramesses II from Tanis; see Pierre Montet, "Les statues de Ramsès II à Tanis," in *Mélanges Maspero*, vol. 1, pt. 2, Mémoires publiés par les membres de l'Institut français d'archéologie orientale du Caire 66 (Cairo: IFAO, 1966), 497–508, pl. II.

15. Compare, e.g., the sistra in Maria Mogensen, *La Glyptothèque Ny Carlsberg: La collection égyptienne* (Copenhagen: F. Bagge, 1930), pls. XXXI, LXXII; Hans Hickman, *Instruments de musique*, CG 101 (Cairo: IFAO, 1949), pl. XLIX, no. 69310.

16. Habachi, "Tell Basta," pl. XX; Naville, *Bubastis*, 48–52.

17. "Engraved underneath the Hathor capitals, in places were they could not be seen, and where it was not possible to engrave them unless the monument was lying on the ground and had not yet been raised" (Naville, *Bubastis*, 47).

18. H. Bakry, "A Family of High Priests of Alexandria and Memphis," *MDAIK* 28 (1972): pl. XXII.

19. The cartouches of Ramesses II and Osorkon II are so similar that altering only a few signs in the Ramesses cartouche would result in that of Osorkon II.

16 Sarcophagus Lid of the Chief Physician Psamtek

Saqqara, south of the pyramid of Unas
Late 26th Dynasty, c. 575–525 B.C.
Basalt
L: 249 cm (98 in.)
Phoebe A. Hearst Museum
of Anthropology, University
of California, Berkeley, 5-522

This massive lid belonged to the inner
anthropoid sarcophagus of Psamtek, the chief
physician and "overseer of Libyans," who is
thought to have been active during the reign
of Amasis, for he dedicated a stela to the Apis
bull which is stylistically consistent with others
known from this period.[1] The decoration of
the lid resembles others from the same time:
the broad face with its placid expression,
heavy lappet wig, curled divine beard, elaborate *wesekh* collar, and sharply incised text
and decorative details. Although many of
these elements had been the stock-in-trade
of coffin and sarcophagus carvers for centuries, the work of the Saite craftsmen is
distinguished by its scale, a predilection for
dark stones that take a glossy finish, and
the use of iron tools, which enabled the relief
sculptors to etch thin, straight lines.

The tomb of Psamtek[2] comprised a free-standing, vaulted rectangular chamber that was constructed at the bottom of a deep, almost square shaft excavated in the desert plateau in the precinct of the 5th Dynasty pyramid of Unas. This chamber was nearly filled by a huge outer limestone sarcophagus. While all visible surfaces of the chamber were covered with religious texts, the outer sarcophagus carried only one horizontal line, which contained the name and titles of Psamtek himself. The inner basalt sarcophagus had been inserted into the limestone case, but both lids were found propped up on stone supports, showing that the tomb had never been used, and the three canopic niches carved into the north, east, and west walls of the chamber were empty.

In both its decoration and construction the tomb of Psamtek embodied the revivalist tendencies of the Late Period. The texts in the tomb chamber included extracts from the Pyramid Texts (Old Kingdom), traditional offering lists, and the Book of the Dead (New Kingdom), while the large size of the sarcophagi (relative to that of the burial chamber itself) and the methods of supporting their lids have late Middle Kingdom parallels. Stone from the Unas pyramid itself was used in the tomb's fabrication.

The sarcophagus was excavated in 1900 by the Egyptian Antiquities Service, directed by Alexandre Barsanti and Gaston Maspero. William Randolph Hearst acquired it while in Egypt with George A. Reisner in early 1900.

TRANSLATION OF INSCRIBED TEXT:

(1) Words to be spoken: O Osiris, chief physician and overseer of the Libyans Psamtek, Horus has commanded (to) his children, so that they hasten (?) to you, without there being a retreater among them when they support you. (2) Your mother Nut spreads herself over you in her name of "Shetpet"; she has caused you to be a god without opposition, in your name of "God." (3) She has protected you from the lord of evil, in her name of "great protectress," the Osiris chief physician and overseer of the Libyans Psamtek. (4) You are the greatest of her children. Geb is merciful to you, for he has loved you; he has protected you; he has restored your head to you; he has caused Thoth to reassemble you, so that which pertained to you (i.e., death) ceases to exist. (5) O spirits, Anubis has granted the protection of the burial of Osiris, the protection of the burial of the chief physician Psamtek. (6) Words spoken by Imseti: "I will be your protection!" (7) Words spoken by Duamutef: "I will be your protection!" (8) Words spoken by Maaiotef: "I will be your protection!" (9) Words spoken by Horus-Khenti-Ierty: "I will be your protection!" (10) Words spoken by Isis: (11) "O, Osiris chief physician Psamtek, (12) I, your sister Isis, will be your protection!" (13) O spirits, Anubis has granted the protection of the burial of Osiris, the protection of the burial of Osiris the chief physician Psamtek. (14) Words spoken by Hapi: "I will be your protection!" (15) Words spoken by Kebehsenuef: "I will be your protection!" (16) Words spoken by Kheribakef: "I will be your protection!" (17) Words spoken by Anubis, the great god, lord of burial: "I will be your protection!" (18) Words spoken by Nephthys: (19) "I enclose my brother Osiris the chief physician (20) Psamtek, so that his body might not cease to be!" (21) Words spoken: O Osiris the chief physician and overseer of the Libyans Psamtek, they have come to you, (22) Isis and Nephthys, in Sais. Their divinity is in you, in your name of "sole god."

CK

BIBLIOGRAPHY Gaston Maspero and Alexandre Barsanti, "Fouilles autour de la pyramide d'Ounas (1899–1900)," *ASAE* 1 (1900): 149–88; Albert B. Elsasser and Vera-Mae Fredrickson, *Ancient Egypt*, exh. cat. (Berkeley: Robert H. Lowie Museum of Anthropology, University of California, 1966), 80 (detail); F. H. Stross and Albert B. Elsasser, "*The Doctor*": A 26th Dynasty Sarcophagus Lid, exh. brochure (Berkeley: Robert H. Lowie Museum of Anthropology, University of California, 1973).

NOTES
1. Paris, Musée du Louvre IM.4084; for references, see PM, vol. 3 (2d ed.), 811, which provides the name of Psamtek's father, Harsiese.
2. For references to the tomb of Psamtek, see ibid., 649.

17 Double-Bird "Pelta" Palette

Naga el-Deir, cemetery 7000,
grave N7008
Predynastic, Naqada I to Naqada IIab
period (c. 3900–3650 B.C.)
Siltstone, ostrich eggshell
7.6 x 12.3 cm (3 x 4⅞ in.)
Phoebe A. Hearst Museum
of Anthropology, University
of California, Berkeley, 6-4746

Unlike a rhomboidal palette found in the same grave, this object most likely did not function like full-sized Egyptian palettes, which were used to grind coloring matter for adorning the face, body, and other surfaces. The small size, presence of inlays, and lack of a usable grinding area suggest that this palette was worn as a pectoral. It is pierced for suspension through a raised central element at the spot where the contiguous tail feathers of the two birds would normally occur. W. M. Flinders Petrie first applied the term *pelta* to these palettes, whose overall shapes resemble those of Amazonian shields known by the same name.[1] The Egyptian pelta palette originally depicted a reed boat;[2] the birds'-head terminals of the present example represent a relatively late stage in the developmental sequence.

The palette was meticulously ground to a smooth surface on both sides; discoidal beads of ostrich shell were inlaid on one side only. Albert M. Lythgoe, working under George A. Reisner, discovered this piece, along with a second, virtually identical example, at Naga el-Deir during his clearance of cemetery 7000 in 1904–5. The two had been deposited, one directly on top of the other, just behind the lower back of one male body and just in front of a second. Both bodies represent a later stage in the use of the grave. Associated ceramics, as well as similar excavated objects, suggest a date for the deposition of pelta palettes in the middle Predynastic Period (Naqada I–IIab).[3] CK

BIBLIOGRAPHY Albert M. Lythgoe and Dows Dunham, *The Predynastic Cemetery N7000 Naga ed-Dêr*, vol. 4 (Berkeley and Los Angeles: University of California Press, 1965), 2 (fig. 1, 0), 5.

NOTES
1. W. M. Flinders Petrie, *Prehistoric Egypt* (London: British School of Archaeology, 1920), 37.
2. Ibid., 38–39.
3. For the assignment of Naqada I–IIab to the Middle Predynastic, see Fekri A. Hassan, "The Predynastic of Egypt," *Journal of World Prehistory* 2, no. 2 (1988): 138–40.

18 Bowl

El-Mamariya, burial 41
Predynastic, Naqada I period
(c. 3800–3600 B.C.)
Ceramic
7.3 x 17.8 (diam) cm (2⅞ x 7 in.)
The Brooklyn Museum, Excavations
of Henri de Morgan, 1906–7,
07.447.40

This bowl, like other Predynastic objects from the Brooklyn Museum (cat nos. 19–22, 25, 26), was excavated by Henri de Morgan during the seasons of 1906–7 and 1907–8. It belongs to a type described by W. M. Flinders Petrie as White Cross-Lined or C-ware.[1] The reddish brown, polished bowl is decorated with yellow-white calcareous clay paint, which was applied with a fiber brush before firing.[2] The interior of the bowl is decorated with five irregularly spaced, multilineal V-shaped patterns; four parallel zigzag lines fill the interstice. No close parallel has been found for the design.

The decoration of this ware, characteristic of late Naqada I–early Naqada II,[3] usually consists of geometric patterns and plantlike shapes. While the immediate purpose of motifs such as triangles, rectangles, and zigzags is clearly decorative, they may originally have had symbolic meaning. The presence of this ware in graves and settlements from the Aswan region north to Asyut bears witness to the early expansion of the Naqada I culture.

The technical simplicity and the varied, original decoration of C-ware pottery suggest that it was not mass-produced but that its manufacture spread by means of individual contact. Regional painting styles may have existed during the Naqada I period.[4] BM

BIBLIOGRAPHY Henri de Morgan, "L'Egypte primitive (suite)," *Revue de l'Ecole d'anthropologie de Paris* 19 (1909): fig. 127, no. 4; Winifred Needler, *Predynastic and Archaic Egypt in the Brooklyn Museum*, Wilbour Monographs 9 (Brooklyn: Brooklyn Museum, 1984), 184, fig. 22.

NOTES
1. W. M. Flinders Petrie, *Corpus of Prehistoric Pottery and Palettes*, British School of Archaeology in Egypt and Egyptian Research Account 32 (London: Quaritch, 1921), fig. 19B; see also W. Kaiser, "Zur inneren Chronologie der Naqadakultur," *Archaeologia Geographica* 6 (1957): 67–77.
2. Needler, *Predynastic and Archaic Egypt*, 183.
3. Ibid.; see also Rosemarie Drenkhahn, *Die Handwerker und ihre Tätigkeiten im alten Ägypten* (Wiesbaden: Harrassowitz, 1976); Diana Craig Patch, "The Origin and Early Development of Urbanism in Ancient Egypt: A Regional Study" (Ph.D. diss., University of Pennsylvania, 1991); Renée Friedman and Barbara Adams, eds., *The Followers of Horus: Studies Dedicated to M. A. Hoffman, 1944–1990*, Egyptian Studies Association Publication 2, Oxbow Monograph 20 (Oxford: Oxbow Books, 1992); Dorothea Arnold and Janine Bourriau, eds., *An Introduction to Ancient Egyptian Pottery*, fasc. 1, *Techniques and Traditions of Manufacture in the Pottery of Ancient Egypt*, Deutsches archäologisches Institut, Abteilung Kairo, Sonderschrift 17 (Mainz: Philipp von Zabern, 1993); P. Ballet, ed., *Cahiers de la céramique égyptienne: Ateliers des potiers et productions céramiques en Egypte* (Cairo: IFAO, 1993).
4. See E. Finkenstaedt, "Regional Painting Styles in Prehistoric Egypt," *ZÄS* 107 (1980): 116–20.

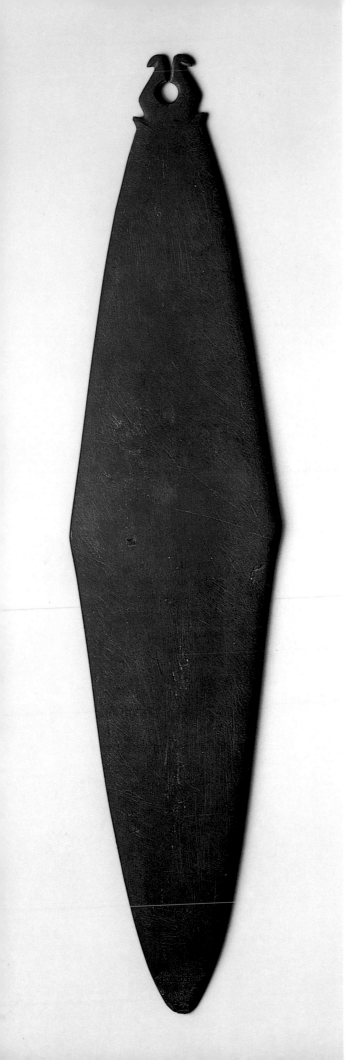

19 Palette with Stylized Birds

El-Mamariya, burial 35
Predynastic, late Naqada I to early
Naqada II period (3600–3400 B.C.)
Schist
L: 66.1 cm (26 in.)
The Brooklyn Museum, Excavations
of Henri de Morgan, 1906–7,
07.447.600

This palette has a simple, rhomboid shape, decorated at one tip with two highly stylized birds that stand on small, earlike projections.[1] The same motif is found on a palette and a comb from Mostagedda[2] and may be related to the fertility goddess.[3] As with other objects of practical use, it is difficult to determine to what extent religious beliefs and superstitions influenced the forms and shapes of these palettes.

The surface of the palette is somewhat hollowed in the center, probably from repeated use. With the exception of beads, schist palettes, which were used by both men and women, are the most popular personal articles found in Predynastic burials. Many palettes still have traces of green malachite, a copper ore pulverized for eye paint. Deposited with the palettes were small lumps of malachite and smooth natural pebbles to serve as grinding stones.[4] Two other minerals have been found on Predynastic palettes: galena, a dark grayish lead ore that became the common material for eye paint in dynastic times, and red ocher, an iron oxide, possibly used as rouge. Green eye paint is sometimes found on Predynastic figures of humans (see cat. no. 23). BM

BIBLIOGRAPHY Henri de Morgan, "L'Egypte primitive (suite)," *Revue de l'Ecole d'anthropologie de Paris* 19 (1909): 299, fig. 128, no. 1; idem, "Report on Excavations Made in Upper Egypt during the Winter, 1907–1908," *ASAE* 12 (1912), 33; Elisabeth Riefstahl, *Toilet Articles from Ancient Egypt* (Brooklyn: Brooklyn Museum, 1943), pl. I (center); Winifred Needler, *Predynastic and Archaic Egypt in the Brooklyn Museum,* Wilbour Monographs 9 (Brooklyn: Brooklyn Museum, 1984), 320, no. 252.

NOTES
1. A similar form has been identified as "the horns and ears of the fertility goddess" by Elise J. Baumgartel (*The Cultures of Prehistoric Egypt,* vol. 2 [London: Oxford University Press, 1960], 83).
2. In a grave dated to Petrie's Amratian; reproduced in Guy Brunton, *British Museum Expedition to Middle Egypt, First and Second Years, 1928, 1929: Mostagedda and the Tasian Culture* (London: Quaritch, 1937), grave 1825, pl. 43, no. 3. The comb is less securely dated; see ibid., grave 1800, pl. 42, no. 51.
3. Brunton considered the motif to be a result of stylistic confusion (ibid.).
4. E.g., see Needler, *Predynastic and Archaic Egypt,* 293, no. 205.

20 Fish Palette

El-Mamariya (no. 69), burial 95
Predynastic, early Naqada II period
(c. 3600–3400 B.C.)
Schist
L: 17 cm (6¾ in.)
The Brooklyn Museum, Excavations
of Henri de Morgan, 1906–7,
07.447.611

This palette is in the form of a tilapia, a
freshwater African fish. The gills, fins, and
spines of the tail are drawn in incised lines
on both faces; both eyes were hollowed for
inlay, now missing. The small tail,[1] once
broken off, is now repaired at the base.
The obverse surface is in good condition;
the reverse is worn and pitted.

Fish palettes are fairly common throughout the Naqada II period. In Naqada III the
shape was often simplified into a small ellipti-
cal plaque.[2] A similar palette with the same
diminutive triangular tail and vestigial fins
is now in Berlin (Ägyptisches Museum no.
12887).[3]

First used merely to supplement the
delineation of the animal represented in outline, carved decoration on the surface of
cosmetic palettes gradually proliferated, as
this fish palette illustrates. Similar palettes
with more elaborate carving[4] foreshadow the
great commemorative monuments culminat-
ing in the Narmer Palette.[5] BM

BIBLIOGRAPHY Elizabeth Riefstahl, *Toilet Articles
from Ancient Egypt* (Brooklyn: Brooklyn Museum,
1943), 2 (upper center); Winifred Needler, *Predynastic
and Archaic Egypt in the Brooklyn Museum*, Wilbour
Monographs 9 (Brooklyn: Brooklyn Museum, 1984),
323, no. 258.

NOTES
1. Cf. another tilapia fish palette in the Brooklyn
Museum from the Abbott collection; illustrated in
Riefstahl, *Toilet Articles*, no. 6; Needler, *Predynastic
and Archaic Egypt*, 252, no. 138.
2. See, e.g., Brooklyn Museum no. 09.889.196, in
Needler, *Predynastic and Archaic Egypt*, 326, no. 262,
fig. 262.
3. Excavated in Naqada; see *Ägyptisches Museum,
Berlin* (Berlin: Staatliche Museen, 1967), no. 136,
from burial 1414.
4. Such as the Min and Hathor palettes (London,
British Museum no. 35501; Cairo, Egyptian Museum
JE 34173); reproduced in Henri Asselberghs, *Chaos
en Beheersing: Documenten uit Aeneolithisch Egypte*
(Leiden: E. J. Brill, 1961), 329, figs. 117, 118, pls.
LXII, LXIII.
5. See Mohamed Saleh and Hourig Sourouzian, *The
Official Catalogue: The Egyptian Museum, Cairo*
(Mainz: Philipp von Zabern, 1987), no. 8 (JE 32169,
CG 14716).

21 Jar with Two Tubular String-Hole Handles

El-Adaima, tomb 23
Predynastic, Naqada II period
(c. 3600–3400 B.C.)
Ceramic
14 x 11.2 (diam) cm (5½ x 4⅜ in.)
The Brooklyn Museum, Excavations
of Henri de Morgan, 1906–7,
07.447.431

During the Naqada II period C-ware (see cat. no. 18) was replaced by a type of pottery both technically superior and more conventional in its decoration. In contrast to the individually made C-ware, this pottery was mass-produced in workshops from hard desert clay. It quickly came to dominate the market for luxury vessels. The buff-on-red decoration of the earlier C-ware was now reversed; on Naqada II pottery the background is beige with motifs painted in reddish brown ocher. While there is evidence that the two types coexisted at the beginning of Naqada II,[1] the older red-polished village pottery gradually became obsolete.

From the very beginning, this ware imitated the shapes and textures of more costly stone vessels. This jar is decorated with spiral shapes that imitate the natural markings of hard stone, in this case, red and cream breccia.[2] This is one of several formal patterns used to suggest stone surfaces. BM

BIBLIOGRAPHY Winifred Needler, *Predynastic and Archaic Egypt in the Brooklyn Museum*, Wilbour Monographs 9 (Brooklyn: Brooklyn Museum, 1984), 203, no. 54.

NOTES
1. See Helene Kantor, "The Final Phase of Predynastic Culture: Gerzean or Semainian?" *JNES* 3 (1944): 79–80.
2. See for example, Needler, *Predynastic and Archaic Egypt*, 242–43, no. 121 (35.1314).

22 Female Figurine

El-Mamariya, burial 2
Predynastic, Naqada IIa period,
c. 3600 B.C.
Terra-cotta
H: 34 cm (13⅜ in.)
The Brooklyn Museum, Excavations
of Henri de Morgan, 1906–7,
07.447.502

Discovered by Henri de Morgan at el-Mamariya with five other very similar fragmentary figurines from other tombs and a sixth rare intact specimen, this female image is one of the very few objects of its type from an authorized excavation.[1] The nature of the figure and the meaning of her pose are not certain. Is she a mortal, a deity, an abstraction, or a fertility symbol? What is the significance of her upraised hands? Is she a dancer or a mourner? Many similar two-dimensional representations of women are found on Naqada II painted pottery, but they all have hemispherical, unmodeled heads. The beaklike face on this figurine presents another problem. Perhaps it represents a goddess with whom a particular bird was associated, just as the hawk and the ibis were symbols of the gods Horus and Thoth, respectively. Bird-shaped or bird-headed depictions of goddesses, however, are uncommon. Perhaps the beaky face is part of an overall abstraction. The legs are summarily indicated, and the feet are not modeled at all.

The full breasts and buttocks have led some to suggest that the figurine may have connotations of fertility or sexuality, which were intimately connected in ancient Egypt. Whatever their symbolism, figurines of this type appear to have had great significance. Similar females on painted pottery are generally represented as larger than the accompanying males, and in ancient Egyptian art scale is an index of importance. DS

BIBLIOGRAPHY Winifred Needler, *Predynastic and Archaic Egypt in the Brooklyn Museum*, Wilbour Monographs 9 (Brooklyn: Brooklyn Museum, 1984), 338, no. 268.

NOTES
1. The other five are Brooklyn Museum nos. 07.447.500–501, 07.447.503–4, 07.447.515; the intact figurine is 07.447.505. All six are published in Needler, *Predynastic and Archaic Egypt*, nos. 268–73.

23 Male Figure

Possibly from Naqada[1]
Predynastic, Early Naqada II
(c. 3600–3400 B.C.)
Terra-cotta
H: 15.7 cm (6⅛ in.)
The Brooklyn Museum, Charles
Edwin Wilbour Fund, 35.1269

Among the funerary equipment in Predynastic burials, human figures are among the rarest of artifacts. They seem to have represented a number of different beliefs, fulfilling diverse if somewhat obscure functions. Male figures are particularly scarce.

This male figurine has a birdlike head, stump arms, an incised girdle at the waist, and a penis sheath.[2] The "legs" are separated by a vertical line in the front and back. Below the waist a long, white garment was indicated in white paint.

The figurine is made of gray terra-cotta that was originally covered by a red ocher wash.[3] A black resinous substance on the back of the head and shoulders is all that remains of the headdress.[4] On each side of the head a long, black line indicating the eyes is surrounded by green malachite paint. The statuette, once broken at the waist, has been repaired.

As its provenance is not clear, this figure cannot be precisely dated. Two similar bird-headed statuettes with stump arms and penis sheaths have been found in an early Predynastic burial near Mahasna.[5] Furthermore, the terra-cotta statuettes seem to be related to bearded ivory figures with stump arms and penis sheaths that date to Naqada I.[6] In its attitude and proportions, however, this figure is more closely related to terra-cotta female statuettes that date to Naqada II.[7] A thermoluminescence test dated it to c. 6000–3100 B.C.[8] BM

BIBLIOGRAPHY Friedrich von Bissing, "Les débuts de la statuaire en Egypte," *Revue archéologique* 15 (1910): 246, figs. 6, 7; James H. Breasted, *Egyptian Servant Statues* (Washington, D.C.: Bollingen, 1948), 99, pl. 95a; Peter J. Ucko, *Anthropomorphic Figurines of Predynastic Egypt and Neolithic Crete with Comparative Material from the Predynastic Near East and Mainland Greece*, Royal Anthropological Institute Occasional Papers 24 (London: A. Szmidla, 1968), no. 169; Winifred Needler, *Predynastic and Archaic Egypt in the Brooklyn Museum*, Wilbour Monographs 9 (Brooklyn: Brooklyn Museum, 1984), 343–44, no. 274.

NOTES
1. The figure's former owner, Friedrich von Bissing, claimed that the figurine had been found at Naqada. The piece was purchased by the Brooklyn Museum in 1935.
2. The penis sheath worn by this figure is documented as early as the painting of the hunter on the Moscow C-ware dish (Pushkin Museum no. 4777); see Needler, *Predynastic and Archaic Egypt*, 344. The development of this garment throughout the Predynastic Period has been studied by Ucko, *Anthropomorphic Figurines*. For illustrations, see also Henri Asselberghs, *Chaos en Beheersing: Documenten uit Aeneolithisch Egypte* (Leiden: E. J. Brill, 1961), pls. 6, 9, 17.
3. Needler, *Predynastic and Archaic Egypt*, 343.
4. Similar black resin is found on the back of the head of a female figurine in the Brooklyn Museum (no. 07.447.505); see ibid., 336, no. 267.
5. John Garstang, *Mahasna and Bet Khallaf*, British School of Archaeology in Egypt and Egyptian Research Account 7 (London: Quaritch, 1903), pl. III.
6. Such as Brooklyn Museum no. 35.1268; illustrated in Needler, *Predynastic and Archaic Egypt*, 344, no. 275. A similar ivory figure comes from a Naqada I burial at Mahasna; see Edward R. Ayrton and W. L. S. Loat, *Predynastic Cemetery at El Mahasna*, Egypt Exploration Fund, 31st Memoir (London: Quaritch, 1911), pl. XI, fig. 1.
7. Brooklyn Museum nos. 07.447.505, 07.447.502, 07.447.504; illustrated in Needler, *Predynastic and Archaic Egypt*, 267–70, nos. 267, 268, 270. Two other bird-headed male statuettes, in the Ashmolean Museum, Oxford, and the Ipswich Borough Council Museum and Art Galleries, also suggest a date in the early Naqada II period; see Ucko, *Anthropomorphic Figurines*, 448, pl. IV, fig. 28, and 470–71, pl. XXVIII, fig. 170.
8. Needler, *Predynastic and Archaic Egypt*, 344.

24 Frog-Shaped Vessel

Naga el-Deir, grave N7304
Predynastic, Naqada IId period
(c. 3400–3300 B.C.)
Limestone, lapis lazuli, ostrich eggshell
4 x 8.4 cm (1 ⅝ x 3 ¼ in.)
Phoebe A. Hearst Museum
of Anthropology, University
of California, Berkeley, 6-17171

This beguiling piece was discovered during George A. Reisner and Albert M. Lythgoe's 1903–4 excavation of the Predynastic cemetery 7000 at Naga el-Deir, in what had been originally an extremely well endowed burial. Although the body had been plundered out, the remaining materials, which included a yellow limestone cylinder seal engraved with fish and crosshatching motifs (PAHMA 6-3499), were sufficiently distinctive to allow the grave to be dated with some precision.[1]

The frog vessel might have been used for cosmetics and must have been a prized possession, for it was executed with skill from valuable materials. The vessel surface, flat rim, and lug handles for suspension were well smoothed; the body was inlaid with small pieces of lapis lazuli and the eyes formed from ostrich eggshell beads. The ancient Egyptians viewed the reproductive abilities of frogs with wonder (the tadpole was adopted as the hieroglyph for the number one hundred thousand),[2] and the frog became the symbol for Heqet, a birth goddess whose priesthood was among the earliest known.[3] It is no surprise, then, that many representations of frogs are known from the Early Dynastic Period alone.[4] Although other examples of this vessel type are known,[5] this one, more than any other, suggests that its artist viewed his finished creation with amusement, for the frog sits balanced not upon its legs but its rounded belly, with its paddlelike appendages suspended in midair.

CK

BIBLIOGRAPHY Helene Kantor, "Further Evidence for Early Mesopotamian Relations with Egqt," *JNES* 11 (1952): 242, 245, pl. XXIII; Albert M. Lythgoe and Dows Dunham, *The Predynastic Cemetery N7000 Naga ed-Dêr* (Berkeley and Los Angeles: University of California Press, 1965), 179, 181–82, figs. 78e, 78g, 79a; Albert B. Elsasser and Vera-Mae Fredrickson, *Ancient Egypt*, exh. cat. (Berkeley: Robert H. Lowie Museum of Anthropology, University of California, 1966), 28; Richard A. Fazzini, *Images for Eternity: Egyptian Art from Berkeley and Brooklyn*, exh. cat. (San Francisco: Fine Arts Museums of San Francisco; Brooklyn: Brooklyn Museum, 1975), 12–13, no. 9; Ali el-Khouli, *Egyptian Stone Vessels: Predynastic Period to Dynasty III* (Mainz: Philipp von Zabern, 1978), vol. 2, 740, no. 5628, vol. 3, pl. 140B.

NOTES
1. Originally dated by Kantor ("Further Evidence," 246, pls. XX–XXII, figs. 1, 2) to SD 55–60 (later Gerzean), N7304 was subsequently assigned to Naqada IIc by Werner Kaiser ("Zur inneren Chronologie der Naqadakultur," *Archaeologia Geographica* 6 [1957]: 75, n. 63). The most recent discussion of the grave's date is that of Patricia Podzorski ("Predynastic Egyptian Seals of Known Provenience in the R. H. Lowie Museum of Anthropology," *JNES* 47 [1988]: 261–62), who accepts Renée Friedman's reassessment of N7304 as belonging to Naqada IId ("Spatial Distribution in a Predynastic Cemetery: Naga ed-Dêr 7000" [M.A. thesis, University of California, Berkeley, 1981], 128).
2. Alan H. Gardiner, *Egyptian Grammar: Being an Introduction to the Study of Hieroglyphs*, 3d ed., rev. (London: Oxford University Press, 1957), 475, I.8.
3. L[aszlo] K[askosy], *LÄ*, vol. 2, col. 1124; Nigel Strudwick, *The Administration of Egypt in the Old Kingdom* (London: Kegan Paul International, 1985), 184–85.
4. See, e.g., A. Jeffrey Spencer, *Catalogue of Egyptian Antiquities in the British Museum*, vol. 5, *Early Dynastic Objects* (London: British Museum Press, 1980), 14, nos. 5, 6 (EA 54372, 66837), pl. 4. The Hearst Museum also possesses an unprovenanced example, purchased by Reisner at Coptos (PAHMA 6-17305).
5. Kantor, "Further Evidence," pls. XXIII–XXIV; el-Khouli, *Egyptian Stone Vessels*, vol. 2, 740, nos. 5629–30, vol. 3, pl. 140P; Barbara G. Aston, *Ancient Egyptian Stone Vessels*, Studien zur Archäologie und Geschichte Ägyptens 5 (Heidelberg: Heidelberger Orientverlag, 1994), type 24, 98.

25 Jar with Two Wavy Handles

Abu Zaidan, tomb 69
Predynastic, Naqada III period
(c. 3400–3200 B.C.)
Serpentine
H: 14.1 cm (5½ in.)
The Brooklyn Museum, Excavations
of Henri de Morgan, 1907–8,
09.889.31

This elongated vessel made of colorful green
stone with dark veins is distinguished by two
long, wavy ridges at the shoulder, which are
pierced in the center for suspension. Pottery
jars of similar shape from the Naqada II
period often have wavy handles with string
holes for suspension.[1] This jar, though made
of hard stone and thus impractical to carry,
imitates the form of such vessels.

The tradition of carving hard stone, for
which Egyptian masters were famed, began
with these stone vessels of the Predynastic
Period. Their manufacture proliferated in the
Naqada III period. Although stone carvers
sometimes imitated the shapes of earlier
ceramic ware, they also introduced a number
of exciting innovations by selecting hard
stone according to its quality and color
and polishing it to achieve highly decorative
surfaces.[2] During Naqada III the Egyptians
began using copper tools, including the drill
with two weights attached to a handle, which
became the sign for *art* and *craft* in the hieroglyphic script.[3]

Among the pottery shapes imitated by
early stone vessels was the popular wavy-
handled jar. This type first appeared in
Palestine sometime before Early Bronze I;[4]
it made its way to the Egyptian Delta with
settlers from Palestine sometime during the
Naqada II period[5] and remained a favorite
type throughout Naqada III.[6] BM

BIBLIOGRAPHY Henri de Morgan, "L'Egypte primi-
tive (suite)," *Revue de l'Ecole d'anthropologie de Paris*
19 (1909): 273–74, figs. 132 (in situ), 133; Helene
Kantor, "The Final Phase of Predynastic Culture:
Gerzean or Semainian?" *JNES* 3 (1944): 128; John D.
Cooney, *Egyptian Art in the Brooklyn Museum Col-
lection* (Brooklyn: Brooklyn Museum, 1952), no. 3;
Winifred Needler, *Predynastic and Archaic Egypt in
the Brooklyn Museum*, Wilbour Monographs 9
(Brooklyn: Brooklyn Museum, 1984), 242, no. 122.

NOTES
1. See, e.g., three wavy-handled pottery jars in the
Brooklyn Museum (nos. 07.447.1310, 07.447.1311,
09.889.605), illustrated in Needler, *Predynastic and
Archaic Egypt*, 77, fig. 2, nos. 27, 29, 30.
2. See the examples in the Brooklyn Museum (nos.
35.1314, 09.889.11, 09.885.35, 05.320), illustrated
ibid., 243, figs. 121–25.
3. Alan H. Gardiner, *Egyptian Grammar: Being an
Introduction to the Study of Hieroglyphs*, 3d ed.
(London: Oxford University Press, 1957), 518, U25.
4. Early Bronze I correlates to Naqada III; see Helene
J. Kantor, "The Relative Chronology of Egypt and Its
Foreign Correlations before the Late Bronze Age," in
Chronologies in Old World Archaeology, ed. R. W.
Ehrich (Chicago: University of Chicago Press, 1965),
7–8.
5. Ibid., 8.
6. See, e.g., similar vessels from Gerza (W. M. Flinders
Petrie, Gerald A. Wainwright, and Ernest MacKay,
The Labyrinth: Gerzeh and Mazghuneh, British School
of Archaeology in Egypt and Egyptian Research
Account 21 [London: Quaritch, 1912], pl. 8, no. 2)
and Tarkhan (W. M. Flinders Petrie, Gerald. A. Wainwright and Alan H. Gardiner, *Tarkhan I and Memphis
V*, British School of Archaeology in Egypt and Egyptian Research Account 23 [London: Quaritch, 1913],
pl. 1, no. 2). See also W. M. Flinders Petrie, *Prehistoric Egypt*, British School of Archaeology in Egypt
and Egyptian Research Account 31 (London: Quaritch, 1920), pl. 39, nos. 82–84.

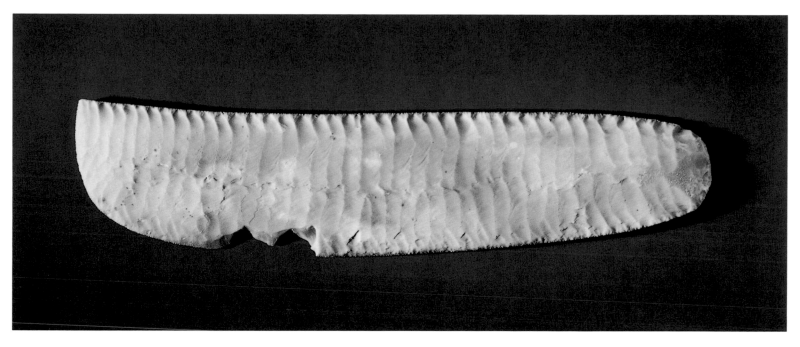

26 Knife

Abu Zaidan, burial 102
Predynastic, Naqada III period,
c. 3400–3200 B.C.
Flint
H: 28.8 cm (11⅜ in.)
The Brooklyn Museum, Excavations
of Henri de Morgan, 1907–8,
09.889.119

Discovered by Henri de Morgan at Abu Zaidan, south of Edfu, during his 1907–8 excavations on behalf of the Brooklyn Museum, this double-edged, finely serrated knife is an excellent example of the ripple-flake technique frequently encountered on Predynastic blades. Several flakings were involved. First, the flint was roughed out for shape and smoothed on both surfaces. Next, one side was carefully flaked over the burnishing in a wave or ripple pattern perpendicularly to the top and bottom, which became the edges of the blade. Finally each edge received fine, precise flaking along the entire length of each side to produce a serrated cutting knife. In technique this blade is identical to the famous knife with an ivory handle, which de Morgan also found at Abu Zaidan.[1] Both demonstrate the skill of artists of the Naqada III period in producing fine ripple flaking over a polished surface. DS

BIBLIOGRAPHY Winifred Needler, *Predynastic and Archaic Egypt in the Brooklyn Museum*, Wilbour Monographs 9 (Brooklyn: Brooklyn Museum, 1984), 272–73, no. 167.

NOTES
1. Needler, *Predynastic and Archaic Egypt*, 268–71, no. 165; Richard A. Fazzini et al., *Ancient Egyptian Art in the Brooklyn Museum* (Brooklyn: Brooklyn Museum, 1989), no. 4

27 Bowl Inscribed for King Scorpion

Hierakonpolis
Dynasty 0, c. 3000 B.C.
Calcite, Egyptian blue
6.4 x 12.1 (diam) cm (2½ x 4¾ in.)
Museum of Fine Arts, Boston,
98.1011

The success of the Egypt Exploration Fund led W. M. Flinders Petrie to found a similar organization through University College, London, which he named the Egyptian Research Account.[1] Like the EEF, the Egyptian Research Account provided American museums with shares of its finds in exchange for support. It was particularly important for its work in sites of the Predynastic and Early Dynastic Periods.

The most important account site was the great necropolis and temple of Hierakonpolis.[2] The wealth of material from excavations conducted first by James E. Quibell and continued by Frederick W. Green between 1897 and 1899 was distributed to museums in England, Belgium, and the United States.[3] Objects inscribed for the earliest kings of Egypt added much to our knowledge of this shadowy period in history.

This calcite bowl is inscribed with the name of King Scorpion, who is generally placed before Narmer in the sequence of rulers. Like many vessel inscriptions of the period, it is roughly cut on the body of the vase. This example is rare in retaining its original Egyptian blue pigment.[4] PL

BIBLIOGRAPHY James E. Quibell and Frederick W. Green, *Hierakonpolis*, vol. 2 (London: Quaritch, 1902), pl. XLVIIIa (center).

NOTES
1. Margaret Drower, *Flinders Petrie: A Life in Archaeology* (London: Victor Gollancz, 1985), 224–25.
2. James E. Quibell, *Hierakonpolis*, vol. 1 (London: Quaritch, 1900); Quibell and Green, *Hierakonpolis*, vol. 2.
3. Barbara Adams, *Ancient Hierakonpolis: Supplement* (Warminster: Aris and Phillips, 1974), 133.
4. Distinct from blue Egyptian faience, Egyptian blue is a crystalline substance formed from copper or copper ore when heated with silica sand and sodium or potassium.

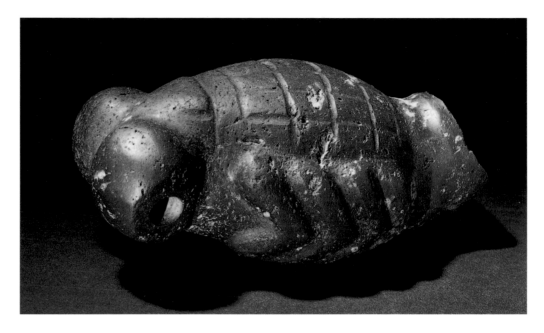

28 Scorpion

Hierakonpolis, Main Deposit
Dynasty 0, c. 3000 B.C.
Hematite
4.5 x 6.2 x 11.3 cm (1¾ x 2½ x 4½ in.)
The University of Pennsylvania Museum
of Archaeology and Anthropology,
E3844

This small figure of a scorpion, the tail now unfortunately gone, was discovered in the so-called Main Deposit at Hierakonpolis by the British expedition headed by James E. Quibell and Frederick W. Green for the Egyptian Research Account. The University of Pennsylvania Museum was an early supporter of this organization, just as it was of the Egypt Exploration Fund, largely through the efforts of Sara Yorke Stevenson, the first curator of the museum's Egyptian and Mediterranean Section.[1]

Apparently the cast-off offerings of the site's Early Dynastic temple, a large number of objects in the Main Deposit, including this scorpion, date from the era of the founding of the ancient Egyptian state. Among the objects were such important documents of Egypt's early history as the King Scorpion mace head and the Narmer mace head, as well as the Narmer Palette, the key monument of Early Dynastic art.

Several of the objects contained in the deposit display a scorpion motif. In addition to the King Scorpion mace head and the present example, these included a scorpion of glazed faience, the tail of a rock crystal scorpion, a vase with scorpion motifs in raised relief, and another vase with scorpion handles.[2] While each of these objects could have been a votive offering to a deity associated with the scorpion, such as the goddess Selket, it is tempting to associate them with the protodynastic King Scorpion.

Reportedly discovered at the northeast end of the chamber containing the Main Deposit, this example shows four carefully articulated legs on each side of the body, with the two eyes deeply drilled, probably for the insertion of inlays made from other materials. The scorpion's back has been carved with five vertical incised lines crossed by six horizontal lines, the whole forming a cross-hatched pattern. This tantalizing object is evocative of the earliest period of the dynastic art of ancient Egypt. GS

BIBLIOGRAPHY James E. Quibell and Frederick W. Green, *Hierakonpolis*, vol. 2 (London: Quaritch, 1902), pl. 48a.

NOTES
1. David O'Connor and David Silverman, "The University Museum in Egypt: The Past," *Expedition* 21 (Winter 1979): 5–7.
2. Quibell and Green, *Hierakonpolis*, 30, 32, pls. XIX, XVII.

29 Censer

Qustul, cemetery L, grave 24
A-Group, c. 3000 B.C.
Indurated clay
8.8 x 14.9 (diam) cm (3½ x 5⅞ in.)
The Oriental Institute, University of
Chicago, 24069

This platform for burning incense was excavated in cemetery L at Qustul, Nubia. Known as the Qustul Censer, this important historical document may bear the first known depiction of a royal figure from either Egypt or Nubia. Its decoration has been interpreted as evidence that the tradition of kingship in Africa began not in Egypt but in Lower Nubia. Qustul is considered to be the burial place of early kings because of the comparatively large size and richness of twenty-three of its tombs.

The sides of the censer are decorated with themes related to early kingship in Egypt. The motifs include a palace façade, a rosette, animal motifs, and three ships, which bear a bearded figure wearing a tall headdress, seated on a throne and holding a flail; a bound prisoner; and a feline(?). Based on a study of Early Dynastic iconography, Bruce B. Williams dated the censer, which he considered to be of Nubian manufacture, to the period between Naqada II and III, prior to the traditionally accepted date for the unification of Egypt.[1] Others, however, would argue that, since a considerable amount of pottery recovered from royal tombs was clearly imported from Egypt, the censer too was made in Egypt and sent to Nubia as a gift from the northern kings.[2] If so, the censer reflects not Nubian kingship but Egyptian monarchy. Even if the censer is of Nubian manufacture, excavations by Günter Dreyer in cemetery U at Abydos have revealed royal tombs that predate the manufacture of the Qustul Censer,[3] indicating that the tradition of kingship in Egypt is older than that reflected by the Nubian tombs of cemetery L. ET

BIBLIOGRAPHY Keith Seele, "University of Chicago Oriental Institute Nubian Expedition: Excavations between Abu Simbel and the Sudan Border: Preliminary Report," *JNES* 33 (1974): 35–39; C. DeVries, "Communication Concerning the Work of the Oriental Institute Nubian Expedition," in *Nubia: Récentes recherches: Actes du Colloque nubiologique international au Musée national de Varsovie*, ed. Kazimierz Michalowski (Warsaw: Musée national, 1975), 18–21; C. DeVries, "The Oriental Institute Decorated Censer from Nubia," in *Studies in Honor of George R. Hughes* (Chicago: Oriental Institute, University of Chicago, 1976), 55–74; Steffen Wenig, *Africa in Antiquity: The Arts of Ancient Nubia and the Sudan*, vol. 2, *The Catalogue*, exh. cat. (Brooklyn: Brooklyn Museum, 1978), 24–25, 117; Bruce B. Williams, *Excavations between Abu Simbel and the Sudan Frontier*, pt. 1, *The A-Group Royal Cemetery at Qustul: Cemetery L*, OINE 3 (Chicago: Oriental Institute, University of Chicago, 1986), 138–45, 147, 172–74, 182, pls. 34, 38; David O'Connor, *Ancient Nubia: Egypt's Rival in Africa*, exh. cat. (Philadelphia: University Museum, University of Pennsylvania, 1993), 21–22, fig. 2.4.

NOTES
1. Williams, *The A-Group Royal Cemetery*, 144, 182; idem, "The Lost Pharaohs of Nubia," *Archaeology Magazine* 33 (September–October 1980): 12–21.
2. O'Connor, *Ancient Nubia*, 21–22.
3. Günter Dreyer, "Umm el-Qaab: Nachuntersuchungen im frühzeitlichen Königsfriedhof 5./6. Vorbericht," *MDAIK* 49 (1993): 34–35; idem, "A Hundred Years at Abydos," *Egyptian Archaeology*, no. 3 (1993): 12.

30   A-Group Bowl

Qustul, cemetery W, tomb 10
A-Group, c. 3000–2900 B.C.
Ceramic
33 x 50.8 cm (13 x 20 in.)
The Oriental Institute,
University of Chicago, 23771

The people of the Nubian A-Group culture created some of the finest pottery of the Nile Valley. Many examples are conical and painted in imitation of baskets. Most have blackened, finely burnished interiors. Referred to as eggshell ware because of the thinness of their walls, these luxury vessels are so delicate that they may have been produced primarily to indicate the status of their owners, rather than for more practical purposes.

This vessel was one of seven fine conical bowls recovered from the richly furnished tomb of an adult female. One bowl was filled with red ocher, which was used as a cosmetic. A palette and grinding stone had been placed before the face of the deceased. The tomb also contained several examples of pottery imported from Egypt, indicating trade and contact between the two cultures.

Both this bowl and the censer (cat. no. 29) were unearthed in excavations directed by Keith Seele for the University of Chicago at Qustul in 1962–64. ET

BIBLIOGRAPHY Bruce B. Williams, *Excavations between Abu Simbel and the Sudan Frontier*, pts. 2–4, *Neolithic, A-Group, and Post-A-Group Remains from Cemeteries W, V, S, Q, T, and a Cave East of Cemetery K*, OINE 4 (Chicago: Oriental Institute, University of Chicago, 1989), 55, pl. 15d.

31 Cylindrical Vase with Inscription of King Narmer

Abydos, tomb B6
1st Dynasty, c. 2900 B.C.
Calcite
26.9 x 20.5 (diam) cm (10⅝ x 8⅛ in.)
The University of Pennsylvania
Museum of Archaeology
and Anthropology, E9510

This cylindrical vase, which the University of Pennsylvania Museum of Archaeology and Anthropology received from the Egypt Exploration Fund, is inscribed with the name of one of the first rulers of a united Egyptian state, King Narmer. It comes from the pioneering excavations W. M. Flinders Petrie conducted at Abydos (1899–1903), a site that had just been "excavated" by the Frenchman Emile Amélineau. Through his exacting methods Petrie recovered much important material either overlooked or discarded by Amélineau and provided countless clues for the historical and cultural reconstruction of the earliest period of ancient Egyptian history.

The present vase was found in a tomb near the one Petrie believed to have been King Narmer's.[1] Of it he wrote: "The most important example of the rope band is the great vase of Narmer."[2] This vessel type displays a "rope" or cord carved in raised relief around the neck of the jar, just below a prominent rim. George A. Reisner, who subsequently studied the types of stone vessels produced during the Early Dynastic Period and the Old Kingdom, considered this sort of vessel not only typical of the 1st Dynasty but also nearly as common as flat-bottomed stone bowls in burials of the era.[3] He also noted that most examples found in earlier tombs have straight, vertical sides and a wider shape than later jars, features that can be observed in the Narmer vase.[4]

Beneath the rope band the name of King Narmer is carved with two hieroglyphic signs, a distinctive fish that has the phonetic value "*nar*" and a chisel, phonetic "*mer*," both contained within a representation of a palace façade surmounted by a Horus falcon. Petrie found this inscription "coarser than on the slate carvings," but he also noted that "the hawk is much like that on the great slate [the Narmer Palette]; the deeply curved top is usual under Narmer, though only occasional under Aha, and then flatter, and is never seen under later kings."[5] GS

BIBLIOGRAPHY W. M. Flinders Petrie, *The Royal Tombs of the Earliest Dynasties*, pt. 2 (London: Egypt Exploration Fund, 1901), 4, 5, 19, 44, pls. II (3), LII (359).

NOTES
1. Petrie, *Royal Tombs*, 5.
2. Ibid., 44.
3. George A. Reisner, *Mycerinus: The Temples of the Third Pyramid at Giza* (Cambridge: Harvard University Press, 1931), 143.
4. Ibid.
5. Petrie, *Royal Tombs*, 19.

32 Stela of King Qaa

Abydos, Umm el-Qaʿab, tomb of Qaa
Late 1st Dynasty, c. 2770 B.C.
Basalt
143 x 66 x 24.1 cm
(56¼ x 26 x 9½ in.)
The University of Pennsylvania
Museum of Archaeology
and Anthropology, E6878

An impressive monument from the close of Egypt's 1st Dynasty, this stela was discovered on the east side of the tomb of King Qaa at Abydos. The stela had been broken, and its two surviving sections were recovered separately. Emile Amélineau found the lower section, and W. M. Flinders Petrie, working at Abydos for the Egypt Exploration Fund, subsequently excavated the upper portion bearing the king's Horus name. (The Horus name identified the king as the earthly embodiment of the ancient celestial god.) The two sections were reunited at the University of Pennsylvania in 1903.[1] This is, in fact, one of two stelae, the other (now in Cairo) also found by Amélineau. Near the section Petrie discovered were several stone vessels, one of which is inscribed "priest of King Qaa."[2] This evidence suggests that the funerary cult of King Qaa was conducted between the two flanking stelae, with offerings of various sorts being presented, presumably, on an offering table.

Although the stela has been reconstructed and considerably restored in modern times, the hieroglyphs forming the king's name are largely intact. Carved in raised relief, they reflect the powerful simplicity of the artistic style of the 1st Dynasty. The tail, legs, and talon of the Horus falcon are boldly indicated, as are the fingers and thumb of the hieroglyph in the form of a human hand and arm[3] which is part of the king's name. The stela also displays a raised-relief border. GS

View of Umm el-Qaʿab, the area of the royal tombs of the 1st and 2d Dynasties.

BIBLIOGRAPHY W. M. Flinders Petrie, *The Royal Tombs of the Earliest Dynasties*, pt. 2 (London: Egypt Exploration Fund, 1901), 6, 15, 26; idem, *Abydos*, vol. 1 (London: Egypt Exploration Fund, 1902), 6, pl. V; PM, vol. 5 (1937), 86; W. B. Emery, *Archaic Egypt* (Harmondsworth: Penguin Books, 1961), 88 (see also fig. 52); David O'Connor, "Abydos and the University Museum: 1898–1969," *Expedition* 12 (Fall 1969): 30 (ill.); Michael A. Hoffman, "The City of the Hawk: Seat of Egypt's Ancient Civilization," *Expedition* 18 (Spring 1976): 38, ill. no. 1.

NOTES
1. Petrie, *Abydos*, 6. The University of Pennsylvania Museum of Archaeology and Anthropology's registration card for the object records the dates that the two sections were received.
2. See Petrie, *Royal Tombs*, pl. IX, no. 12.
3. See Alan H. Gardiner, *Egyptian Grammar: Being an Introduction to the Study of Hieroglyphs*, 3d ed., rev. (London: Oxford University Press, 1966), 454, D36.

the White Crown of Upper Egypt. Facing the king's Horus name is the ancient vulture goddess of el-Kab, Nekhebet, who holds the hieroglyphic symbol for union clutched tightly in a talon. Beneath her is a circle, which encloses the hieroglyphs *bš*, perhaps meaning "rebel(s)." Above the group is the phrase "within Nekheb (el-Kab)," presumably meant as an epithet of Nekhbet. The four hieroglyphs at the viewer's right traditionally have been read "the year of fighting the northern enemy."[4]

The inscription and the vase's findspot combine to suggest that it was a votive object. It probably once contained a valuable commodity and was donated to a deity in return for success in battle against a northern enemy. As such, it is an important document of the civil war that is thought to have taken place at the end of the 2d Dynasty and the close of the Early Dynastic Period.[5] GS

BIBLIOGRAPHY James E. Quibell and W. M. Flinders Petrie, *Hierakonpolis,* pt. 1 (London: Egyptian Research Account, 1900), 11, pls. XXXVI (bottom), XXXVII, XXXVIII (bottom); James E. Quibell and Frederick W. Green, *Hierakonpolis,* vol. 2 (London: Egyptian Research Account, 1902), 43–44; PM (1937), vol. 5, 195 (with additional citation); W. B. Emery, *Archaic Egypt* (Harmondsworth: Penguin Books, 1961), 99–100, fig. 63; Michael Hoffman, "The City of the Hawk: Seat of Egypt's Ancient Civilization," *Expedition* 18 (Spring 1976): ill. no. 4.

NOTES
1. Some scholars believe Khasekhem and Khasekhemwy, the last two kings of the 2d Dynasty, to be identical; others disagree. See, e.g., Emery, *Archaic Egypt,* 98, and Michael A. Hoffman, *Egypt before the Pharaohs* (New York: Alfred A. Knopf, 1979), 348–50.
2. Quibell and Petrie, *Hierakonpolis,* vol. 1, 11.
3. Quibell and Green, *Hierakonpolis,* vol. 2, 43–44.
4. Quibell and Petrie, *Hierakonpolis,* vol. 1, 11; Quibell and Green, *Hierakonpolis,* vol. 2, 44; Emery, *Archaic Egypt,* 99. The idea of the "northern rebels" actually fighting within Nekheb seems somewhat unlikely to the present writer and hence the suggested association with Nekhbet.
5. Emery, *Archaic Egypt,* 98–99.

33 Vase of King Khasekhem

Hierakonpolis, Main Deposit
2d Dynasty, c. 2650 B.C.
Calcite
H: 80 cm (31½ in.)
The University of Pennsylvania
Museum of Archaeology
and Anthropology, E6878

Among the votive objects of 2d Dynasty date discovered in the Main Deposit at Hierakonpolis were three bearing nearly identical inscriptions, each with the name of King Khasekhem, the penultimate—and perhaps also the ultimate—king of that dynasty.[1] These objects were a granite jar sent to the Egyptian Museum, Cairo; a calcite bowl in the Ashmolean Museum, Oxford; and this massive calcite vase.[2] The vase was found standing upright, on the revetment, or wall, and "its mouth was closed by a flat earthenware dish."[3]

While the vase is noteworthy for its impressive size, its historical interest lies in its inscription. This shows, on the viewer's left, the Horus name of King Khasekhem, which appears within the customary palace façade surmounted by a Horus falcon, who wears

34 Three Copper Tools

Naga el-Deir, grave N1513
Early Dynastic Period, 2d Dynasty
(c. 2770–2649 B.C.)
Copper
Phoebe A. Hearst Museum
of Anthropology, University
of California, Berkeley

A *Adze Blade*
L: 24.8 cm (9¾ in.); W: 8 cm (3¼ in.);
TH: .4 cm (⅛ in.)
6-87

B *Axe Blade*
L: 16 cm (6¼ in.); W: 15 cm (5⅞ in.);
TH: .3 cm (³⁄₃₂ in.)
6-88

C *Adze Blade*
L: 19.5 cm (7⅝ in.); W: 3.5 cm (1⅜ in.);
TH: .45 cm (³⁄₁₆ in.)
6-89

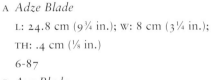

Unlike model implements placed in ancient Egyptian tombs of later periods, many graves of the Predynastic and Early Dynastic Periods have yielded full-sized copper tools that demonstrate both the skills of the metalsmiths of those times and the sheer quantity of copper available to them. These large, heavy blades also provide a clearer view of the woodworkers of the Early Dynastic Period, whose axes hewed timber for architectural construction (beams and columns for the roofing and supports of tombs, palaces, and houses) and for the fabrication of seagoing and Nile ships. Chisels and adzes were used for smaller-scale projects (private, royal, and divine sculptures and furniture for temples, tombs, and dwellings) or the finishing stages of structures and boats.

These three copper tools were discovered on the floor of the main chamber of grave N1513 at Naga el-Deir; they had been placed immediately before the face of the person buried therein. This tool deposit made up only a small portion of the grave goods interred in this tomb, which yielded more items than any other tomb excavated by George A. Reisner in cemetery 1500. CK

BIBLIOGRAPHY George A. Reisner, *The Early Dynastic Cemeteries of Naga ed-Dêr*, vol. 1, University of California Publications, Egyptian Archaeology 2 (Leipzig: J. C. Hinrichs, 1908), 48–52 (description of tomb), 48, fig. 83 (plan), pl. 40c (photograph of copper tools).

35 Stone Vessels and a Knife

Naga el-Deir
Early Dynastic Period, 2d Dynasty
(c. 2770–2649 B.C.)
Phoebe A. Hearst Museum of Anthropology, University of California, Berkeley

A

A *Pressure-Flaked Crescent-Shaped Blade*
Northwest side chamber of tomb N1514
Flint
L: 31.5 cm (12⅜ in.)
6-262

B *Model Spouted Vessel*
Main chamber of tomb N1571
Tuff
5 x 7.3 cm (2 x 2⅞ in.)
6-358

C *Cosmetic Case in the Form of a Bovine Head with Swivel Construction*
Tomb N1605
Siltstone
W: 6.5 cm (2½ in.); L: 6.5 cm (2½ in.)
6-686ab

D *Cosmetic Jar Made in Two Parts*[1]
Main chamber of tomb N1571
Tuff body, siltstone rim and shoulder
Body: 4 x 5.7 (diam) cm (1⅝ x 2¼ in.)
Shoulder: 1 x 5.7 (diam) cm (⅜ x 2¼ in.)
6-357, 6-357a

E *Squat Cylinder Jar*
Northeast storage chamber of tomb N1513
Calcite
8 x 12.5 (diam) cm (3⅛ x 4⅞ in.)
6-103

F *Tall Cylinder Jar with Rope Trim beneath Rim*
Main chamber of tomb N1572
Calcite
24.4 x 13 (diam) cm (9⅝ x 5⅛ in.)
6-580

G *Tall Piriform Jar with Rounded Rim*
Northeast storage chamber of tomb N1513
Calcite
27 x 17 (diam) cm (10⅝ x 6¾ in.)
6-123

H *Jar with Rolled Rim*
Northeast storage chamber of tomb N1513
Calcite
12 x 7.5 (diam) cm (4¾ x 3 in.)
6-141

I *Globular Jar*
Northeast storage niche of tomb N3013
Calcite
8.5 x 13 (diam) cm (3⅜ x 5⅛ in.)
6-836

J *Small Bowl with Sharp Shoulder*
Northeast storage chamber of tomb N1513
Calcite
4.5 x 12.5 (diam) cm (1¾ x 4⅞ in.)
6-120

B–D

E–J

K *Plate with Incurved Rim*
Northeast storage chamber of
tomb N1513
Siltstone
4.5 x 28.2 (diam) cm (1¾ x 11⅛ in.)
6-105

L *Oval Bowl*
Northeast storage chamber of
tomb N1513
Tuff or siltstone
H: 8 cm (3⅛ in.); W: 10 cm (3⅞ in.);
L: 15 cm (5⅞ in.)
6-109

M *Bowl with Incurved Rim*
Southeast storage chamber of
tomb N1514
Tuff or siltstone
8 x 25.5 (diam) cm (3⅛ x 9⅞ in.)
6-219

N *Model Cylinder Jar with Rope Trim
beneath Rim*
Tomb N1584
Tuff or siltstone
4.3 x 3 cm (1¾ x 1¼ in.)
6-621

All the burials from which these vessels
derive were large, corbel-vaulted tombs of
2d Dynasty date. The superstructures con-
sisted of rubble-filled, rectangular mastabas
with niches along at least three of their
mud-brick sides. The subterranean burial
apartments—which comprised a main, centrally positioned funerary chamber and two
or more subsidiary storage chambers—were
reached by a rock-cut stairway. Even in their
plundered state, it is clear that these tombs
were lavishly furnished. Stone vessels were
present in virtually all instances. Often of
exquisite workmanship and design, they
reflect both the wealth of the tomb owner
and the skill of the craftsmen responsible for
their execution. CK

BIBLIOGRAPHY 35A: George A. Reisner, *The Early
Dynastic Cemeteries of Naga ed-Dêr*, vol. 1, Univer-
sity of California Publications, Egyptian Archaeology 2
(Leipzig: J. C. Hinrichs, 1908), 112 (Type II), pl. 40b.
35B: Reisner, *Early Dynastic Cemeteries*, 43–44, 110,
pl. 41c; Barbara G. Aston, *Ancient Egyptian Stone
Vessels* (Heidelberg: Heidelberger Orientverlag, 1994),
120 (Type 75). 35C: Reisner, *Early Dynastic Cemeter-
ies*, 54–55, pls. 34a, 41c; Aston, *Ancient Egyptian
Stone Vessels*, 126 (Type 91). 35D: Reisner, *Early
Dynastic Cemeteries*, 43–44, 105, pl. 41c; Aston,
Ancient Egyptian Stone Vessels, 123 (Type 86). 35E:
Reisner, *Early Dynastic Cemeteries*, 49, 101, pl. 47b;
Aston, *Ancient Egyptian Stone Vessels*, 105 (Type 37).
35F: Reisner, *Early Dynastic Cemeteries*, 54, 101, pl.
51a; Aston, *Ancient Egyptian Stone Vessels*, 103
(Type 32). 35G: Reisner, *Early Dynastic Cemeteries*,
49–50, 105, pl. 46b; Aston, *Ancient Egyptian Stone
Vessels*, 122 (Type 82). 35H: Reisner, *Early Dynastic
Cemeteries*, 49–50, 105, pl. 46b; Aston, *Ancient
Egyptian Stone Vessels*, 100(?) (Type 25). 35I: Reis-
ner, *Early Dynastic Cemeteries*, 74–75, 105, pl. 72b;
Aston, *Ancient Egyptian Stone Vessels*, 123 (Type 84).
35J: Reisner, *Early Dynastic Cemeteries*, 49–50, 107,
pl. 47a; Aston, *Ancient Egyptian Stone Vessels*, 130
(Type 106). 35K: Reisner, *Early Dynastic Cemeteries*,
49, 101, pl. 46b; Aston, *Ancient Egyptian Stone
Vessels*, 113 (Type 52). 35L: Reisner, *Early Dynastic
Cemeteries*, 49–50, 101, pl. 46b; Aston, *Ancient
Egyptian Stone Vessels*, 109–10 (Type 46). 35M:
Reisner, *Early Dynastic Cemeteries*, 45, 109, pl. 48b;
Aston, *Ancient Egyptian Stone Vessels*, 112 (Type 51).
35N: Reisner, *Early Dynastic Cemeteries*, 53, 102,
pl. 41c.

NOTES
1. Four vertical stripes on the body correspond with
four grooves on the shoulder and mark the original
position of the bindings that secured the parts of the
vessel together.

36 Magic Set and Wand of Khufu

Giza, Menkaure valley temple
4th Dynasty, reign of Khufu
(c. 2551–2528 B.C.)
Limestone, basalt, quartz, flint
Cups: H: 3.5–4 cm (1⅜–1¼ in.)
Dummy vessels: H: 11 cm (4⅜ in.)
Wand: H: 17.5 cm (6⅞ in.)
Museum of Fine Arts, Boston,
11.767–72, 11.765

This magic set consists of four conical cups, one of quartz crystal and three of black basalt; two tall-necked "dummy" vessels (vessels not hollowed out), one of limestone and one of black basalt; and a flint wand inscribed for Khufu.[1] The wand may have been a particular keepsake because of its association with the great king. Similar wands were found within the Menkaure complex, one uninscribed, also from the valley temple, and a fragment of one inscribed for the "mother of the king, Khamerernebty."[2]

Such sets were used in the "opening of the mouth" funeral ceremony that was performed to reanimate the body of the deceased. These rituals could be conducted for sculptural and relief representations of the departed as well as the actual corpse, and so the sets are found in tombs, mortuary chapels, and temples.[3] This particular set was undoubtedly used on the statues in the Menkaure temple.

The group was found under the remains of a large oval copper tray, which George A. Reisner theorized had been used by plunderers to dump material. The vessels were discovered in the correct order known from intact groups, suggesting that they might have been held in place on a wooden tray, which subsequently decayed. PL

BIBLIOGRAPHY George A. Reisner, *Mycerinus: The Temples of the Third Pyramid at Giza* (Cambridge: Harvard University Press, 1931), 233–34, pls. 61f, 65b.

NOTES
1. Reisner, *Mycerinus*, 233–34, pls. 61f, 65b.
2. Ibid., 233.
3. Ann Macy Roth, "Model Equipment with a Peseshkef," in *Mummies and Magic: The Funerary Arts of Ancient Egypt*, exh. cat. ed. Sue D'Auria, Peter Lacovara, and Catharine Roehrig (Boston: MFA, 1988), 81.

37 Tablet with the Names of Oils

Giza, tomb G4733e
Old Kingdom (c. 2575–2134 B.C.)
Calcite
.8 x 19.5 x 9.2 cm (½ x 7¾ x 3⅝ in.)
Museum of Fine Arts, Boston, 31.976

This small rectangular tablet was made to hold a drop of each of the seven sacred oils used in the embalming process and to anoint the body during religious rites.[1] Oils also were important as foodstuffs and as offerings in temples. The modern equivalents of these substances are largely unknown, but most oils, particularly those imported from Libya or the Levant, were very costly.[2] Much like modern olive oil,[3] these oils were distinguished by their origin and by grade.

The seven oils named on the tablet are *seti-heb* oil, *heknu* oil, *sefeti* oil, *ni-chenem* oil, *tewat* oil, the best *ash* oil, and the best *tiehenu* oil. These oils could be represented in the tomb by these tablets, by lists of their names, depictions of jars, or actual containers placed in the burial chamber. PL

BIBLIOGRAPHY Nigel Strudwick, "Oil Tablet," in *Mummies and Magic: The Funerary Arts of Ancient Egypt*, exh. cat., ed. Sue D'Auria, Peter Lacovara, and Catharine Roehrig (Boston: MFA, 1988), 81–82.

NOTES
1. Strudwick, "Oil Tablet," 81–82.
2. William J. Darby, Paul Ghalioungui, and Louis Grivetti, *Food: The Gift of Osiris* (London and New York: Academic Press, 1977), 776–89.
3. Jacobus J. Janssen, *Commodity Prices from the Ramessid Period: An Economic Study of the Village of Necropolis Workmen in Thebes* (Leiden: E. J. Brill, 1975), 330–37.

38 Slab Stela of the Royal Acquaintance Nofer

Giza, tomb G1207
4th Dynasty, reign of Khufu
(c. 2551–2528 B.C.)
Limestone, pigment
38.1 x 50.8 x 8.3 cm (15 x 20 x 3¼ in.)
Phoebe A. Hearst Museum
of Anthropology, University
of California, Berkeley, 6-19801

A slab stela is a monolithic, self-contained funerary relief bearing a representation of the tomb owner seated at an offering table, a text identifying the owner, and an enumeration of offerings. A short-lived phenomenon, these stela were restricted to the reign of Khufu (whose fragmentary reliefs provide close parallels for the slab stela's low raised-relief style) and to the cemeteries surrounding his pyramid at Giza. They are relatively rare; just over three dozen are known (four are preserved in the Hearst Museum).[1] Although this stela has lost most of its original pigment, sufficient traces remain to reconstruct the basic color scheme: red for the dress, yellow for skin, blue-green and red for the offerings, and black for the hair and detailing.

The slab stela of Nofer was found in situ in her funerary chapel, a simple, multichambered, mud-brick structure erected against the east wall of her stone mastaba. Installed in a niche cut into the face of the mastaba, the stela constituted the connecting element between the tomb and the cult activities carried out in the chapel. The exceptional quality of the stela's execution indicates its importance in effecting Nofer's continued existence; it is almost certainly a product of the royal workshops. Its composition is clear and unambiguous: the offering table, with its contents enumerated above, assumes center position, flanked by the seated figure of Nofer and an extensive list of her garments (the "linen list"[2]). Four items that had been included in offering lists since before the inception of the Old Kingdom are, however, conspicuously absent: bread, beer, oxen, and fowl. It is clear that they should have been carved in the space below and to the right of the tall offering stand, which for some reason remained blank.

TRANSLATION OF INSCRIBED TEXT:
(1) The royal acquaintance Nofer (2) Cool water, purification (with) natron pellets, (3) purification (with) 1 incense pellet, cakes of green eye paint, (4) cakes of black eye paint, wine, (5) zizyphus fruit, one loaf of zizyphus-fruit bread, persea-fruit, (6) carob beans, and cakes of green sekhet (a ground fruit).

(Below offering stand)
1,000 alabaster vessels and 1,000 items of clothing. (At right: the linen list is divided into four horizontal sections, in descending order of fabric quality)
(1) 1,000 pieces of idemy linen[3] (the very finest quality) in each of the following widths: h-100(?)-, 9-, 8-, 7-, and 6-breadth.
(2) 1,000 pieces of (royal) linen[4] in each of the following widths: h-, 100-, 9-, 8-, 7-, 6-, 5-, 4-, and double-breadth.
(3) 1,000 pieces of fine linen[5] in each of the following widths: h-,100-, 9-, 8-, 7-, 6-, 5-, 4-, and double-breadth.
(4) 1,000 pieces of heavy linen in each of the following widths: 100-, 9-, 8-, 7-, 6-, 5-, 4-, double-, and single-breadth.

CK

BIBLIOGRAPHY Henry Frederick Lutz, *Egyptian Tomb Steles and Offering Stones of the Museum of Anthropology and Ethnology of the University of California*, University of California Publications, Egyptian Archaeology 4 (Leipzig: J. C. Hinrichs, 1927), 1, 15, pl. 2; George A. Reisner, *A History of the Giza Necropolis*, vol. 1 (Cambridge: Harvard University Press, 1942), 190, 395, pl. 18(b); Albert B. Elsasser and Vera-Mae Fredrickson, *Ancient Egypt*, exh. cat. (Berkeley: Robert H. Lowie Museum of Anthropology, University of California, 1966), 50–51; Henry G. Fischer, "Redundant Determinatives in the Old Kingdom," *MMA Journal* 8 (1973): 15–16, fig. 14; *Journey to the West: Death and the Afterlife in Ancient Egypt*, exh. cat. (Berkeley: Robert H. Lowie Museum of Anthropology, University of California, 1979), cover, 4; Donald B. Spanel, *Through Ancient Eyes: Egyptian Portraiture*, exh. cat. (Birmingham, Ala.: Birmingham Museum of Art, 1988), 48–49.

NOTES
1. For other slab stelae excavated at Giza, see Reisner, *Giza Necropolis*, vol. 1, pls. 17–20; and William S. Smith, "The Old Kingdom Linen List," *ZÄS* 71 (1935): 134–49.
2. On the Old Kingdom linen list, see Smith, "Linen List," 134–49; and Paule Posener-Krieger, *Les archives du temple funéraire de Néferirkarê-Kakäi (Les papyrus Abousir)*, vol. 2, Bibliothèque d'étude 65, no. 2 (Cairo: IFAO, 1976), 342.
3. For the reading *jdmj*, see Smith, "Linen List," 136ff; Alan H. Gardiner, "Two Hieroglyphic Signs and the Egyptian Words for 'Alabaster' and 'Linen,'" *BIFAO* 30 (1930): 175; and Elmar Edel, "Beitrage zum ägyptischen Lexikon VI," *ZÄS* 102 (1975): 24ff.
4. On the reading and meaning of *sesher* in the combination *sesher-nesut*, "royal linen" (*byssus*), see Gardiner, "Two Hieroglyphic Signs," 173–76.
5. For the reading and meaning of *shemayet-nofru*, see Edel, "Beitrage VI," 14; Gardiner, "Two Hieroglyphic Signs," 175; and Posener-Krieger, "Archives," 364.

39 Menkaure

Giza, Menkaure valley temple
4th Dynasty, reign of Menkaure
(c. 2490–2472 B.C.)
Calcite
28.5 x 16 cm (11¼ x 6½ in.)
Museum of Fine Arts, Boston, 09.203

George A. Reisner's excavations of the pyramid complex of Menkaure yielded a tremendous quantity of sculpture that had originally been erected in the associated mortuary and valley temples.[1] Unfortunately most of the statuary had been ritually buried or moved as the temple fell into disuse, so determining the original decorative program of the temples is difficult. In addition, there appear to have been some modifications in the design of the sculptures.

This portrait head of King Menkaure, discovered in his valley temple, belonged to one of four statues found flanking the entrance to the inner sanctum. The statues had all been broken apart, but it was possible to reassemble one example, now in the Egyptian Museum, Cairo.[2]

Although all similar in design, the sculptures vary in degree of completeness.[3] The most finished head has an elaborately pleated *nemes* headcloth;[4] the others are simpler. Like the series of triad sculptures depicting Menkaure with various deities,[5] they appear to have been intentionally left in varying stages of finish.

As with the colossal calcite statue of Menkaure in the Museum of Fine Arts, Boston (09.204),[6] the iconographic composition of the Boston head seems to have been deliberately altered, resulting in the rather odd proportions of the piece. Judging by the foreshortened profile of the head and the inset, recarved ears, the *nemes* headcloth was cut away. The rough, unfinished treatment of the hair, contrasted with the finished state of the rest of the piece, also suggests such a transformation. The revised hairstyle was probably intended to be a series of "corn rows," similar to those discovered recently on a statue of Neferefre at Abusir.[7]

The reason for these design changes is difficult to determine; it might, however, be mirrored in an architectural redesign seen in the pyramid temple of Menkaure.[8] Although Reisner suggested that the head might represent Menkaure's son and successor, Shepseskaf,[9] there is no evidence to support this, and the features of the king in this portrait are in keeping with other known likenesses of Menkaure. PL

BIBLIOGRAPHY George A. Reisner, *Mycerinus: The Temples of the Third Pyramid at Giza* (Cambridge: Harvard University Press, 1931), 112, pls. 52–53; William S. Smith, *Ancient Egypt as Represented in the Museum of Fine Arts, Boston*, 4th ed. (Boston: MFA, 1960), 46, 51, fig. 27; G. Godron, "Une tête de Mycerinus du Musée de Boston," *BIFAO* 62 (1964): 59–61.

NOTES
1. Reisner, *Mycerinus*, 108–24, pls. 7–8.
2. Ibid., pl. 48.
3. Ibid., 110–12.
4. Ibid., pl. 50.
5. E. L. B. Terrace, "A Fragmentary Triad of King Mycerinus," *BMFA* 59, no. 316 (1961): 40–49.
6. See Peter Lacovara and C. Nicholas Reeves, "The Mycerinus Colossus Reconsidered," *RdE* 38 (1987): 111–14.
7. Mohamed Saleh and Hourig Sourouzian, *Official Catalogue: The Egyptian Museum, Cairo* (Mainz: Philipp von Zabern, 1987), no. 38.
8. Ibid., 114.
9. Cf. William S. Smith, *A History of Egyptian Painting and Sculpture in the Old Kingdom* (London: Oxford University Press, 1946), 33–35.

40 Stone Vessels

Giza, Menkaure valley temple
1st to 4th Dynasty
(c. 2920–2465 B.C.)
Museum of Fine Arts, Boston

A *Plain Cylinder Jar*
Calcite
10.5 x 7.2 (diam) cm (4⅛ x 2⅞ in.)
11.548

B *Spheroidal Jar with Horizontal Handles*
Serpentine
6.8 x 19 (diam) cm (2⅞ x 7½ in.)
11.1148

C *Swelling-Shoulder Jar*
Calcite
15 x 12 (diam) cm (5⅞ x 4¾ in.)
11.409

D *Swelling-Shoulder Jar with Handles*
Porphyry
9.5 x 12.2 (diam) cm (3¾ x 4⅞ in.)
11.429

E *Conical Bowl*
Diorite
12.2 x 12.1 (diam) cm (4¾ x 4¾ in.)
11.1736

F *Vessel with External Rim*
Diorite
5.5 x 9.8 (diam) cm (2¼ x 3⅞ in.)
11.461·

G *Spouted Fancy-Shape Vase*
Calcite
12.5 x 6.1 (diam) cm (4¾ x 2⅜ in.)
11.454

H *Flat-Bottomed Dish*
Calcite
6 x 16 (diam) cm (2⅜ x 6¼ in.)
11.1157

In addition to sculpture, George A. Reisner discovered a large cache of stone vessels at the valley temple of Menkaure, some deposited in the temple's storerooms. While many vessels had been smashed and broken when they were placed in the magazines, it was possible to reconstruct more than five hundred individual examples.

The vessels were made from a variety of hard and soft stones and included a number of unfinished specimens.[1] Although Reisner assumed that the majority dated to the reign of Menkaure (2490–2472 B.C.), many are of types that belong to the Early Dynastic Period and not the Old Kingdom.[2] In addition, of the few inscribed vessels, none mentions Menkaure, although two mention the 2d Dynasty ruler Hetepsekhemwy (one of these over an erased inscription of Raneb), and two have the name of Sneferu.[3] Predynastic examples include two trumpet-footed vases of the Naqada I period (MFA 11.1191, 11.1163). It would appear that many of the vessels, like those from the step pyramid complex, were taken from earlier tombs and temples and redeposited in the Menkaure temple.[4]

This selection of vessels includes the more common Early Dynastic Period types such as the swelling-shoulder jar (cat. no. 40C), the serpentine spheroidal jar (cat. no. 40B), and the porphyry jar (cat. no. 40D). Lesser-known Old Kingdom examples include the calcite cylinder jar with splay foot (cat. no. 40A), the fancy-form bowl (cat. no. 40H), and the spouted hourglass-form vase (cat. no. 40G). The diorite bowl (cat. no. 40F) copies the shape of the carinated pottery bowls of the 4th Dynasty. PL

BIBLIOGRAPHY George A. Reisner, *Mycerinus: The Temples of the Third Pyramid at Giza* (Cambridge: Harvard University Press, 1931), 178–99; Barbara A. Green, "Ancient Egyptian Stone Vessels: Materials and Forms" (Ph.D. diss., University of California, Berkeley, 1989).

NOTES
1. Reisner, *Mycerinus*, 178–99. I would like to thank Richard Newman of the Department of Object Conservation and Scientific Research, MFA, Boston, for analysis of the stone types represented in these vessels.
2. Cf. Ali el-Khouli, *Egyptian Stone Vessels: Predynastic Period to Dynasty III* (Mainz: Philipp von Zabern, 1978).
3. Reisner, *Mycerinus*, 178–99.
4. Mohamed Saleh and Hourig Sourouzian, *Official Catalogue: The Egyptian Museum, Cairo* (Mainz: Philipp von Zabern, 1987), no. 20.

This marvelous rendering of a naked boy is one of the finest private sculptures Reisner discovered at Giza. The youth is depicted in the manner traditional for young boys: naked, with the tip of his right index finger (now restored) poised between his lips. The customary youthful sidelock worn by prepubescent children is, however, not present. Although sometimes cited as one of the earliest and best depictions of a young boy,[1] this statue, like all the finest examples of ancient Egyptian art, creates a tension between naturalism and stylization. The overlarge head, projecting ears, slightly stooped posture, and rounded abdomen acutely reproduce the physical characteristics of youth, but the painstakingly executed facial features are identical to those found on sculptures of adults. The boy is shown uncircumcised, for this rite was not performed until puberty.[2] (At the same time his sidelock would be removed, and his hair would be allowed to grow naturally.)

The rarity of this depiction's quality is matched by that of its survival.[3] Although numerous wooden statues of Old Kingdom date have survived from Saqqara, few have been found, even partially intact, at Giza due to the site's infestation since ancient times with termites. To these intruders can be attributed the loss of the boy's lower limbs.

Unlike most 5th Dynasty tomb statuary excavated by Reisner at Giza, this piece was discovered not in the *serdab* (a sealed statue chamber located in the mastaba superstructure) but in the main subterranean burial chamber of tomb G1152, leaning against the south end of the rock-cut sarcophagus. No inscription has survived from the tomb; therefore, the identity of the boy—and his relationship to the original tomb owner— remains unknown. CK

41 Statue of a Boy
Giza, tomb G1152
5th Dynasty (c. 2465–2323 B.C.)
Acacia wood
H: 45.7 cm (18 in.)
Phoebe A. Hearst Museum
of Anthropology, University
of California, Berkeley, 6-19768

Statue leaning against rock-cut sarcophagus in burial chamber of tomb G1152.

BIBLIOGRAPHY Henry Frederick Lutz, *Egyptian Statues and Statuettes in the Museum of Anthropology of the University of California,* University of California Publications, Egyptian Archaeology 5 (Leipzig: J. C. Hinrichs, 1930), 27, pls. 39–40; William S. Smith, *A History of Egyptian Painting and Sculpture in the Old Kingdom* (London: Oxford University Press, 1946), 59, pl. 23c–d; Albert B. Elsasser and Vera-Mae Fredrickson, *Ancient Egypt,* exh. cat. (Berkeley and Los Angeles: University of California Press, 1966), 36; Albert B. Elsasser, *Treasures of the Lowie Museum,* exh. cat. (Berkeley: Robert H. Lowie Museum of Anthropology, University of California, 1968), 83 (detail); William S. Smith, *The Art and Architecture of Ancient Egypt,* 2d ed., rev. by William K. Simpson (Baltimore and Harmondsworth: Penguin Books, 1981), 139, fig. 134.

NOTES
1. Smith, *Art and Architecture,* p. 139.
2. On the rite of circumcision, see, most recently, Ann Macy Roth, *Egyptian Phylaes in the Old Kingdom: The Evolution of a System of Social Organization,* Studies in Ancient Oriental Civilization 48 (Chicago: University of Chicago Press, 1991), 62ff.
3. Depictions of naked boys, whether alone or as part of a family group, are not rare in the Old Kingdom. For a statuette of a boy from G2009, now in Boston, see Smith, *History of Painting and Sculpture,* pl. 24d, and Edward Brovarski, in *Mummies and Magic: The Funerary Arts of Ancient Egypt,* exh. cat., ed. Sue D'Auria, Peter Lacovara, and Catharine Roehrig (Boston: MFA, 1988), 89. See also the example from the Egyptian Museum, Cairo (CG 126), in Ludwig Borchardt, *Statuen und Statuetten von Königen und Privatleuten in Museum von Kairo, Nr. 1–1294,* vol. 1, CG 53 (Berlin: Reichsdruckerei, 1911), 96–97, pl. 29 (5th Dynasty).

the image of a dark-haired, light amber-skinned lady decked out for eternity in a white sheath banded with red and green and adorned with a similarly hued broad collar, bracelets, and anklets.

George A. Reisner discovered the statue of Isran in a pit of Giza tomb G1402 along with a larger-scale representation of the overseer of craftsmen Sabu and his son Ptahirek (PAHMA 6-19803).[2] It is possible, though not at all certain (in the absence of corroborating inscriptions), that the three might have constituted a family group. CK

BIBLIOGRAPHY Henry Frederick Lutz, *Egyptian Statues and Statuettes in the Museum of Anthropology of the University of California*, University of California Publications, Egyptian Archaeology 5 (Leipzig: J. C. Hinrichs, 1930), 18, pls. 27b, 28a.

NOTES
1. On the title *mjtr.t*, which indicates a lower-echelon employee attached to the palace (such as a weaver), see William A. Ward, *Index of Egyptian Administrative and Religious Titles of the Middle Kingdom* (Beirut: American University of Beirut, 1982), 94.
2. For the statue of Sabu and Ptahirek, see William S. Smith, *A History of Egyptian Painting and Sculpture in the Old Kingdom* (London: Oxford University Press, 1946), pl. 22a; Lutz, *Egyptian Statues and Statuettes*, 19–20, pl. 30b.

42 Statue of the Lady Isran

Giza, tomb G1402
5th to early 6th Dynasty,
c. 2465–2255 B.C.
Limestone, pigment
39.4 x 15.4 x 24.6 cm
(15½ x 6⅛ x 9¾ in.)
Phoebe A. Hearst Museum
of Anthropology, University
of California, Berkeley, 6-19802

The short column of text running down the proper right side of the blocklike seat identifies this seated woman as "the *mjtr.t*[1] Isran." The simple, heavy wig; broad facial planes; lack of modeling; heavy ankles; and spatulate feet are all indications of the artist's competence, if not inspiration. Yet Isran's impassive countenance and serene pose convey a simple charm, which would be even more compelling had the original colors survived. Even in its present state, however, one can discern

43 Pair Statue of Khakare and Ankhremenes

Giza, tomb G1314
5th to early 6th Dynasty,
c. 2465–2255 B.C.
Limestone, pigment
39.5 x 10 x 17.5 cm (15⅛ x 4 x 6⅞ in.)
Phoebe A. Hearst Museum
of Anthropology, University
of California, Berkeley, 6-19780

To best view this statue of the "palace hairdresser" (or wigmaker) Khakare and his son Ankhremenes, one must stand in a strictly frontal position, echoing the precise stance of the figures. If one stands too far to either side, essential elements of the composition are lost. When seen from the proper right side, the diminutive figure of Ankhremenes is obscured by his father's out-thrust leg; when one stands at the statue's left, Khakare's entire right side vanishes. Even small-scale Egyptian statuary has the power to compel the viewer to adopt its orientation.

Khakare's statue is an unusual juxtaposition of inexact proportioning and carefully executed details, such as the painstakingly delineated wig, eyes, kilt, and legs. Particularly interesting is a rare depiction of the ends of the kerchief, whose center Khakare grasps in his right fist, carved in relief against the back slab. The statue was discovered by George A. Reisner in the *serdab* of a Giza mastaba that also contained a stone architrave inscribed simply with Khakare's name, repeated nine times.[1]

Specialists concerned with the toilette of the elite were in a position of some influence because of their immediate physical proximity to these individuals. Khakare was not an "inspector" (supervisor) of other cosmeticians or hairstylists, so we can assume that he did not actually attend the person of the king, whose body, being divine, was potentially dangerous to those who had close contact with him. It is more likely that Khakare was in the service of mid- to low-ranking courtiers; it is tempting to suggest that the care with which his wig is depicted in this statue was prompted by his occupational interests.

TRANSLATION OF INSCRIBED TEXT:
(1) The hairdresser (or wigmaker) of the great house, Khakare (2) His eldest son, Ankhremenes

CK

BIBLIOGRAPHY Henry Frederick Lutz, *Egyptian Statues and Statuettes in the Museum of Anthropology of the University of California,* University of California Publications, Egyptian Archaeology 5 (Leipzig: J. C. Hinrichs, 1930), 13–14, pl. 22; William S. Smith, *A History of Egyptian Painting and Sculpture in the Old Kingdom* (London: Oxford University Press, 1946), 65–66; Albert B. Elsasser and Vera-Mae Fredrickson, *Ancient Egypt,* exh. cat. (Berkeley: Robert H. Lowie Museum of Anthropology, University of California, 1966), 46.

NOTES
1. Henry G. Fischer, "The 'Inspector of Youths' Nfr-n-Hwfw," *Oudheidkundige Mededeelingen uit het Rijksmuseum van Oudheden te Leiden* 41 (1960): 8, cf. fig. 3.

44 Statue of Itjetka

Giza, tomb G1214
Late 5th to mid 6th Dynasty,
c. 2426–2246 B.C.
Limestone, pigment
41 x 10.2 x 17 cm (16⅛ x 4 x 6¾ in.)
Phoebe A. Hearst Museum
of Anthropology, University
of California, 6-19772

This standing depiction of Itjetka was discovered in situ in the *serdab* of tomb G1214 together with a seated representation of a man named Katjesu (PAHMA 6-19770).[1] The two images were clearly executed by the same artist and probably represent a double commission; they might depict members of the same family. As neither Itjetka's nor Katjesu's name is accompanied by a title, they are likely to have been fairly low-ranking members of Old Kingdom "society"—a position consistent with the workmanlike quality of their statues.

Although a significant amount of pigment remains on Itjetka's statue, it was even more vividly colored when first discovered by George A. Reisner. In addition to the standard applications of black (wig, brows, eye details, negative space, and top of the base), red (dress, jewelry details, and inscription), yellow (skin, base rims, and rear of the back slab), and white (dress and, possibly, jewelry), her toenails are tinted a saucy pink. CK

BIBLIOGRAPHY Henry Frederick Lutz, *Egyptian Statues and Statuettes in the Museum of Anthropology of the University of California*, University of California Publications, Egyptian Archaeology 5 (Leipzig: J. C. Hinrichs, 1930), 18–19, pls. 28b, 29a; William S. Smith, *A History of Egyptian Painting and Sculpture in the Old Kingdom* (London: Oxford University Press, 1946), 65 (1214,2); Albert B. Elsasser and Vera-Mae Fredrickson, *Ancient Egypt*, exh. cat. (Berkeley: Robert H. Lowie Museum of Anthropology, University of California, 1966), 34–35; Richard Fazzini, *Images for Eternity: Egyptian Art from Berkeley and Brooklyn*, exh. cat. (San Francisco: Fine Arts Museums of San Francisco; Brooklyn: Brooklyn Museum, 1975), 133, no. 22.

NOTES
1. For the accompanying statue of Katjesu, see Lutz, *Egyptian Statues and Statuettes*, 12, pl. 18; Smith, *A History of Egyptian Painting and Sculpture*, 65 (G1214 [1]); and Elsasser and Fredrickson, *Ancient Egypt*, 53.

45 Pair Statue from the
Tomb of Ikhetneb

Giza, tomb G 1206
Mid to late 5th Dynasty,
c. 2426–2323 B.C.
Limestone, pigment
74 x 35 x 26.5 cm
(29⅛ x 13¾ x 10⅜ in.)
Phoebe A. Hearst Museum
of Anthropology, University
of California, Berkeley, 6-19775

The lintel over the chapel door of the tomb in which this uninscribed pair statue of a man and his wife was discovered in Giza mastaba G1206 bore the name of the "royal acquaintance" and "inspector of *wa'b*-priests" Ikhetneb. Because the chapel had been walled up to serve as a *serdab* containing this limestone statue, together with five wooden statues, however, the statue deposit may represent a later use of the tomb. One of two offering basins (cat. no. 46) that were discovered in situ, sunk into the ground immediately in front of the walled-up chapel, was inscribed for the "prophet of Khufu," "royal acquaintance," and "inspector of *wa'b*-priests" Senenu. Because the walling-up of the chapel has been thought to be contemporary with the placement of the offering basins, this pair statue has occasionally been referred to as Senenu and his wife.

The two figures, rendered in gender-specific poses, stand close together, the placement of the male on the viewer's right accommodates the different poses of the woman (standing) and the man (striding). The male figure slightly overlaps his consort in order to facilitate her embrace; her left arm encircles his back, with the hand coming to rest on his left shoulder. According to photographs made at the time of the statue's discovery, its color was almost perfectly preserved. Today almost all that remains is a portion of the man's broad collar on his proper right shoulder. The statue is the work of a competent, though not exceptionally talented artist. The facial features are well formed and set in broad, round faces. More attention has been paid to the fairly well modeled torsos and arms than to the legs and feet, which are over-large and somewhat crude. The back slab rises nearly to the top of the heads but has been cut back behind the exterior shoulders. CK

BIBLIOGRAPHY Henry Frederick Lutz, *Egyptian Statues and Statuettes in the Museum of Anthropology of the University of California*, University of California Publications, Egyptian Archaeology 5 (Leipzig: J. C. Hinrichs, 1930), 22–24, pls. 35, 35[a]; Albert B. Elsasser and Vera-Mae Fredrickson, *Ancient Egypt*, exh. cat. (Berkeley: Robert H. Lowie Museum of Anthropology, University of California, 1966), 41; *Journey to the West: Death and the Afterlife in Ancient Egypt*, exh. cat. (Berkeley: Robert H. Lowie Museum of Anthropology, University of California, 1979), 21.

46 Offering Basin of Senenu

Giza, tomb G1206
Mid to late 5th Dynasty,
c. 2426–2323 B.C.
Limestone, pigment
20 x 57.5 x 36.2 cm
(7⅞ x 22⅝ x 14¼ in.)
Phoebe A. Hearst Museum
of Anthropology, University
of California, Berkeley, 6-19752

This impressive offering basin is inscribed for the "inspector of *wa'b*-priests" and "prophet of Khufu" Senenu. It was dedicated by his son, a certain Akhethetep, who, to judge from the inscription, inherited some of his father's titles. The text encircling the rim begins in the upper right corner and ends at the lower left, with the large, seated figure holding a baton of office.[1] The main wish expressed is for Senenu to receive burial in the necropolis. The hieroglyphic signs are for the most part well spaced, finely proportioned, and well carved; they were originally enhanced by black pigment.

George A. Reisner discovered the basin sunk into the ground immediately before the walled-up chapel of Giza mastaba G1206, over whose door a drum lintel bore the name of Ikhetneb. It is reasonable to assume that Ikhetneb was the original owner of the tomb and that the walling-up of the chapel to serve as a *serdab* for five wooden and one stone statue (cat. no. 45) represents a reuse of the tomb by Akhethotep on behalf of his father, Senenu. A second, uninscribed offering stone holding seven separate basins was found, also sunk into the floor, beside the first. The open area in front of the chapel thus was converted into an exterior chapel for the perpetuation of his cult.

TRANSLATION OF INSCRIBED TEXT:
(1) An offering that the King (and) Anubis, who is before the divine booth, gives: burial in the western cemetery, (after) a very fine old age, with the great god [for] the royal acquaintance and inspector of wa'b-*priests, Senenu; (2) the controller of phylae-members, district administrator and prophet of (Khufu), Senenu. (3) It was his eldest son, the inspector of ships, controller of young work-gang recruits, inspector of* wa'b-*priests, controller of phylae-members, and district administrator, Akhethotep, who made this for him.*

CK

BIBLIOGRAPHY Henry Frederick Lutz, *Egyptian Tomb Steles and Offering Stones of the Museum of Anthropology and Ethnology of the University of California,* University of California Publications, Egyptian Archaeology 4 (Leipzig: J. C. Hinrichs, 1927), 1, 12, 15, no. 4, pl. 3; Albert B. Elsasser and Vera-Mae Fredrickson, *Ancient Egypt,* exh. cat. (Berkeley: Robert H. Lowie Museum of Anthropology, University of California, 1966), 52.

NOTES
1. Two examples in the Egyptian Museum, Cairo (CG 1323, CG 1353), have the inscription arranged in a similar manner, running around the rim; CG 1353 also has a text terminating in a large, seated male determinative. See Ludwig Borchardt, *Denkmäler des Alten Reiches (ausser den Statuen) in Museum von Kairo, Nr. 1295–1808,* vol. 1, CG 97 (Berlin: Reichsdruckerei, 1937), 10, pl. 4, and 24–25, pl. 6.

47 Funerary Furniture of Impy

Giza, tomb of Impy, G2383
6th Dynasty (c. 2323–2150 B.C.)
Copper
Museum of Fine Arts, Boston

Unplundered tomb of Impy with sarcophagus and copper funerary furniture.

A *Beaker with Flaring Rim*
13 x 9.8 (diam) cm (5¼ x 3⅞ in.)
13.2942

B *Model Spouted Bowl and Stand*
6 x 12 cm (2⅜ x 4¼ in.)
13.2944

C *Censer*
9 x 6.4 (diam) cm (3½ x 2½ in.)
13.2930

D *Inscribed Basin*
14 x 25 (diam) cm (5¼ x 9⅞ in.)
13.2940

E *Ewer*
17 x 12 (diam) cm (10⅛ x 4¼ in.)
13.2941

F *Model Jar*
5 x 4.2 (diam) cm (2 x 1¼ in.)
13.2957

G *Model* Hes *Vase*
9 x 2.2 (diam) cm (3½ x ⅞ in.)
13.2938e

H *Model Table*
12 x 18.5 cm (4¾ x 7¼ in.)
13.2938a

I *Model Dish*
1.5 x 6.2 (diam) cm (1/2 x 2½ in.)
13.3237

J *Model Basin*
2.8 x 6.4 (diam) cm (3¼ x 2½ in.)
13.2954

At the end of 1912 George A. Reisner began clearing the great mastaba complex of the Senedjemib family, near the northeastern corner of the pyramid of Khufu. The associated tomb shafts had all been badly plundered, save one that had been blocked with twenty-five feet of precisely fitted stone blocks. After carefully removing these, the expedition came upon the unplundered tomb of Impy, son of the royal architect Nekhebu.

The tomb contained a beautifully inscribed cedar coffin housing the badly deteriorated mummy of Impy wearing an elaborate gold and faience broad collar, necklaces, and a gilded copper bracelet and belt. Even more remarkable was the profusion of copper vessels and model vessels found in the tomb. These included pitchers and basins, cups, bowls, dishes, jars, censers, and model offering tables and stands.[1]

These objects were made of almost pure copper, and most had been cold-hammered into shape.[2] The technique of manufacture is reflected in the simple, angular forms of the pieces, a style copied in stone and pottery vessels. A craftsman cut, cold-hammered, and annealed the table into shape from a single sheet of copper. To make the jars and beakers, sheets of copper were bent to form cylinders; separate bases were cut from copper sheets and hammer-welded to the bottoms of the cylinders. The little dishes were hammered into a mold to give them a uniform shape. The ewer has a spout formed from a piece of folded copper, with another copper sheet for the top. The spout and top were then riveted to the shoulder of the ewer, over a hole punched into its side.[3]

The great quantity of copper vessels in Impy's tomb contrasts sharply with the tomb of Queen Hetepheres of the 4th Dynasty, which contained only pottery vessels of similar form.[4] Other finds of valuable metal vessels from the 6th Dynasty point to the wider distribution of wealth at this period.[5] PL

BIBLIOGRAPHY William S. Smith, *Ancient Egypt as Represented in the Museum of Fine Arts, Boston*, 4th ed. (Boston: MFA, 1960), 64–67, fig. 38.

NOTES
1. George A. Reisner, "New Acquisitions of the Egyptian Department: A Family of Builders of the Sixth Dynasty," *Museum of Fine Arts Bulletin* 11 (November 1913): 53–66.
2. Analysis conducted by James Muhly in 1979, archives of the Research Laboratory of the Museum of Fine Arts, Boston, through the courtesy of Arthur Beale.
3. Deborah Schorsch, "Copper Ewers of Early Dynastic and Old Kingdom Egypt—an Investigation of the Art of Smithing in Antiquity," *MDAIK* 48 (1992): 145–59.
4. George A. Reisner and William S. Smith, *A History of the Giza Necropolis*, vol. 2, *The Tomb of Hetepheres, the Mother of Cheops* (Cambridge: Harvard University Press, 1955), 60–89.
5. Ali Radwan, *Die Kupfer- und Bronzegefasse Ägyptens* (Munich: C. H. Beck, 1983), 58–80.

48 Female Statuettes

Naga el-Deir, cemetery 100,
tomb N43/202
Late Old Kingdom to early
First Intermediate Period,
c. 2246–2120 B.C.
Wood, gesso, paint
Phoebe A. Hearst Museum
of Anthropology, University
of California, Berkeley

A *Tall Nude Female Figure with
Carved Wig*
40.5 x 7.5 cm (16 x 3 in.)
6-15215

B *Nude Female Figure*
26.5 x 6.5 cm (10⅜ x 2½ in.)
6-15218

These two statuettes are typical of many produced during the late Old Kingdom and into
the First Intermediate Period, particularly
in provincial areas.[1] Because the women are
depicted naked, with their pubic hair carefully indicated, and because such statuettes
are rarely inscribed, these examples have
been thought to represent female servants,
concubines, or other women of relatively low
status. This hypothesis is probably correct
in most cases; a similar nude female statuette
from Naga el-Deir, also in the Hearst
Museum (6-12120+16133), is, however,
identified as a "sole royal ornament."[2]
Clearly this genre could be adapted to serve
more than one purpose.

The larger and finer of the two—whose
distinguishing features are a carved wig,
strong facial lines, and a long, graceful
body—was made from two pieces of wood
(only the proper right arm is separate) and
tenoned onto the wooden base. The smaller
statuette was carved from a single piece of
wood and similarly secured to its base. Both
statuettes received a thin coat of gesso before
being painted in black, red-brown, and
white. The women sport extremely short
hairstyles and have exaggeratedly long limbs.
Other female statuettes from this assemblage
were painted yellow, the more usual skin
color for women, and exhibited more compact proportions.

The two images were among nineteen
wooden statues and statue groups discovered
by George A. Reisner in 1902–3, wedged
tightly around a simple, uninscribed wooden
coffin in the burial niche at the bottom of
Naga el-Deir shaft tomb N43.[3] Probably also
associated with this assemblage is a niche
containing two model funerary boats, three
model groups,[4] and one standing male figure,
designated by Reisner as tomb N202; hence
the dual designation of this tomb complex as
N43/202. CK

Statuettes positioned around coffin in tomb N43/202
as found in 1902.

BIBLIOGRAPHY 48A: Albert B. Elsasser and Vera-
Mae Fredrickson, *Ancient Egypt*, exh. cat. (Berkeley:
Robert H. Lowie Museum of Anthropology, University of California, 1966), 60; Richard Fazzini, *Images
for Eternity: Egyptian Art from Berkeley and Brooklyn*, exh. cat. (San Francisco: Fine Arts Museums of
San Francisco; Brooklyn: Brooklyn Museum, 1975),
37, no. 28.

NOTES
1. For a parallel, see MMA 58.125.3, in *Metropolitan
Museum Guide* (New York: MMA, 1993), 94, no. 16.
An example of lesser quality is in the collection of
University College, London (UC 16658); see Anthea
Page, *Egyptian Sculpture: Archaic to Saite from the
Petrie Collection* (London: University College, 1976),
17, no. 19.
2. The base of this statuette, which is smaller than either
of the examples illustrated here, is inscribed "One
honored before the great god, the sole royal ornament
Shepset."
3. George A. Reisner, "The Work of the Expedition of
the University of California at Naga-ed-Der," *ASAE* 5
(1904): 108, pl. VI.1 (the photograph is reversed). For
the food preparers model from N43 (PAHMA 6-17161),
see Elsasser and Fredrickson, *Ancient Egypt*, 56–57.
4. Reisner, "Naga-ed-Der," 108, pl. IV.1. For one of
the boats from N202 (PAHMA 6-17156), see Elsasser
and Fredrickson, *Ancient Egypt*, 35.

49 Stela of Satnetinheret

Naga el-Deir
9th to early 11th Dynasties,
c. 2134–2060 B.C.
Limestone, pigment
66 x 40 x 11.5 cm (26 x 15¾ x 4½ in.)
Phoebe A. Hearst Museum
of Anthropology, University
of California, Berkeley, 6-19881

This simple, rectangular funerary stela depicting the "sole royal ornament" and "priestess of Hathor" Satnetinheret was dedicated by her husband, a provincial official named Heny. The form of her name, "Lady of Onuris," honors the ancient hunter and warrior god of the 8th Upper Egyptian (Thinite) nome (province),[1] whom Greek mythology identified with the giant Antaeus. Satnetinheret stands before an assortment of offerings, holding a mirror up to her face, a gesture that, because of the mirror's reflective properties (one of its ancient Egyptian designations is "face see-er"), is probably connected with the process of rebirth.[2] Four lines of hieroglyphic text above her head contain a standard offering formula and give special prominence to the lady's titles and honorific epithets[3]—to such a degree that two additional columns of text, providing more detail about her food offerings, had to be squeezed into the lower right portion of the stela.

The decorative style of this stela—with its irregularly carved and spaced hieroglyphic signs, rather finicky decorative details, and gravity-defying offering pile—connect it with a group of similar works from Naga el-Deir and the Girga district,[4] which, in turn, have close stylistic affinities with monuments created at centers farther south, at Dendera[5] and Thebes.[6] It was at Thebes that the new 11th Dynasty was emerging under Nebhepetre Mentuhotep, who would reunite Egypt around 2040 B.C. and bring to an end the social and artistic decentralization of the First Intermediate Period.

TRANSLATION OF INSCRIBED TEXT:
(1) An offering that the King (and) Anubis, who is upon his mountain and in the place of embalming, the lord of the sacred land give: (2) Invocation-offerings for the sole royal ornament and priestess of Hathor, one honored (3) and beloved of Hathor, one (most?) beautiful of (female) ornaments in the expressed opinion of the pillars (of the community), the jmy-t-wr.t *priestess (4) among the noblewomen,[7] Satnetinheret. (5) Dedicated (literally "made") by the mayor, sole companion, and lector-priest Heny: 1,000 of bread and beer, 1,000 oxen, (6) 1,000 fowl, 1,000 of everything for the sole [royal ornament] and priestess of Hathor, his beloved wife, Satnetinheret.*

CK

BIBLIOGRAPHY Henry Frederick Lutz, *Egyptian Tomb Steles and Offering Stones of the Museum of Anthropology and Ethnology of the University of California*, University of California Publications, Egyptian Archaeology 4 (Leipzig: J. C. Hinrichs, 1927), 16, no. 28, pl. 15; Dows Dunham, *Naga ed-Dêr Stelae of the First Intermediate Period* (Oxford: Oxford University Press, 1937), 44–45, no. 31; Richard Fazzini, *Images for Eternity: Egyptian Art from Berkeley and Brooklyn*, exh. cat. (San Francisco: Fine Arts Museums of San Francisco; Brooklyn: Brooklyn Museum, 1975), 30–31, no. 31.

NOTES
1. W[olfgang] S[chenkel], "Onuris," *LÄ*, vol. 4, cols. 573–74.
2. For the use and symbolism of mirrors, see Christine Lilyquist, *Ancient Egyptian Mirrors: From the Earliest Times through the Middle Kingdom*, Münchner ägyptologische Seminar 27 (Berlin: Deutscher Kunstverlag, 1979). The ancient Egyptian terms for mirrors are discussed on 65–71; the association of mirrors with "sole royal ornaments," on 98; and the mirror as a symbol of rebirth, on 98–99.
3. Female figures possessing their own stelae during this period are well attested from provincial sites in Upper Egypt; see several examples in the Museum of Fine Arts, Boston: R. Lephrohon, *Stelae I* (Mainz: Philipp von Zabern, 1985), 2, 72–4 (MFA 12.1478); 2, 103–5 (MFA 25.627); 2, 122–4 (MFA 25.673); 2, 134–36 (MFA 25.677).
4. Stylistically the depiction of Satnetinheret is virtually identical to that on two other stelae in the Hearst Museum (6-2042, 6-1576), also from Naga el-Deir (Lutz, *Egyptian Tomb Steles*, 18, nos. 34, 38, pls. 18, 20), as well as to stela 16956 in the Oriental Institute, Chicago (Dunham, *Stelae*, 102–4, no. 84, pl. XXXII), possibly from Ginga. Satnetinheret's stela can be associated with Jürgen Settgast's "polychrome group" of Naga el-Deir stelae ("Materialien zur Ersten Zwischenzeit I," *MDAIK* 19 [1963], 14–15), which can be dated around the time of Theban incursions into the Abydos area in the early 11th Dynasty (Edward Brovarski, "Naga [Nag']-ed-Dêr," *LÄ*, vol. 4, cols. 308–9).
5. For stylistically related stelae from Dendera, see examples in Lephrohon, *Stelae I*.
6. Some of the preunification monuments of the Theban 11th Dynasty with the closest connections with the Naga el-Deir stelae are those of Wahankh Intef II and Megegi and Queen Nefru. For the former (MMA 13.182.3, 14.2.7), see William C. Hayes, *The Scepter of Egypt*, vol. 1, *From the Earliest Times to the End of the Middle Kingdom* (New York: MMA, 1953), 151–53, figs. 90–91; for the latter, see Fazzini, *Images for Eternity*, 48, no. 32-2.
7. Henry G. Fischer, "A Daughter of the Overlords of Upper Egypt in the First Intermediate Period," *Journal of the American Oriental Society* 76 (1956): 106–7.

50 Reef Knot Bracelet

Sheikh el-Farag, tomb 5045
First Intermediate Period, c. 2100 B.C.
Gold wire
4 x 5 cm (1 ⅝ x 2 in.)
Diam of wire: .4 cm (¼ in.)
Museum of Fine Arts, Boston,
24.1807

This gold wire bracelet from Sheikh el-Farag was found in situ on the left wrist of an adult buried in a rectangular rock-cut grave. Situated on the east bank of the Nile in Upper Egypt, Sheikh el-Farag was one of a series of cemeteries excavated by George A. Reisner in 1923–24. The First Intermediate Period tombs in cemetery 5000 were largely destroyed, and this wrist ornament, from tomb 5045, was the only item retrieved from the burial. A comparable bracelet from Mostagedda was found on the wrist of a woman.[1] Both are made from two thin strips of sheet metal, which were twisted and rolled into one-millimeter wires. The knots were sealed with solder, and the ends of the wires curved and soldered so that the open bangles appear to made from a single piece of metal.

The reef knot has a basic psychological appeal in that it integrates opposites into a satisfying whole. This role of the knot in ancient Egypt was noted by Gertie Englund, who observed its centrality and unifying function on the side panels of Old Kingdom thrones.[2] Here the knot binds the antithetically placed and ideologically opposite figures of Horus and Seth as they tug on cords formed from the two plants symbolic of Upper and Lower Egypt. The tendency of the "two lands" to split into separate entities was a legitimate source of anxiety, and it was only under the exercise of strong, central kingship that the land along the Nile maintained its integrity. In this respect the enthroned king is the mighty, magical force that binds north to south, and the knot, a tangible expression of that cohesion.

Representations of the reef knot as a separate amuletic element are first found in burials of the First Intermediate Period. At that time many images associated with kingship were adopted by private individuals as part of a general trend toward democratization of the afterlife. Depictions of the knot typically take the form of a central motif on wire bracelets, although the knot is occasionally represented in three-dimensional form on the dorsa of design amulets.[3]

Reef knot bracelets of precious metal continued to be made during the Middle Kingdom.[4] Added to the knot repertoire were clasps of sheet gold, some ingenious in design. Many fine examples of this adaptation were found among the jewels belonging to princesses buried at Dashur and Lahun.[5] More common were two-dimensional knots featured as part of the base design of scarabs.[6]

Scarabs with knot motifs persisted in popularity throughout the Second Intermediate Period, although representations are often schematic and debased.[7] There are sporadic examples of knot beads and cowroids with bases inscribed with knots terminating in four uraei during the early 18th Dynasty.[8] This knot with snakes was later adopted and popularized by the Greeks in the fourth century B.C. YM

NOTES

1. Carol Andrews, *Catalogue of Egyptian Antiquities in the British Museum*, vol. 6, *Jewellery I: From the Earliest Times to the Seventeenth Century* (London: British Museum, 1981), no. 276, pl. 24.
2. Gertie Englund, "The Treatment of Opposites in Temple Thinking and Wisdom Literature," in *The Religion of the Ancient Egyptians: Cognitive Structures and Popular Expressions* (Uppsala: Acadamiae Ubsaliensis, 1989), 78.
3. W. M. Flinders Petrie, *Buttons and Design Amulets* (London: British School of Archaeology in Egypt, 1925), no. 322.
4. Cyril Aldred, *Jewels of the Pharaohs* (London: Thames and Hudson, 1971), 190–92, 195, pls. 34, 36, 44.
5. A matched pair were discovered on the forearms of the deceased in a 12th Dynasty tomb (κ8) at Buhen; see David Randall-MacIver and Charles Leonard Wooley, *Buhen* (Philadelphia: University Museum, University of Pennsylvania, 1911), 201.
6. W. M. Flinders Petrie, Guy Brunton, and M. A. Murray, *Lahun*, vol. 2 (London: British School of Archaeology in Egypt, 1920), pl. LXV, no. 411.
7. R. S. MacAlister, *The Excavation of Gezer*, vol. 3 (London: John Murray, 1912), pl. 206, no. 16.
8. Bertrand Jaeger, *Essai de classification et datation des scarabées Menkheperre* (Fribourg: Editions universitaires, 1982), 79, no. 333.

51 Jewelry Group

Mesheikh, graves 127, 140
Middle Kingdom, c. 1990 B.C.
Electrum, amethyst, carnelian,
garnet, faience
Disk: diam: 3.2 cm (1¼ in.)
Carnelian beads and amulets:
L (string): 44 cm (17⅜ in.)
Amethyst beads and amulets:
L (string): 71.5 cm (28⅛ in.)
Museum of Fine Arts, Boston,
12.1247–49

George A. Reisner and his team of excavators recovered numerous beads and amulets from the late-third- to early-second-millennium and Middle Kingdom cemeteries at Mesheikh. While the tombs were heavily plundered, the burials yielded a range of jewelry forms and materials that characterize these periods in Egypt.

When beads and amulets were found in the debris of a burial chamber, it was Reisner's policy to string like materials together. Hence, all beads and amulets of amethyst were strung together, all pierced carnelian items were treated as one unit, and so forth. This was the situation in graves 127 and 140 at Mesheikh.

A Middle Kingdom jewelry group from Naga el-Deir, found in situ on the deceased, can serve as a model for the distribution and placement of the beads and amulets.[1] The hardstone necklaces from this burial were composed of graduated beads of the same material. A silver uraeus pendant and a thin silver disk were found in the neck region.

Two stone scarabs were strung on a bracelet of assorted beads, and a green jasper scarab was worn as a finger ring on the left hand.

While we will never know how the beads and amulets were deposited in graves 127 and 140, it is likely that there were at least two hardstone necklaces of the same material, an electrum disk amulet at the neck, and one or more bracelets of mixed stone beads, scarabs, and a recumbent lion. Two small sacred-eye beads and a finely carved miniature shell, all of carnelian, attest to the skillfulness of the stone carver. YM

NOTES
1. Sue D'Auria, Peter Lacovara, and Catharine Roehrig, *Mummies and Magic: The Funerary Arts of Ancient Egypt*, exh. cat. (Boston: MFA, 1988), 117–18.

52 Relief Showing a Crocodile

Deir el-Bahri, mortuary temple
of Nebhepetre Mentuhotep[1]
Middle Kingdom, 11th Dynasty,
reign of Nebhepetre Mentuhotep
(c. 2061–2010 B.C.)
Limestone, pigment
31 x 74.9 x 9.8 cm (12¼ x 29½ x 3⅞ in.)
The Johns Hopkins University,
Archaeological Collection, 9211

This relief featuring that fierce denizen of
the Nile, the crocodile, came to the Johns
Hopkins University's archaeological collection through the Egypt Exploration Fund and
the efforts of James Teackle Dennis, a loyal
friend of the university who worked with
Edouard Naville at Deir el-Bahri. The excavations centered on the mortuary temples
of Hatshepsut, of the New Kingdom, and of
Nebhepetre Mentuhotep, founding monarch
of the Middle Kingdom. The present relief,
from the latter structure, was found during
the second or third season of the excavations
(1904–6).[2] It may have come from a representation of the king hunting along the Nile and
in the desert.[3] It is also possible that it was
once part of a complex scene that showed
Nebhepetre's fleet as it advanced against
his enemies in his successful quest to reunify
Egypt. Several other fragments of relief sculpture from this impressive scene are preserved
in other collections, including some at Yale
University which were also acquired through
the Egypt Exploration Fund.[4]

The crocodile rests at the bottom of the
Nile, away from the boats and sailors toiling
upon the river's surface. He has plunged
below to enjoy his meal, a fish held between
his powerful jaws. The teeth are ragged and
menacing, and the thick hide is indicated by
a crosshatched pattern. The water is represented by diagonal, wavy lines, some of which
still retain traces of blue pigment. At the
extreme right is the tail fin of a fish, perhaps
a *bolti*. The relief is broken into three adjoining fragments. GS

BIBLIOGRAPHY Ellen Reeder Williams, *The Archaeological Collections of the Johns Hopkins University*
(Baltimore: Johns Hopkins University Press, 1984), 15.

NOTES
1. The reliefs of this temple have been studied by
Dieter Arnold of the Metropolitan Museum of Art,
and his insights are especially worthy of note; see
Dieter Arnold, *Der Temple des Königs Mentuhotep
von Deir el-Bahari*, vol. 2, *Die Wandrelief des Sankt-
tures* (Mainz: Philipp von Zabern, 1974).
2. Williams, *Archaeological Collections*, 15.
3. Ibid.
4. Gerry D. Scott, III, *Ancient Egyptian Art at Yale*
(New Haven: Yale University Art Gallery, 1986),
62–65, nos. 28–31.

53 Necklaces of Princess Mayet

Deir el-Bahri, mortuary temple
of Nebhepetre Mentuhotep,
MMA pit 18
11th Dynasty, c. 2045 B.C.
The Metropolitan Museum of Art,
Rogers Fund and Edward S. Harkness
Gift, 1922

A *Necklace*
Gold ball beads
L: 61 cm (24 in.)
22.3.320

B *Necklace*
Carnelian beads
L: 45 cm (17¾ in.)
22.3.321

C *Two-Strand Necklace*
Carnelian, dark blue glass, silver and
rock crystal beads and amulets
L: 76 cm (28¾ in.)
22.3.323

D *Four-Strand Necklace*
Silver; carnelian; blue paste; feldspar,
amethyst, and green jasper beads
and amulets; and an unidentified
(nonamber) resin bead[1]
L: 67 cm (26⅜ in.)
22.3.324

The shrines of six king's wives formed part of one of the earliest phases of the temple of Nebhepetre Mentuhotep, datable to before reunification. Herbert E. Winlock found two of the burials associated with these shrines, those of Ashayet and Mayet.[2]

Mayet—though buried with a group of women sharing the titles "king's wife," "sole royal ornament," and "priestess of Hathor"—was in fact only a child of about five.[3] She was buried in a plain limestone sarcophagus containing two simple, rectangular wooden coffins. Her small body had been lengthened with padding, and her head covered with a large mask. While linen was being wrapped around her shoulders and head, lovely, bright necklaces were inserted between the layers.

These delicate necklaces, whose original stringings—and, in some cases, original thread—were perfectly preserved, are, along with the jewelry of Wah,[4] basic to our knowledge of jewelry of the period. It seems likely that Mayet wore these necklaces during her life, and indeed the gold ball-bead and ring-bead necklaces show signs of wear.

The hollow gold ball beads with small tube extensions at the holes belong to a type of gold or silver necklace whose special technological requirements, rarity, and occurrence in *frises d'objets* ("friezes of objects" painted on the interior of coffins) seem to indicate a particular significance or value.[5] The multistrand necklaces include amulets and an eclectic mix of lustrous and rare materials, including dark blue imperfect glass, silver, and rock crystal.[6] MH

BIBLIOGRAPHY Herbert E. Winlock, "Excavations at Thebes," *BMMA* 17 (November 1921): pt. 2, 51–53, figs. 28–30; William C. Hayes, *The Scepter of Egypt*, vol. 1, *From the Earliest Times to the End of the Middle Kingdom* (New York: MMA, 1953), 162, 229, fig. 144; N. E. Scott, "Egyptian Jewelry," *BMMA* 22 (March 1964): 225 (fig. 4), 228–29.

NOTES
1. C. W. Beck, Amber Research Laboratory, Vassar College, 1991 (analysis report in MMA files).
2. For Winlock's own account, see *Excavations at Deir el Bahri, 1911–31* (New York: Macmillan, 1942), 31–46, where he gives references to Naville's work. For a full understanding of the temple and its building phases, see Dieter Arnold, *The Temple of Mentuhotep at Deir el-Bahri*, The MMA Egyptian Expedition 21 (New York: MMA, 1979), esp. 39–45 (chart on 45), and his earlier *Der Tempel des Königs Mentuhotep von Deir el-Bahari*, vol. 1 (Mainz: Philipp von Zabern, 1974).
3. Recent opinion tends to the view that the function of these women was chiefly religious; see D. Franke, "Review of *Essays on Feminine Titles of the Middle Kingdom and Related Subjects* by William A. Ward," *JEA* 76 (1990): 231, for the most recent bibliography on the subject.
4. See the account of the unwrapping of Wah's mummy in Winlock, *Excavations at Deir el Bahri*, 223–28. Wah's burial, like that of Meketre, whom he served, is now dated to the very early 12th Dynasty.
5. Deborah Schorsch, "The Gold and Silver Necklaces of Wah: A Technical Study of an Unusual Metallurgical Joining Method," in *Conservation of Ancient Egyptian Materials*, vol. 2 (forthcoming). For an additional example of this type of necklace, formerly in the collection of the duke of Northumberland, see sale cat., Sotheby's, London, 9 July 1974, no. 38.
6. For "imperfect glass," see Christine Lilyquist and R. H. Brill, *Studies in Early Egyptian Glass* (New York: MMA, 1993), 6, n. 9.

54 Relief of Mentuhotep III

Armant[1]
Middle Kingdom, reign of Sankhkare
Mentuhotep (c. 2010–1998 B.C.)
Limestone
80.1 x 135 x 11.5 cm
(31½ x 53⅛ x 4½ in.)
The Brooklyn Museum,
Charles Edwin Wilbour Fund, 37.16E

With the reunification of Egypt in the 11th Dynasty, southern artists rediscovered the great Memphite monuments of the Old Kingdom. As a result, the severe southern style was modified by the more naturalistic and refined artistic tradition of the north.[2]

This raised relief of King Sankhkare Mentuhotep evokes the great royal reliefs of the Old Kingdom in a conscious revival of what was then considered Egypt's golden age.[3] The wafer-thin raised relief; elegant,

modulated contours; and attention to detail reflect the finest Memphite traditions, while the elongated proportions and crisp outlines of the figures reveal the influence of southern art. This blend of the robust vitality of the south with the grace and refinement of the north produced a new style that would be emulated by later generations.

On the left, under the outstretched wing of the Horus falcon, Mentuhotep, wearing the ceremonial beard and the Red Crown of the Delta, performs a ritual dance.[4] To the right, the king, now wearing the *nemes* headdress, faces the goddess Iunyt. She holds out to him the *was* scepter of dominion. Above, the scene is symbolically reproduced: a falcon, symbolizing the king, receives the scepter from a cobra, a manifestation of the goddess.

Subtle differences in details such as the treatment of the ears can be seen between the figures on the left and right.[5] This indicates that at least two artisans were working side by side.[6] BM

BIBLIOGRAPHY T. G. H. James, *Corpus of Hieroglyphic Inscriptions in the Brooklyn Museum*, vol. 1, Wilbour Monographs 6 (Brooklyn: Brooklyn Museum, 1974), 36–37; Richard Fazzini, *Images for Eternity: Egyptian Art in Brooklyn and Berkeley,* exh. cat. (San Francisco: Fine Arts Museums of San Francisco; Brooklyn: Brooklyn Museum, 1975), no. 35; Richard Fazzini et al., *Ancient Egyptian Art in the Brooklyn Museum* (Brooklyn: Brooklyn Museum, 1989), no. 18.

NOTES
1. According to Henry Abbott, who purchased the relief sometime before 1852 (ex-collection New-York Historical Society).
2. Henry G. Fischer, "An Example of Memphite Influence in a Theban Stela of the Eleventh Dynasty," *Artibus Asiae* 22 (1959): 240–52.
3. Fazzini, *Images for Eternity,* 44.
4. The dance was possibly connected with the ritual of rejuvenation celebrated during the *heb-sed* (jubilee) festival; a similar representation is found in the reliefs of King Djoser in the funerary complex at Saqqara; see Kurt Lange and Max Hirmer, *Egypt: Architecture, Sculpture, Painting in Three Thousand Years,* 4th ed. (London and New York: Phaidon, 1968), pl. 15, and also ibid., 49, fig. 35.
5. James Romano, in Fazzini et al., *Ancient Egyptian Art,* no. 19.
6. Ibid.

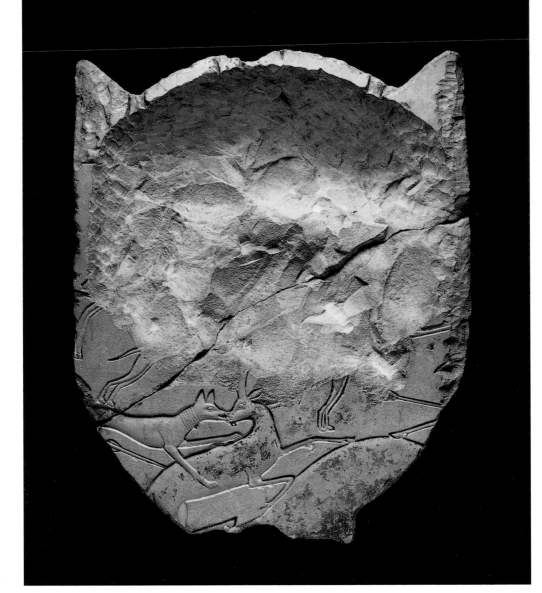

55 Hunting in the Desert

Deir el-Bahri, tomb of Khety (TT 311)
11th Dynasty, c. 2020 B.C.
Limestone
45 x 35.5 cm (17¾ x 14 in.)
The Metropolitan Museum of Art,
Rogers Fund, 1923, 23.3.173

Herbert E. Winlock found the tombs of many
great nobles of the 11th and early 12th
Dynasties arranged along the northern cliffs
of Deir el-Bahri, looking down over the
approach avenue and funerary complex
of King Nebhepetre Mentuhotep. Located
nearest the king's complex was the tomb of
Khety, chancellor for Nebhepetre Mentuhotep
from at least soon after reunification until
sometime after year 40.[1]

Sometime after the reign of Ramesses II
the tomb became a limestone platter factory,
supplied by the fine white limestone slabs
lining the walls of the entry passage and
statue chamber. Only fragments of the original decoration survive, and only one relief
fragment actually remained in its place in the
bottom course of the passage. The themes of
the decoration were more or less traditional,
and the relief cutting itself is comparable to
the relief styles identified in other postunification and late monuments of the king.[2]

The original sunk-relief scene is still dis-
cernable on this large fragment, which was
being reworked into a platter. Frightened
gazelles flee from raining arrows and ferocious

hunting dogs. At the bottom, in the best-
preserved area, a hound in a woven red
leather collar leaps onto the back of a gazelle
and grabs its muzzle with jagged teeth. The
gazelle's forelegs collapse on the slope of
a rose-colored desert hillock.

The carver employed stylistic innovations that appear sporadically in this period.
Ground lines are used sparingly, thereby
creating a spatial illusion, and animals are
depicted in the "flying gallop" to heighten
the animation of the chase.

A number of vertical lines above the
register line at the top of the fragment indicate that the chase was positioned beneath
a different type of scene. A separate relief

fragment from the hunting scene indicates
that it was positioned over an offering depiction of sealed and tied unguent jars. MH

BIBLIOGRAPHY Herbert E. Winlock, "The
Museum's Excavations at Thebes," BMMA 18
(December 1923): pt. 2, 18 (for the tomb of Khety in
general, see 11–19); William C. Hayes, The Scepter of
Egypt, vol. 1, From the Earliest Times to the End of
the Middle Kingdom (New York: MMA, 1953), 164.

NOTES
1. For Khety's dates, see James Allen, "Some Theban
Officials of the Early Middle Kingdom," forthcoming
in Studies in Honor of William K. Simpson (Boston:
MFA).
2. Rita Freed, "The Development of Middle Kingdom
Egyptian Relief Sculptural Schools of Late Dynasty
XI with an Appendix on the Trends of Early Dynasty
XII" (Ph.D. diss., New York University, 1984), 55,
164–65, chart I.

56 Female Head

Deir el-Bahri, tomb of Khety (TT 311)
11th Dynasty, c. 2020 B.C.
Hardwood
H: 6 cm (2⅜ in.)
The Metropolitan Museum of Art,
Rogers Fund, 1926, 26.3.104A

In the debris of Khety's tomb were found
sparse fragments of tomb equipment. Among
these were remains of several statuettes: arms
of hardwood and pine, a fragment of a pine
head, and the wonderful hardwood head
shown here.[1]

The small head is beautifully worked.
The inlaid brows, pencil thin and delicately
curved, contain remnants of a resinous inlay
material. Large, wide eyes were once set with
copper sockets and, presumably, stone inlays.
The rounding of the eyelids near the nose is
subtly indicated. The muscles of the cheeks
swell out from delicate depressions by the
nose, the full lips are encircled by a vermilion
line (marked edge) and surrounded by soft
flesh, and the small, round chin leads to a full
throat. Beneath the perfectly fitted echeloned
hairstyle the contours of the skull are visible.
The hairstyle strongly indicates that the head
is a female rather than Khety himself.[2]

By combining the large, expressive features and vigorous facial modeling with the
dense, controlled ornamentation of the head,
the sculptor created an artwork taut with
energy. In the context of the stylistic development of 11th Dynasty sculpture, this small
head represents the fullest potential of the
local Theban style.[3] MH

BIBLIOGRAPHY William C. Hayes, *The Scepter of
Egypt*, vol. 1, *From the Earliest Times to the End of
the Middle Kingdom* (New York: MMA, 1953), 164,
210; Herbert E. Winlock, "The Museum's Excavations
at Thebes," *BMMA* 23 (February 1928): sec. 2, 24,
fig. 27; Dorothea Arnold, "Amenemhat I and the Early
Twelfth Dynasty at Thebes," *MMA Journal* 26 (1991):
28–29, figs. 39–41.

NOTES
1. The very incomplete group of arms apparently
belonged to male statuettes and offering bearers.
A statue base found in the statue chamber there was
larger in scale than any of the recovered statuary
fragments.
2. Arnold, "Amenemhat I," 28–29. The excavators
originally associated the head with one of the male
arms.
3. Ibid., esp. 27–32.

Chamber of the tomb of Khety, photographed by
Harry Burton, 1922. The wall paintings show funerary
offerings, including, at left, a mirror, spears, an axe,
bows, and rolls of linen.

Excavation of the tomb of Meketre, under the direction of Herbert E. Winlock of the Metropolitan Museum of Art.

57 Group of Relief Fragments

Sheikh Abd el-Qurna,
tomb of Meketre (TT 280)
Early 12th Dynasty, 1990–1985 B.C.
Limestone, pigment
The Metropolitan Museum of Art,
Rogers Fund and Edward S. Harkness
Gift, 1920, 20.3.162, 20.3.163,
31.3.170; Rogers Fund, 1927,
31.3.174, 31.3.176

The tomb of Meketre was excavated into an extremely friable stratum of shale in the cliffs behind Sheikh Abd el-Qurna hill in western Thebes. Because of the poor quality of the stone, the walls were faced with limestone blocks, which were decorated with painted relief. Eventually the weak stone of the cliff collapsed, destroying the chambers within. The larger pieces of limestone facing were undoubtedly carted away and used for other purposes, while the smaller fragments were gradually buried beneath tons of debris. But even these fragments were a stunning discovery when the tomb was cleared. The craftsmanship of both the carving and the painting is of the highest quality. The delicately modeled contours of the cow's head in the unpainted fragment demonstrates the consummate skill of the sculptor. The painter's ability is evident in the careful rendering of the bird's wing, the marking on the bull hide, and the beaded collar. The shading of color in the bird's feathers is a detail not usually seen at Thebes until much later in the 12th Dynasty. CR

BIBLIOGRAPHY Henry G. Fischer, "Flachbildkunst des Mittleren Reiches," in *Das alte Ägypten,* ed. Claude Vandersleyen, Propyläen Kunstgeschichte 15 (Berlin: Propyläen, 1975), xxvi, 294, 300; Dorothea Arnold, "Amenemhat I and the Early Twelfth Dynasty at Thebes," *MMA Journal* 26 (1991): 21–32.

58 Water Jar with Lid
Lahun, tomb of
Princess Sithathoryunet
12th Dynasty, reign of Amenemhat III
(c. 1844–1797 B.C.)
Calcite
55.8 x 26.7 (diam) cm (22 x 10½ in.)
The Metropolitan Museum of Art,
Rogers Fund, 1921, 21.2.62

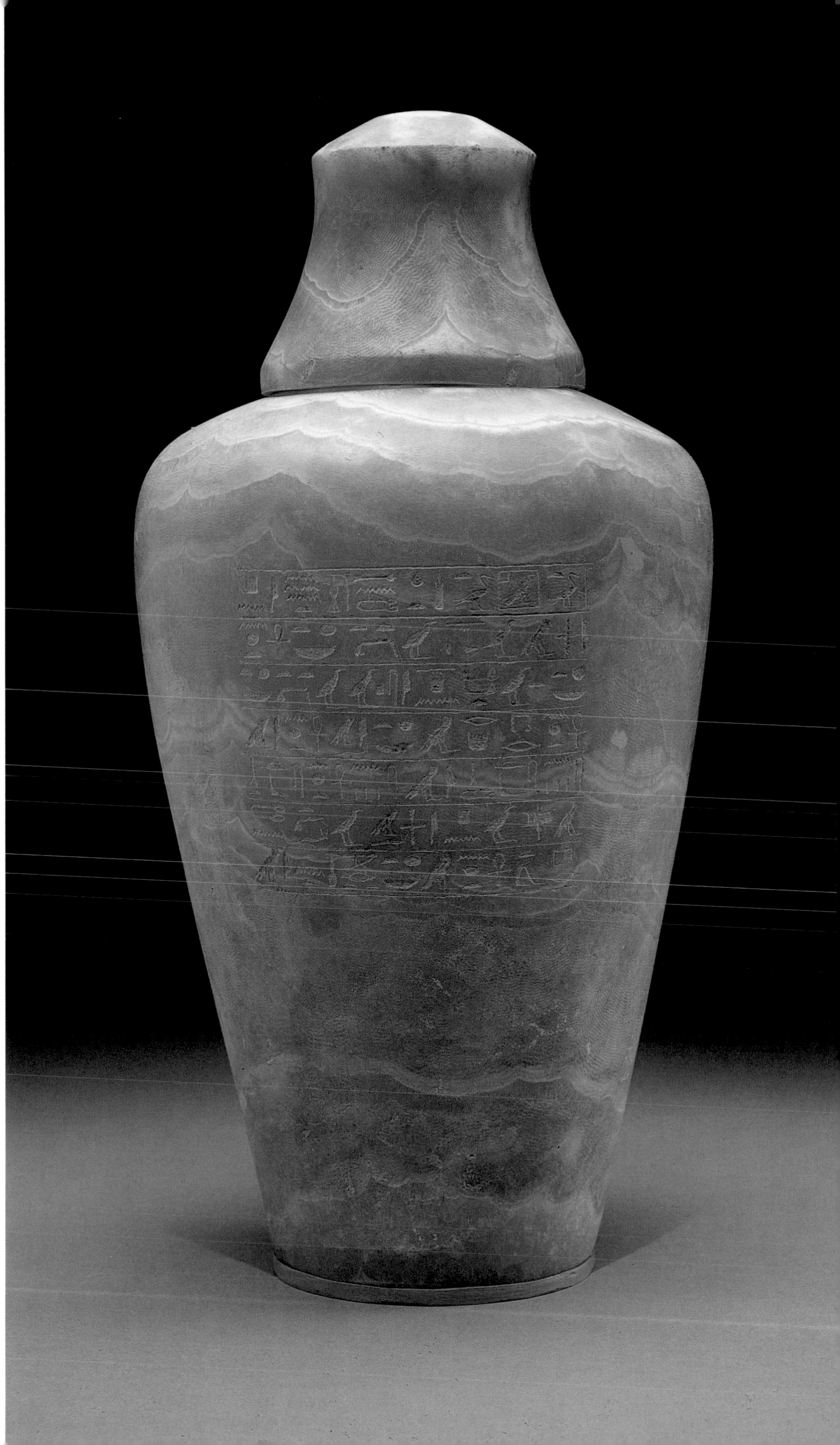

The tomb of princess Sithathoryunet was discovered in 1913 by the British School of Archaeology near the pyramid of Senwosret II, and she is thought to have been his daughter. In 1919–20, while doing additional work in the tomb, W. M. Flinders Petrie found a small chamber hidden behind the stone sarcophagus of the princess. This chamber, like the rest of the tomb, had been entered by robbers in ancient times, but they left behind this superb water jar of calcite. With its elegant proportions and artistic use of the natural banding of the stone, this monumental vessel and its bell-shaped lid are exquisite examples of the mastery of ancient Egyptian craftsmen. The jar and lid imitate the shape of a type of container used for hand washing in the Old Kingdom and usually made of metal or clay when employed in a domestic setting. By the 12th Dynasty this type of vessel was used only in rituals for pouring libations, as the inscription on this example suggests:[1]

Princess Sithathoryunet, receive these, your cool waters, in the earth, which beget everything living. For they are everything given by the earth, which [itself] begets everything living and from which everything comes. May you come to live through them. May you be restored through them. May you come to live and be restored through the air in it (the earth), and may it beget you so that you emerge alive in everything you desire and that it may be to your good.

CR

BIBLIOGRAPHY W. M. Flinders Petrie, Guy Brunton, and M. A. Murray, *Lahun*, vol. 2 (London: British School of Archaeology in Egypt, 1923), 15–16, pls. XXV.7, XXVI; William C. Hayes, *The Scepter of Egypt*, vol. 1, *From the Earliest Times to the End of the Middle Kingdom* (New York: MMA, 1953), 325, fig. 214.

NOTES
1. Part of this entry is based on unpublished label copy written by Dorothea Arnold for the special exhibition *Pharaoh's Gifts: Stone Vessels from Ancient Egypt*. The inscription was translated by James P. Allen for this exhibition, which was on view at the Metropolitan Museum of Art from August 9, 1994, through January 29, 1995.

59　Relief of a Foreigner Throwing a Spear

Lisht, pyramid complex of Senwosret I
12th Dynasty, c. 1950 B.C.
Limestone, pigment
22 x 22 cm (8⅝ x 8⅝ in.)
The Metropolitan Museum of Art,
Rogers Fund, 1913, 13.235.3

A register line crosses this small fragment above its middle. Above the line one can see two yellow-painted legs, the right one bent. In the lower scene a man is ready to hurl a spear held aloft in his left hand. He has a thick mop of hair with traces of red; a long, pointed beard; and pinched, seamed features; his skin shows traces of yellow. These characteristics mark him as a non-Egyptian, a foreigner. Directly in front of his beard, the point or corner of an object is visible. The

end of another spear touching the register line in front of his own spear indicates the presence of another armed man.

A battle is apparently taking place. The figure in the upper register is perhaps kneeling or collapsing, and the man in the lower register is part of a fighting troop. The rendering of his hair and skin does not match the traditional Egyptian depiction of any particular ethnic group, although there are similarities to representations of desert people and foreigners from the northeast found in middle Egyptian tombs of the 12th Dynasty. But the pointed object in front of the foreigner's face helps identify him as a Semitic warrior, as it is clearly the edge of a shield exactly like the shields with slightly curving corners carried by Semites in the battle scene from the Theban tomb of Intef.[1]

Foreign enemies are typically shown being dominated, with some individual resistance here and there; a group would not normally be shown persisting against the Egyptians. The exception seems to be enemy troops depicted in battle on a fortress wall, from which they throw stones and launch missiles. It may be that the foreigner on this fragment stood on the walls of a fortress ready to cast his spear into besieging Egyptian troops. The slightly downward inclination of his upper body supports this conjecture.

While it is by no means certain that this fragment is part of such a depiction, it raises the possibility that a large battle and siege scene existed at the pyramid of Senwosret I, a scene, furthermore, related in important respects to Theban 11th Dynasty battle representations and not simply derived from Old Kingdom prototypes in the area. It could be that the tradition of such scenes is stronger than suspected.[2]

The fragment was found in the area of the causeway of the Senwosret I pyramid complex at Lisht. Selective reexcavation has found no decisive evidence for any relief decoration in the causeway; this fragment and other fine low-relief fragments showing heads of foreigners perhaps belonged to a scene in the temple, either in the *pr-wrw* (entrance hall) or the court.[3]　MH

NOTES
1. See the shield carried by the figure on the ramparts of the fort, and others in the third register of the battle scene, in Brigitte Jarôs-Deckert, *Das Grab der Inj-it.f* (Mainz: Philipp von Zabern, 1984), color pl. and folding pl. 2, discussed on 40–44. See also the shields carried by a foreign support troop in tomb 17 (Khety) at Beni Hasan, in Percy Newberry, *Beni Hasan*, vol. 2 (London: EEF Archaeological Survey, 1893), pl. 15.
2. See Jarôs-Deckert, *Das Grab der Inj-it.f*, 44–47, for an important discussion of the development of battle representations in the Middle Kingdom. See also Alan Schulman, "The Battle Scenes of the Middle Kingdom," *JSSEA* 12 (1982): 165–83.
3. Dieter Arnold, *The South Cemeteries of Lisht*, vol. 1, *The Pyramid of Senwosret I*, The MMA Egyptian Expedition 22 (New York: MMA, 1989), 18–20. I thank Dorothea Arnold and Dieter Arnold for discussing this relief.

60 Shawabti of Bener

Lisht, pyramid complex of Senwosret I
Middle Kingdom, c. 1820–1750 B.C.
Calcite, pigment
18.5 x 6 cm (7¼ x 2⅜ in.)
The Metropolitan Museum of Art,
Rogers Fund, 1944, 44.4.5

Excavated in 1909 by the Metropolitan Museum of Art expedition working at Lisht, this small funerary statue, made for the "hall-keeper of the palace," Bener, formed the centerpiece of a model burial. It was found wrapped in linen and lying on its side in a miniature coffin, with a little pot at its feet. The statue is a mummiform representation of its owner, an image enhanced in this case by the natural veins of the stone, which encircle the body like mummy wrappings. Paint was used only to define the eyes and to fill the incised hieroglyphs on the body.

Bener's statue is one of the earliest examples of a genre of funerary art that became increasingly popular after the Middle Kingdom. Such images, known as shawabtis, shabtis, or ushebtis, were meant to substitute for their owner in the afterlife, and their responsibilities are often spelled out in a text carved on the statue itself. The inscription on

Bener's shawabti reads: "Recitation: hall-keeper of the palace, Bener, says: O shawabti! If I am assigned to any work there [in the necropolis], as a man to his duties—to plant fields, to irrigate riverbanks, to transport sand from west to east—'Here am I!' you shall say." The text also features truncated hieroglyphs of living beings, mutilated to prevent them from doing harm to the statue. JA

BIBLIOGRAPHY William C. Hayes, *The Scepter of Egypt*, vol. 1, *From the Earliest Times to the End of the Middle Kingdom* (New York: MMA, 1953), 350; Hans Schneider, *Shabtis: An Introduction to the History of Ancient Egyptian Funerary Statuettes*, vol. 1 (Leiden: Rijksmuseum van Oudheden, 1977), 92, 183, fig. 6; Dieter Arnold, *The South Cemeteries of Lisht*, vol. 1, *The Pyramid of Senwosret I*, The MMA Egyptian Expedition 22 (New York: MMA, 1988), 36, pl. 13; James Allen, *Funerary Inscriptions from Lisht*, The MMA Egyptian Expedition (New York: MMA, forthcoming).

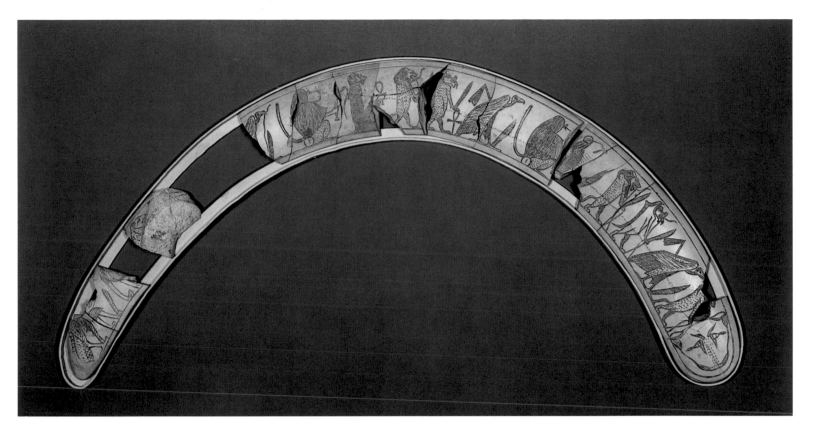

61 Amuletic Wand

Lisht, South Cemetery, outer court area, shaft 5004

13th Dynasty, c. 1750 B.C.

Hippopotamus ivory

L: 32.5 cm (12¾ in.)

The Metropolitan Museum of Art, Rogers Fund, 1908, 08.200.19

This amuletic wand with leopard-head terminal shows a formidable array of deities and demons: upright lions, vultures, the composite goddess Taweret, a frog, an ape, a seated cloaked lion-headed figure, an ape with a lamp, a fragment of a seated(?) lion, and the fragments of two emblems, one consisting of a lion head on two legs, the other of a jackal head on two legs. All these figures are associated with the cycle of myths detailing the birth and travels of the sun god, and the two emblems seem to signify the god himself. The demons assist the sun god against the fiends who are his enemies; their function here is indicated by the knives and protective *sa* signs they hold. The fiends are represented by the snakes in the mouths of some of the demons.[1]

Amuletic wands marshal the same demonic forces that assisted the sun god to aid in the analogous struggles of vulnerable children and mothers to survive and of the newly dead to be reborn. This wand is specifically inscribed on the reverse for the first function: "Words said by the numerous guardians: We have come to extend our protection herewith upon the healthy child, Minhotep, may he live, be prosperous and healthy, born by the princess Sat-Sobek, may she live, be prosperous and healthy." Like some others, the knife is worn at the tip by use, perhaps in some kind of incantatory rite.

The knife itself is beautifully engraved in a dense style. The closely spaced figures are depicted with a high degree of variegated detailing, which distinguishes, for example, between the feathering of the vulture's wings and that of the wing tips, and between the near and farther legs.

The piece was found by the Metropolitan Museum Egyptian Expedition in 1907–8 in the fill of pit 5004 in the outer court of the Senwosret I pyramid complex and may have belonged to the burial in that pit. Ongoing reexcavation and close study have made it clear that the huge cemeteries of the Middle Kingdom capital of Itjtawy were used by officials throughout the 12th and 13th Dynasties.[2] The knife in fact belongs to a type datable to the early 13th Dynasty. MH

BIBLIOGRAPHY Georg Steindorff, "The Magical Knives of Ancient Egypt," *The Journal of the Walters Art Gallery* 9 (1946): 106, n. 41; Hartwig Altenmüller, "Ein Zaubermesser des Mittleren Reiches," *SAK* 13 (1986): 1–27, esp. 22–24, fig. 4 (earlier arrangement of the fragments); Dieter Arnold, *The South Cemeteries of Lisht*, vol. 3, *The Pyramid Complex of Senwosret I*, The MMA Egyptian Expedition 25 (New York: MMA, 1992), 47, 69–70, pls. 82–84a (present arrangement).

NOTES
1. Amuletic wands, also called magic knives because of their shape, have been studied by Hartwig Altenmüller, who has identified the figures on this wand (see "Ein Zaubermesser").
2. Arnold, *Pyramid Complex of Senwosret I*, 41.

62 Fragment of a Relief

Abydos
Middle Kingdom, 12th to 13th
Dynasty, c. 1991–1640 B.C.
Limestone
42.3 x 21.5 cm (16⅝ x 8½ in.)
The University of Pennsylvania
Museum of Archaeology
and Anthropology, 69-29-56

One of the many productive projects undertaken by the University of Pennsylvania–Yale University Expedition to Egypt has been the reconstruction of the so-called cenotaphs, or memorial structures, erected by various elite families during the Middle Kingdom at the site of Abydos.[1] The cenotaphs, varying from fairly large chapels to very small examples, demonstrate a broad range of socioeconomic status among the dedicators.[2] The chapels appear to have been intended to allow the deceased and his or her family to benefit eternally from the religious rituals conducted at Abydos for such funerary deities as Osiris and Khentyimentiu.

This fragmentary relief recovered by the expedition is representative of cenotaph stelae from Abydos. Only the lower section, however, is preserved. The top surviving register shows two groups of three figures that confront each other. Five are male, and one, on the viewer's extreme left, is female, as traces of her long, close-fitting garment and the resulting close spacing of her feet demonstrate.

The male figures wear knee-length kilts (although this detail is preserved only for the figures advancing from the viewer's right).

Below this fragmentary register are three seated figures, two female and one male. The seated male figure wears a short beard, a broad collar, and a full wig that is swept behind the ears. The two female figures wear traditional close-fitting sheaths and long wigs. Their jewelry consists of broad collars and armlets. They are identified by brief texts above their heads as: "the lady of the house Satet" (left) and "the lady of the house Kuyu" (center). Their male companion appears to be identified as "Shemsuem . . . the justified."[3] In front of the seated figures is a short offering list, or "menu." The offerings desired are (viewer's left to right, top to bottom): "Two cups of water, one loaf of bread, one cake, one savory offering, two measures of beans, two cuts of roast beef, two bottles of wine, and two jars of beer." GS

NOTES
1. For the cenotaphs and their importance, see William K. Simpson, *The Terrace of the Great God at Abydos: The Offering Chapels of Dynasties 12 and 13* (New Haven: Peabody Museum of Natural History, Yale University; Philadelphia: University Museum, University of Pennsylvania, 1974); David O'Connor, "The Present, Abydos: The University Museum–Yale University Expedition," *Expedition* 21 (Winter 1979): 46–47; idem, "The 'Cenotaphs' of the Middle Kingdom at Abydos," *Mélanges Gamal Eddin Mokhtar*, vol. 2 (Cairo: IFAO, 1985), 161–77.
2. See O'Connor, "The 'Cenotaphs,'" 168.
3. The name and its orthography seem unusual.

63 Window Stela from a Cenotaph

Abydos
Middle Kingdom, 11th to 13th
Dynasty, c. 2040–1640 B.C.
Limestone
22.3¹ x 14 cm (8¾ x 5½ in.)
The University of Pennsylvania
Museum of Archaeology
and Anthropology, 69-29-135

Window stelae were probably placed in the walls of the cenotaphs, or memorial structures, built at Abydos by many pious families during the Middle Kingdom. Through the rectangular opening a statue representing the owner could observe the religious rituals conducted at the site, which were deemed beneficial for the spirit of the deceased.

View of north Abydos with mud-brick cenotaph chapels in the middle ground.

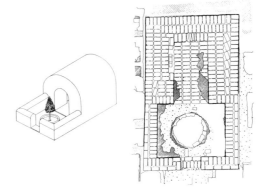

Reconstruction and plan of vaulted cenotaph chapel.

Only a portion of such a stela is preserved here, and it was excavated by the University of Pennsylvania–Yale University Expedition in 1969, codirected by William K. Simpson and David O' Connor. The statue opening occupies the center stela, and brief texts appear in somewhat irregular registers around it. These have been translated by the excavator as: "Kissing the ground before Khenty-khety [Osiris]" and "Seeing the beauty of Wepwawet at the first coming forth . . . by the revered one, Ukhotep."[2] The stela further records the name of Ukhotep's mother, Hotep, and a male relative, Snefer-ptah. GS

BIBLIOGRAPHY David O'Connor, "The Present, Abydos: The University of Pennsylvania–Yale University Expedition," *Expedition* 21 (Winter 1979): 49, fig. 6.

NOTES
1. This is the present restored height.
2. O'Connor, "The Present, Abydos," 49.

64 Statue Base from a Cenotaph

Abydos
Middle Kingdom, 12th to 13th
Dynasty, c. 1991–1640 B.C.
Limestone, pigment
3.7 x 6.5 x 16 cm (1½ x 2⅝ x 6¼ in.)
D (recess): 1.8 cm (⅞ in.)
The University of Pennsylvania
Museum of Archaeology
and Anthropology, 69-29-147

Ancient Egyptian statues, especially those carved in hard stones, were occasionally set into separate statue bases carved in wood or limestone. The practice dates at least to the 4th Dynasty of the Old Kingdom.[1] Such statue bases were typically inscribed, and it seems likely that at least some of the many uninscribed statues that survive from ancient Egypt were originally set into a separate statue base that identified the name and title of the now-anonymous owner.

This statue base has a recess with straight back and sides and a curving front. Two brief hieroglyphic texts surround the recess. The first, a standard offering text, reads right to left and is oriented toward the viewer. The second text, giving the statue owner's filiation, also reads right to left but is oriented toward the statue. The hieroglyphs are carved in sunk relief and filled with bright blue pigment.

TRANSLATION OF INSCRIBED TEXT:
(1) An offering that the king gives to Osiris, the lord of Abydos, that he may grant invocation offerings of bread and beer, beef and fowl, for the ka of Aba-em-hotep(?), (2) engendered by Iot, the justified.

GS

NOTES
1. E.g., the statues of King Djedefra's sons; see William S. Smith, *A History of Egyptian Painting and Sculpture in the Old Kingdom* (London: Oxford University Press, 1946), 33.

65 Statue of the Gardener Merer

Buhen, tomb κ8
Middle Kingdom, late 12th to 13th
Dynasty, c. 1840–1640 B.C.
Diorite
H: 28 cm (11 in.)
University of Pennsylvania Museum
of Archaeology and Anthropology,
E10751

Sculpture was an integral part of the burial equipment provided for private individuals of sufficient means throughout ancient Egypt's long history. The ancient Egyptians believed that a sculptural image, whether a two-dimensional relief or a three-dimensional statue, furnished an abode for a spiritual aspect of the deceased owner. Animated through appropriate ritual, the sculptural image was rendered able to receive its indwelling spirit, which was then sustained by the funerary cult practiced at the tomb.

During the Middle Kingdom sculptural images of private individuals were created for both temple settings and a funerary context. In each case the intent was to provide a locus where the indwelling spirit of the deceased could receive the offerings believed essential for a continued existence after death.

This sculpture was discovered in a relatively substantial private tomb (κ8) at Buhen, an ancient Egyptian fortress town in Nubia. Although the tomb had been plundered, the burial chamber remained largely intact. When David Randall-MacIver and Charles Leonard Woolley of the University of Pennsylvania's Eckley B. Coxe Jr. Expedition discovered the tomb in February 1909, the remains of its ancient owner still wore a considerable amount of jewelry. This included a ring with a scarab, the base of which was inscribed with the name of the 12th Dynasty king Amenemhat III. Outside the burial chamber, in a central passageway, the excavators discovered this statue.[1]

Stylistically the statue reflects such characteristics of later Middle Kingdom sculpture in the round as the use of a hard, dark stone; the depiction of a long, voluminous overkilt; and the choice of a compact pose that draws the various parts of the body, including the limbs, into a tight, rigid mass. These elements combine to suggest a considerable interest in the durability of sculptural form on the part of both artists and patrons during the Middle Kingdom.

The statue shows the owner striding, with the left foot advanced. His shaved pate has been dramatically carved. The large, prominent ears are emphasized by deeply recessed areas at the temples. The lips are relatively thin, and the mouth and jaw firm. Eyebrows are modeled in relief. A square-topped back pillar rises from the statue base to a point midway up the back. The garment's waistband is moderately high, rising to a point approximately midway between the abdomen and the breasts.

The statue base is inscribed with two horizontal lines of hieroglyphic text along its upper front surface. An additional horizontal line is inscribed on its front side edge. The inscription reads:

(1) an offering that the king gives to Ptah-sokar for the ka of (2) the gardener Merer, (3) born of the lady of the house, Neferu.

The hieroglyphs of the inscription are much more crudely cut than the highly competent carving of the rest of the sculpture. Given that uninscribed statues could be set into separately carved statue bases (see cat. no. 64), one wonders whether this statue was originally carved for a more august person, who was perhaps associated with Buhen, and later appropriated for its present owner, Merer, during the unsettled times at the close of the Middle Kingdom. In addition, it is not absolutely certain that the statue and the remains of the occupant of tomb K8 can be identified as the same individual (although this is likely), as the outer chambers of the tomb had been disturbed in antiquity.[2] GS

BIBLIOGRAPHY David Randall-MacIver and Charles Leonard Woolley, *Buhen* (Philadelphia: University Museum, University of Pennsylvania, 1911), 192, 200–1, 234, pls. 72–73; David O'Connor and David Silverman, "The Egyptian Collection," *Expedition* 21 (Winter 1979): 35, fig. 52; idem, *The Egyptian Mummy: Secrets and Science*, exh. cat. (Philadelphia: University Museum, University of Pennsylvania, 1980), 25, fig. 18.

NOTES
1. The findspot, marked with an asterisk, is illustrated in a line drawing in Randall-MacIver and Woolley, *Buhen*, 200.
2. The excavators noted: "With the exception of F [the burial chamber] all the chambers had been completely rifled in ancient days"; see ibid.

66　C-Group Pottery

The Oriental Institute,
the University of Chicago

A *Bowl*
Adindan, cemetery K, tomb 63
C-Group IIA, 2050–1700 B.C.
Ceramic, pigment
17 x 30 (diam) cm (6¾ x 11¾ in.)
23135

B *Bowl*
Adindan, cemetery T, tomb 223
C-Group, 1900–1650 B.C.
Ceramic, pigment
25.9 x 35.3 (diam) cm (10¼ x 13⅞ in.)
23452

The C-Group culture of lower Nubia flourished during a period roughly paralleling the Egyptian Middle Kingdom and Second Intermediate Period. The C-Group people decorated their pottery in a variety of styles, including a figurative decoration that alludes to the importance of cattle to this culture. Cow motifs were also employed to decorate tall, thin stone stelae that were erected around the perimeter of some private tombs of the C-Group. The cow might be a symbol of wealth and hence related to cattle cults found in other areas of sub-Saharan Africa. It might also be related to the Egyptian bovid-form deities Bat and Hathor. Several bowls decorated with cows were excavated at Adindan. Another is in the collection of the Egyptian Museum, Cairo (JE 89989), and fragments of a third are in Chicago (Oriental Institute 30262).

C-Group pottery is more frequently decorated with incised lines and motifs. The bowl with a blackened ground and geometric herringbone pattern (cat. no. 66A) is characteristic of the IIA period of C-Group ware.

As is typical of C-Group pottery from Adindan, these examples were not made on a pottery wheel. The potter formed the vessel by pressing clay against the slope of a depression in the ground while gradually turning the clay mass. ET

BIBLIOGRAPHY 66A: Bruce B. Williams, *Excavations between Abu Simbel and the Sudan Frontier*, pt. 5, *C-Group, Pan Grave, and Kerma Remains at Adindan Cemeteries T, K, U, and J*, OINE 5 (Chicago: Oriental Institute, University of Chicago, 1983), 218, pls. 15B, 40A. 66B: Keith Seele, "University of Chicago Oriental Institute Nubian Expedition: Excavations between Abu Simbel and the Sudan Border, Preliminary Report," *JNES* 33 (1974): 27, 28, fig. 14; C. DeVries, "Communication Concerning the Work of the Oriental Institute Nubian Expedition," in *Nubia: Récentes recherches: Actes du Colloque nubiologique international au Musée national de Varsovie*, ed. Kazimierz Michalowski (Warsaw: Musée national, 1975), 18; Steffen Wenig, *Africa in Antiquity: The Arts of Ancient Nubia and the Sudan*, vol. 2, *The Catalogue*, exh. cat. (Brooklyn: Brooklyn Museum, 1978), 137, no. 32; Williams, *C-Group, Pan Grave, and Kerma Remains*, 102–5, pls. 17A, 19, 46.

67 Kerma Pottery

Kerma
Classic Kerma period/
late Second Intermediate Period
(c. 1640–1550 B.C.)
Ceramic
Museum of Fine Arts, Boston

Kerma tumulus KIII after excavation. These vessels were found in subsidiary graves cut into the extensive royal tumulus.

A *Red-Polished Bottle*
  Tomb K317
  16.2 x 10 (diam) cm (6⅜ x 3⅞ in.)
  21.3083

B *Collared Jar*
  Tomb K312
  28 x 26 (diam) cm (11 x 10¼ in.)
  20.2095

C *Black-Topped Bowl*
  Tomb K316
  9.1 x 17 (diam) cm (3⅝ x 6¾ in.)
  20.2093

D *Rilled Black Beaker*
  Tomb K308
  17.7 x 11.2 (diam) cm (7 x 4⅜ in.)
  20.2094

E *Black-Topped Beaker*
  Tomb K316
  10.4 x 13.1 (diam) cm (4⅛ x 5⅛ in.)
  20.2096

Paralleling the C-Croup culture of Lower Nubia, Kerma culture, centered south of the third cataract of the Nile, flourished at a time when the power of Egypt was declining. The hallmark of the Kerma culture was the production of fine, black-topped pottery made in elegant shapes. The familiar bell- or tulip-shaped beakers, well known from examples found not only in Nubia but also in Egypt itself,[1] were recovered by the hundreds in the later tumuli and monuments at Kerma.[2] Kerma ceramics are made of a fine Nile silt fabric with very fine vegetable inclusions, suggesting an admixture of animal dung.

Although remarkably thin and regular, these pots were handmade and not thrown on a wheel, as was most contemporary Egyptian pottery. The exterior, and often the interior as well, was slipped and burnished to a high gloss. The beakers were then fired mouth downward in a kiln, where they were partially covered by fuel. Iron in the surface of the buried mouth of the vessel, thus starved for oxygen, was reduced to form black ferrous oxide, while iron in the body of the beaker, in contact with the air inside the kiln, oxidized to form red ferric oxide. The high temperatures at the surface of the fuel layer are thought to have created the silvery band that often separates the two colors.[3] The firing atmosphere could be manipulated to fire all black or all red vessels as well.

The Kerma artisans were particularly inventive with the shapes of their wares. The delicate beaker form could be opened up to produce a graceful bowl or repeated, as in the case of the "rilled" beaker, to represent a nested stack of beakers.

While most pottery found in the graves at Kerma appears to have been made specifically for burial, some utilitarian vessels were occasionally included, such as the collared jar (cat. no. 67B), which evidences a great deal of wear at the rim and traces of burning and wear at the base. PL

BIBLIOGRAPHY George A. Reisner, *Excavations at Kerma, Parts IV–V*, Harvard African Studies 6 (Cambridge: Peabody Museum, Harvard University, 1923), 320–504; William S. Smith, *Ancient Egypt as Represented in the Museum of Fine Arts, Boston*, 4th ed. (Boston: Museum of Fine Arts, 1960), 98, fig. 61; Steffen Wenig, *Africa in Antiquity: The Arts of Ancient Nubia and the Sudan*, vol. 2, *The Catalogue*, exh. cat. (Brooklyn: Brooklyn Museum, 1978), 155–59; Peter Lacovara, in *Kerma, royaume de Nubie*, exh. cat., ed. Charles Bonnet (Geneva: Musée d'art et d'histoire, 1990), 213, no. 264.

NOTES
1. Janine Bourriau, "Nubians in Egypt during the Second Intermediate Period: An Interpretation Based on the Ceramic Evidence," in *Studien zur altägyptischen Keramik*, ed. Dorothea Arnold (Mainz: Philipp von Zabern, 1981), 25–40.
2. Peter Lacovara, "The Internal Chronology of Kerma," *Beiträge zur Sudanforschung* 2 (1987): 51–74.
3. H. Hodges, "Black-Topped Pottery: An Empirical Study," in *Ancient Egyptian Ceramics: Colloquium on Ancient Egyptian Ceramics II: Non-Typological Approaches to Ceramic Material*, ed. Peter Lacovara (Boston: Museum of Fine Arts, 1982), 31–33.

68 Furniture Inlays

Kerma
Classic Kerma period/late Second
Intermediate Period
(c. 1640–1550 B.C.)
Hippopotamus ivory
Museum of Fine Arts, Boston

A *Taweret*
   Tomb K1053
   10.3 x 4.5 cm (4⅛ x 1¾ in.)
   13.4220e
B *Flying Ostrich*
   Tomb K1095
   9 x 8.2 cm (3½ x 3¼ in.)
   20.1321a
C *Flying Giraffe*
   Tumulus KIII
   6.8 x 3.2 cm (2¾ x 1¼ in.)
   20.1547b
D *Bustard*
   Tomb K308
   4 x 3.5 cm (1½ x 1⅜ in.)
   20.2098
E *Fox*
   Tomb K1090
   2.8 x 9.8 cm (1¼ x 3⅞ in.)
   20.2099
F *Lion*
   Tomb K407
   3.5 x 8.9 cm (1⅜ x 3½ in.)
   20.2100
G *Goat Nibbling a Tree*
   Tomb K439
   Goat: 8 x 3 cm (3¼ x 1¼ in.)
   Tree: 7 x 1 cm (2¾ x ¾ in.)
   20.1372a, b

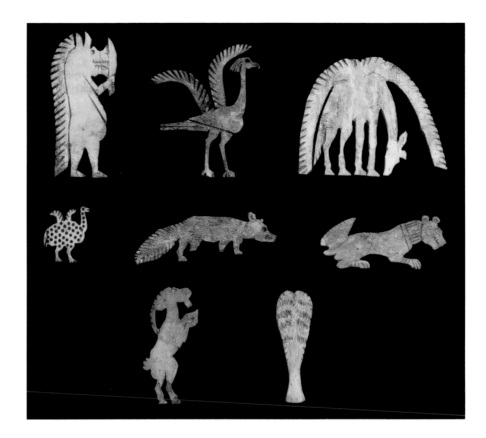

Unlike the ancient Egyptians, who placed the preserved bodies of their dead in coffins, the Kerma Nubians were not mummified but were buried lying on beds. In the more important tombs of the classic period, these beds were elaborately carved and decorated.[1] A number had footboards inlaid with ivory carvings of geometric designs, which were later supplanted by figures of animals. The animals were usually grouped in three uniform rows and combined local fauna with fantastic creatures or representations of Egyptian deities such as Taweret. Depicted as a hippopotamus with a crocodile's tail and the paws of a lion, Taweret was regarded as a protective household deity in Egypt and probably served the same function here.[2]

Similar rows of animals were depicted on the funerary chapels at Kerma and must also have had the function of protecting the deceased.[3]

Traces of red paint and a darker inlay material show that the inlays were originally even more detailed. They were inset in the acacia wood footboards with pegs or gypsum plaster. Particularly interesting is the design of a goat nibbling at a tree, a motif derived from ancient Near Eastern art.[4] PL

BIBLIOGRAPHY Dows Dunham, "An Experiment in Reconstruction at the Museum of Fine Arts, Boston," *JEA* 26 (1940): 137; William S. Smith, *Ancient Egypt as Represented in the Museum of Fine Arts, Boston,* 4th ed. (Boston: Museum of Fine Arts, 1960): 100–101, figs. 63, 64; Steffen Wenig, *Africa in Antiquity,* vol. 2, *The Catalogue,* exh. cat. (Brooklyn: Brooklyn Museum, 1978), 146–47; Brian Curran, "Les incrustations en ivoire," in *Kerma, royaume de Nubie,* exh. cat., ed. Charles Bonnet (Geneva: Musée d'art et d'histoire, 1990), 143, 217–22.

NOTES
1. George A. Reisner, *Excavations at Kerma, Parts IV–V,* Harvard African Studies 6 (Cambridge: Peabody Museum, Harvard University, 1923), 265–71.
2. Rolf Gundlach, "Thoeris," *LÄ,* vol. 6 (1986), cols. 494–97.
3. Peter Lacovara, "The Funerary Chapel at Kerma," *Cahiers de recherches de l'Institut de papyrologie et d'égyptologie de Lille* 8 (1986): 49–58.
4. Cf. E. L. B. Terrace, "Lid of a [Syrian] Stone Pixis," *BMFA* 59, no. 318 (1961): 119.

69 Ribbed Ball-Bead Necklace

Kerma, tumulus KIII, grave 332
Classic Kerma period
(c. 1640–1550 B.C.)
Blue-glazed faience
L (string): 41 cm (16⅛ in.)
Diam (beads): 3–4 cm (1⅛–1⅝ in.)
Museum of Fine Arts, Boston,
20.1720

This blue-glazed faience necklace consists of thirteen graduated, ribbed ball beads. They were found in a rectangular grave containing a bed burial and two sacrificial bodies. George A. Reisner recorded numerous beads of carnelian, faience, glazed quartz, and gold associated with the main burial. Several thousand faience disk beads were positioned around the waist; many were attached to leather fragments thought to be remnants of a skirt. Another mass of beads, primarily of carnelian, glazed quartz, and faience, were located around the neck region. The ribbed beads, described as forming one necklace, were among them.[1]

Reisner described the ribbed bead from Kerma as "a corrugated ball-bead . . . made by cutting shallow grooves radiating from the ends of the hole." He noted their restriction to burials in large tumuli and their typical material, faience, although four isolated beads of blue-glazed quartz were also excavated.[2] Undoubtedly the ribbed ball beads were made at Kerma, as the remains of a sizable faience factory are well documented.[3]

While Reisner placed KIII at the beginning of the classic Kerma sequence, it was later determined to be the last of the great royal tombs (see photograph, p. 161).[4] In addition to the royal burial, this tumulus contained the graves of high-ranking individuals, some of whom were buried on beds, richly adorned and accompanied by human sacrifices.

Necklaces of large, spherical beads were an especially popular adornment in Meroitic times. Numerous representations show kings, queens, and deities wearing both close-fitting and long-strand ball-bead necklaces. YM

BIBLIOGRAPHY George A. Reisner, *Excavations at Kerma, Parts I–III*, Harvard African Studies 5 (Cambridge: Peabody Museum, Harvard University, 1923), 168–69.

NOTES
1. George A. Reisner, *Excavations at Kerma, Parts I–III*, 168–69.
2. George A. Reisner, *Excavations at Kerma, Parts IV–V*, Harvard African Studies 6 (Cambridge: Peabody Museum, Harvard University, 1923), 118.
3. Ibid., 135.
4. Peter Lacovara, "The Internal Chronology of Kerma," *Beiträge zur Sudanforschung* 2 (1987): 51–74.

70 Blue-Glazed
Quartz Beads
Kerma, tumulus KIII, burial K309
Classic Kerma period
(c. 1640–1550 B.C.)
Blue-glazed clear quartz (rock crystal)
L (string): 100 cm (39⅜ in.)
Diam: .6–1.0 cm (¼–⅜ in.)
Museum of Fine Arts, Boston,
20.1716

George A. Reisner excavated literally thousands of blue-glazed quartz beads at Kerma. They were associated with sacrificial burials in the long corridors as well as subsidiary graves in the great tumuli.[1] In the debris above the plundered main burial in grave K421 alone, more than 3,800 glazed quartz beads were discovered with hundreds of faience ring beads. Since groups of faience beads were still attached to fabric, Reisner speculated that this mass of beads might originally have adorned an elaborate garment.[2] More typically, however, the glazed quartz beads were interspersed with other beads or amulets around the neck region of the deceased.[3] The glazed beads are almost always spherical, range from .5 to 1 centimeter in diameter, and rarely were arranged in graduated order.

Reisner's field records indicate that blue-glazed quartz beads from K309 were part of a 266-bead girdle that perhaps included a bell-shaped copper alloy pendant (MFA 20.1806).

Because the burial, which included a primary bed burial and at least one sacrificial victim, had been plundered, ownership of the jewelry could not be determined.[4] One hundred seventy-eight beads were subsequently strung together and accessioned as a unit by the Museum of Fine Arts.

Although the glazing of hard stones, including cryptocrystalline quartzes, was practiced by prehistoric cultures of the Nile Valley,[5] it achieved an unrivaled popularity at Kerma during the classic phase. Deposits of milky and clear quartz were abundant in the third cataract region, and in the vicinity of KI, where Reisner located the remains of an extensive faience factory, excavators discovered several piles of natural crystals.[6] These would have been especially appropriate for the manufacture of beads and small amulets. The adaptation of actual crystals— bored width-wise, glazed blue, and worn as central pendants around the neck[7]— demonstrates that the crystal itself served some amuletic role[8] and explains why a material easily fractured during firing[9] was so frequently chosen over faience. YM

NOTES
1. For the numerous and varied objects of blue-glazed quartz, see George A. Reisner, *Excavations at Kerma, Parts IV–V*, Harvard African Studies 6 (Cambridge: Peabody Museum, Harvard University, 1923), 49–55.
2. George A. Reisner, *Excavations at Kerma, Parts I–III*, Harvard African Studies 5 (Cambridge: Peabody Museum, Harvard University, 1923), 212.
3. One necklace (MFA 13.3969) found in situ (K1067) is composed of a silver cylindrical amulet case, carnelian ball beads, two faience star-shaped beads, and blue-glazed quartz ball beads.
4. Reisner, *Excavations at Kerma, Parts I–III*, 149.
5. J. C. Payne, *Catalogue of the Predynastic Egyptian Collection in the Ashmolean Museum* (Oxford: Clarendon Press, 1993), 204–5.
6. One large group was found in a basket (KI, room Y1); see Reisner, *Excavations at Kerma, Parts IV–V*, 92.
7. Three blue-glazed natural crystal pendants were among the jewels recovered from Kerma; see ibid., 132, nos. 1, 5, 6.
8. Clear quartz (rock crystal) is almost universally regarded as a magical material; see G. F. Kunz, *The Magic of Jewels and Charms* (Philadelphia: J. B. Lippincott, 1915), 153–57.
9. Reisner noted many broken beads in the KI area. No doubt the glazing of quartz as well as the manufacture of faience took place at this site.

71 Fly Pendant

Kerma, tumulus X, burial K1061
Classic Kerma period
(c. 1640–1550 B.C.)
Copper alloy
8.5 x 4.2 x .4 cm (3⅜ x 1⅝ x ⅛ in.)
Museum of Fine Arts, Boston,
13.4006

George A. Reisner excavated four pairs of fly pendants at Kerma. Two pairs came from heavily plundered graves (KB5; K325); the others were found around the neck region of men additionally adorned with bronze and ivory daggers (burials K401, K1061). Reisner described all flies as pierced through the head and those in situ as having been suspended on strings around the neck.[1] On the body in the sacrificial corridor (K401), the pendants were originally part of a necklace composed of eleven small cylindrical beads of gold sheet,[2] while the flies from K1061 were either part of or associated with a string of forty-one blue-glazed quartz beads.[3]

Fly pendants appear early in the amuletic repertoire of the Nile Valley.[4] Those of Pre-dynastic date are usually 1 to 2 centimeters in size,[5] carved from hard stone, and strung with beads and other amulets. A small golden fly and several dozen cylinder beads of gold sheet found in an A-Group royal burial at Qustul may represent the earliest example from a Nubian context.[6] The significance of these early flies is unknown, though the precious materials from which they were crafted and the funerary contexts in which they were found suggest a combined social and religious function.

It is difficult to determine whether the large, paired fly pendants from Kerma derive from earlier models or developed independently. Both the early Qustul pendant and K401 flies were associated with cylindrical gold beads, but that relationship may be little more than coincidental. We do know that at Kerma and Buhen the pendants are always large, paired, and often worn by armed males around the neck. A fragment depicting a bound Nubian warrior adorned with a fly (MFA 19.12.13), as represented on a granite sphinx of Amenhotep II from the Amun temple complex at Gebel Barkal,[7] gives an idea of how these pendants might have been worn.[8] YM

BIBLIOGRAPHY George A. Reisner, *Excavations at Kerma, Parts IV–V*, Harvard African Studies 6 (Cambridge: Peabody Museum, Harvard University, 1923), 348–49.

NOTES
1. George A. Reisner, *Excavations at Kerma, Parts I–III*, Harvard African Studies 5 (Cambridge: Peabody Museum, Harvard University, 1923), 131–32, pls. 44, 53.
2. Reisner, *Excavations at Kerma, Parts IV–V*, 196.
3. Ibid., 348–49.
4. For a serpentine fly from Armant, see R. Mond and O. H. Myers, *Cemeteries of Armant I* (London: Oxford University Press, 1937), 80.
5. An exception is a five-centimeter fly of glazed steatite from Hemamieh; see Guy Brunton, *Qau and Badari I* (London: British School of Archaeology in Egypt, 1927), 16, pl. 17.
6. Bruce B. Williams, *Excavations between Abu Simbel and the Sudan Frontier*, pt. 1, *The A-Group Royal Cemetery at Qustul, Cemetery L*, OINE 3 (Chicago: Oriental Institute, University of Chicago, 1986), 306, pl. 110.
7. Dows Dunham, *The Barkal Temples* (Boston: MFA, 1970), 25, no. 3.
8. I am grateful to Peter Lacovara for bringing this fragment in storage to my attention.

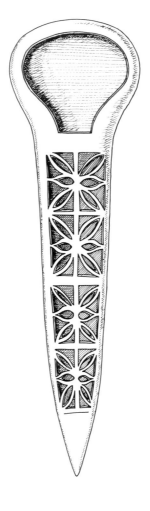

butt combined with a long, thin, gracefully tapering blade—evolved from daggers of the Middle Kingdom with lunate handles.[2] The openwork floral design of the sheath was cut with great delicacy from a piece of leather, whose two sides were folded over and laced up the back. A horizontal piercing on the back probably once held laces for tying around the waist.

A similar dagger dating to the same period was found in the Ahotep treasure.[3] Early in the New Kingdom such daggers were replaced with ones with handles cast as part of the blade for added strength.[4] PL

BIBLIOGRAPHY 72A: Albert B. Elsasser and Vera-Mae Fredrickson, *Ancient Egypt*, exh. cat. (Berkeley: Robert H. Lowie Museum of Anthropology, University of California, 1966), 67.

NOTES
1. Peter Lacovara, "The Hearst Excavations at Deir el-Ballas: The Eighteenth Dynasty Town," in *Studies in Ancient Egypt, the Aegean, and the Sudan: Essays in Honor of Dows Dunham*, ed. William K. Simpson and Whitney M. Davis (Boston: MFA, 1981), 120–24.
2. Wolfgang Schenkel, "Dolch," in *LÄ*, vol. 1 (1975), 1113–16.
3. Friedrich W. von Bissing, *Ein Thebanischer Grabfund aus dem Anfang des Neuen Reichs*, 2d ed. (Bad Honnef: LTR Verlag, 1982), pl. III 5.
4. Schenkel, "Dolch," 1114.

72 Dagger and Sheath

Deir el-Ballas, North Palace
Early 18th Dynasty, c. 1550–1525 B.C.

A *Dagger*
Bronze, ivory
L: 23.5 cm (9¼ in.)
Phoebe A. Hearst Museum of Anthropology, University of California, Berkeley, 6-17311

B *Dagger Sheath*
Leather
L: 27.8 cm (10⅝ in.); w: 6.7 cm (2⅝ in.)
Museum of Fine Arts, Boston, 47.1682

This dagger and leather sheath were discovered in George A. Reisner's excavations for the Hearst Expedition at Deir el-Ballas, the location of a late Second Intermediate Period royal city belonging to the Theban pharaohs. The palace and houses of the court officials were abandoned in the early 18th Dynasty, presumably after the Hyksos expulsion. A number of actual weapons, as well as votive model weapons in painted clay, were found in and around the royal residence, designated the North Palace by Reisner.[1]

Its remarkably good state of preservation suggests that the dagger must actually belong to the sheath, which was found nearby. The elegant shape of this poniard—round ivory

73 Shawabti of Seniu

Thebes, "Seankhkare" cemetery,
near MMA 1021
18th Dynasty, c. 1525–1450 B.C.
Glazed steatite, black paint
29 x 8 x 5 cm (11⅜ x 3⅛ x 2 in.)
The Metropolitan Museum of Art,
Rogers Fund, 1919, 19.3.206

This shawabti, or funerary statue, was made
for the chief steward and scribe Seniu. One
of the finest of its kind, it is particularly
remarkable for the careful delineation of the
facial features. The wig was painted over
the glaze. At some point, perhaps while it
was being made, the shawabti broke in two
and was carefully rejoined with three round
dowels of steatite.

The shawabti was discovered in two
pieces, high in the cliffs south of Deir el-
Bahri. Although the burial of Seniu himself
has not been found, his titles and the artistic
style and quality of this piece indicate that he
served the royal household of the early 18th
Dynasty. The inscription on the shawabti's
body is chapter 6 of the Book of the Dead,
a version of the "shawabti spell" almost identical with that inscribed on the shawabti of
Bener (cat. no. 60). JA

BIBLIOGRAPHY William C. Hayes, *The Scepter of
Egypt*, vol. 2, *The Hyksos Period and the New Kingdom, 1675–1080 B.C.* (New York: MMA, 1959), 59,
fig. 29; Hans Schneider, *Shabtis: An Introduction to
the History of Ancient Egyptian Funerary Statuettes*,
vol. 1 (Leiden: Rijksmuseum van Oudheden, 1977),
92, 188.

74 Tuthmoside Battle Relief

Asasif, mortuary temple of Ramesses IV
18th Dynasty, reign of Tuthmosis III,
Hatshepsut, or Amenhotep II
(1479–1401 B.C.)
Sandstone, pigment
61 x 115 x 40 cm (24 x 45 x 15¾ in.)
The Metropolitan Museum of Art,
Rogers Fund, 1913, 13.180.21

This beautifully painted relief was discovered during the Metropolitan Museum of Art's 1912–13 season at Asasif, Thebes, where it had been reused in the foundations of Ramesses IV's unfinished mortuary temple. Herbert E. Winlock assigned the block's original use to an unspecified monument of Ramesses II.[1] The relief portrays defeated Syrians under the bellies of royal chariot horses.

Although scholars long believed that monumental royal battle reliefs originated in the 19th Dynasty,[2] they are now known to have existed earlier.[3] Stylistic and iconographic features of the relief point to a Tuthmoside date, probably from the reign of Amenhotep II. The costumes of the Syrians, especially the *galibeyeh*-like garment, are identical to those worn by Syrians in Theban tomb scenes from the first half of the 18th Dynasty.[4] By the reign of Amenhotep III this type of garment had completely disappeared and was replaced by a brightly colored, elaborately decorated costume wound in layers of material around the body.[5] The physiognomy of the figures is rendered in a manner consistent with art during the reign of Amenhotep II. The philtrum is depicted on two figures, while the nose and eyes are consistent with royal and private relief sculpture from Amenhotep's reign.[6] Finally, the low inclination of the charging horses and the absence of streamers dangling below their groins and bellies point to a mid-18th Dynasty date.[7] Streamers are portrayed on every example of royal chariot teams in battle from the reign of Amenhotep III onward,[8] but not on an example from the reign of Tuthmosis IV. This block, then, represents further evidence that monumental battle reliefs already existed in the first half of the 18th Dynasty. PB

BIBLIOGRAPHY Howard Carter and Percy E. Newberry, *The Tomb of Thoutmosis IV* (Westminster: A. Constable, 1904), pls. x–xi; Herbert E. Winlock, "Excavations at Thebes in 1912–13," *BMMA* 9 (November 1914): 22–23; J. B. Pritchard, "Syrians as Pictured in the Paintings of the Theban Tombs," *Bulletin of the American Schools of Oriental Research*, no. 122 (1951): 36–41; Bernard Bruyère, *Deir el Médineh année 1926: Sondage au temple funéraire de Thotmès II* (Cairo: IFAO, 1952), 40–42, pls. ii, IV; G. A. Gaballa, *Narrative in Egyptian Art* (Mainz: Philipp von Zabern, 1976), 99; Karol Myśliwiec, *Le portrait royal dans le bas-relief du Nouvel Empire*, Travaux du Centre d'archéologie méditerranéenne de l'Académie polonaise des sciences 18 (Warsaw: Editions scientifique de Pologne, 1976), 61, figs. 106–10; Peter F. Dorman, "Egyptian Art," *BMMA* 41 (Winter 1983–84): 42–43, no. 42.

NOTES
1. Winlock, "Excavations at Thebes," 22–23; Hayes, *Scepter of Egypt*, vol. 2, 339–40.
2. Gaballa, *Narrative in Egyptian Art*, 99.
3. E.g., under Tuthmosis II; see Bruyère, *Deir el Médineh*, 40–42, pls. ii, IV.
4. Pritchard, "Syrians," 38 (B).
5. Ibid., 41 (type C); cf. Donald B. Redford, in *The Akhenaten Temple Project*, vol. 2, *Rwd-Mnw and Inscriptions* (Toronto: University of Toronto Press, 1988), 21–22.
6. Myśliwiec, *Le portrait royal*, 61, figs. 106–10.
7. Carter and Newberry, *Tomb of Thoutmosis IV*, pls. x–xi.
8. Mohamed Saleh and Hourig Sourouzian, *Official Catalogue: The Egyptian Museum, Cairo* (Mainz: Philipp von Zabern, 1987), no. 143.

Mortuary temple of Hatshepsut at Deir el-Bahri, photographed in 1995.

75 Kneeling Statue of Hatshepsut

Deir el-Bahri, mortuary temple
of Hatshepsut
18th Dynasty, reign of Hatshepsut
(c. 1473–1458 B.C.)
Granite, pigment
77 x 33 x 50 cm (30⅛ x 13 x 19⅝ in.)
The Metropolitan Museum of Art,
Rogers Fund, 1923, 23.3.1

Of the handful of women who ruled Egypt during pharaonic times, Maatkare Hatshepsut had the longest reign and left the most monuments. She ruled for about twenty-two years, first as regent for, then as senior coruler with, her nephew and stepson, Tuthmosis III. During excavations by the Metropolitan Museum of Art in the Deir el-Bahri area, thousands of statue fragments were uncovered in two great depressions in front of Hatshepsut's mortuary temple. It was soon evident that statues once decorating the temple's façade and courtyards had been deliberately smashed and buried. The excavators theorized that a vindictive Tuthmosis III had taken revenge upon his aunt by destroying her images and removing her name wherever it occurred on monuments, and this rather simplistic explanation is the one most often found in popular publications even today. Later discoveries, however, suggest that the destruction occurred some twenty years after Hatshepsut's death.[1] Although we can only speculate about Tuthmosis's motivation in destroying the monuments, the long delay is more suggestive of political expediency than personal vengeance.

Unlike larger statues, which had been smashed into hundreds of pieces, a group of small kneeling figures had merely been broken into large chunks. In several cases the entire head and the features of the face were left unmutilated. The only portions missing from this example are the original base and part of the feet. Hatshepsut kneels in a position of offering. She wears the garb of a king, including the royal beard, the *shendyt* kilt, and the *khat* headcloth with a uraeus at the forehead. She holds a libation jar decorated with a *djed* pillar, a symbol of stability. CR

BIBLIOGRAPHY Herbert E. Winlock, *BMMA* supp. (December 1923): 32–33, figs. 27, 28; William C. Hayes, *The Scepter of Egypt*, vol. 2, *The Hyksos Period and the New Kingdom, 1675–1080 B.C.* (New York: MMA, 1959), 97; Roland Tefnin, *La statuaire d'Hatshepsout: Portrait royal et politique sous la 18e dynastie*, Monumenta Aegyptiaca 4 (Brussels: Fondation égyptologique reine Elisabeth, 1979), 88–97; Wilfried Seipel, *Gott, Mensch, Pharao: Viertausend Jahre Menschenbild in der Skulptur des alten Ägypten.* (Vienna: Kunsthistorisches Museum, 1992), 228–41.

NOTES
1. For a thorough discussion of the evidence, see Peter F. Dorman, *The Monuments of Senenmut: Problems in Historical Methodology* (London and New York: Kegan Paul International, 1988), chap. 3, esp. 63–65.

76 Objects from Foundation Deposits

Deir el-Bahri, mortuary temple of Hatshepsut

18th Dynasty, reign of Hatshepsut (c. 1473–1458 B.C.)

The Metropolitan Museum of Art

A *Brick Mold*
Wood
11.7 x 27.7 x 6.2 cm (4⅝ x 10⅞ x 2½ in.)
Rogers Fund, 1922, 22.3.252

B Setep *Instrument*
Wood
H: 6.1 cm (2⅜ in.); L: 27.1 cm (10⅝ in.); TH: 1 cm (⅜ in.)
Rogers Fund, 1925, 25.3.42

C *Model Bivalve Shell*
Calcite
7.3 x 12.4 x 3.5 cm (2⅞ x 4⅞ x 1⅜ in.)
Rogers Fund, 1927, 27.3.400

D *Lidded Jar*
Calcite
Jar: 12 x 7.6 (diam) cm (4⅜ x 3 in.)
Edward S. Harkness Gift, 1926, 26.7.1433

E *Adze*
Wood, bronze, modern leather
L: 19.6 cm (7¾ in.)
W (blade): 5.1 cm (2 in.)
Gift of the Egypt Exploration Fund, 1896, 96.4.7

F *Knot Amulet*
Wood
5.3 x 15.2 x 1.5 cm (2⅛ x 6 x ⅝ in.)
Rogers Fund, 1925, 27.3.398

G *Axe*
Wood, bronze
L: 55 cm (21⅝ in.)
Blade: 10.7 x 10.8 x 1.4 cm (4¼ x 4¼ x ½ in.)
Rogers Fund and Edward S. Harkness Gift, 1925, 25.3.129

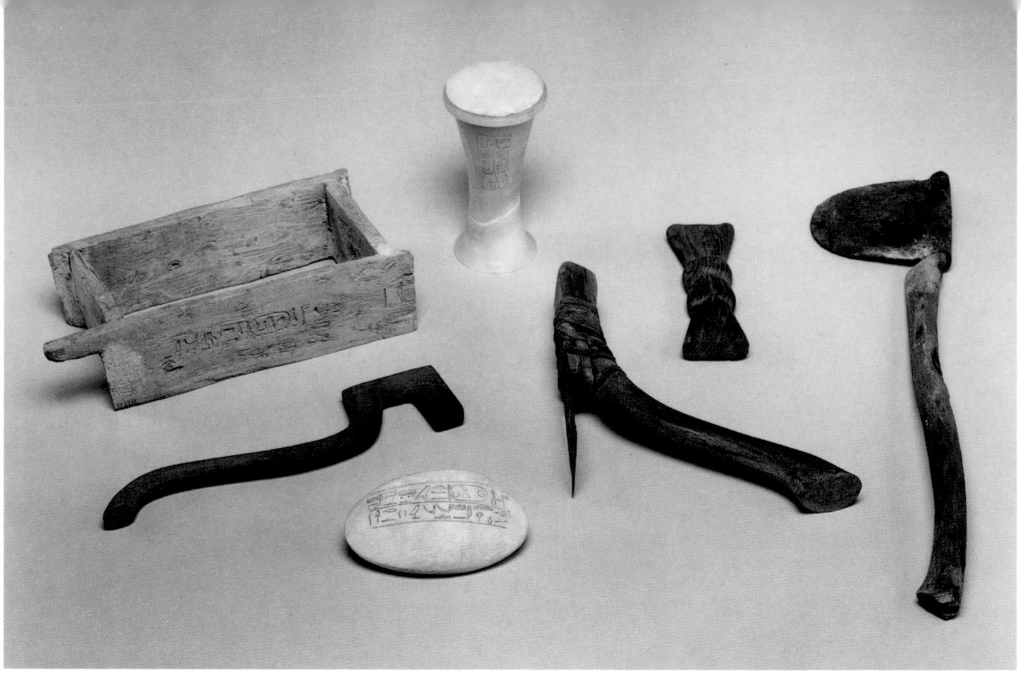

The burying of foundation deposits was an important part of the ceremonial "stretching of the cord," the ritual laying out of the plan of an official building. The deposits symbolically ensured the stability of the structure and, in the case of a funerary monument, guaranteed the continuity of offerings for the spirit of the deceased. To this end, building tools and materials were included for the continued repair of the building. Small offerings of fruit and grain, choice portions of slaughtered oxen, jars of precious oils, and ritual implements were included for the replenishment of the mortuary cult.

Fourteen foundation deposits have been discovered around the perimeter of Hatshepsut's mortuary temple at Deir el-Bahri. The objects had been placed in pits lined with mud brick. The first was found during the Egypt Exploration Fund's excavation of the temple in the 1890s. Two more were uncovered by Howard Carter and Lord Carnarvon during their excavations in the Asasif plain in front of the temple in 1910–11. In the 1920s the Metropolitan Museum of Art found another eight intact deposits and three that had been robbed.

The artifacts in this group were chosen from several deposits. Among them is a model clamshell of calcite with the inscription "The good goddess, Maatkare, she made [it] as her monument for her father, Amun-Re, at the stretching of the cord over Djeser-Djeseru-Amun (an abbreviation of the temple's name), which she did while alive." Also included are a wood brick mold; an adze and an axe with their original metal blades, one fastened with leather thongs; a calcite unguent jar; a wooden knot; and a *setep* instrument, used in the "opening of the mouth" ritual, which was performed to allow a god or the spirit of the dead to benefit from the funerary offerings. Most of these pieces are inscribed with the throne name of Hatshepsut and the epithet "beloved of Amun who is in Djeser-Djeseru." CR

BIBLIOGRAPHY Herbert F. Winlock, *Excavations at Deir el-Bahri, 1911–1931* (New York: Macmillan, 1942), 153; William C. Hayes, *The Scepter of Egypt*, vol. 2, *The Hyksos Period and the New Kingdom, 1675–1080 B.C.* (New York: MMA, 1959), 84–85, figs. 46–47; James Morris Weinstein, *Foundation Deposits in Ancient Egypt* (Ann Arbor, Mich.: University Microfilms, 1973), 151–64.

77 Fragment from Obelisk of Hatshepsut

Karnak, temple of Amun, pylon 5
18th Dynasty, reign of Hatshepsut
(c. 1473–1458 B.C.)
Red granite
106 x 42 x 46 cm (41¾ x 16½ x 18⅛ in.)
Museum of Fine Arts, Boston, gift
of the heirs of Francis Cabot Lowell,
1975, 75.12

To demonstrate her power as well as her devotion to Amun, Hatshepsut commissioned two majestic red granite obelisks for the temple of Amun-Re at Karnak.[1] The obelisks once stood 97½ feet tall, and their pyramidion tops would have been covered with gleaming sheet gold.[2] The northern obelisk still stands; the southern one lies shattered on the ground. This fragment of relief came from the fallen obelisk.

Created in connection with Hatshepsut's *sed* festival (a jubilee reaffirming a king's right to rule) in year 16 of her reign, the obelisks were strategically positioned between the fourth and fifth pylons in the hall of her father, Tuthmosis I, to further strengthen her association with him.[3] A queen was literally the king's wife, but Hatshepsut chose to be more than a wife, a ruler in her own right. Therefore, she was often depicted as a male in full royal regalia. Here she has a male torso and wears the pharaoh's traditional pleated *shendyt* kilt, double crown over a head cloth, ceremonial beard, and *wesekh* collar.

Originally eight horizontal registers on each face of the obelisk depicted scenes of Hatshepsut and Tuthmosis III making offerings to various deities. By comparing its iconography with that of reliefs on the northern obelisk, William S. Smith determined that this fragment is from one of the four lowest registers on either the north or west side of the southern obelisk.[4] Another fragment from the southern obelisk is in the collection of the Museum of Fine Arts, Boston (75.13). On both faces of this corner fragment, Amun-Re is depicted crowned with the traditional double-falcon feathers. JH

BIBLIOGRAPHY William S. Smith, "Two Fragments from Hatshepsut's Karnak Obelisk," *BMFA* 40 (1942): 45–48; Labib Habachi, "Two Grafiti from the Reign of Queen Hatshepsut," *JNES* 16 (1957): 88–104; idem, *The Obelisks of Egypt* (New York: Scribner's, 1977), pl. 13; Wilfried Seipel, "Hatshepsut I," *LÄ*, vol. 2 (1977), cols. 1045–51; K. Martin, "Obelisk," *LÄ*, vol. 4 (1981), cols. 542–45; L. Gabolde, "A propos de deux obélisques de Thouthmosis II, dédiés à son père Thouthmosis I et érigés sous le règne d'Hatshepsout-pharaonen à l'ouest du IVe pylone," *Cahiers de Karnak* 8 (1987): 143–58; H. Fischer, "Twice Inscribed Obelisks," *Göttingen Miszellen* 122 (1991): 29–30; R. Hillinger and C. Loeben, *Obelisken* (Landshut, 1992).

NOTES
1. This was the second pair of obelisks that Hatshepsut commissioned. According to an inscription on the base, it took seven months to cut the obelisks from the Aswan quarry (see note 2 below).
2. A relief in the south colonnade of Hatshepsut's mortuary chapel at Deir el-Bahri depicts a pair of obelisks that Hatshepsut had commissioned earlier to stand farther to the east at Karnak. These two obelisks are seen in relief scenes on blocks from her now-dismantled Red Chapel at Karnak. See Habachi, "Two Grafiti," 95–96.
3. William C. Hayes, *The Scepter of Egypt*, vol. 2, *The Hyksos Period and the New Kingdom, 1675–1080 B.C.*, 3d printing (New York: MMA, 1978), 101. One of the inscriptions on the shaft of the northern obelisk states that Hatshepsut "made it as her monument for her father, Amun . . . (when) she celebrated [for] him the first occurrence of the sed-festival."
4. Smith, "Two Fragments," 46.

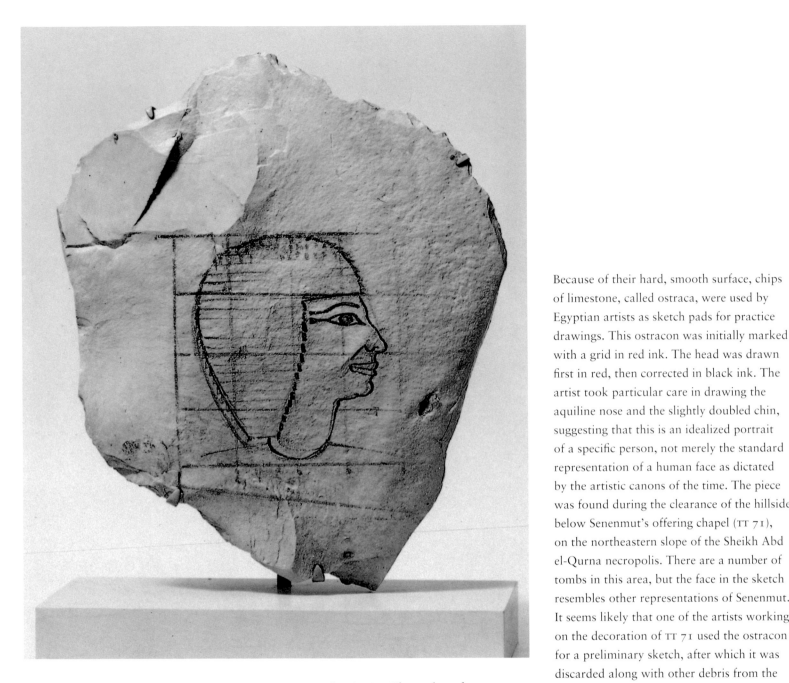

Because of their hard, smooth surface, chips of limestone, called ostraca, were used by Egyptian artists as sketch pads for practice drawings. This ostracon was initially marked with a grid in red ink. The head was drawn first in red, then corrected in black ink. The artist took particular care in drawing the aquiline nose and the slightly doubled chin, suggesting that this is an idealized portrait of a specific person, not merely the standard representation of a human face as dictated by the artistic canons of the time. The piece was found during the clearance of the hillside below Senenmut's offering chapel (TT 71), on the northeastern slope of the Sheikh Abd el-Qurna necropolis. There are a number of tombs in this area, but the face in the sketch resembles other representations of Senenmut. It seems likely that one of the artists working on the decoration of TT 71 used the ostracon for a preliminary sketch, after which it was discarded along with other debris from the tomb's construction. CR

BIBLIOGRAPHY William C. Hayes, *Ostraka and Name Stones from the Tomb of Sen-Mut (No. 71) at Thebes* (New York: MMA, 1942), 9, no. 1, pl. I; idem, *The Scepter of Egypt,* vol. 2, *The Hyksos Period and the New Kingdom, 1675–1080 B.C.* (New York: MMA, 1959), 110.

78 Artist's Sketch of Senenmut

Sheikh Abd el-Qurna, below the tomb of Senenmut (TT 71)
18th Dynasty, reign of Hatshepsut
(c. 1473–1458 B.C.)
Limestone
22.5 x 18 x 3.5 cm (8⅞ x 7⅛ x 1⅜ in.)
The Metropolitan Museum of Art,
Rogers Fund, 1936, 36.3.252

79 Canopic Jar Lid

Deir el-Bahri, tomb of Senenmut
(TT 353)
18th Dynasty, reign of Hatshepsut
(c. 1473–1458 B.C.)
Terra-cotta (Nile B clay)
11.5 x 14.8 (diam) cm (4½ x 5⅞ in.)
The Metropolitan Museum of Art,
Rogers Fund, 1927, 27.3.559

This is probably a lid for a canopic jar, one of four that would have held the internal organs of the deceased.[1] The face was modeled by hand with great care, making this one of the finest examples of its type. The lid was found inside a tomb (TT 353) discovered by the Metropolitan Museum of Art during excavations in the valley in front of the temple of Hatshepsut at Deir el-Bahri. Funerary texts on the walls of the one decorated tomb chamber identified the owner as Senenmut, one of Hatshepsut's most important courtiers. Among Senenmut's many titles was that of "overseer of works," and he is generally identified as the architect of her temple. Because of its inscriptions and plan, the tomb has been identified as the burial element of Senenmut's funerary complex, which also included an offering chapel built some distance away in the nobles' necropolis on Sheikh Abd el-Qurna hill. CR

BIBLIOGRAPHY William C. Hayes, *The Scepter of Egypt*, vol. 2, *The Hyksos Period and the New Kingdom, 1675–1080 B.C.*, rev. ed. (New York: MMA, 1990), 112; Peter F. Dorman, *The Tombs of Senenmut: The Architecture and Decoration of Tombs 71 and 353* (New York: MMA, 1991), 148–49, pls. 87a–b, d.

NOTES
1. But see Dorman, *The Tombs of Senenmut*, where the author questions this identification.

80   Heart Scarab of Hatnofer

Sheikh Abd el-Qurna,
tomb of Hatnofer (SAE 71)
18th Dynasty, reign of Hatshepsut,
c. 1465 B.C.
Serpentine and gold
Scarab: 6.6 x 5.3 x 2.8 cm
(2⅝ x 2⅛ x 1⅛ in.)
Chain: L: 77.5 cm (30½ in.)
The Metropolitan Museum of Art,
Rogers Fund, 1936, 36.3.2

The heart scarab was a regular part of the burial equipment that accompanied the mummy into its coffin. It was usually placed directly over the heart, either wrapped in the mummy bandages or, as in this case, suspended from a chain around the neck. In this position the scarab served both as a source of rebirth and as a permanent form of the heart itself.

The Egyptians considered the heart to be the seat of all thought and emotion. As such, it was the vehicle through which the deceased was judged in the afterlife, where it was weighed against the abstract notion of *ma'at* (order). Because the scarab could be a substitute for the heart, it had to be coached to respond like the heart itself would. This is the purpose of chapter 30B of the Book of the Dead, which was regularly inscribed on the bottom of heart scarabs and addressed to both the mummy's heart and the heart scarab. Hatnofer's version reads:

Hatnofer says: Heart of my mother, heart of my mother! Heart of my [present] form! Don't stand up against me as a witness. Don't create an obstacle against me in the Council. Don't make opposition against me before the keeper of the scales [of judgment]. You are my life force in my body, my creator who makes my limbs sound. When you go to the good place to which we travel, don't make my name smell bad to the court of the living, so that it may go well for us and for the jury, and so that the judge may be happy. Don't tell lies against me beside the god. See: your [own] reputation is [involved].

Hatnofer was the mother of Senenmut, perhaps the most influential official of the female pharaoh Hatshepsut. This scarab, discovered on Hatnofer's mummy, is a particularly fine example of the genre and a good illustration of the wealth that Senenmut's family commanded. Its green stone and gold bezel and chain fit perfectly the specification for such objects recorded in the Book of the Dead: "a scarab of serpentine, banded in gold, with a chain of gold or silver." JA

BIBLIOGRAPHY Ambrose G. Lansing and William C. Hayes, "The Museum's Excavations at Thebes," *BMMA* 32 (January 1937): pt. 2, 20, fig. 34; William C. Hayes, *The Scepter of Egypt*, vol. 2, *The Hyksos Period and the New Kingdom, 1675–1080 B.C.* (New York: MMA, 1959), 224–25, fig. 133.

A classic Egyptian private sculpture type, the block statue reduces the form of the body to a simple cubic mass from which only the head, the hands, and occasionally the feet protrude. A cloak envelops the rest of the body, which is seated comfortably on the ground with legs drawn up to the chest and arms crossed over the knees.

The owner of this block statue, Sitepehu, was high priest (overseer of prophets) in the Thinite nome, the Egyptian state in which Abydos was located. Like Amenemhat (see cat. no. 82), Sitepehu lived during the reign of Hatshepsut, and his facial features similarly reflect a certain likeness to those of his monarch. Sitepehu seems to have taken part in the transportation of Hatshepsut's obelisk, as his name appears in the scene of this event at Hatshepsut's temple at Deir el-Bahri.[1]

The statue was discovered in Sitepehu's tomb at Abydos, placed opposite the central doorway. A lengthy text appears on the front and sides of his garment. In addition to an appeal to Osiris and passages concerning the afterlife, the text appeals to Onuris, principal deity of the Thinis. The sculpture is notable for its large size and its well-preserved state. The face and hands retain much of their traditional red-brown color, and the rich black of the wig framing the face and the treatment of eyes enliven the statue. GS

81   Statue of Sitepehu

Abydos, cemetery D, tomb 9
New Kingdom, 18th Dynasty, reign of
Hatshepsut (c. 1473–1458 B.C.)
Sandstone, pigment
82.5 x 43.5 x 58 cm
(32½ x 17⅛ x 22⅞ in.)
University of Pennsylvania Museum
of Archaeology and Anthropology,
E9217

BIBLIOGRAPHY David Randall-MacIver and Arthur C. Mace, *El Amrah and Abydos* (London: Egypt Exploration Fund, 1902), 65, 71, 84, 85, 94, 95, 97, pls. 32, 33; Kurt Sethe, *Urkunden der 18. Dynastie: Historisch-biographische Urkunden* (Leipzig: J. C. Hinrichs, 1905), vol. 1, 516–20; Lee Horne, ed., *Introduction to the Collections of the University Museum* (Philadelphia: University Museum, 1985), 21, no. 9.

NOTES
1. See Sethe, *Urkunden*, vol. 1, 517; James H. Breasted, *Ancient Records of Egypt*, vol. 2 (New York: Russell and Russell, 1962), 138.

82 Statue of Amenemhat

Buhen, temple of Horus
New Kingdom, 18th Dynasty, reign of
Hatshepsut (c. 1473–1458 B.C.)
Diorite
37 x 23 cm (14⅝ x 9 in.)
University of Pennsylvania Museum
of Archaeology and Anthropology,
E1098

Following Middle Kingdom precedent, New Kingdom private individuals of sufficient means and rank often placed statues of themselves in the temples of their god. The concept behind this practice was probably twofold: to establish a surrogate that would maintain the statue owner's devotion to the deity throughout eternity and to provide a locus in which a spiritual aspect of the deceased could share eternally in the temple offerings and rituals. This sculpture of the Egypto-Nubian official Amenemhat is such a temple statue.

Dedicated in the temple of Horus at Buhen, a site in Nubia near the second cataract, the sculpture shows Amenemhat seated on the ground in an asymmetric pose, with one leg drawn up to the body and the other folded back beneath it. The legs cross at the ankles, while the hands rest comfortably, palms down, on the thighs.

Amenemhat wears a simple, knee-length kilt that has a waistband or belt at the top. He also wears a full, flaring, shoulder-length wig, swept back behind the ears. Typical of the early New Kingdom, this wig harks back to Middle Kingdom precedent, reminding the viewer that this statue, like much of early New Kingdom sculpture, probably took its inspiration from the artistic accomplishments of the Middle Kingdom.

Found in a cache of three sculptures near the north wall of the town of Buhen, this sculpture was believed by the excavators to have been moved from its original position and left in this spot.[1] Also found were a block statue of the same owner and a seated sculpture belonging to another individual which also shows a debt to Middle Kingdom sculpture prototypes.[2] The three statues were most likely dedicated in the nearby temple of Horus of Buhen before being cached at some later date.[3]

Inscriptions on other monuments[4] indicate that Amenemhat was apparently a local Nubian chieftain who also served the Egyptian monarch Hatshepsut as an official and scribe. His sculpture displays the heart-shaped face and aquiline nose associated with Hatshepsut and her successor, Tuthmosis III. The eyebrows and eyelids are modeled in relief, and the corners of the mouth are drilled. Particularly accomplished is the modeling of the musculature and bony structure of the lower legs, while the positioning of the feet is well worked out for the statue type.

Five vertical lines of incised hieroglyphic text appear on the lap, a single horizontal line of text is incised around the back of the kilt, and a single horizontal text register appears on the front top surface of the statue base. All three inscriptions are offering texts. In addition, the owner's name and his title, scribe, appear on the right upper arm. GS

BIBLIOGRAPHY David Randall-MacIver, "Egyptian Section, The Eckley B. Coxe Junior Expedition," *Museum Journal* 1, no. 2 (1910): 27–28; David Randall-MacIver and Charles Leonard Woolley, *Buhen* (Philadelphia: University Museum, University of Pennsylvania, 1911), 108–9, pl. 36; Hermann Ranke, "A Contemporary of Queen Hatshepsut," *University Museum Bulletin* 8 (January 1940): 29–30, pl. IX; PM, vol. 7 (1952), 138; Jacques Vandier, *Manuel d'archéologie égyptienne* (Paris: A. et J. Picard, 1958), vol. 3, 450, 679; David O'Connor, "Ancient Egypt and Black Africa—Early Contacts," *Expedition* 14 (Fall 1971): 8, fig. 2; David O'Connor and David Silverman, *The Egyptian Mummy: Secrets and Science* (Philadelphia: University Museum, University of Pennsylvania, 1980), 29, no. 24.

NOTES
1. Randall-MacIver and Woolley, *Buhen*, 108.
2. Ibid., 108–11, pls. 36, 37.
3. Ranke believed that the statues might have been removed as a result of the fall or death of Hatshepsut, but this is quite uncertain (see "A Contemporary of Queen Hatshepsut," 29–30).
4. Randall-MacIver and Woolley, *Buhen*, 110

83 Funerary Equipment of Tuthmosis IV

Thebes, Valley of the Kings, tomb of
Tuthmosis IV
18th Dynasty, reign of Tuthmosis IV
(c. 1401–1391 B.C.)
Faience
Museum of Fine Arts, Boston,
gift of Theodore M. Davis

A *Throw Stick*
L: 26 cm (10¼ in.); W: 4.1 cm (1⅝ in.)
03.1086

B *Ankh*
23.5 x 12.8 cm (9¼ x 5 in.)
03.1089

C *Model Papyrus Roll*
L: 14 cm (5½ in.); diam: 2.8 cm (1¼ in.)
03.1095

D *Large Jar*
19 x 16 (diam) cm (7½ x 6¼ in.)
03.1103

E *Model* Hes *Vase*
11 x 4.2 cm (4¼ x 1⅝ in.)
03.1096

F *Shawabti*
H: 18.5 cm (7¼ in.)
03.1098

Theodore M. Davis, a successful New Yorker
who funded a number of excavations,
obtained a permit to work in the Valley
of the Kings from 1903 to 1912.[1] With Percy
Newberry and then with Howard Carter,
he made a number of extraordinary discoveries, including the intact tomb of Yuaa and
Thuiu, and the tombs of Horemheb, Siptah,
Hatshepsut, and Tuthmosis IV.[2]

The scraps of burial goods recovered
from the latter royal tombs hint at the splen-
dors later found in the tomb of Tutankhamun.
Many of the magical figures, the arms of the
throne, the elaborate fan and royal chariot,
all stripped of their gilding, are paralleled by
intact pieces in the tomb of Tutankhamun.[3]

In the tomb of Tuthmosis IV Davis
found numerous fragments of faience vases
and model tomb equipment left behind by
tomb robbers. These included model papyrus
rolls, ankhs, *hes* vases, and throw sticks,
as well as shawabtis and vessels. All these
objects were made of bright blue faience
with details added in a deep violet manganese pigment. Some are inscribed with the
prenomen (throne name) of Tuthmosis IV in
a cartouche surmounted by the epithet "Lord
of the Two Lands." The faience vessels were
probably made expressly for burial. PL

BIBLIOGRAPHY Theodore M. Davis, *The Tomb
of Thutmosis IV* (Westminster, England, 1904).

NOTES
1. John A. Wilson, *Signs and Wonders upon Pharaoh:
A History of American Egyptology* (Chicago: University of Chicago Press, 1964), 115–23.
2. C. Nicholas Reeves and John H. Taylor, *Howard
Carter before Tutankamun* (London: British Museum
Press, 1992), 71–77.
3. C. Nicholas Reeves, *The Complete Tutankhamun*
(London: Thames and Hudson, 1990), 41, 170–73,
188–87, 200–201.

84 Shawabti Figure of Hekanefer

Toshka East, tomb 1
New Kingdom, late 18th Dynasty,
c. 1330–1300 B.C.
Serpentine
19 x 6.3 cm (7½ x 2½ in.)
Peabody Museum of Natural History,
Yale University, 222265

During the intensive efforts to explore the archaeological remains of ancient Nubia before they were submerged by the creation of Lake Nasser behind the Aswan High Dam, the University of Pennsylvania–Yale University Expedition to Egypt investigated several sites, including Toshka. During much of the New Kingdom, from about 1460 to 1070 B.C., Toshka served as the center of one of three Egyptian-governed provinces in Lower Nubia.[1] There the expedition, headed by William K. Simpson, excavated three rock-cut tombs during its 1961–62 season. Tomb 1 belonged to Hekanefer, prince of Miam. This ancient Nubian prince is a fascinating historical figure who was undoubtedly a leader of his people as well as a faithful friend of Egypt, having received a portion of his education at the pharaoh's court, as reflected in the title "child of the nursery," which is proudly displayed in his tomb.[2]

In addition, Hekanefer can be located with some precision in the chronology of ancient Egypt since he appears in a painting in the Theban tomb of Huy, viceroy of Nubia during the reign of Tutankhamun (c. 1333–1323 B.C.).[3] In the painting Hekanefer leads a procession of Nubians and kneels in respect before the viceroy. He is dressed in a fashion that blends Egyptian costume with Nubian, with features traditionally associated with the depiction of Nubians, including a dark flesh color, full lips, and curly hair.[4]

These features are markedly absent in this shawabti discovered by the Pennsylvania-Yale expedition in the fill of a pit associated with Hekanefer's burial chamber.[5] Rather, the figure is carved in a style readily associated with Egyptian sculpture from the close of the 18th Dynasty. This led the excavators to suggest that the shawabti might be the product of a Theban workshop.[6] Such could certainly be the case, although skilled craftsmen must have resided in Nubia at this time.

The shawabti figure is crisply carved, with the facial features well worked. The arched eyebrows, heavy eyelids, prominent nose with slightly flaring nostrils, fleshy cheeks, and broad, firm jaw have been given considerable attention. Details are sharply incised, as are the hands, the agricultural implements they hold, and the seven surviving registers of hieroglyphic text, which give Hekanefer's name, his title as prince of Miam, and a slightly irregular version of chapter six of the Book of the Dead.[7]

The present volume contains two representations of Nubian nobles, each rendered in the prevailing Egyptian artistic style of their day. That of Amenemhat (cat. no. 82) is from the beginning of the 18th Dynasty, and this example is from the dynasty's close. Taken together, they are eloquent testimony to the close link between Egypt and Nubia, and to Egypt's cultural ascendancy throughout the 18th Dynasty. GS

BIBLIOGRAPHY William K. Simpson, *Heka-nefer and the Dynastic Material from Toshka and Arminna* (New Haven: Peabody Museum, Yale University; Philadelphia: University Museum, University of Pennsylvania, 1963), 14–15, pl. VIIa–c, fig. 10; Gerry D. Scott, III, *Ancient Egyptian Art at Yale*, exh. cat. (New Haven: Yale University Art Gallery, 1986), 110–11, no. 61 (with additional bibliography).

NOTES
1. David O'Connor, *Ancient Nubia: Egypt's Rival in Africa* (Philadelphia: University Museum, University of Pennsylvania, 1993), 60–61.
2. See Simpson, *Heka-nefer*, 5, 24–27.
3. For the identification of the owner of the Hekanefer tomb and shawabti figure with the tomb painting in the tomb of Huy, see ibid., 2. For the tomb of Huy (TT 40), see PM, vol. 1, pt. 1, 75–78. The relevant portion of the tomb painting is also reproduced in Simpson, *Heka-nefer,* as the frontispiece.
4. The Egyptian representation of ethnicity deserves further study.
5. Simpson, *Heka-nefer*, 14.
6. Ibid., 15.
7. See ibid., fig. 10, right.

(throne name) or nomen (family name) of Ay. Such deposits identified for perpetuity the king who founded the temple and magically protected the structure.

The use of faience name plaques in foundation deposits can be traced back to the Middle Kingdom.[1] From that time to the reigns of Hatshepsut and Tuthmosis III, small plaques, inscribed or molded with the royal name, were inserted into actual mud bricks, which, in turn, were left in the foundation pit. In later times larger faience plaques, generally eight to fourteen centimeters in length, were deposited directly in the foundation trenches.[2]

The foundation pits at the Ay temple were located at the sides of doors and at the corners of the building, much like modern cornerstones.[3] Clean sand, a symbol of purity, was poured into the hole and around the offerings.

TRANSLATION OF INSCRIBED TEXTS:
85A: King of Upper and Lower Egypt, Lord of the Two Lands, Kheperkheperure-ir-Ma'at, son of Re, the God's father, Ay, divine ruler of Thebes, beloved of Amun-Re, lord of heaven. 85B: Kheperkheperure-ir-Ma'at (prenomen of Ay).

ET

BIBLIOGRAPHY Harold Nelson and Uvo Hölscher, *Work in Western Thebes, 1931–33*, OIC 18 (Chicago: University of Chicago Press, 1934), 117–18, fig. 61; Uvo Hölscher, *The Excavation of Medinet Habu*, vol. 2, *The Temples of the Eighteenth Dynasty*, OIP 41 (Chicago: Oriental Institute, University of Chicago, 1939), 85–87, 91, fig. 73, pl. 54F; James M. Weinstein, "Foundation Deposits in Ancient Egypt" (Ph.D. diss., University of Pennsylvania, 1973), 219–21.

NOTES
1. Faience name plaques were first attested in the deposits of Amenemhat I and Senwosret I at Abydos and at the pyramid of Senwosret I at Lisht; see Weinstein, "Foundation Deposits," 46–47.
2. Ibid., 126–33, 421–22.
3. See ibid., 220, no. 227, for Weinstein's reconsideration of the placement of the deposits, which Hölscher thought were at the sides of ramps but might be at the sides of doors.

85 Name Plaques

Medinet Habu, mortuary temple of Ay
18th Dynasty, reign of Ay
(c. 1323–1319 B.C.)
Faience
The Oriental Institute,
University of Chicago

A H: 2.6 cm (1 in.); L: 15.5 cm (6⅛ in.);
w: 7.6 cm (3 in.)
14710
B H: 3.3 cm (1¼ in.); L: 10 cm (4 in.);
w: 6 cm (2⅜ in.)
14706

The location of the mortuary temple of King Ay was unknown until 1930, when the Oriental Institute dug into the northwest corner of the mound to the north of the temple of Ramesses III at Medinet Habu. That trench revealed mud bricks stamped with the cartouche of King Ay.

Little of the temple remained. But Uvo Hölscher, field director of the excavation, painstakingly traced the foundation trenches of the mud-brick and stone walls to reconstruct the plan. In the course of the work nine foundation deposits were discovered. They contained pottery, including small baked clay dishes inscribed with hieratic texts and filled with food offerings, thousands of small faience amulets in the form of food offerings and protective signs, tools and model tools of copper and bronze, stone hand mills, beads, and faience plaques with the prenomen

86 Ostracon with Selket and Taweret

Medinet Habu, debris of the mortuary
temple of Ay and Horemheb
Late 18th Dynasty, reign of Ay or
Horemheb (c. 1323–1307 B.C.)
Limestone, pigment
7.3 x 8.5 x 3 cm (2⅞ x 3⅜ x 1⅛ in.)
The Oriental Institute,
University of Chicago, 15595

This ostracon, bearing a sketch of a stela, is decorated with a scene of two deities associated with birth. To the right is a scorpion, the symbol of the goddess Selket, "she who allows the throat to breath," a reference to her ability to guard against the venom of a scorpion's sting. Here Selket has been anthropomorphized by the addition of human arms and hands. To the left is the goddess Taweret, a fantastic combination of hippopotamus, crocodile, and lion, who was responsible for the purification of the spirit (*ka*) after birth or rebirth[1] and for the protection of children. Both figures are shown inside a shrine, perhaps an indication of a birth arbor. This small stela may have been a votive offering to the two deities to ensure safe birth.

Because the stela was excavated from a disturbed archaeological context in the ruins of the mortuary temple of Ay and Horemheb, the date of its manufacture can only be approximated. Although a small, informal piece, the painting was carefully executed in two stages. The draft of the design in red pigment is still visible under the black outline and final colorful pigments. ET

NOTES
1. Bernard Bruyère, *Rapport sur les fouilles de Deir el Médineh 1935–40*, pt. 3 (Cairo: IFAO, 1952), 82.

87 Doorjamb with
King Merneptah Smiting
Foreigners
Memphis, palace of Merneptah
19th Dynasty, reign of Merneptah
(c. 1224–1214 B.C.)
Limestone
104.4 x 56 cm (41⅛ x 22 in.)
The University of Pennsylvania
Museum of Archaeology
and Anthropology, E17527

Reconstruction of interior of palace of Merneptah. Watercolor by Mary Louise Baker, 1920, University of Pennsylvania Museum.

Clarence S. Fisher of the University of Pennsylvania conducted archaeological excavations at the ancient site of Memphis from 1915 to 1923. There he discovered an important, though still largely unpublished, structure belonging to the fourteenth son and ultimate successor of Ramesses II, Merneptah. Usually termed a palace, the structure was burned at a relatively early date, sealing off much archaeological data.[1] The palace most likely was closely connected with the religious structures in the area, and Fisher recovered a number of votive objects of Ramesside date at the site (see cat. nos. 88, 89).

This limestone doorjamb displays an image as old as dynastic Egypt, the triumphant pharaoh smiting his enemies. The image can be traced back to the very foundation of the ancient Egyptian state and that great commemorative monument, the Narmer Palette. Here King Merneptah is shown moving forward. He wears the double crown of Upper and Lower Egypt, the royal beard, the *shendyt* kilt, sandals, and bull's tail associated with deities and the king. His jewelry consists of a broad collar and elaborate girdle, bracelets, and armlets. In his near hand he raises his weapon, a combination mace and axe, to dispatch two supplicating Asiatics, whom he holds by their hair. To further seal the fate of these two, the king's pet feline, perhaps a lioness and therefore an embodiment of the lion goddess Sekhmet, springs forward to maul the fallen foe.

Before the king are two cartouches of Merneptah and the epithets "lord of the thrones of the Two Lands (Egypt)" and "lord of diadems." Written horizontally beneath the cartouches is the phrase "given life and dominion like Re." Between the king's head and his raised arm is the phrase "Horus, strong of arm." Behind him is an interesting combination of hieroglyphs and other images. At the top the royal falcon god Horus wears twin plumes; behind him a sun disk is encircled by a uraeus. The Horus falcon is perched on a rectangle, not unlike a palace façade, within which is written, "The lord of every festival, like Atum." At the base of the rectangle two human arms seem to emerge from a staff, suggesting that the whole should be seen as a sort of sacred standard. The near arm holds an ankh (emblem of life) and a *ma'at* feather (symbolizing righteousness),

while the far arm holds its own standard, a divine head with beard and uraeus, surmounted by the rebus *ka-nesut* (king's *ka*, or spirit). The entire scene appears beneath an extended *pt* sign (for heaven), and the remains of two vertical columns of hieroglyphic text read "[king Mernept]ah, given all life" and "[king Mernept]ah, forever." GS

BIBLIOGRAPHY *Man and Animals*, exh. cat. (Philadelphia: University Museum, University of Pennsylvania, 1984), 63 (ill.); Lee Horne, ed., *Introduction to the Collections of the University Museum* (Philadelphia: University Museum, University of Pennsylvania, 1985), 24 (ill.), no. 14.

NOTES
1. David O'Connor and David Silverman, "The University Museum in Egypt," *Expedition* 21 (Winter 1979): 26.

88 Fragment of an Ex-Voto to Ptah

Memphis

19th Dynasty (c. 1307–1196 B.C.)

Limestone

23 x 21 x 8 cm (9 x 8¼ x 3⅛ in.)

The University of Pennsylvania Museum of Archaeology
and Anthropology, E13579

Discovered by the University of Pennsylvania's Eckley B. Coxe Jr.
Expedition in 1915, this fragment preserves the upper portion
of a stela dedicated to the creator god Ptah of Memphis. The deity is
seated; behind him once stood his consort, the lioness-headed goddess
of war and vengeance, Sekhmet. Only her hand and staff remain.
Before Ptah is a brief hieroglyphic inscription, "He who gives life to
the Two Lands," while between Ptah and Sekhmet are the brief hieroglyphic labels, "Sekhmet the mighty" and "Ptah, lord of heaven."

Although only partially preserved, Ptah is shown with his usual
mummiform body, from which his hands emerge to grasp his divine
scepter. At the top of the scepter the hieroglyphs for life, dominion,
and stability appear. Ptah wears bracelets on both wrists, a broad
collar, and a necklace counterpoise. The god's eye, eyebrow, ear, lips,
and beard strap are each carefully indicated, and he displays his usual
close-cropped hair (or close-fitting cap) and divine beard.

The number of votive stelae recovered by the expedition at Memphis suggest that the area once functioned, at least in part, as a votive
shrine. This fragment, carved in raised relief, was part of a stela probably
given to the god as a plea for divine aid or as a token of thanks. GS

89 Ex-Voto to Ptah

Memphis

19th Dynasty (c. 1307–1196 B.C.)

Limestone, pigment

27 x 18 cm (10⅝ x 7⅛ in.)

The University of Pennsylvania Museum of Archaeology
and Anthropology, E13632

This rather crude, round-topped stela bears incised figures of Ptah and
Nefertem, both deities associated with ancient Memphis. Ptah is mummiform and wears a broad collar, necklace counterpoise, mummy tabs,
and close-cropped hair or tight-fitting cap. His hands emerge from the
mummiform body to grasp his divine scepter, which also appears to
incorporate the ankh. Remains of red paint are preserved on both the
figure of Ptah and his scepter, and traces of light blue appear on the
beard and strap, with a darker hue on the head. A curved line above
Ptah's head suggests that the figure might have been conceived as
standing in a shrine or pavilion.

The second deity, Nefertem, wears a knee-length kilt and strides
forward. In his far hand he holds a double-plumed scepter; an ankh is
in his near hand. He wears a traditional long wig, a distinctive crown,
a broad collar, and a breast covering. Like the figure of Ptah, that of
Nefertem preserves traces of red pigment on the body and light blue on
the beard.

The unsophisticated nature of the carving probably indicates that
the stela is an ancient Egyptian example of "folk art," which mimics
the courtly style for the benefit of a much humbler clientele. It was discovered by Clarence S. Fisher's expedition to Memphis in 1919. GS

90 Bakenwerel, Chief of Police in Western Thebes

Medinet Habu, northwest corner of
the Small Temple
Late 20th Dynasty, c. 1127 B.C.
Brown granite
28.7 x 14.6 x 17 cm
(11¼ x 5¾ x 6¾ in.)
The Oriental Institute,
University of Chicago, 14663

This statue represents a man named Bakenwerel, the chief of police of western Thebes at the end of the 20th Dynasty. He sits on a rounded cushion, his legs drawn up before him, and wears the elaborately pleated male dress of the late New Kingdom, with mid-length pleated sleeves. The center section of his kilt forms a raised panel before his legs. His wig is a row of curls reaching his shoulders. In his right hand he holds a head of lettuce, a symbol of rebirth.

The identity of the statue is established by inscriptions on the front and back: "Chief of the Medjay" (front); "Chief of the Medjay in the west of Thebes, Bakenwerel, justified" (back). During the New Kingdom a police corps known as the Medjay, initially Nubian, but later made up of Egyptians, maintained security on the west bank of the Nile. Throughout most of this period two chiefs codirected the Medjay and reported directly to the vizier or to the First Prophet of Amun.

Bakenwerel is known from the Papyrus Abbott, in which he is mentioned as a member of a commission sent to investigate the robbery of royal tombs in the sixteenth year of the reign of Ramesses IX.[1] ET

NOTES
1. Papyrus Abbott (1.10), in T. Eric Peet, *The Great Tomb Robberies of the Twentieth Egyptian Dynasty* (Oxford: Clarendon Press, 1930), 37.

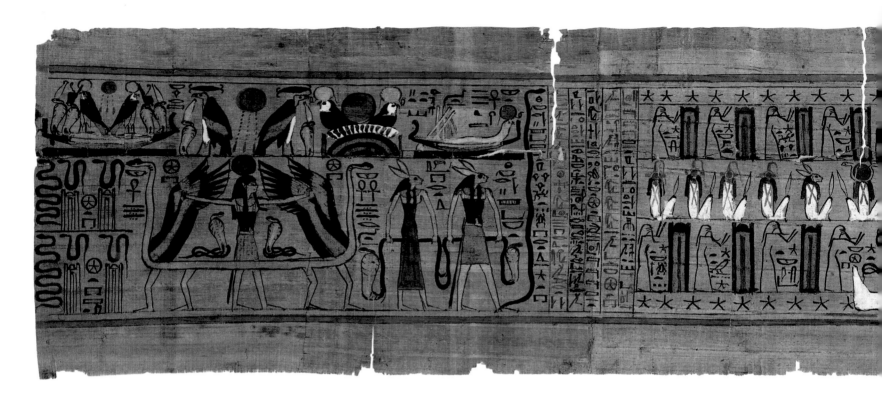

91 Netherworld Papyrus
Deir el-Bahri, tomb 60, pit 4
21st Dynasty, c. 1000–945 B.C.
Papyrus, ink, paint
24 x 119.5 cm (9½ x 47 in.)
The Metropolitan Museum of Art,
Rogers Fund, 1925, 25.3.31

Gautsoshen was a Theban housewife and a singer in temple ceremonies honoring Amun-Re, king of the gods. Her burial in a pit tomb in the Theban necropolis was rather modest but included two beautiful examples of illustrated funerary papyri of the late 21st Dynasty.

The more colorful of the two is this papyrus containing three scenes depicting the netherworld to which Gautsoshen's spirit traveled at night with the sun. On the right, Gautsoshen stands before the mummified figure of Osiris, king of the netherworld, and

Selket, one of four goddesses who protect the mummy. On the left, the sun descends into the netherworld, where it will meet the mummified body of Osiris. The other figures in this scene are denizens of the netherworld; the twin lions represent the two horizons in which the sun sets and rises, and the sun itself appears between them. The final scene, in two registers, shows various aspects of the sun's journey through the netherworld. The text, in four vertical columns, explains the purpose of the papyrus: "May this great god, ruler of the west . . . cause the secret gates of the necropolis to open to Gautsoshen . . . so that she may come forth as she wishes." JA

BIBLIOGRAPHY Herbert E. Winlock, "The Egyptian Expedition, 1924–1925," *BMMA* 21 (March 1926): pt. 2, 24, 28–31; N. Rambova, ed., *Mythological Papyri*, trans. Alexandre Piankoff, Bollingen Series 40, 3 (New York: Pantheon, 1957), frontispiece, 181–85, pl. 24; William C. Hayes, *The Scepter of Egypt,* vol. 2, *The Hyksos Period and the New Kingdom, 1675–1080 B.C.* (New York: MMA, 1959), 228; Siegfried Schott, *Zum Weltbild der Jenseitsführer des Neuen Reiches,* Nachrichten der Akademie der Wissenschaften in Göttingen, Philologische-historische Klasse (Göttingen: Vandenhoek und Ruprecht, 1965), no. 11, 188; Andrzej Niwinski, *Studies on the Illustrated Funerary Papyri of the 11th and 10th Centuries B.C.,* Orbis Biblicus et Orientalis 86 (Freiburg: Universitätsverlag, 1989), 346.

92 Lintel

Memphis, building of Ankhefenmut
21st Dynasty, reign of Siamun
(c. 978–959 B.C.)
Limestone, pigment
58.9 x 93 x 18.8 cm (23¼ x 36⅝ x 7⅜ in.)
The Carnegie Museum of
Natural History, 3755-1b

This fragment of a doorway lintel depicts a priest worshiping before King Siamun, represented by his inscribed name and epithets "strong bull" and "beloved (of the goddess) Ma'at." The priest is identified by a hieroglyphic text inscribed above his upraised hand as "Ankhefenmut, son of Hatiay."[1] Behind the figure three columns of inscription continue his titles, including "overseer of the secrets in the Memphis temple, scribe of the temple of the estate of Ptah, and prophet of Ptah."[2] The priest kneels, holding a delicately carved ostrich feather fan in his left hand; his right hand is raised in adoration of Siamun. Ankhefenmut's long kilt and sash billow forward as he kneels, with one fringed end of the sash falling behind his right foot.[3]

Carved from limestone to adorn one of several entrances to a mud-brick building dating to the reign of this little-known pharaoh, the relief was executed with attention to detail, apparent in the fan, sandals, and carefully rendered features of the priest.

Although much of ancient Memphis has not been systematically excavated due to flooding and the encroachment of the modern village of Mit Rahina, the western section of the main temple complex was unearthed by W. M. Flinders Petrie for the British School of Archaeology in Egypt between 1908 and 1913. Although Petrie attributed the structure containing the lintel to King Siamun,[4] others have identified Ankhefenmut as the donor of the building, based on his repeated depictions and his dedicatory inscription of the building to "Amun, lord of lapis-lazuli."[5]

The other half of the lintel, now in the Carnegie Museum of Natural History, repeats the worship scene in roughly mirror image. Other lintels from this 21st Dynasty building are now in museum collections in London, Cairo, Manchester, Copenhagen, and Philadelphia.[6] NT

BIBLIOGRAPHY "Pharaoh's Door Lintel Comes to Pittsburgh," *Pittsburgh Gazette*, 14 April 1923; Diana Craig Patch, *Reflections of Greatness: Ancient Egypt at the Carnegie Museum of Natural History*, exh. cat. (Pittsburgh: Carnegie Museum of Natural History, 1990), 77–78.

NOTES
1. See Patch, *Reflections of Greatness*, 77–78, for transliteration and translation of name and titles from the left portion of the lintel (3755-1a).
2. Ibid.
3. For a clear depiction of an arching kilt on a seated figure, see Sue D'Auria, Peter Lacovara, and Catharine Roehrig, *Mummies and Magic: The Funerary Arts of Ancient Egypt*, exh. cat. (Boston: MFA, 1988), 159, fig. 110.
4. W. M. Flinders Petrie, *Memphis I* (London: British School of Archaeology, 1909), 12–13, pls. 30, 31; and idem, *The Palace of Apries (Memphis II)* (London: British School of Archaeology, 1909), 14–15, pl. 24.
5. Kenneth A. Kitchen, *The Third Intermediate Period in Egypt (1100–650 B.C.)* (Warminster: Aris and Phillips, 1973), 279, nn. 214–16; Karol Myśliwiec, *Royal Portraiture of the Dynasties XXI–XXX* (Mainz: Philipp von Zabern, 1988), 12–13.
6. London, British Museum 1470; Cairo, Egyptian Museum JE 40033; Manchester Museum 4933; Copenhagen, Ny Carlsberg Glyptotek AEIN.1012; Philadelphia, University of Pennsylvania Museum of Archaeology and Anthropology E14349.

93 Hearing Ear Stela

Medinet Habu, in debris,
south of the Ramesside Pool
22d to 26th Dynasty (c. 945–525 B.C.)
Limestone, pigment
8 x 5.7 x 2.1 cm (3⅛ x 2¼ x ⅞ in.)
The Oriental Institute,
University of Chicago, 16718

Stelae decorated with ears, as well as models of ears in faience or metal, have been recovered from many sites in Egypt, including Thebes (Medinet Habu, Deir el-Bahri), Faras, and, in the Sinai, at Serabit el-Khadem.[1] Brief inscriptions on some examples refer to a god who "hears petitions," confirming that the ears are those of a god to whom prayers are directed on behalf of a petitioner. Although supplicants appealed to several gods, and even deceased kings and queens, Ptah was most commonly invoked.[2] These small stelae, even when dedicated to a single god, often have multiple pairs of ears, perhaps an allusion to the superhuman effectiveness of the god's hearing.

The belief that individuals could solicit divine help is attested not only by small artifacts but also by shrines, usually on the back exterior walls of temples. Such shrines were referred to as "places of hearing petitions."

This tradition continued throughout Egyptian history, as indicated by the decoration on the back wall of the Ptolemaic period temple at Kom Ombo (c. 204 B.C.), which is adorned with two ears and a figure of the goddess Ma'at.

This example was discovered not in the temple at Medinet Habu but among the ruins of houses from the Third Intermediate Period, suggesting that it was used as part of the religion of common people and not the official temple cult. Since ear stelae date to as early as the mid-18th Dynasty,[3] such artifacts cannot be used as evidence for the rise of personal piety in the Ramesside period. ET

NOTES
1. Geraldine Pinch, *Votive Offerings to Hathor* (Oxford: Griffith Institute, Ashmolean Museum, 1993), 246–50, 259, pls. 2, 6, 8, 14, 55, 56.
2. Ibid., 249, 260–64.
3. Ibid., 249.

94 Ostraca

Abydos
Late New Kingdom to Third
Intermediate Period, 19th to 25th
Dynasty, c. 1307–664 B.C.
Ceramic
The University of Pennsylvania
Museum of Archaeology
and Anthropology

A *Sherd with Osiris*
12.2 x 18 cm (4¾ x 7⅛ in.)
69-29-563

B *Sherd with Osiris and Two Cobras*
11 x 20 cm (4⅜ x 7⅞ in.)
69-29-568

C *Sherd with Male Deity*
13 x 11 cm (5⅛ x 4⅛ in.)
69-29-559

D *Sherd with Two Cobras*
6 x 10.5 cm (2⅛ x 4⅛ in.)
69-29-615

During the 1967 season of the University of Pennsylvania–Yale University Expedition to Egypt, some fifty of these rather enigmatic sherds were discovered. They all had once belonged to red or brown ware bowls of roughly the same shape. Drawings in black or white pigment (ink?) appeared on the inner surface.[1] The excavator reported that the group showed "various gods, sometimes standing on boats and sometimes with their names written in hieroglyphics. Some sherds from similar bowls had a single line of hieratic text."[2]

The first example (cat. no. 94A) shows Osiris depicted in white. He wears the white crown, divine beard, broad collar, necklace counterpoise, and mummy tabs, and holds a divine *was* scepter. A single vertical line of hieroglyphs before the god reads, "Osiris, foremost of the Westerners," and once might have been completed by the further epithet, "the Lord of Abydos," as in cat. no. 94D.

The second (cat. no. 94B) depicts a mummiform Osiris, drawn in black, standing on two cobras, who raise their heads. The god wears the *atef* crown, a broad collar and necklace counterpoise, mummy tabs, and a divine beard. His hands clutch the divine *was* scepter as well as the regal crook and flail.

A third decorated sherd (cat. no. 94C) displays a well-drawn male deity (perhaps Amun?) rendered in black. The god wears a long divine beard, a full wig, armlets, bracelets, a sleeveless top, and a short kilt with pleated apron panel. He holds an ankh in his near hand.

The last example (cat. no. 94D) shows the rearing heads of two cobras in black. Above them appear the hieroglyphs for "the lord of Abydos." A vertical line ends in a partial ellipse behind the serpents. This, when taken with another partially preserved vertical line at the far left of the fragment, suggests that the two serpents rear up in a protective gesture before the god Osiris, who holds his divine *was* scepter in front of him. He was probably once more fully identified by the label text as "Osiris, lord of Abydos," written in a single vertical column of hieroglyphs. The original composition was no doubt similar to that of cat. no. 94B.

As a group, the objects are unusual and probably functioned in some votive manner. Although it cannot be demonstrated with any degree of certainty, the bowls presumably once contained some form of offering dedicated to Osiris and other deities. Whether they were broken as part of the offering ritual or were simply dedicated to the god and broken by later circumstance is unknown. At present these bowls seem to be unique to the site of Abydos, where some were also recovered by the early collector Giovanni Anastasi (1780–1857).[3] GS

BIBLIOGRAPHY David O'Connor, "Abydos: A Preliminary Report of the Pennsylvania–Yale Expedition, 1967," *Expedition* 10 (Fall 1967): 16–17; idem, "Pennsylvania-Yale Expedition to Egypt I: Abydos 1967," *ARCE Newsletter* 63 (October 1967): 3; idem "The Present, Abydos: The University Museum–Yale University Expedition," *Expedition* 21 (Winter 1979): 46–47.

NOTES
1. O'Connor, "Abydos: A Preliminary Report," 16.
2. Ibid.
3. O'Connor, "The Present, Abydos," 47.

95 Animal Figurines

Abydos
Late New Kingdom to Third
Intermediate Period, 19th to 25th
Dynasty (c. 1307–664 B.C.)
Ceramic
The University of Pennsylvania
Museum of Archaeology
and Anthropology

A *Cobra*
   H: 7.5 cm (3 in.)
   69-29-881
B *Head of a Ram*
   H: 6.4 cm (2½ in.)
   69-29-855

These two somewhat curious objects are almost certainly votive objects connected with local piety at Abydos. Fashioned from simple mud, each of these animal shapes is associated with several ancient Egyptian deities. The first example is formed as a coiled cobra, which rears its head. The serpent's eyes and tongue are articulated, the latter made separately and attached, and the mouth is incised. Also incised is a triangular area beneath the head at the jowl. A single vertical line of incised hieroglyphic text is inscribed down the front of the snake's throat, but it has been damaged.

The second example represents a ram's head. The eyes, nose, and mouth are each articulated, as are the horns and ears. The eyeballs were probably added separately, and the mouth was rendered by a simple incised line. Like the bowl fragments in the exhibition (cat. no. 94), these objects so far appear to be unique to Abydos.[1] GS

BIBLIOGRAPHY David O'Connor, "Abydos: A Preliminary Report of the Pennsylvania-Yale Expedition, 1967," *Expedition* 10 (Fall 1967): 16; idem, "Pennsylvania-Yale Expedition to Egypt I: Abydos 1967," *ARCE Newsletter* 63 (October 1967): 3.

NOTES
1. O'Connor, "Pennsylvania-Yale Expedition," 3.

Amunirdis, daughter of the Nubian pharaoh Kashta, held the title God's Wife of Amun. In that capacity she was entrusted with the administration of Egypt on behalf of her father, who lived at the Nubian capital, Napata. Amunirdis and perhaps five other Nubian women, who held the same office in Thebes, were buried in a series of tomb chapels located to the east of the first pylon of the Ramesses III temple at Medinet Habu. The chapels were robbed in antiquity. Georges Daressy partially cleared them in 1895, and in 1928–29 the Oriental Institute again excavated them. In the course of this later work, other funerary equipment, originally from the tomb chapels, was recovered from throughout the temple area, where it had been scattered by ancient tomb robbers.

In a side room of the burial chamber of Amunirdis, excavators found approximately thirty large pottery jars, which contained black matter, fragments of papyrus, and smaller plates, jars, and cups—presumably remains from the embalming of Amunirdis. The chamber also contained corners of a metal bedstead that may have been used in the preparation of the mummy. Many objects inscribed for Amunirdis and other God's Wives, including this shawabti, were found in a stone-lined basin about fifty meters from the chamber, just to the south of the Small Temple. ET

BIBLIOGRAPHY Uvo Hölscher, *The Excavation of Medinet Habu*, vol. 2, *The Temples of the Eighteenth Dynasty*, OIP 41 (Chicago: University of Chicago Press, 1939), 39–40; idem, *The Excavation of Medinet Habu*, vol. 5, *Post-Ramessid Remains*, OIP 66 (Chicago: University of Chicago Press, 1954), 23.

96 Shawabti of Amunirdis

Medinet Habu, basin to the south
of the 18th Dynasty Temple
25th Dynasty, reign of Kashta
(c. 770–750 B.C.)
Serpentine, pigment
H: 22.2 cm (8¾ in.)
The Oriental Institute,
University of Chicago, 14198

97 Miniature Situla

El-Kurru, tomb of Queen Tabiry
(tomb KU53)
Napatan period, c. 710 B.C.
Amethystine quartz
3.5 x 2.4 (diam) cm (1⅜ x 1 in.)
Museum of Fine Arts, Boston, 21.306

A model situla of pale amethystine quartz was excavated by George A. Reisner from the royal cemetery at el-Kurru, burial site of the ancestral and early Napatan rulers. It later appeared in the site report as from KU53, the tomb of Queen Tabiry, one of the wives of Piye.[1] Many fine amulets were recovered from this plundered burial, including several of unusual stones.[2]

The vessel, missing its wire handle and bored through the neck for suspension, was erroneously published as rose quartz.[3] It falls into that category of miniature vessels of semi-precious stone that appear in the Nile Valley as early as the late Predynastic Period.[4] Smaller yet are those pendants of colored stone representing globular and pointed vessels.[5]

The situla appears in tribute scenes as well as private tombs of the Egyptian 18th Dynasty.[6] In the latter the vessels are linked with the milk ritual and have the characteristic curved metal handle whose ends pass through two suspension hoops attached to the rim. Once through the hoops, the ends of the handle are sharply bent and project outward. Although the form of the body of the container changed over time, the handle and its suspension apparatus remained relatively constant.

Although representations of situlae appear on Egyptian mortuary stelae of the Third Intermediate Period, actual examples are absent from the archaeological record. In her topological analysis of situlae, Miriam

Lichtheim describes a vessel "with narrow neck, distinct shoulder, and flat or slightly rounded base" as a variant of the common Late Period type.[7] The two miniature vessels from el-Kurru point to a 25th Dynasty date for this form. The date may be earlier if two pendants also found in KU53 were heirlooms. It is not known whether these objects were imported or made in Nubia, but it is clear that in the Napatan state, milk, which was linked to the notions of sustenance, revitalization, and rebirth, performed a vital function.[8] A gilded silver pendant of a queen suckled by a goddess from the burial of another of Piye's wives (MFA 24.928)[9] and the spouted silver milk vessel inscribed for Queen Khensa from KU4[10] demonstrate the privileged status these royal Kushite women held. Hence, the model situla, with its royal connotations and amuletic properties, was a fitting jewel for a wife of Piye. YM

NOTES

1. In the photographic plate this object is placed among the finds from KU53 with a question mark. The text notes: "Not registered. Rose quartz miniature vase. Height 3.5 cm. Not located in records, but perhaps from KU 53." Perhaps the presence of another model situla of mottled red and green agate (MFA 24.651) led Dunham to assign this amuletic pendant to KU53. See Dows Dunham, *The Royal Cemeteries of Kush*, vol. 1, *El Kurru* (Cambridge: Harvard University Press, 1950), 88, pl. 59c.

2. Examples include a finely sculpted marble cat with pierced ears (MFA 21.305) and a brown jasper falcon with double crown (19-3-1338).

3. The vessel was recently examined by Richard Newman of the Research Lab, Museum of Fine Arts, Boston, who detected small amounts of ferric iron and an absence of titanium, the metallic element responsible for the pink hue associated with rose quartz, a mineral not found along the Nile Valley.

4. A unprovenanced amethyst vase with sheet-gold rim now in Berlin is considered to be Gerzean in date. See J. C. Payne, "An Early Amethyst Vase," *JEA* 60 (1974): 79–81. For an Early Dynastic amethystine quartz bowl (Oxford, Ashmolean Museum E135), see Emile Amelineau, *Les nouvelles fouilles d'Abydos, 1896–1897*, vol. 2 (Paris: E. Leroux, 1902), 254, pl. 21.

5. For a pair of Early Dynastic vase-shaped pendants, see Henri Frankfort, "The Cemeteries of Abydos: Work of the Season, 1925–26," *JEA* 16 (1930): 215, pl. 2. For globular pendants of the same date, see Cecil M. Firth, *Archaeological Survey of Nubia, 1908–1909* (Cairo: National Printing Department, 1912), pl. 37a.

6. Miriam Lichtheim, "Oriental Institute Museum Notes—Situla No. 11395 and Some Remarks on Egyptian Situlae," *JNES* 6 (April 1947): 171.

7. Ibid., 174, pl. IV, no. 14.

8. Janice Yellin, "Egyptian Religion and the Formation of the Napatan State," paper delivered at the International Nubian Studies Conference, Lille, France, 1994.

9. See Dunham, *El Kurru*, 82, pl. 55.

10. Ibid., 32, pl. 64c/2.

98 Mut Pendant

El-Kurru, tomb of Queen
Nefrukekashta (ku52)
25th Dynasty, late 8th century B.C.
Cast silver
10.8 x 2 x 2.2 cm (4¼ x ¾ x ⅞ in.)
Museum of Fine Arts, Boston, 21.322

Large gold and silver pendants depicting deities were popular items of adornment during the Third Intermediate Period[1] and remained in style in Nubia throughout the Napatan and Meroitic periods. George A. Reisner recovered three such pendants, made of silver and representing goddesses, from the plundered burial of Queen Nefrukekashta, a wife of Piye.[2] The largest and most dramatic is a small sculpture depicting the goddess Mut.[3]

The goddess is shown wearing a plain, close-fitting dress; a tripartite wig; and the double crown representing Upper and Lower Egypt, with a uraeus surmounted by a sun disk and horns. The surface of the crown of Lower Egypt is enhanced by multiple rows of punctate impressions. Mut's jewels include a broad collar, armbands, wristlets, and anklets bordering the hemline. A strong midline axis is accentuated by arms that closely approximate the body. The left foot is slightly advanced.

The pendant is formed primarily of cast silver. A copper-enriched solder secures the nearly square silver sheet base, the double 1.5 millimeter silver wire suspension hoops at the rear of the double crown, and the coil of the crown of Lower Egypt. YM

BIBLIOGRAPHY Dows Dunham, *The Royal Cemeteries of Kush*, vol. 1, *El Kurru* (Cambridge: Harvard University Press, 1950), 81–85, pls. 60A–B, 70B.

NOTES
1. H. Stierlin and Christiane Ziegler, *Tanis: Vergessene Schätze der Pharaoen* (Munich: Hirmer, 1987), pls. 61, 62.
2. Dunham, *El Kurru*, 81–85.
3. Ibid., 81, pl. 60A–B.

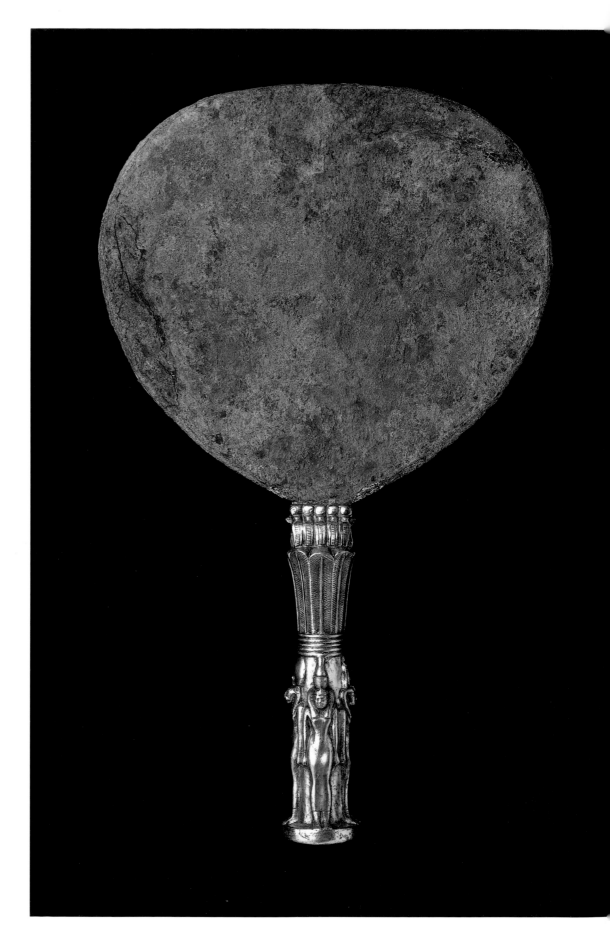

99 Mirror of Shabako

El-Kurru, pyramid of Shabako (KU15)
25th Dynasty, reign of Shabako
(c. 712–698 B.C.)
Bronze mirror, gilded silver handle
H: 32.9 cm (12⅞ in.)
Handle: H: 14.3 cm (5⅝ in.)
Museum of Fine Arts, Boston, 21.318

An item of beauty and function, the mirror also had highly symbolic religious and funerary meaning. Its ability to re-create life by reflecting one's image linked the mirror with rebirth or regeneration.[1] Its round shape and light-reflecting surface gave it obvious solar and lunar symbolism.[2] The religious significance of mirrors in Nubia is evident in their placement in royal burials from the time of the Kerma tumuli[3] and throughout the Napatan and Meroitic periods.

At el-Kurru George A. Reisner excavated the burials of five of the Nubian kings of Egypt as well as those of many of their ancestors and relatives. Among the scant remains left in Shabako's pyramid, he found this bronze mirror with gilded silver handle on the floor, near the northeast corner of chamber B.[4]

The thick bronze disk on Shabako's mirror is not perfectly round; it is flattened, like the sun nearing the horizon. The finely modeled handle is in the form of a palm column; individual palm fronds encircle its top. Above this a square abacus is surrounded by a frieze of uraei crowned with sun disks.[5] The base of the handle flares out into a disk incised on the bottom with a sixteen-petal rosette design.[6]

The disk serves as a base for four standing female figures, executed in high relief, which encircle the handle.[7] The figures, one lion-headed and three human, are similarly clad in close-fitting sheaths, and they wear anklets and bracelets summarily indicated by two parallel lines. Their slender bodies are not unlike those found in depictions of Egyptian goddesses, but the faces are executed in the indigenous Kushite style.[8]

The lion-headed goddess crowned with a large sun disk and uraeus is likely Hathor-Tefnut, a daughter of Re. She stands opposite a figure representing the queen, or God's Wife, crowned with a distinctive set of small horns and a sun disk overlaying two tall

falcon feathers.[9] The other two figures, in the more important positions, aligned with the front and back faces of the disk, are Hathor, crowned with a sun disk with horns, and Mut,[10] with her characteristic double crown. In fact, the mirror handle displays four images of the same goddess, Hathor. Each figure shares the aspect of Hathor as divine mother of the god.[11] Kings, as the sons of Amun, were considered to be born of Mut, which gave her the status of the king's earthly mother.[12] As the wife of Amun, the God's Wife also shared the earthly mother role.[13]

Two other Nubian mirrors with sculpted handles, each with four figures modeled in the round in high relief, have been found in royal tombs. One belonged to King Amaninatakelebte (r. 538–519 B.C., MFA 21.338),[14] and the other to King Nastasen (r. 335–315 B.C., Khartoum, Sudan National Museum 1374). The mirror of Amaninatakelebte has a similar palm column handle with four male figures: the king, Amun-Re, and two hawk-headed figures, likely representing two forms of the solar god.[15] The mirror of Nastasen has two male and two female figures: Amun-Re, a falcon-headed solar god, Mut, and Hathor.[16]

In Egyptian mirror offering scenes described by Constance Husson, the king offers mirrors to aspects of Hathor as well as to various forms of the solar god.[17] While Egyptian religious beliefs cannot be indiscriminately superimposed onto Nubian iconography, it seems likely that the Nubian images are related to Hathor and the solar god, both of whom have long been associated with the mirror. This grouping of rulers and deities elevates mirrors in Nubia to a status unmatched in Egypt. JH

BIBLIOGRAPHY Günther Roeder, *Ägyptische Bronzewerke* (Glückstadt: J. J. Augustin, 1937), fig. 652 b3, pl. 79f.; Dows Dunham, *The Royal Cemeteries of Kush*, vol. 1, *El Kurru* (Cambridge: Harvard University Press, 1950), 57, pl. LXII.

NOTES
1. Christine Lilyquist, "Mirrors," in *Egypt's Golden Age: The Art of Living in the New Kingdom, 1558–1085 B.C.*, exh. cat., ed. Edward Brovarski, Susan Doll, and Rita Freed (Boston: MFA, 1982), 184; mirrors have been found wrapped in the bandages of the deceased (idem, *Ancient Egyptian Mirrors: From the Earliest Times through the Middle Kingdom*, Münchner ägyptologische Seminar 27 [Berlin: Deutscher Kunstverlag, 1979], 42, n. 468).
2. C. Müller, "Spiegel," in *LÄ*, vol. 5 (1984), 8, col. 1148; for solar and lunar significance in religious offerings, see Constance Husson, *L'offerand du miroir dans les temples égyptiens de l'époque gréco-romain* (Lyon: Audin, 1977), chaps. 2, 3.
3. Lilyquist, *Ancient Egyptian Mirrors*, 46, 141–44, figs. 69, 82–89.
4. Dunham, *El Kurru*, 57, pl. XVI.C; the mirror is unregistered and was given no field number.
5. Three other royal Nubian mirrors also have the square abacus: two in Boston (MFA 24.961 [Meroe], 21.338 [Amaninatakelebte]) and one in Khartoum (Sudan National Museum 1374 [Nastasen]).
6. The same type of pattern is seen on the base of the gold cylinders found in King Aspelta's tomb.
7. Dunham, *El Kurru*, 57, pl. LXII. The figures were intended to be viewed in an upright position, yet such mirrors cannot stand unsupported. P. Munro notes a series of ten mirrors, found at Memphis and identified as Kushite, which have scenes etched on them of a female making offerings before the goddess Mut ("Eine Gruppe spätägyptischer Bronzespiegel," *ZÄS* 95 [1969]: pls. I–VIII). Each is on a rectangular stand. It is conceivable that the mirrors' sculpted handles once had some type of base to support them, possibly of wood.
8. This figure is quite similar in proportion and style of execution to the silver amulet of the goddess Mut (cat. no. 98).
9. M. Gitton and J. Leclant, "Gottesgemahlin," in *LÄ*, vol. 2 (1976), col. 796.
10. A mirror from Meroe is inscribed with a standing female making offerings to a seated goddess Mut; see Dunham, *El Kurru*, 447, fig. 241d.
11. According to Husson (*L'offerand du miroir*, 252), other goddesses who also share this aspect of Hathor are Mut, Opet, Sobeket-Neith, and Nepthys.
12. Karl-Heinz Priese, *The Gold of Meroe* (New York: MMA; Mainz: Philipp von Zabern, 1993), 34. The mirror itself is a sacred offering to the goddess Mut in the Kushite period, as indicated by a series of mirrors dedicated to Mut found at Mit Rahina; see Munro, "Eine Gruppe spätägyptischer Bronzespiegel," pls. I–VIII.
13. Gitton and Leclant, "Gottesgemahlin," cols. 795, 799. See the names in the second cartouches of the God's Wives.
14. Dows Dunham, *The Royal Cemeteries of Kush*, vol. 2, *Nuri* (Boston: MFA, 1955), 155, fig. 117, pl. XCI.
15. The mirror of Nastasen has a disk resting on a crescent, uniting solar and lunar imagery.
16. Dunham, *Nuri*, 247–49, pl. XCII.
17. The forms include Horus of Edfu, Harsomtus, Harpocrates, Harsises, Horakhty, Soped, and Shu (Husson, *L'offerand du miroir*, 252).

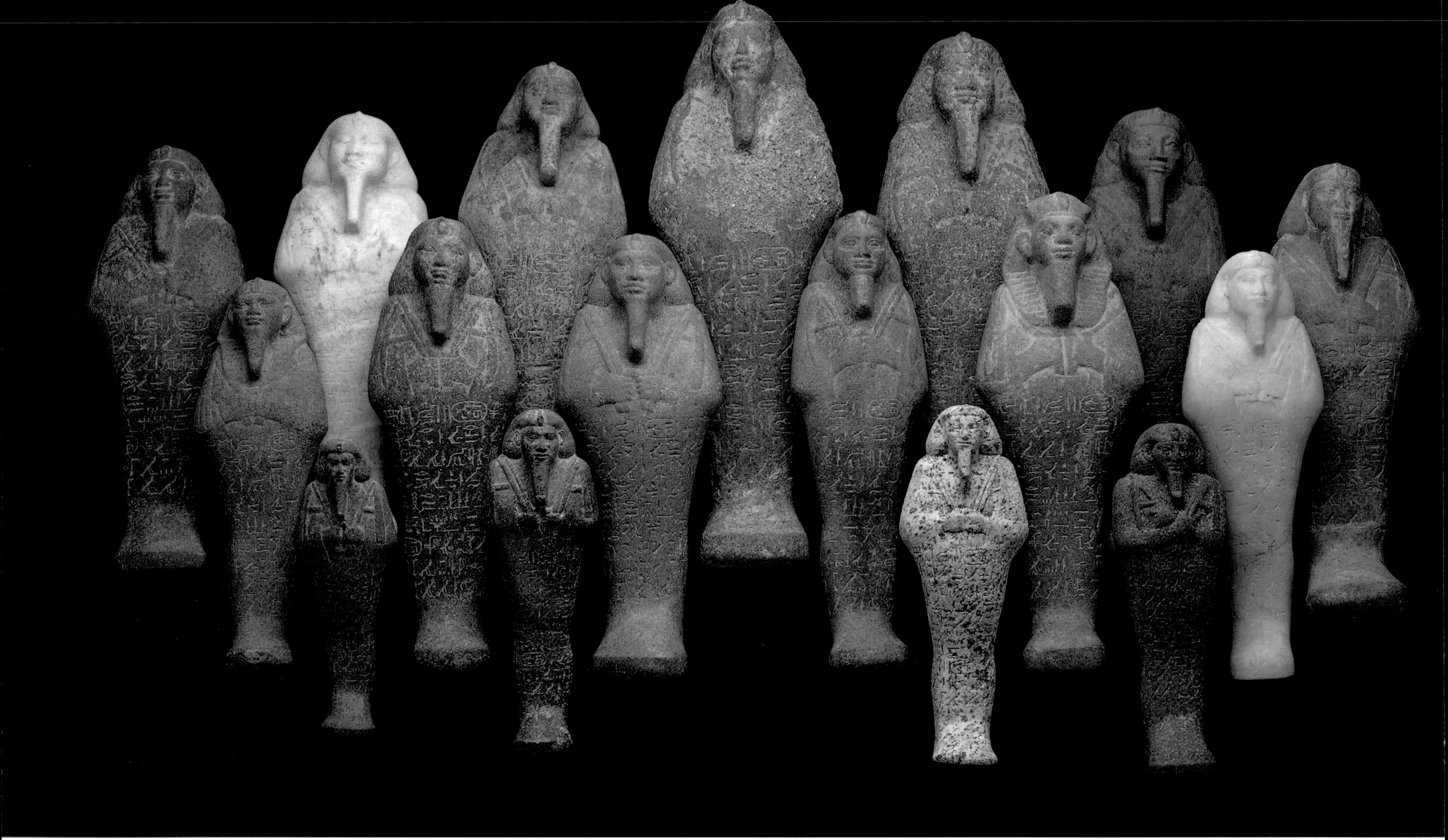

100 Shawabtis of Taharqa

Nuri, pyramid I, tomb of Taharqa
25th Dynasty, reign of Taharqa
(c. 690–664 B.C.)
Museum of Fine Arts, Boston

A *Shawabti*
Ankerite
37 x 13.3 x 7.3 cm (14⅝ x 5¼ x 2⅞ in.)
20.228, HU-MFA 17-2-1325

B *Shawabti*
Calcite
34 x 12.6 x 7.7 cm (13⅜ x 5 x 3 in.)
21.2921, HU-MFA 17-2-1600

C *Shawabti*
Ankerite
33 x 13 x 6.8 cm (13 x 5⅛ x 2⅝ in.)
21.2959, HU-MFA 17-2-490

D *Shawabti*
Ankerite
35.3 x 12.8 x 8.1 cm (13⅞ x 5 x 3¼ in.)
21.11854, HU-MFA 17-3-300

E *Shawabti*
Ankerite
44.5 x 15.5 x 7.9 cm
(17½ x 6⅛ x 3⅛ in.)
21.11855, HU-MFA 17-2-483

F *Shawabti*
Ankerite
35.7 x 10.4 x 6.2 cm (14 x 4⅛ x 2½ in.)
21.11856, HU-MFA 17-2-1768

G *Shawabti*
Ankerite
33.2 x 11.5 x 6.1 cm
(13⅛ x 4½ x 2⅜ in.)
21.11857, HU-MFA 17-2-1536

H *Shawabti*
Ankerite
41.5 x 14.2 x 8.4 cm (16⅜ x 5⅝ x 3¼ in.)
21.11858, HU-MFA 17-3-302

I *Shawabti*
Ankerite
36 x 12.3 x 8.3 cm (14⅛ x 4⅞ x 3¼ in.)
21.11859, HU-MFA 17-2-486

J *Shawabti*
Ankerite
39.2 x 13.3 x 7.1 cm
(15⅜ x 5¼ x 2¾ in.)
21.11860, HU-MFA 17-2-1531

K *Shawabti*
Ankerite
33.8 x 13.1 x 6.4 cm
(13¾ x 5⅛ x 2½ in.)
21.11861, HU-MFA 17-2-1230

L *Shawabti*
Syenite
30 x 9.9 x 5.6 cm (11⅞ x 3⅞ x 2¼ in.)
20.231, HU-MFA 16-12-168

M *Shawabti*
Calcite
33 x 10.5 x 6.1 cm (13 x 4⅛ x 2⅜ in.)
20.216, HU-MFA 17-2-536

N *Shawabti*
Syenite
25.2 x 9 x 5 cm (9⅞ x 3½ x 2 in.)
20.232, HU-MFA 17-2-1493

O *Shawabti*
Syenite
22.2 x 7.4 x 4.4 cm (8¾ x 2⅞ x 1¾ in.)
20.234, HU-MFA 17-2-419

P *Shawabti*
Stone
26.4 x 9.7 x 5.6 cm (10⅜ x 3⅞ x 2¼ in.)
21.3015, HU-MFA 17-2-567

Q *Shawabti*
Granite
25.9 x 8 x 6.1 cm (10¼ x 3⅛ x 2⅜ in.)
21.2997, HU-MFA 17-2-410

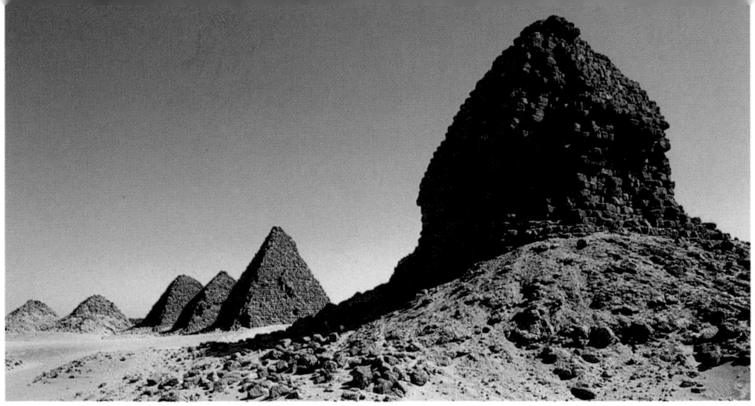
Royal pyramids at Nuri, with the pyramid of Anlamani in foreground.

In the tomb chamber of King Taharqa, members of the Harvard-Boston Expedition found as many as 1,070 stone shawabtis.[1] Originally they stood in rows three deep, lining the walls of the burial chamber, a common placement for Nubian shawabtis. Most had been disturbed by robbers and were scattered about the chamber and corridors. Ranging in height from twenty-five to sixty centimeters, the shawabtis are made from various stones, primarily ankerite, calcite, granite, and serpentine. The shawabtis of Taharqa are assigned to five groups on the basis of headdress, hand position, and types of insignia or implements they carry.[2]

All were inscribed with a variant[3] of the usual shawabti spell in nine, ten, or eleven horizontal rows of incised hieroglyphs, covering the front and sides of the torso:[4]

May the Osiris, King Taharqa, true of voice, be illuminated. He says: "Oh this shawabti, if one counts, if one calls, or if one reckons King Taharqa, true of voice, at his duty, now indeed an obstacle is implanted therewith, as a king at his duty. 'Here I am!' shall you say. If one counts off, at any time that has to be spent there, to make the fields arable, to irrigate the riparian lands, and to transport sand from the west to the east and vice versa. If one seeks King Taharqa, true of voice, to do all works that are to be done there in the god's land, 'I shall do it, here I am,' you shall say 'namely me in the god's land, [for] I am you.'"

Unlike their Egyptian counterparts, Nubian shawabtis[5] were made mainly for royal burials, where, in some cases, they are found in greater numbers (the tomb of Senkamunisken, for example, held 1,277). Nubian shawabtis also show greater variation in materials, typology, and size than is found in the Egyptian repertoire, as the examples from Taharqa's tomb demonstrate.

The iconography of the Kushite shawabtis uniquely blends Egyptian and Nubian motifs.[6] Curiously the double uraeus, which is ubiquitous on royal Nubian sculpture, is found only on the shawabtis of King Senkamunisken. There were some borrowings from Egyptian shawabtis, but no single type was used as a model. At the very least, the Nubian craftsman desired to create a distinctive style, separate from the Egyptian.[7]

For the funerary statuettes of Taharqa craftsmen returned to hard stone, which, in Egypt, had not been a popular material for shawabtis since the New Kingdom.[8] Also revived on Taharqa's shawabtis was the use of one broad and one narrow hoe, which had been customary in the New Kingdom but had completely died out in the Third Intermediate Period. The *nemes* headdress, crook, flail, *tyet*, and *djed* found on Taharqa's shawabtis had not been commonly seen since the Ramesside period in Egypt. Textual variants were borrowed from the New Kingdom as well.[9] The small double bags held over each shoulder are not seen on the Egyptian examples and were not used in Nubia after Taharqa's reign.[10] JH

BIBLIOGRAPHY Dows Dunham, *The Royal Cemeteries of Kush*, vol. 2, *Nuri* (Boston: MFA, 1955), 9–10, 256, 281, pl. CXL, figs. 197, 200.

NOTES
1. Dunham, *Nuri*, 10.
2. Of the shawabtis included here, cat. nos. 99A and 99L fall into Dunham typology I-1-a, cat. nos. 99B–K and M–P are II-1-b, and cat. no. 99Q is II-2-b.
3. Ibid., fig. 200. The textual modification using the clause including "to seek" distinguishes the Taharqa shawabti spell. See Joyce L. Haynes and R. J. Leprohon, "Napatan Shawabtis in the Royal Ontario Museum," *JSSEA* 17, nos. 1–2 (1987): 27; Leprohon suggests that this expression may be used with the idea of seeking or demanding payments in kind as well as the general collecting of taxes.
4. For a discussion of the iconography of Nubian shawabtis, see Jacques F. Aubert and Liliane Aubert, *Statuettes égyptiennes: Chaouabtis, ouchebtis* (Paris: Librairie d'Amérique et d'Orient, 1974).
5. Hans Schneider, *Shabtis: An Introduction to the History of Ancient Egyptian Funerary Statuettes*, vol. 1 (Leiden: Rijksmuseum van Oudheden, 1977), version VIIB.
6. Haynes and Leprohon, "Napatan Shawabtis," 24, nn. 43, 45.
7. Ibid., 22.
8. Ibid., 23, n. 25.
9. Schneider, *Shabtis*, 119, 147.
10. After Taharqa's time each shawabti carried one bag suspended by a cord over the shoulder. This single bag remained a standard feature of Kushite shawabtis. While the single bag is also seen on Saite shawabtis, the Kushite one is frequently distinguished by short tassels hanging from its lower edge.

101 Rosette Buttons

Nuri, tomb of King Talakhamani
(Nu16)
Napatan period, 6th to 5th century B.C.
Sheet gold
Small rosettes: .2 x 1.6 (diam) cm
(1/16 x 5/8 in.)
Large rosettes: 2 x 2.6 (diam) cm
(3/4 x 1 in.)
Museum of Fine Arts, Boston, 20.267,
20.272–73, 20.280, 20.282–83,
20.305–9

The royal tombs at Nuri contained rosette buttons of varying shape, manufacture, and size. Most numerous were small, flat, eight-lobed ornaments made of gold sheet with chased petals and a central boss. The edges of these stylized buttons were bent downward to obscure the gold attachment rings soldered to the underside.

Other floral buttons from Nuri are deeper and resemble a blossom in early or full bloom. They are usually made of gold sheet modeled into the desired shape over a stone form. Long tubes of sheet metal were soldered onto the backs of these larger buttons to prevent the floral heads from drooping when applied to a textile.

Despite the extensive plundering of the royal tombs at Nuri, clusters of rosettes survived in several burials. George A. Reisner recovered eighty-six flat rosettes from the

tomb of King Talakhamani (c. 435–431 B.C.).[1] Other buttons belonging to Talakhamani are tridimensional, with seven to eight petals and tubular attachments on the back.[2] An earlier king, Amaniastabarka, was also buried with multiples of the small, flat type in addition to the larger, sculpted forms.[3]

A painting of King Tanwetamani (664–653 B.C.) in the burial chamber of his pyramid at el-Kurru (Ku16) gives us an idea of how the small, flat rosette buttons were worn. Painted in gleaming yellow against a band of red and white squares, the ruler wears a single diagonal line of rosettes. These appear to be sewn onto a dyed leather or cloth strip crossing the torso. It is not clear whether the buttons continue around the back of the band. Flat and tridimensional rosettes may also have adorned headbands. A representation of a Meroitic queen shows the royal lady wearing a circular head ornament decorated with alternating stars and eight-lobed rosettes.[4]

The rosette undoubtedly had solar associations in Nubia during the first millennium. In the early Napatan tombs at el-Kurru, many faience pendants depict scarabs with sun disks. The solar orb in these amulets is typically represented as a multipetaled blossom with a central boss.[5] YM

BIBLIOGRAPHY Dows Dunham, *The Royal Cemeteries of Kush*, vol. 2, *Nuri* (Boston: MFA, 1955), 208, fig. 160.

NOTES
1. Dunham, *Nuri*, 208, fig. 160.
2. Twenty-eight of these larger buttons were found in the floor debris of the middle chamber beneath the pyramid.
3. King Amaniastabarka was an early-fifth-century B.C. ruler. In the debris of the room adjacent to his burial chamber (Nu2), excavators found seventeen flat rosettes, five large rosettes, and five undecorated gold buttons; see Dunham, *Nuri*, 167–69.
4. This queen, whose name was not recovered, lived during the latter half of the second century B.C.; see Dows Dunham, *The Royal Cemeteries of Kush*, vol. 3, *Decorated Chapels of the Meroitic Pyramids at Meroe and Barkal* (Boston: MFA, 1952), pl. 10B.
5. Thirteen of these pendants were found in Ku53, the tomb of Queen Tabiry, wife of Piye; see Dows Dunham, *The Royal Cemeteries of Kush*, vol. 1, *El Kurru* (Cambridge: Harvard University Press, 1950), 87, pl. 49.

Selection of bronze figurines recovered from the Osiris grave.

102 Statuettes of Osiris

Medinet Habu, northwest corner
of Eastern High Gate, so-called
Osiris grave
25th to 26th Dynasty (c. 770–525 B.C.)
Serpentine
The Oriental Institute,
University of Chicago

A H: 12 cm (4¾ in.)
14302
B H: 14.5 cm (5¾ in.)
14301

The precinct of Medinet Habu was strongly associated with the worship of Osiris, the god of the afterlife. Over several centuries pilgrims brought hundreds of statues of Osiris to the holy site as offerings. Some were deposited in pits. One pit, which excavators termed the Osiris grave, was located at the northwest corner of the Eastern High Gate. Located 2 meters below ground, this deposit, over a meter deep, contained hundreds of bronze and stone statues and fragments of statues of Osiris. Metal plumes from Osirid crowns, thirty centimeters long, indicate that some statues, whose bodies were perhaps made of wood, must have been nearly 1.5 meters tall. Many figures retained traces of gilding. Another cache of Osiris statues was discovered under the floor of the Great Temple in 1895–96 by Georges Daressy.[1]

The nature of the Osiris grave is not entirely clear. It may be a cachette, a repository for statues cleared from the temple sometime before 100 B.C. and given an honorable burial within the temple precinct. But almost all the statues portray Osiris, and stylistically they are all quite similar, though they can be divided into particular groupings. This suggests that, unlike the statues of the Karnak cachette, which were manufactured over a span of nearly one thousand years, the Medinet Habu Osiris figures were made over a short period in one workshop, perhaps at, or near, Medinet Habu.

TRANSLATION OF INSCRIBED TEXT (102B):
Osiris, Wenefer the good god. May he give life, prosperity, health, and strength to Aatamun, son of Nesy, at Medinet Habu.

ET

BIBLIOGRAPHY 102B: Uvo Hölscher, *The Excavation of Medinet Habu*, vol. 2, *The Temples of the Eighteenth Dynasty*, OIP 41 (Chicago: University of Chicago Press, 1939), 40; idem, *The Excavation of Medinet Habu*, vol. 5, *Post-Ramessid Remains*, OIP 66 (Chicago: University of Chicago Press, 1954), pl. 19G.

NOTES
1. Under the floor of room 45; Georges Daressy, *Médinet Habou* (Cairo: Service des antiquités de l'Egypte, 1897), 170.

103 Osiris

Medinet Habu, south side of
18th Dynasty Temple, tomb 5
26th Dynasty (c. 664–525 B.C.)
Schist
H: 19 cm (7½ in.)
The Oriental Institute,
University of Chicago, 14292

During the Third Intermediate Period private burials were dug in the area east of the first pylon of the Great Temple and south of the Small Temple of Hatshepsut, perhaps in imitation of the processional way through the necropolis of the Asasif leading to the Amun shrine at Deir el-Bahri. Although the Medinet Habu tombs were robbed in antiquity, they still supply valuable information about the period.

Tomb 5 was a stone-faced burial chamber with a brick-lined antechamber. Only two uninscribed "dummy" canopic jars escaped the attention of looters, and the body itself was destroyed. The tomb was dubbed the "Tomb of the Monkey," for the skeleton of a small ape, perhaps the pet of the tomb owner, was found in the southeast corner. Among the remaining furnishings of the tomb were many small shawabtis. The tomb also contained many bronze and a few stone Osiris figurines, which apparently were thrown into the tomb after it was plundered in the Ptolemaic era.

The use of schist and the fine finishing of this statue are characteristic of the craftsmanship of the Saite period. ET

BIBLIOGRAPHY Uvo Hölscher, *The Excavation of Medinet Habu,* vol. 5, *Post-Ramessid Remains,* OIP 66 (Chicago: University of Chicago Press, 1954), 30.

104 Statue of Osiris

Giza, tomb G7792A
26th Dynasty, c. 664–525 B.C.
Green schist
55 x 21 x 15.5 cm (21⅝ x 8¼ x 6⅛ in.)
Museum of Fine Arts, Boston,
29.1131, HU-MFA 28-4-76

George A. Reisner's excavations in Giza are
most frequently remembered for his work
in the Old Kingdom pyramid fields, but he
also cleared countless Late Period shafts and
tombs. These tombs contained many valuable
Late Period objects, such as the basalt sarcophagus of Kheper-Re (MFA 30.834), and
a wealth of inscriptional information derived
from the more than four thousand shawabtis
belonging to Late Period notables.

One of the finest pieces from Giza of this
period is this upper part of a statue of a
standing Osiris. The deity is identified by his
customary regalia of cloak, crook, flail, and
atef crown. The crown with uraeus is flanked
by two striated ostrich plumes. The body of
the rearing cobra, behind the head, is looped
in a figure-eight pattern, a feature that
Bernard V. Bothmer attributed to the first
half of the sixth century B.C.[1] The ceremonial
beard is plaited and attached by a clearly
defined chin strap. Around the neck is an
elaborate multistrand *wesekh* collar with a
bottom row of drop beads. The color of the
stone itself reflects the role of Osiris, whose
image was frequently executed in green to

suggest his role as the renewer of all life. Green was associated with the new growth of vegetation and, by extension, life, rebirth, and resurrection. This finely polished piece reveals the hand of a master craftsman of the Saite period.

Reisner excavated the statue in April 1928 "from pit G7792A in filling."[2] It was not found in situ.[3] The inscription on the obelisk-shaped back pillar,[4] incised in two vertical columns with crisp lines, indicates that the statue was dedicated by an official, the "royal acquaintance" Ptahirdis.[5]

TRANSLATION OF INSCRIBED TEXT:
(1) Adoring Osiris, paying honor to the ka *of the lord of Rosetau, by the Osiris, the royal acquaintance, Ptahirdis,*[6] *true of voice, son of Wepemsaef, true of voice, engendered by Merptahit[es]*[7] *. . . [Osiris] (2) Lord of Rosetau, one great of power, the eldest, the father of the gods, one who created that which is loved. May you give me bread, beer, and all good things. May you rescue me from all things evil. May you give me power . . .*[8]

JH

BIBLIOGRAPHY Dows Dunham, "The Late Period Gallery Rearranged," *BMFA* 29 (1931): 26; William S. Smith, *Ancient Egypt as Represented in the Museum of Fine Arts, Boston* (Boston: MFA, 1946), 156; PM, vol. 3, pt. 1 (1974), 204, 291; Joyce Haynes, *Padihershef: The Egyptian Mummy*, exh. cat. (Springfield, Mass.: George Walter Vincent Smith Art Museum, 1984), 39, fig. 7; Sue D'Auria, Peter Lacovara, and Catharine H. Roehrig, eds., *Mummies and Magic: The Funerary Arts of Ancient Egypt*, exh. cat. (Boston: MFA, 1988), 237–38; Christiane Zivie-Coche, *Giza au premier millénaire: Autour du temple d'Isis dame des pyramides* (Boston: MFA, 1991), 263, 264, 277, 288.

NOTES
1. Bernard V. Bothmer, *Egyptian Sculpture of the Late Period, 700 B.C.–A.D. 100* (Brooklyn: Brooklyn Museum, 1960), 58; a close parallel is the green schist head of Osiris (no. 50, pl. 46), dated to 590–570 B.C.
2. HU-MFA object register, Egypt IX, Giza 28-3-1 to 30-1-99, MFA archives.
3. A green schist statue of a seated Osiris was found in Saqqara in the tomb of a high official named Psametik. It is noteworthy that it too was found in a pit within his tomb, where later objects had been added to the original funerary equipment; see Mohamed Saleh and Hourig Sourouzian, *Official Catalogue: The Egyptian Museum, Cairo* (Mainz: Philipp von Zabern, 1987), no. 252 (CG38358); Georges Daressy, *Statues de divinités,* CG 29 (Cairo: IFAO, 1906), 96–97, pl. 19. Also note that a basalt statue of Amun (H: 1.4 m; CG 38001) was discovered, according to vague records, "with Chephren statues, found in the pit of the temple of Giza" (ibid., 1).

4. Obelisk-shaped back pillars that taper to a point behind the head are a common feature of the Late Period; see the statue of Osiris in Bothmer, *Egyptian Sculpture of the Late Period,* 57–58, no. 50, pl. 46.
5. A tomb belonging to a Ptahirdis, also a "royal acquaintance," is located near the sphinx, but without a complete genealogy of the tomb owner, it is not possible to ascertain whether this is the same individual. A shawabti fragment of a Ptahirdis, born of Mer-Ptah (HU-MFA 24-11-358), was found in the debris east of pyramid GIb.
6. Hermann Ranke, *Die ägyptischen Personennamen,* vol. 1 (Glückstadt: J. J. Augustin, 1935), 138.16.
7. Ibid., 156.11.
8. Ptahirdis dedicated this statue to the local form of the god Osiris, the lord of Rosetau; for a discussion, see Zivie-Coche, *Giza au premier millénaire,* 264.

105 Offering Table of Pabasa

Asasif, tomb of Pabasa (TT 279)
26th Dynasty, reign of Psamtik I
(c. 664–610 B.C.)
Granite
20.5 x 71 x 81 cm (8⅛ x 28 x 31⅞ in.)
Metropolitan Museum of Art, 22.3.2,
Rogers Fund and Edward S. Harkness
Gift, 1922

Pabasa was mayor of Thebes at the beginning of the Saite period, a rare time of political stability and cultural distinction during Egypt's first millennium B.C. His tomb was excavated by the Metropolitan Museum of Art under the direction of Ambrose Lansing in 1919.[1] This impressive slab, which once stood in the center of the courtyard of Pabasa's tomb, is representative of Saite art in its confidence, its quality of execution, and its copying of earlier forms—in this case, offering tables of the Middle and New Kingdoms, some thousand years older.

Pabasa's table was the focus of daily offerings of food and drink made by priests or visitors to the tomb for his life force (*ka*). Its top is carved with images of bread, joints of meat, fowl, and fruit, as well as two jars for beer and water. The table itself is shaped like the hieroglyph for "offering" (a reed table with a conical loaf of bread); the groove in its projecting end would allow libations to run off.

The hieroglyphic inscriptions across the top and down either side of the table contain a prayer taken from the ancient Pyramid Texts, to be recited as the offerings were made:

Oh, Osiris . . . Pabasa, justified! May Re in the sky be well disposed to you and make the Two Goddesses well disposed to you. May the night be well disposed to you. May the day be well disposed to you. May the "Offering that the King Gives" be well disposed to you.

Oh, Osiris . . . [Pabasa, justified!] May offerings be what is brought to you. May offerings be what you see. May offerings be what you hear. May offerings be before you. May offerings be behind you. May offerings be with you.

The prayer, only traces of which are visible, was deliberately erased by Pabasa's opponents sometime after his burial, to prevent his spirit from enjoying the benefits of offerings. JA

NOTES
1. See Ambrose Lansing, "The Egyptian Expedition, 1916–1919," *BMMA* 15 (July 1920): pt. 2, 16–24.

106 Group of Bronze Statuettes

Giza, Tomb G7632, hall A1 (except cat. no. 106E, from pit 7632A, AVI)
27th to 30th Dynasty (c. 525–343 B.C.)
Bronze
Museum of Fine Arts, Boston

A *Apis Bull*
H: 6.6 cm (2⅝ in.)
MFA 27.986, HU-MFA 25-2-740

B *Isis and Horus*
H: 8.7 cm (3⅜ in.)
MFA 27.985, HU-MFA 25-2-737

C *Cat*
H: 9 cm (3½ in.)
MFA 27.987, HU-MFA 25-2-739

D *Osiris*
H: 25.5 cm (10 in.)
27.982, HU-MFA 25-2-733

E *Harpocrates*
H: 12.8 cm (5 in.)
MFA 27.983, HU-MFA 25-2-897

F *Imhotep*
H: 13.6 cm (5⅜ in.)
MFA 27.984, HU-MFA 25-2-840

Small bronze statuettes of divinities are common to most museum collections, but few come from scientifically excavated contexts. This group, discovered by the Harvard University–Museum of Fine Arts expedition to Giza, is particularly interesting because it is provenanced. Such bronzes were often buried as votive deposits in and around temples and other sacred sites. George A. Reisner found the group in hall A1 of G7632, a Late Period tomb with multiple chambers cut in the limestone escarpment. The tomb is located in the mastaba field east of the great pyramid of Khufu, on the east side of the large mastaba of Ankhkhaf (G7510). The numerous Late Period tombs at Giza indicate the renewed status of this area as a favored burial ground.

The offering of a statuette to a deity was a common custom in the Late Period, and most bronze statuettes were intended for dedication in a shrine. This group is atypical not only for its deposit in a burial but also for the diversity of deities represented. It is far more typical to find a single god or group of related gods at a site, such as the group of bronze lepidotus fish, sacred to Osiris, which Reisner found at Mesheikh.[1] Perhaps this cache represents a votive deposit made after the tombs were robbed.[2]

The sacred Apis bull was represented in this cache wearing a sun disk on his head and a saddle bordered front and back by incised winged sun disks. A tang for attachment protrudes from the base.

The goddess Isis, venerated as the divine mother, is shown nursing her son Horus. She is crowned with the classic sun disk and horns. A tang for attachment to a wooden throne projects from the seat of the goddess.

The seated cat has carefully delineated features, with incised markings indicating fur. Around the neck is a beaded choker as well as an aegis pectoral on a strand of cowroid beads. The ears are pierced; the jewelry found on statuettes of cats was, however, meant primarily as adornment for cult statues. Pet cats did not necessarily wear such things in real life.[7] This seated cat likely represents the goddess Bastet, the lady of Busiris.

The statuette of the seated Osiris is by far the largest and the most finely crafted of the group. It represents the god mummified, his hands protruding from the wrappings to hold the crook and flail. He is crowned with two ostrich plumes and a sun disk surmounting the curled horns of a longhorn sheep. Jutting out from the base is a tang, for attachment probably to a wooden base, long since decayed. A hieroglyphic text is inscribed on the back, right side, and front of the base: "May Osiris give life to Wadjetirdis,[3]

daughter of Ankhit,[4] born of the lady of the house Asetemkhebit."[5]

The child god Harpocrates (Hor-Pa Khred, or Horus the Child), is shown nude with the sidelock of youth. He holds his finger to his mouth, a gesture symbolic of childhood.

Imhotep, the architect of Djoser's step pyramid complex in Saqqara, was deified as the god of wisdom and learning in the Late Period. This fine-featured figure sits with an inscribed papyrus scroll open on his lap. The hieroglyphs on the scroll read: "Imhotep the great, son of Ptah, born of Ankhkhred."[6]

JH and PL

BIBLIOGRAPHY 106D: Christiane Zivie-Coche, *Giza au premier millénaire: Autour du temple d'Isis, dame des pyramides* (Boston: MFA, 1991), 265. 106F: *Master Bronzes: Selected from Museums and Collections in America*, exh. cat. (Buffalo: Buffalo Fine Arts Academy, 1937), no. 47.

NOTES
1. Sue D'Auria, Peter Lacovara, and Catharine Roehrig, eds., *Mummies and Magic: The Funerary Arts of Ancient Egypt*, exh. cat. (Boston: MFA, 1988).
2. A number of other bronzes came from hall A1: a standing Osiris with gold leaf (MFA 27.989); a small Osiris (MFA 25.2.738); a seated Harpocrates (MFA 27.982); a large composite deity (MFA 25.2.735); a small composite deity (MFA 25.2.736); a small Bastet (MFA 27.987); and a striding Apis (MFA 27.986). In addition to the bronzes, Reisner recovered a large faience Sekhmet amulet (MFA 27.997); a shawabti (MFA 25.2.744); a faience *udjat* eye amulet (MFA 25.2.745); three barrel beads (MFA 25.2.746); and two cylinder beads (MFA 25.2.747). There were also numerous intact and fragmentary small pottery vessels; see "Giza Diary," vol. 15, 16 February 1925, MFA archives.
3. See "Bastet-ir-dis," in Hermann Ranke, *Die ägyptischen Personennamen*, vol. 1 (Glückstadt: J. J. Augustin, 1935), 90.7.
4. Ibid., 63.3.
5. Ibid., 4.3.
6. Cf. "Ankh-khred-nefer," ibid., 66.8.
7. Jaromír Málek notes an exception in the painted scene in the Ramesside tomb of Penbuy and Kasa (TT10), where a domestic cat is shown wearing a collar and earrings (*The Cat in Ancient Egypt* [London: British Museum Press, 1993], 102).

107 Female Feline with Lotus above Falcon Heads

Mendes
Late Period to Ptolemaic period
(664–30 B.C.)
Limestone
28 x 41.6 x 9.5 cm
(11 x 16⅜ x 3¾ in.)
The Brooklyn Museum, gift of the Egyptian Antiquities Organization, 80.7.7

An expedition to Mendes, sponsored by New York University's Institute of Fine Arts, discovered this relief in 1965. According to field records, the relief was found in debris over and around the ruins of Mendes's Level I Saite temple platform.[1] Unfortunately this establishes neither the relief's date nor its specific original provenance. Its precise subject matter also remains a question.

Some observers have noted stylistic affinities between the relief's feline and sixth-century B.C. leopards from the classical world.[2] Without denying the existence of some extremely bold Egyptian reliefs in earlier eras, it has also been suggested that this aspect of the work could argue for a Ptolemaic or Roman period date.[3] In a 1993 gallery reinstallation the Brooklyn Museum labeled the relief as a Ptolemaic(?) image of the goddess Mafdet(?). Since that time research on this unusual piece has noted the relationship of cats to the lotus, including the occasional use of the latter as a replacement in several iconographic contexts for a Hathor head.[4] Moreover, and without attempting to link them in time, we have come to wonder if there could be a relationship between the Mendes relief and some New Kingdom representations of transom windows with rows of bewigged falcon heads (sometimes in bold relief), which are potential symbols of the celestial in association with cats or sphinxes.[5] As with these windows, it seems reasonable to relate this feline to Hathor or the other goddesses who could be depicted as felines and to the association of these goddesses with the sun and the protection of the solar deity.[6] RF

BIBLIOGRAPHY Richard Fazzini, "The Reinstallation of the Brooklyn Museum's Egyptian Collection," *Minerva* 5, no. 1 (1994): 42, fig. 8.

NOTES
1. The relief came to light at coordinates X170.5, Y158 of a grid established for the temple. For maps with the temple's remains and this grid, see Donald Hansen, "Mendes 1965 and 1966 I: The Excavations at Tell el Rubʻa," *JARCE* 6 (1967): pls. III, IV.
2. E.g., those of Mary Comstock and Cornelius Vermeule, *Sculpture in Stone: The Greek, Roman, and Etruscan Collections of the Museum of Fine Arts, Boston* (Boston: MFA, 1976), 251, nos. 387–88.
3. For such bold relief, see, e.g., Cyril Aldred et al., *L'Egypte du crépuscule: De Tanis à Meroe, 1070 av. J.-C.–IVe siècle apr. J.C.* (Paris: Gallimard, 1980), 22, fig. 7; 89, fig. 70; and the comments of Robert S. Bianchi et al., *Cleopatra's Egypt: Age of the Ptolemies*, exh. cat. (Brooklyn: Brooklyn Museum, 1988), 242, no. 131.
4. E.g., Erik Hornung et al., *Skarabäen und andere Siegelamulette aus Basler Sammlungen*, Ägyptische Denkmäler in der Schweiz 1 (Mainz: Philipp von Zabern, 1976), 249, no. 293.
5. E.g., Eugène Warmenbol and Florence Doyen, "Le chat et la maîtresse: Les visages multiples d'Hathor," in *Les divins chats d'Egypte: Un air subtil, un dangereux parfum*, ed. L. Delvaux and Eugène Warmenbol (Leuven: Editions Peeters, 1991), 62, 65, 67, figs. 28, 31, 33 (a cat with frontal face with some formal affinities to our relief); Uvo Hölscher, *The Excavation of Medinet Habu*, vol. 3, *The Mortuary Temple of Ramesses III*, pt. 1, OIP 54 (Chicago: University of Chicago Press, 1941), 49 and pl. 37. For a recent summary history of such windows, see Maarten Raven, "A Transom-Window from Tuna El-Gebel," *Oudheidkundige Mededelingen uit het Rijksmuseum van Oudheden te Leiden* 69 (1989): 51–61, which mentions some 25th to 26th Dynasty archaizing examples that seem to lack feline images (60–61).
6. E.g., Warmenbol and Doyen, "Le chat et la maîtresse," 60–67; Raven ("A Transom-Window," 61) mentions that both the cat and the falcon head may be related to solar power. See also Herman te Velde, "The Cat as Sacred Animal of the Goddess Mut," in *Studies in Egyptian Religion Dedicated to Professor Jan Zandee*, ed. M. Heerma van Voss et al. (Leiden: E. J. Brill, 1982), 127–37; Michèle Broze, "Le chat, le serpent et l'arbre-ished (Chapitre 17 du Livre des Morts)," in Delvaux and Warmenbol, eds., *Les divins chats d'Egypte*, 109–15; and Jaromír Málek, *The Cat in Ancient Egypt* (London: British Museum Press, 1993), 73–111.

Three registers of decoration on the sides and back, set above a niched dado, increase in size from top to bottom and are separated by horizontal bands of rectangles in alternating colors. The top register is painted in a meander pattern; the middle with alternating hieroglyphic mottos for "protection" and "stability"; and the lowest register with figural decoration. On each of the two sides the painted images of three mummiform divinities hold strips of cloth for wrappings, and the rear of the shrine is protected by Osiris, here appearing as the deified *djed* pillar. He wears the *atef* crown and is flanked by pendant uraei bearing the emblems of Isis and Nephthys on their heads.[2]

The rather cartoonlike expressions of the divinities have counterparts on the religious papyri of the Ptolemaic period and suggest that this chest be dated accordingly.

TRANSLATION OF INSCRIBED TEXT:
(Left) Words spoken by Anubis, lord of the sacred land.

(Right) Words spoken by Anubis, who is before the divine booth.

CK

NOTES
1. On the development of the canopic chest, see Katzaryna Dobrowolska, "Génèse et évolution des boîtes à vases-canopes," *Etudes et travaux* 4 (1970): 73–85.
2. An almost identical canopic chest is in the collection of the University of Tübingen; see Emma Brunner-Traut and Helmut Brunner, *Die ägyptische Sammlung der Universität Tübingen* (Mainz: Philipp von Zabern, 1981), 256, no. 977, pl. 139. The date assigned, "Spätzeit" (Late Period), is too broad, however.

108 Canopic Box

Naga el-Deir
Ptolemaic period, c. 300–31 B.C.
Wood, gesso, paint
49 x 21.5 x 27.5 cm
(19¼ x 8½ x 10⅞ in.)
Phoebe A. Hearst Museum
of Anthropology, University
of California, Berkeley, 6-17149ab

This canopic chest represents the final stage in the development of the receptacle for the viscera, the earliest dated examples of which come from the 4th Dynasty.[1] The box is constructed in the form of a shrine with inward-slanting sides with a cavetto cornice. Its flat lid supports a three-dimensional image of a recumbent mummified falcon, the funerary divinity Sokar. The decoration of the front simulates a building or sanctuary entrance: directly beneath the cornice, three winged disks lie one above the other, over a pair of double sealed doors. The doors are inscribed with the name and epithets of Anubis, "the divine embalmer."

109 Mummy Mask

Tebtunis (Tell Umm el-Breigat)
Ptolemaic period,
3d to 1st centuries B.C.
Cartonnage (linen and gesso),
pigment, gilding
36.5 x 26.5 x 18 cm
(14⅛ x 10⅜ x 7⅛ in.)
Phoebe A. Hearst Museum
of Anthropology, University
of California, Berkeley, 6-20107

This gilded and painted mask was placed directly over the head of a wrapped mummy. The facial features are highly conventionalized and not in any way a true portrait. So stylized are the features, in fact, that it is not possible to assign this mask to either sex. The brown line that separates the visage from the rest of the mask was added to reinforce its identification with the hieroglyphic sign for *face*, which is always depicted, unlike most complex signs having to do with the human body, in frontal view.

The color scheme and simplicity of design suggest that the mask was made in the Ptolemaic period.[1] Although cartonnage masks continued to be produced in Roman times, especially in the area between Akhmim and Abydos in Upper Egypt,[2] the later examples tend to cover more of the upper body and to be more elaborately embellished.[3] Here only the gilded face imparts a sense of richness. Otherwise decoration is limited to the small area between the lappets of the wig, where the broad collar is typically exposed; even this remains unfinished.[4] CK

NOTES

1. Günter Grimm, *Die römischen Mumienmasken aus Ägypten* (Wiesbaden: F. Steiner, 1974), 100.

2. Ibid.

3. Ibid., 54 and n. 93, mentions PAHMA 6-20104, a slightly more elaborate example than 6-20107, as from Tebtunis, on the basis of the statement in Albert B. Elsasser and Vera-Mae Fredrickson, *Ancient Egypt*, exh. cat. (Berkeley: Robert H. Lowie Museum of Anthropology, University of California, 1966), 77.

4. Although cartonnage masks may appear virtually identical, there is a surprising amount of variation, even among the least elaborate types. A mask at the University of Heidelberg (2938), e.g., is more elaborate but not gilded; see Erika Feucht et al., *Vom Nil zum Neckar: Kunstschätze Ägyptens aus pharaonischer und koptischer Zeit an der Universität Heidelberg* (Heidelberg: Ägyptologisches Institut, Heidelberg Universität, 1986), 92 (color plate), 127–28, no. 284. A mask in a private collection in Switzerland is very similar to the Hearst Museum piece, but a broad collar with falcon-head terminals has been added; see *Geschenk des Nils: Ägyptische Kunstwerk aus schweizer Besitz* (Basel: Ägyptologisches Seminar, Basel Universität, 1978), 96, no. 340.

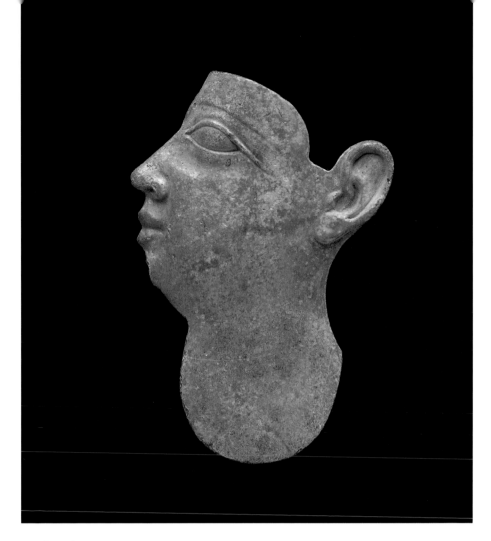

popular in Egypt during the Ptolemaic and early Roman periods, when they were used to decorate cartonnage.[9]

This jasper head from Meroe is unique for its large size[10] and mottled beige color.[11] Whether part of a larger construction or in its present form when imported into Nubia, the inlay is a highly valued object in its own right. JH and YM

BIBLIOGRAPHY Dows Dunham, *The Royal Cemeteries of Kush*, vol. 5, *The West and South Cemeteries at Meroe* (Boston, MFA, 1963), fig. 168.

NOTES
1. The contents of this tomb were summary; see Dunham, *The West and South Cemeteries*, 259, fig. 168.
2. For a similar Ptolemaic head of opaque red glass in the Cleveland Museum of Art, see John D. Cooney, "Intaglios, Cameos, and Related Works," *Bulletin of the Cleveland Museum of Art* 55 (April 1968): 117, fig. 6. Robert S. Bianchi has identified three datable glass inlay types with special reference to profile heads; see "Those Ubiquitous Glass Inlays from Pharaonic Egypt: Suggestions about Their Functions and Dates," *Journal of Glass Studies* 25 (1983).
3. Ahmed Yousef Moustafa, "The Golden Belt of Prince Ptah-Shepses," *ASAE* 54 (1956): 149–51.
4. The hieroglyphic belt buckle of Queen Nefertari (MFA 04.1955) has red glass and red jasper inlays. The color, rather than the chemical composition of the material, seems of paramount importance here.
5. See Kamal El Mallakh and Arnold Brackman, *The Gold of Tutankhamen* (New York: Newsweek Books, 1978), 318, no. 123.
6. Milada Vilimkova, *Egyptian Jewelry* (Prague: Svoboda, 1969), nos. 42, 43.
7. Christiane Ziegler et al., *Tanis: L'or des pharaons*, exh. cat. (Paris: Association française d'action artistique, 1987), 238, no. 78.
8. Bianchi, "Those Ubiquitous Glass Inlays," 31–32.
9. Robert S. Bianchi, "Those Ubiquitous Glass Inlays, Part II," *BES* 5 (1983): 9–29.
10. Head inlays of semiprecious stones, often from jewels, tend to range in height from 1 to 3 centimeters, while glass inlays are often larger. For an opaque red glass head 20.3 centimeters in height, see Sidney M. Goldstein, *Pre-Roman and Early Roman Glass in the Corning Museum of Glass* (Corning, N.Y.: Corning Museum of Glass, 1979), 66, no. 166.
11. Color was invested with symbolic meaning in the ancient world. In a manner reminiscent of the yellow jasper head fragment of Queen Tiye at the Metropolitan Museum of Art (26.7.1396), perhaps the beige stone was selected as the appropriate color for a queen.

110 Head Inlay of a Royal Figure

Meroe, tomb W323
304–30 B.C.
Mottled beige jasper
6.7 x 4.5 x .6 cm (2⅝ x 1¾ x ¼ in.)
Museum of Fine Arts, Boston, 24.548

In the plundered remains of tomb W323[1] George A. Reisner recovered a highly polished, finely modeled, beige jasper inlay of a royal face in profile. Although the tip of the chin is missing, the fleshy cheeks, nasolabial fold, long neck with rounded base, and pursed mouth fit the standard Ptolemaic type found on comparable glass inlays from Egypt.[2]

The use of semiprecious stones as an inlay material in the Nile Valley predates recorded history. The inlaid gold belt buckle of Ptahshepses[3] demonstrates that the cutting and fitting of colored stones to represent parts of the human body in profile was already established by the late Old Kingdom. The technique was regularly employed during the Middle Kingdom and into the New Kingdom, when stone and glass inlays occasionally appeared on the same jeweled object.[4]

During the New Kingdom artisans substituted opaque colored glass for stone, as seen in red glass heads of Tutankhamun and Ankhesenamun inlaid into the young king's gilded throne[5] and in the blue glass profiles of goddesses featured in a number of pectorals from the same tomb.[6] A red jasper head of Seti I in the Museum of Fine Arts, Boston (1940.72), indicates the continued use of this highly prized material.

Head inlays of carnelian, lapis lazuli, and green feldspar were very much in vogue during the Third Intermediate Period at Tanis,[7] while figural glass substitutes are associated with several shrines from the Saite-Persian period.[8] Glass inlays of varying types, including profile heads, were especially

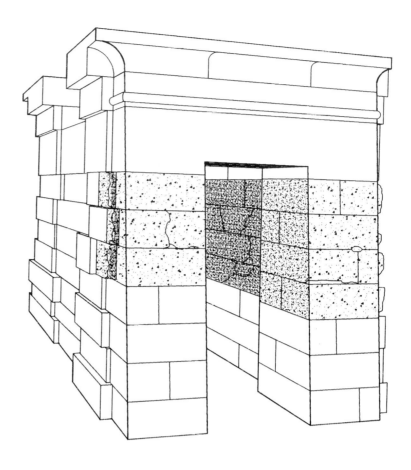

111 Temple Gateway

Coptos
Ptolemaic period, reign of
Ptolemy VIII (Euergetes II)
(170–163, 145–116 B.C.)
Sandstone, pigments
Extant size: H: 190 cm (74¾ in.)
Reconstructed size: 524 x 458 x 378 cm
(206¼ x 180¼ x 148¾ in.)
H of typical block: 48 cm (18⅞ in.)
Museum of Fine Arts, Boston,
24.1632–33

In May and June of 1923 Dows Dunham of
the Museum of Fine Arts, Boston, excavated
for twelve days at Coptos in Upper Egypt.
His short visit was remarkably productive.
Sent to the site because of reports of illicit
digging, Dunham selected several areas where
antiquities were rumored to have been found
and set to work. By the second day his team
had begun unearthing an assemblage of sandstone blocks dating to the Ptolemaic period.
These blocks, assigned to Boston by Egypt's
Department of Antiquities, belong to a
temple gateway.[1]

The blocks were found not at the gateway
site but as foundation fill for a later structure.
The gateway may originally have formed
part of the great temple of Min and Isis, the
largest and northernmost of three temple com-
plexes at Coptos.[2] The place of reuse was
close to that temple, on its north side, between
the temple proper and its sacred lake.

The gateway dates to the reign of
Ptolemy VIII (Euergetes II), who belonged to
the dynasty of Macedonian Greeks who ruled
Egypt for three centuries after Alexander
the Great conquered the country in the late
fourth century B.C. In part to solidify control
over their subjects, these rulers paid for temples to be built in the local style in honor of
Egyptian gods. Ptolemy VIII was a particularly prolific builder. He rebuilt the Opet
temple at Karnak and sponsored construction
projects at Edfu, Dendera, Medamoud,
Philae, Medinet Habu, and Deir el-Bahri,
among other sites, as well as at Coptos.

On the gateway are scenes in sunk relief
showing Ptolemy VIII making offerings to
various members of the Egyptian pantheon,
including Min and Isis. Short hieroglyphic
captions accompanying each scene name
the participants and describe their actions.
Besides its extensive Ptolemaic decoration,
the gateway bears texts dating to the reign
of the Roman emperor Nero (A.D. 54–68).
Nero's agents carved the name of their ruler,

"Nero Claudius," in hieroglyphs on the inner
part of the passageway, beneath a series of
cartouches of Ptolemy VIII.[3] The dismantling
and reuse of the blocks in a new location
must have happened after Nero's reign
and can be tentatively attributed to the late
Roman period, perhaps to the third or early
fourth century A.D. The curved arrangement
of the blocks in their secondary position suggests that they belonged to one of the bastion
towers of a late Roman fortification wall.

The gateway has been newly reconstructed by the Museum of Fine Arts
Department of Conservation.[4] Although
Dunham proposed during excavation that
the blocks all originated from the same building, only recently was it recognized that they
once belonged to a single gateway. From
the 1920s until 1995 the twenty-four blocks
were installed in the Museum of Fine Arts in
two units, as elements of a gateway and of
a separate section of temple wall. In the new
reconstruction the former "wall" unit has
been attached behind the previously identified

gateway elements, supplying the rear portion of one jamb. The impetus toward the new installation came from this author's observation that the relief decoration on both sets of blocks was standard for temple gateways. Details of the reliefs and some key measurements suggested that the museum's blocks were from a single gateway. Verification came with the discovery of an archival photograph showing the full shape of a particular block that was partially obscured from view in one part of the old installation. The block had the same unusual profile as a block in the other part of the display and had apparently been its neighbor in the original gateway.

Distinctive details of the architecture make possible some firm statements about adjoining elements that no longer survive. Bosses on the outer edges of the jambs tell us, for instance, that the gateway originally stood in a mud-brick wall, rather than in a stone wall. Another feature, the use of asymmetrical recesses on the passageway, makes it clear that the original wooden door, now missing, would have had a single leaf.

Like much Egyptian architectural decoration, the Coptos gateway reliefs are divided into rows, or registers, of scenes. Ten cult scenes survive, all from the same two registers near the top of the gateway. The theme throughout is typical for Egyptian temple reliefs: the reigning king gives gifts to the gods, who grant him favors in return.

On the gateway's façade Ptolemy makes offerings to two deities in each of four scenes. To Osiris[5] and Isis he offers incense and cool water, while to Horus and Nephthys he gives jars of wine. For Min and a goddess whose name is broken off, his gift is "myrrh for his father."[6] Myrrh, an aromatic ointment, is represented pictorially by a statuette of a reclining sphinx with an ointment jar between its paws. To "Harpocrates the very great, first of Amun"[7] and to "Isis the great,

the eye of Re, mistress of heaven," Ptolemy presents a platter of food. Often the royal gift and a reciprocal divine blessing are directly related. Thus in the scene where Ptolemy presents food, Harpocrates gives him "every good thing every day" (a common designation for food offerings), and Isis endows him with "all offerings and provisions."

On either side of the passageway, near the front, Ptolemy is shown being welcomed into the company of the gods. Thoth embraces the king, while Seshat endows him with the "years of Horus of Pe," or eternal rule. Ornamental motifs and royal names, rather than cult scenes, decorate the inner part of the passageway. Blocks survive here only on the gateway's right side. This was the side against which a door would have rested when the gateway was in use. On the rear face of the gateway, where two scenes remain, Ptolemy is shown offering wine to the earth god, Geb,[8] and giving incense to the sky goddess, Nut.

The carving style displays the robust, highly modeled quality of much Ptolemaic work. Full breasts and protruding bellies, standard for art under the Ptolemies, are in evidence throughout. The sculptors lavished great care on details such as jewelry and headdresses. In general, the carving is more accomplished for the figures and their trappings than it is for the hieroglyphs, perhaps because the small size chosen for many of the texts made them difficult to carve.

The reliefs were originally brightly painted. Enough color is preserved to demonstrate that the painters did not simply fill in carved elements with solid tones but also added many details, such as straps and patterns on garments or stars on sky signs spreading across the tops of the scenes. For some of the repeated ornament on the surface behind the door, painted features provided variety. Thus basket-shaped hieroglyphs

(*nb* signs) supplying the word *all* for a series of emblems of "all life and dominion" are each painted with a different basketweave pattern.

A fire might have led to the second phase of work on the gateway, under Nero.[9] Reddened sandstone at the spot where the wooden door once stood suggests that the door burned, causing the adjacent stone to discolor from heat. A fire would also explain the presence of a block that looks like an ancient repair. The workers who added Nero's name to the passageway perhaps did so as part of a larger restoration project that included replacing the damaged door and repairing the masonry.

The exact location at Coptos where the gateway of Ptolemy VIII was first erected, and where it still stood in Nero's day, remains uncertain. As a gate in a mud-brick wall, it most likely served as an entrance to the enclosure wall of a temple precinct. Because of the gateway's relatively modest dimensions, the precinct of a small subsidiary temple is the most likely location. Assigning the monument to a particular sanctuary is problematic, however, in part because the surviving blocks lack the lowest scenes on the jambs, where resident deities were traditionally shown. DWL

Opposite: Column drum; Coptos; Roman period, reign of Augustus (30 B.C.–A.D. 14); sandstone, pigment, gilding; 55 × 54 (diam) cm (21⅝ × 21¼ in.); Museum of Fine Arts, Boston, 24.1808. This finely painted and gilded column drum depicts Osiris and Isis receiving libations from Emperor Augustus.

Left: Gateway blocks and column drums as found at Coptos, 1923.

BIBLIOGRAPHY George A. Reisner, "Excavations in Egypt and Ethiopia, 1922–1925," *BMFA* 23 (June 1925): 18; *Romans and Barbarians*, exh. cat. (Boston: MFA, 1976), 16, fig. 1.

NOTES
1. Information on the expedition appears in Reisner, "Excavations in Egypt and Ethiopia," 18, and in the Harvard University-Museum of Fine Arts Expedition diary, vol. 4 (unpublished).
2. Claude Traunecker has proposed the southern sanctuary at Coptos as a possible alternative to the great temple for the gateway's original location (personal communication). For site plans of Coptos, see Raymond Weill, "Koptos (campagne de 1910)," *ASAE* 11 (1911): pls. I–II; Claude Traunecker, *Coptos: Hommes et dieux sur le parvis de Geb*, Orientalia Lovaniensia Analecta 43 (Louvain: Peeters Press, 1992): fig. 7.
3. Nero is named in the lowest surviving row of vertical cartouches and the fragmentary text band beneath it. The other royal names on this surface all belong to Ptolemy VIII.
4. Reconstruction of the gateway was directed by Arthur Beale, Department of Conservation, MFA, and Rita Freed, curator of ancient Egyptian, Nubian, and Near Eastern art, MFA. This author provided the research and drawings guiding the reconstruction.
5. Osiris is given the epithet "Foremost of the Mansion of Gold," a standard designation for the god at Coptos. For the "Mansion of Gold" as the Coptite sanctuary of Osiris, see Traunecker, *Coptos*, 98.
6. The goddess is most likely a form of Isis.
7. For the dual role of Harpocrates as the son of Amun and of Osiris, see Laure Pantalacci and Claude Traunecker, *Le temple d'el-Qal'a*, vol. 1 (Cairo: IFAO, 1990), 10.
8. The god's name and the top of his headdress are missing, so the identification of the figure as Geb is tentative. Another, less likely, alternative is that this is Shu, the god of air.
9. Claude Traunecker, personal communication.

112 Statue of an Official

Coptos, Min temple precinct
Ptolemaic to Roman period,
c. 50 B.C.–A.D. 25
Sandstone
112.5 x 38 cm (40½ x 15 in.)
The University of Pennsylvania
Museum of Archaeology
and Anthropology, E975

W. M. Flinders Petrie discovered this statue of an anonymous official near the temenos of the Min temple at Coptos. The tripartite costume, associated with the latter part of the Late Period, consists of a short-sleeved shirt; a wraparound kilt; and a fringed shawl or cloak.[1] The cloak is draped over the left shoulder, and its four folds continue around to the back pillar. The official also wears a diadem of rosette-shaped floral design. His hair is rendered in a somewhat naturalistic fashion at the back and shows two rows of curls at the front, beneath the diadem, which expand to three rows at the temples.

Deeply recessed eyes angle downward and inward at the inner canthi. The upper eyelids are rendered in relief, as are the rather narrow and sharp eyebrows. Although the nose, mouth, and chin are damaged, the lips are full and the corners of the mouth are drilled.

The clenched right hand is held close to the body; the right thumbnail is carefully detailed. The left hand holds the cloak in place. A tall back pillar rises to the neck, its top forming a truncated, flat-topped pyramid behind the head. Its inscription was never completed. The statue's head was broken off at the neck but has been reattached. The sculpture remains broken off at the ankles, and the statue base is missing. GS

BIBLIOGRAPHY W. M. Flinders Petrie, *Koptos* (London: Quaritch, 1896), 22.

NOTES
1. For the garment and the statue type, see Robert S. Bianchi, in *Cleopatra's Egypt: Age of the Ptolemies*, exh. cat. (Brooklyn: Brooklyn Museum, 1988), 66–67, 124–28.

113 Lion

Karanis, house 5016, room F
Roman period, 2d to mid-3d century A.D.
Limestone
H: 24 cm (9⅜ in.); W: 14.5 (5¼ in.);
L: 44.5 cm (17½ in.)
Kelsey Museum of Archaeology,
University of Michigan, 3683

Excavations conducted by the Kelsey Museum of Archaeology for the University of Michigan at the Greco-Roman site of Karanis provide an unique view of rural village life from the mid-third century B.C. to the end of the fifth century A.D. Situated in the Faiyum, an ancient (and modern) agricultural district lying fifty miles southwest of Cairo, Karanis was founded under Ptolemy II Philadelphus (285–246 B.C.) to settle Greek mercenaries within the local population and to exploit the fertile area. The town increased in population and size in the Roman period, reaching a high point in the third and fourth centuries A.D. Documentary evidence indicates at least a partial abandonment of Karanis in the fifth century, although archaeological remains suggest that some habitation continued into the sixth century A.D.

Working over the course of eleven seasons, excavators from the University of Michigan documented hundreds of residences, seventeen granaries, and two temples. Well-preserved finds from Karanis included domestic articles, numerous papyrus documents—including correspondence, public documents, and religious and scientific texts—and a wide range of sculpture, including architectural statuary and objects of personal devotion.

A considerable number of crouching lions, carved from the same local gray limestone used in antiquity as building material,[1] were found during excavations at Karanis. This example was recovered as a surface find from house 5016. A nearly identical lion[2] was discovered nearby in the inner court of the North Temple, leading the excavator, Arthur Boak, to speculate that the two had once formed a pair flanking the entrance to the inner court.[3] The form of a lion posed frontally on a plinth continued traditions documented from the early pharaonic period, when lions were more closely associated with the omnipotence of the pharaoh. Lion sculptures produced during the Greco-Roman period at Karanis are characterized by a schematic treatment of anatomical details[4] and may have served as guardian figures at specific temple sites or domestic or granary shrines.[5] NT

BIBLIOGRAPHY Arthur E. R. Boak, ed., *Karanis: The Temples, Coin Hoards, Botanical and Zoölogical Reports, Seasons 1924–31* (Ann Arbor: University of Michigan Press, 1933), 10, pl. VI (fig. 11), pl. VII (fig. 13); Elaine K. Gazda, *Guardians of the Nile: Sculptures from Karanis in the Fayoum (c. 250 B.C.–A.D. 450)*, exh. cat. (Ann Arbor: Kelsey Museum of Archaeology, University of Michigan, 1978), 18, 24, no. 4.

NOTES
1. Gazda, *Guardians of the Nile*, 18–19, nos. 1–12.
2. Ibid., 23.
3. Boak, *Karanis*, 10; see also pls. VI (fig. 11), VII (fig. 13) for site photograph and lion (25933).
4. Gazda, *Guardians of the Nile*, 18.
5. Ibid., 15.

114 Declaration of Property

Karanis, structure 4017
Roman period, c. A.D. 53
Papyrus, ink
15.6 x 14 cm (6⅛ x 5½ in.)
Special Collections Library, University
of Michigan, 6484

Excavations at Karanis produced a rich
and diverse harvest of archaeological data:
approximately one hundred thousand objects,
twenty-five hundred folders of papyri (many
containing multiple fragments) and some
five thousand ostraca. Probably the best-
documented site of the ancient world, Karanis
is one of the very few places for which we
know the exact findspot of every papyrus or
other written source. The excavators kept a
detailed record of the excavation and carefully labeled the recovered objects.

In 1935, when the first volume of the
ostraca from Karanis was published, the
editor stated that "by means of the ostracon
texts alone it is now possible to trace certain
families through several generations in the
occupancy of some of the houses, and we
may confidently expect that our knowledge
of these families will be considerably increased

by the publication of the contemporaneous
papyri."[1] Although some later scholars tried
to follow this approach, efforts were given
up completely in the early 1970s. In the
early 1990s, however, a team of young papyrologists proposed to study the site "house
to house," by combining archaeological and
textual data from individual structures.[2]

In 1933 excavators discovered structure
4017, which contained, along with other
archaeological objects, several papyri (probably more than fifty fragments) and ostraca
that date primarily from the beginning of the
fourth century A.D. Among the finds was this
papyrus, the only known example to date
from the middle of the first century A.D., or
three centuries earlier than the other recovered
documents, which indicates that the structure
might have been in use for a very long time.

The papyrus, like most papyri from
Karanis, was written in Greek, in about A.D.
53. It is a copy of a property return submitted

by Petheus, the elder son of Petheus, to
Thrakidas, keeper of the property archives
of the Arsinoite nome. Petheus describes
himself as a cultivator on the estate of
the emperor Germanicus and declares a
considerable property in the vicinity of the
villages Psenarpsenesis and Kerkesoucha,
and an olive grove in the vicinity, a house
and other holdings in the village itself, and
still other possessions at another location
in the same village.

TRANSLATION OF TEXT:
Copy of the report.

*To Thrakidas, the gymnasiarch and biblio-
phylax of the archives in the Arsinoite nome
from Petheus, the elder son of Petheus, from
Karanis in the Herakleides division, a farmer
of the estate of Germanicus. There belongs to
me in the Herakleides division near Karanis a
productive olive grove, in which the trees are
old, amounting in all to 11 arouras; and in
the village a house and courtyard in which I
dwell, and the half share of a privately owned
oil press and storehouse, and in another place
another house, buildings and dovecotes; and
near Psenarpsenesis a catoecic allotment of 5
arouras and an olive grove . . . and near
Kerkesoucha . . . . Therefore I have presented
this declaration.*

*Registered in the . . . year of Tiberius
Claudius Caesar Augustus Germanicus, . . .
29. I have signed it . . .*

TG

BIBLIOGRAPHY Elinor Husselman, ed., *Papyri from
Karanis: Third Series*, American Philological Associa-
tion, Philological Monographs 29 (Cleveland: Case
Western Reserve University Press, 1971), 49–50.

NOTES
1. Leiv Amundsen, *Greek Ostraca in the University
of Michigan Collection*, University of Michigan Studies, Humanistic Series 34 (Ann Arbor: University
of Michigan Press, 1935), ix.
2. The first article that has appeared is by P. van
Minnen, "House-to-House Enquiries: An Interdiscipli-
nary Approach to Roman Karanis," *Zeitschrift für
Papyrologie und Epigraphik* 100 (1994): 227–51.

115 Head of Serapis

Karanis, surface find
Roman period, late 2d century A.D.
Serpentine
13.3 x 6.7 x 6.0 cm (5¼ x 2⅝ x 2⅜ in.)
Kelsey Museum of Archaeology,
University of Michigan, 8526

This head is identifiable as the Greco-Egyptian deity Serapis by the five curling locks on his forehead (now broken), free-flowing hairdo and beard, and cylindrical *kalathos* (corn measure) adorned with olive branches. It must originally have been part of a composite statue, judging by indications on its back and neck that it was once inserted into a separate bust or figure.[1]

Long believed to be a political invention of the Ptolemies meant to unite the Greek and Egyptian populations, Serapis is now recognized as a syncretistic god who rose to prominence and was enthusiastically promoted by Ptolemy I Soter.[2] By the end of the Hellenistic period shrines dedicated to Serapis were common throughout Egypt, with principal cult centers in Memphis and Alexandria. A composite of two traditional Egyptian gods—Osiris, the god of the netherworld, and the deified Apis bull from Memphis— Serapis was revered in Roman Egypt as an omnipotent, protective deity (as was his companion, Isis).[3]

In addition to this serpentine head, Serapis was represented at Karanis in several other sculptured versions,[4] a partially conserved wall painting from a private home,[5] and an altar relief from the North Temple bearing the head of "Zeus Ammon Sarapis Helios."[6] NT

BIBLIOGRAPHY Wilhelm Hornbostel, *Serapis* (Leiden: E. J. Brill, 1973), 254, n. 8; 469, pl. CXLIV (no. 232); G. J. F. Kater-Sibbes, *Preliminary Catalogue of Serapis Monuments* (Leiden: E. J. Brill, 1973), 201, no. 1074; Anne E. Haeckl, "Osiris/Serapis," in *The Gods of Egypt in the Graeco-Roman Period*, ed. Anne E. Haeckl and Kate C. Spelman (Ann Arbor: Kelsey Museum of Archaeology, University of Michigan, 1977), 55, no. 39; Elaine K. Gazda, *Guardians of the Nile: Sculptures from Karanis in the Fayoum (c. 250 B.C.–A.D. 450)*, exh. cat. (Ann Arbor: Kelsey Museum of Archaeology, University of Michigan, 1978), 14, 37, no. 28.

NOTES
1. Gazda, *Guardians of the Nile*, 37.
2. John E. Stambaugh, *Sarapis under the Early Ptolemies* (Leiden: E. J. Brill, 1972), 12–13; see also Florence D. Friedman, *Beyond the Pharaohs: Egypt and the Copts in the 2nd to 7th Centuries A.D.*, exh. cat. (Providence: Rhode Island School of Design, 1989), 203. For a discussion of the establishment of the cult of Serapis under Alexander the Great, see Yves Bonnefoy, *Mythologies: A Restructured Translation of Dictionnaire des mythologies et des religions des sociétés traditionnelles et du monde antique*, vol. 1 (Chicago: University of Chicago Press, 1991), 123.
3. Stambaugh, *Serapis*, 4–5.
4. Gazda, *Guardians of the Nile*, 38–39, 53, 56 (nos. 29, 30, 47, 54). For a discussion of Karanis Serapis images, see also Elaine K. Gazda, ed., *Karanis: An Egyptian Town in Roman Times*, exh. cat. (Ann Arbor: Kelsey Museum of Archaeology, University of Michigan, 1983), 40–41.
5. Klaus Parlasca, *Mumienporträts und verwandte Denkmäler* (Wiesbaden: F. Steiner, 1966), 212, pl. 46 (1).
6. Arthur E. R. Boak, ed., *Karanis: The Temples, Coin Hoards, Botanical and Zoölogical Reports, Seasons 1924–31* (Ann Arbor: University of Michigan Press, 1933), 10–12, pl. VII (fig. 15).

116 Bust of Harpocrates

Karanis, house 39, room A
Roman period, early 3d century A.D.
Terra-cotta
12.4 x 8.6 x 6.8 cm (4⅞ x 3⅜ x 2⅝ in.)
Kelsey Museum of Archaeology,
University of Michigan, 6461

One of nineteen terra-cotta figurines of Harpocrates excavated at Karanis, this mold-made image depicts the deity in bust form. Harpocrates, identified by the Greek rendering of his Egyptian name, meaning "Horus the child," is shown as a chubby youth with a tightly braided and coiled sidelock. The features, particularly the eyes, are carefully rendered, the lips are parted, and the small chin barely protrudes from a fleshy neck. The deity wears a square amulet, suspended by an inverted triangular element, which might have been attached to a necklace rendered in paint (and now abraded).[1]

According to Egyptian myth, Harpocrates was conceived by Isis after the murder and regeneration of her husband, Osiris, and thus the infant god served as an emblem of fecundity. His popularity in Karanis and other agrarian areas can be ascribed to his association with fertility and the earth.[2] Terra-cotta figurines of Harpocrates were found in granaries and houses throughout Karanis, as well as in a concentrated find of eight images in the south temple complex.[3]

The high quality of craftsmanship evident in this Harpocrates bust suggests that it might have been a workshop model.[4] Or, as suggested by its find site in a house, this terra-cotta could have been an object of personal devotion from a domestic shrine. NT

BIBLIOGRAPHY Elaine K. Gazda, *Guardians of the Nile: Sculptures from Karanis in the Fayoum (c. 250 B.C.–A.D. 450)*, exh. cat. (Ann Arbor: Kelsey Museum of Archaeology, University of Michigan, 1978), 64, no. 63; Marti Lu Allen, "The Terracotta Figurines from Karanis: A Study of Technique, Style, and Chronology in Fayoumic Coroplastics" (Ph.D. diss., University of Michigan, Ann Arbor, 1985), 380–81, no. 63, pl. 54.

NOTES
1. See Françoise Dunand, *Catalogue des terres cuites gréco-romaines d'Egypte* (Paris: Réunion des musées nationaux, 1990), 105, no. 242, for a similar bust-form terra-cotta Harpocrates bearing a rectangular amulet suspended from a floral garland.
2. Elaine K. Gazda, ed., *Karanis: An Egyptian Town in Roman Times*, exh. cat. (Ann Arbor: Kelsey Museum of Archaeology, University of Michigan, 1983), 38.
3. Ibid.
4. Marti Lu Allen, in Gazda, *Guardians of the Nile*, 58.

117 Three Figurines

Karanis

Roman period, 2d to 5th century A.D.

Terra-cotta

Kelsey Museum of Archaeology,
University of Michigan

A *Couchant Horse*
House 506, room M, level B
6.1 x 2.4 x 7.5 cm (2⅜ x 1 x 3 in.)
KM 6896

B *Standing Dog*
House 114, room C, level B
9.8 x 5.8 x 10.8 cm (3⅞ x 2¼ x 4¼ in.)
KM 6905

C *Standing Horse*
House 507, room B, level B
12.6 x 4.3 x 9.2 cm (5 x 1¾ x 3⅝ in.)
KM 6894

The site of the Roman town of Karanis yielded hundreds of terra-cotta figurines, many of them depicting animals. Although they resemble toys, these mold-made figures most likely held religious significance. Both the standing and seated horses wear parade trappings, perhaps indicating their use as souvenirs or votive figures in connection with specific religious festivals.[1] The long-haired dog figurine, very unlike the Anubis figures seen on contemporary funerary stelae (see cat. no. 122), wears an amulet hanging from its collar, perhaps another indication of religious significance.[2]

The dog figure was made from a three-part mold; the horses both came from two-part molds. All were covered with a lime wash, with details added in black, red, and pink paint, some of which still survives. Many different kinds of terra-cotta animals were found at Karanis. Horses are the most common, followed by dogs and then camels; other animals and birds are much less frequently represented.[3] Significantly none depicts an Egyptian sacred animal; although

the Karanis terra-cottas sometimes represent the same species (cats, dogs, cows, etc.), they never show the iconographic features of the sacred animals. Thus it is unlikely that they were used in connection with animal cults. TW

BIBLIOGRAPHY 117A: Marti Lu Allen, "The Terra-cotta Figurines from Karanis: A Study of Technique, Style, and Chronology in Fayoumic Coroplastics" (Ph.D. diss., University of Michigan, Ann Arbor, 1985), 333, no. 39, pl. 29. 117B: Allen, "Terracotta Figurines from Karanis," 288, no. 19, pl. 15. 117C: ibid., 328, no. 36, pl. 27.

NOTES

1. Marti Lu Allen, in Elaine K. Gazda, *Guardians of the Nile: Sculptures from Karanis in the Fayoum (c. 250 B.C.–A.D. 450)*, exh. cat. (Ann Arbor: Kelsey Museum of Archaeology, University of Michigan, 1978), 60.
2. For related terra-cotta dogs excavated at the Middle Egyptian site of Antinopolis (Antinoe), see Françoise Dunand, *Catalogue des terres cuites gréco-romaines d'Egypte* (Paris: Réunion des musées nationaux, 1990), 287–89.
3. For an idea of the range of types of the Karanis animal terra-cottas, see Elaine K. Gazda, ed., *Karanis: An Egyptian Town in Roman Times*, exh. cat. (Ann Arbor: Kelsey Museum of Archaeology, University of Michigan, 1983), 15, fig. 23.

118 Three Toys

Karanis
Roman period, 2d to 5th century A.D.
Kelsey Museum of Archaeology,
University of Michigan

A *Horse on Wheels*
   House 114, room D, plus surface finds
   Wood with applied pigment
   H: 9.8 cm (3⅞ in.); W: 4.5 cm (1¾ in.);
   L: 17.7 cm (7 in.)
   KM 10034, 10036, 10037, 26404,
   26406 (piece reconstructed from parts
   found in the course of excavation)

B *Doll*
   House 114, room D
   Wood
   12.4 x 3.7 x 1.3 cm (4⅞ x 1½ x ½ in.)
   KM 10003

C *Castanet*
   House 209, room C
   Wood with modern twine
   18.5 x 2.9 x 3.4 cm (7¼ x 1⅛ x 1⅜ in.)
   KM 3534

Since most Egyptian artifacts come from a funerary context, we cannot always be certain whether such objects were used in life. The artifacts from Karanis, however, were found in houses and show signs of wear and use. More than 250 objects in a variety of materials from the Karanis excavations have been classified as toys of some sort; most common are gaming pieces, marbles, dice, and tops. There is also a significant group of wooden toys, of which the present three objects are typical examples.[1]

The wooden horse is one of several wheeled animals and birds discovered at Karanis; this particular example has been reconstructed from several pieces. Such pull toys were common in Greco-Roman Egypt, although they are rarely encountered outside Karanis in such excellent condition. This horse is still functional, lacking only a cord through the hole in its nose with which to pull it.

House C123 and courtyard following excavation.

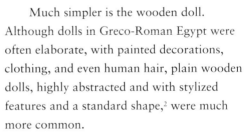

Much simpler is the wooden doll. Although dolls in Greco-Roman Egypt were often elaborate, with painted decorations, clothing, and even human hair, plain wooden dolls, highly abstracted and with stylized features and a standard shape,[2] were much more common.

The castanet is one of approximately fifty musical instruments found at Karanis; these include other castanets, clappers, flutes, bells, and finger cymbals in bronze, bone, and wood.[3] Because of its size and general appearance, this particular castanet is possibly a children's toy rather than an instrument for adults. Unlike modern castanets, which are played in pairs, this one is played alone by grasping the handle and shaking it, causing the loose pieces of wood to strike each other. Although the cord binding the pieces together is modern, the rest of the castanet is original. TW

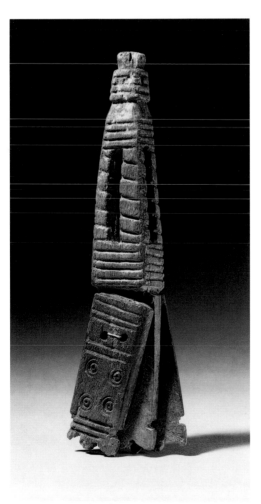

NOTES

1. Other published toys of this sort from Karanis are a toy weaver's comb and a toy chair in Eunice Dauterman Maguire, Henry P. Maguire, and Maggie J. Duncan-Flowers, *Art and Holy Powers in the Early Christian House* (Urbana: University of Illinois Press, 1989), 230–31, nos. 150, 151. In the same volume are examples of dice (no. 144) and a cylindrical box possibly used as a dice cup (no. 141); see 226–27. These and other toys from Karanis (including a toy animal, a top, a model writing desk, and a model lamp) can be seen in group photographs in Elaine K. Gazda, ed., *Karanis: An Egyptian Town in Roman Times*, exh. cat. (Ann Arbor: Kelsey Museum of Archaeology, University of Michigan, 1983), 29–30, figs. 52, 53.
2. For a parallel to this doll from Karanis, see Maguire, Maguire, and Duncan-Flowers, *Art and Holy Powers*, 229, no. 147. Two other Greco-Roman dolls similar to examples from Karanis are in the same publication; one is a carved bone doll with yarn hair wrapped in cloth, while the other is a rag doll representing a swaddled baby (see 228, nos. 145, 146).
3. For two flutes from Karanis, see ibid., 224–25, nos. 139, 140.

119 Two Vessels

Karanis
Roman period, 3d to 4th century A.D.
Glass
Kelsey Museum of Archaeology,
University of Michigan

A *Deep Bowl*
House 42, room J, level C
6.5 x 13.4 (diam) cm (2½ x 5¼ in.)
KM 5913

B *Flask*
House 506, room M, level B
16 x 13 (diam) cm (6¼ x 5⅛ in.)
KM 5943

Karanis has yielded more glass than any other site in Egypt. In addition to a collection of 180 glass vessels from Karanis obtained by purchase from Dr. D. L. Askren before the University of Michigan began excavations,[1] some 1,003 pieces were recovered in the seasons of 1924 and 1929; hundreds of additional pieces were found in subsequent seasons. Like much of the glass from Karanis, these two pieces are well preserved and were found in a good archaeological context in hoards of glass objects. Both pieces were recovered with other glass objects from large pottery storage bins. The glass bowl was found in a storage jar, along with twenty-five other glass vessels, in the basement of a house, while the flask was located in a similar jar covered with a stone mortar, along with glass vessels, a cosmetic jar containing two bone pins, and a glass lamp containing four dice.[2]

The iridescence common to Roman period glass is absent from most Karanis pieces and with good reason: such iridescence was not intentional but is the result of deterioration brought on by moisture. The extremely arid conditions at Karanis that helped preserve wood, papyrus, and textile artifacts similarly kept glass objects from decay. This bowl and flask, then, give a good idea of how ancient glass originally looked. Both pieces lack their original coverings: the glass bowl probably once had a lid (as can be seen from the angle of its inner rim), while the flask was found with a leather cover, long since deteriorated. TW

BIBLIOGRAPHY Donald B. Harden, *Roman Glass from Karanis Found by the University of Michigan Archaeological Expedition in Egypt, 1924–1929* (Ann Arbor: University of Michigan Press, 1936), 107 (no. 233), 210, pls. 8, 18 (no. 601).

NOTES
1. Margaret Cool Root with L. A. McCoy, *Wondrous Glass: Reflections on the World of Rome, c. 50 B.C.–A.D. 650,* exh. cat. (Ann Arbor: Kelsey Museum of Archaeology, University of Michigan, 1982), 9.
2. For photographs of the jar with pins and the lamp containing dice, see ibid., pls. 2, 3.

120 Pair of Statuettes

Tebtunis (Tell Umm el-Breigat),
temple enclosure
Roman period, 1st to 3d centuries A.D.
Calcite, traces of pigment
52 x 14.2 cm (20½ x 5⅝ in.)
Phoebe A. Hearst Museum
of Anthropology, University of
California, Berkeley, 6-20313, 6-20314

Each of these statuettes depicts a naked, wavy-haired youth standing on a drum base; a tiny ram is positioned by one foot. A dagger or short sword, suspended by a diagonal strap across the breast, rests beneath the proper left armpit; in one hand the boy grasps the end of a cloak, which is draped carelessly across his back. One arm, broken away in both instances, was upraised; the other rests upon his hip. The body is arranged in a somewhat unpracticed version of the Praxitelean S-curve, and the proportions and modeling are uneven. The two figures were clearly intended as a pair, for they are virtually mirror images and bear the same inscription, written in retrograde (backward): "Herakles, a knight, dedicated (this statue) as a benefaction." The statuettes were found during Bernard P. Grenfell and Arthur S. Hunt's exploration of the enclosure of the temple dedicated to the crocodile god Sobeknebtunis, which also contained shrines dedicated to other divinities. The precise context of the statues is unknown, but if they served any purpose other than votive, it might have been as lamp or offering holders with the now-lost upraised arms supporting some sort of receptacle.

The identification of the youths is problematic. Although there was a temple dedicated to the youthful god Harpocrates at Tebtunis,[1] the lack of a sidelock argues against this connection. In the Ptolemaic and Roman periods the Egyptian Harpocrates and Greek Herakles became associated;[2] this composite divinity usually has a muscular physique, however. At some time the god Apollo joined the duo, and an Apollo-Harpocrates-Herakles triad is also attested,[3] but, again, little similarity exists between the triple divinity and these youths. According to one Tebtunis papyrus, there was a temple in the area dedicated to the Dioscuri, Castor and Pollux, though not necessarily at Tebtunis;[4] therefore, these twin images could possibly represent the savior twins.

Given the adolescent appearance of the youths and the associated ram, however, the statuettes most likely depict Apollo. In the absence of sufficient documentation, few reliable conclusions can be drawn regarding the 1899–1900 Tebtunis finds. Although subsequent missions have worked at the site in the intervening decades, only since 1988 has a joint expedition of the Institut français d'archéologie orientale and the Papyrological Institute of Milan[5] undertaken a modern, systematic study of the entire site.

TRANSLATION OF INSCRIBED TEXT:
Herakles, a knight, dedicated (this statue) as a benefaction.

CK

BIBLIOGRAPHY Henry Frederick Lutz, *Egyptian Statues and Statuettes in the Museum of Anthropology of the University of California,* University of California Egyptian Expedition Publications 5 (Leipzig: J. C. Hinrichs, 1930), 10–11, pl. 15ab.

NOTES
1. For a short general summary of references on Tebtunis, including information about the main cults, see Helck, in *LÄ,* vol. 6, 245–46.
2. On Herakles-Harpocrates, see Erika Feucht et al., *Vom Nil zum Neckar: Kunstschätze Ägyptens aus pharonischer und koptischer Zeit an der Universität Heidelbergs* (Heidelberg: Ägyptologisches Institut, Universität Heidelberg, 1986), 118–19, no. 286, with reference to Klaus Parlasca, "Herakles-Harpokrates und 'Horos auf den Krokodilen,'" in *Akten des 24. Orientalisten-Kongress in München 1957* (1959): 71–74.
3. On Apollo-Harpocrates-Herakles, see R. E. Wit, *Isis in the Graeco-Roman World* (Ithaca, N.Y.: Cornell University Press, 1971), 214, 217.
4. Papyrus Teb. 39, 14, dated to 114 B.C.; reference from Alan K. Bowman, *Egypt after the Pharaohs, 332 B.C.–A.D. 642: From Alexander to the Arab Conquest* (London: British Museum, 1986), 171, n. 8.
5. For a summary of excavation activity and the first season's results, see Claude Gallazzi, "Fouilles anciennes et nouvelles sur le site de Tebtynis," *BIFAO* 89 (1989): 179ff.

in the Ptolemaic and Roman periods are many and varied, but the single most common type is one that the Greeks called Isis Kourotrophos and the Romans Isis lactans, the mother Isis suckling the infant Horus.[2] This image has resonance in Christian iconography as the immediate forerunner of the Virgin Mary cradling her son Jesus.[3]

This plaque, now much fragmented, originally depicted a seated figure of Isis nursing Horus. Both the goddess's proper left arm and the entire figure of Horus are now missing; her right hand cradles her left breast. Shown here in her typical guise, Isis has curled hair and wears a veil, sleeved chiton, and fringed shawl knotted between her breasts.[4] Although numerous terra-cotta, metal, and stone parallels of this image have survived, plaster examples are extremely rare. This flat plaster figure was formed in a one-piece mold,[5] then gessoed and painted. Isis's hair is yellow, her flesh is pink, and details are picked out in black and green; her garments may have been mostly white. The purpose of this plaque is uncertain, but it was probably dedicated to the goddess, either in one of the central temple precincts at Tebtunis or in a smaller house shrine. CK

121 Votive Plaque

Tebtunis (Tell Umm el-Breigat)
Roman period, 1st to 3d centuries A.D.
Plaster, gesso, pigment
27 x 12 cm (10⅝ x 4¾ in.)
Phoebe A. Hearst Museum
of Anthropology, University
of California, Berkeley, 6-20448

Of all the ancient Egyptian religious cults, that of the goddess Isis eventually achieved the greatest prominence and longevity.[1] From Egypt and the eastern Mediterranean her veneration was carried to Greece, Italy, and Western Europe. Because of her manifold imagery in Egyptian religion—as powerful magician, loyal sister, faithful wife, steadfast widow, and supportive mother—the Greeks and Romans identified her with such diverse divinities as Demeter, Tyche, Artemis (Delos), Hera (Samos), and, via her previous association with Hathor, Aphrodite. Her depictions

NOTES
1. For the immense range of documentation on the Goddess Isis, see, in general, R. E. Wit, *Isis in the Graeco-Roman World* (Ithaca, N.Y.: Cornell University Press, 1971); and, for references, Jean Leclant and G. Clerc, *Inventaire bibliographique des Isiaca (IBIS)*, 4 vols. (Leiden: E. J. Brill, 1972–91).
2. Wit, *Isis*, 216–17.
3. Compare, e.g., the Coptic stela of Mary nursing Jesus (Maria lactans), now in Berlin (inv. no. 4726), in Steffen Wenig, *The Woman in Egyptian Art*, trans. B. Fischer (New York: McGraw-Hill, 1969), 54, 112, no. 112.
4. Among the numerous parallels for Isis's costume, see a statue of Isis from the Luxor Serapeum in Leclant and Clerc, *IBIS*, vol. 3 (1985), pl. III.
5. The technique of plaster modeling is thought to have originated in Egypt; see Jean Marcadé, "A propos des statuettes hellénistiques en aragonite du Musée de Délos," *Bulletin de correspondance hellénique* 76 (1952): 198ff.

122 Funerary Stela of Heraklea and Ares

Terenouthis
Roman period, late 3d to early 4th century A.D.
Limestone, pigment
39.4 x 27.6 cm (15½ x 10⅞ in.)
Kelsey Museum of Archaeology, University of Michigan, 21179

Situated on the western border of the Delta, Terenouthis is noteworthy for its large necropolis dating from the 6th Dynasty to the fourth century A.D. and for the remains of a temple dedicated to Hathor, "Mistress of Mefket," constructed by Ptolemy I Soter and completed by Ptolemy II Philadelphus. Both archaeological and textual sources show particularly extensive activity at the site throughout the Roman period. One season of excavations conducted by the Kelsey Museum of Archaeology during 1935 at Kom Abu Billo (ancient Terenuthis) resulted in the recovery of hundreds of funerary stelae. Distinctive in their format, and often identified as "Terenuthis stelae," these funerary monuments were produced during the first four centuries A.D. and, in their representations of the deceased, combine typical Greco-Roman style with Egyptian elements. Short accompanying texts were inscribed in either demotic or Greek.

The Greek inscription on this example identifies the deceased, "Heraklea, aged 60, (and) Ares, aged 52, year 5 (in the month of) Mechir, day 1. Farewell!" Heraklea is depicted lying on her funerary couch, holding a vessel, while Ares stands beside an incense burner. Both are represented as idealized youths conducting funerary rites. The depictions, typical for Terenouthis stelae, are taken from a relatively limited number of standard poses, all of which have religious significance.

Such representations have some parallels with earlier Egyptian stelae that show the deceased seated before an offering table. Heraklea's offerings are moved under the couch, however, since, according to artistic convention of the time, they could not be represented in front of a forward-facing figure. Although the clothing and hairstyles of the two decedents are distinctly Greco-Roman, the incense burner and the jackal figure, representing the god Anubis, "guardian of the necropolis," are traditional Egyptian elements. The sunk-relief carving technique is also typically Egyptian.[1] NT

BIBLIOGRAPHY Finley A. Hooper, *The Funerary Stelae from Kom Abou Billou* (Ann Arbor: Kelsey Museum of Archaeology, University of Michigan, 1961), pl. 12a (no. 139); R. McCleary, *Portals to Eternity* (Ann Arbor: Kelsey Museum of Archaeology, University of Michigan, 1987), 10, fig. 22.

NOTES
1. For a discussion of Greek and Egyptian motifs in second- to third-century funerary stelae, see Thelma K. Thomas, in Florence D. Friedman, *Beyond the Pharaohs: Egypt and the Copts in the 2nd to 7th Centuries A.D.*, exh. cat. (Providence: Rhode Island School of Design, 1989), 251–53.

123 Funerary Statues

Karanog

Meroitic period, 100 B.C.–A.D. 300

Sandstone

University of Pennsylvania Museum
of Archaeology and Anthropology

A Male *Ba* Statue
Surface find
H: 58 cm (22⅞ in.)
E7018

B Pair *Ba* Statue
Southeast corner of grave 273
H: 46 cm (18⅛ in.)
E7009

C Head from a *Ba* Statue
Surface find
H: 18 cm (7⅛ in.)
E7036

Although the advancing military might of
Assyria forced Egypt's Kushite 25th Dynasty
to fall back to its homeland and relinquish
control of Upper and Lower Egypt, the
dynasty continued to thrive in Nubia. The
subsequent history of the kingdom of Kush
is generally divided into two phases, the
Napatan period (c. 750–270 B.C.) and the
Meroitic period (c. 270 B.C.–A.D. 350).[1]
Two significant changes mark the division
between these eras: the transfer of the royal
cemetery from Napata to Meroe and the shift
from the use of Egyptian as the only written
language to the use of Meroitic.[2]

   Between 1907 and 1910 the University
of Pennsylvania's Eckley B. Coxe Jr. Expedition to Egypt excavated and published
important sites in Nubia, including the
Meroitic town and cemetery of Karanog.[3]
The expedition leaders were David Randall-
MacIver, the University Museum's first
professional Egyptologist (his previous work
at Zimbabwe had demonstrated that its
earliest structures were of medieval date
and built by the indigenous population),
and Charles Leonard Woolley, who went
on to direct excavations at Ur in 1922.[4]

   In the cemetery of Karanog the expedition recovered a remarkable number of
sculptures: "Fragments, heads, and nearly
complete figures found in the cemetery represent an original total of 120 statues."[5]
Although perhaps ultimately derived from
Egyptian sources, these statues represent

a sculptural form largely unique to Meroitic Nubia.[6] Termed *ba* statues by those who first studied them because they resembled the Egyptian method of depicting a spiritual element of the deceased (the *ba*) as a human-headed bird, the statues usually combine human and avian anatomy. Woolley and Randall-MacIver believed that a developmental progression from bird statues to human-headed bird statues to human statues with attached bird feathers and tail could be possible, but, as Steffen Wenig has stated, "Since the tombs have not been securely dated, it is difficult to date the *ba*-statues precisely."[7] In any event, the combination of human and bird into a single image must certainly have been intended to represent some spiritual and otherworldly aspect of the deceased.

The Karanog *ba* statues represent the civil, religious, and economic elite of the ancient town and their relations. They seem to have been placed either in a niche in the burial's pyramid-shaped superstructure or possibly in the offering chamber.[8] Most typical of the type is the single figure, which can be either male or female. The statue of a man

(cat. no. 123A) is naked to the waist except for a strap that passes over his right shoulder. An ankle-length pleated garment, worn under a knee-length kilt with sash, covers his lower body. The right hand is drilled for insertion of a separate staff; the left hand clutches a folded handkerchief or fly whisk carved in raised relief.[9] The characteristic back and tail feathers of a bird extend from the figure's back. The head is a modern restoration.

The pair statue (cat. no. 123B) is more unusual. Both figures are male. Whether they are intended to represent separate individuals or the same man is unknown. The figures stand side by side and share a common, flaring bird back, which may once have been differentiated by painted plumage. The relative proportions and execution are poor, but the statue shares the same basic elements of better-executed examples, including stylized hair and eyes and prominent ears. Both heads are drilled at the top for the insertion of a separately made solar disk. The figures wear low-slung, ankle-length kilts with sashes extending down the front. The feet are flat and poorly modeled, and the heads are joined by reserve space. Arms extend straight at the sides, with the outer hands fisted, but only one figure shows both arms. The missing arm presumably was conceived as placed behind that of his mate. The sculpture has some modern restorations.

The head from a *ba* statue (cat. no. 123C) retains traces of pinkish pigment on the neck, ear, and under the chin, and some gray-black on the hair. The eyes are stylized and emphasized, as are the ears, which are deeply drilled. The nose is also drilled at the nostrils. The lips are full and separated by a downward curving, incised line. The modeling of the rest of the face is rudimentary. The hairline is sharply defined, and a raised area on the top of the head indicates where a sun disk was broken off. GS

BIBLIOGRAPHY 123A: Charles Leonard Woolley and David Randall-MacIver, *Karanog: The Romano-Nubian Cemetery* (Philadelphia: University Museum, University of Pennsylvania, 1910), vol. 1, 239. 123B: ibid., vol. 1, 238, vol. 2, pl. 8. 123C: ibid., vol. 1, 240, vol. 2, pl. 9.

NOTES
1. The Napatan period starts about 750 B.C., before the royal family of Kush became rulers of Egypt. For other overviews, see Karl-Heinz Priese, "The Kingdom of Kush: The Napatan Period," and Fritz Hintze, "The Kingdom of Kush: The Meroitic Period," in *Africa in Antiquity: The Arts of Ancient Nubia and the Sudan*, exh. cat., vol. 1, *The Essays* (Brooklyn: Brooklyn Museum, 1978), 75–105; David O'Connor, *Ancient Nubia: Egypt's Rival in Africa* (Philadelphia: University Museum, University of Pennsylvania, 1993), 70–84.
2. See Priese, "The Napatan Period," 75.
3. See Woolley and Randall-MacIver, *Karanog*; David O'Connor and David Silverman, "The University Museum in Egypt," *Expedition* 21 (Winter 1979): 19–22.
4. See O'Connor and Silverman, "The University Museum"; Warren R. Dawson and Eric P. Uphill, *Who Was Who in Egyptology*, 2d rev. ed. (London: Egypt Exploration Society, 1972), 190 (MacIver), 310–11 (Woolley).
5. Woolley and Randall-MacIver, *Karanog*, 47.
6. The form is remarkably like the small amuletic *ba* figures produced in Egypt during the Late Period, as well as some of the composite deities of the same date. Although no link between them can be demonstrated, the image resembles that of a statue of a New Kingdom monarch in the guise of a falcon in the Musée du Louvre, Paris (E5351), recently illustrated in Christiane Ziegler, *The Louvre: Egyptian Antiquities* (London: Scala Books, 1990), 46. The head of a similar statue is in Brooklyn (58.118); see Richard A. Fazzini et al., *Ancient Egyptian Art in the Brooklyn Museum* (Brooklyn: Brooklyn Museum, 1989), no. 36, with additional discussion and bibliography on the statue type.
7. Steffen Wenig, *Africa in Antiquity*, vol. 2, *The Catalogue*, 88.
8. See ibid.; O'Connor, *Ancient Nubia*, 104.
9. See Woolley and Randall-MacIver, *Karanog*, 48.

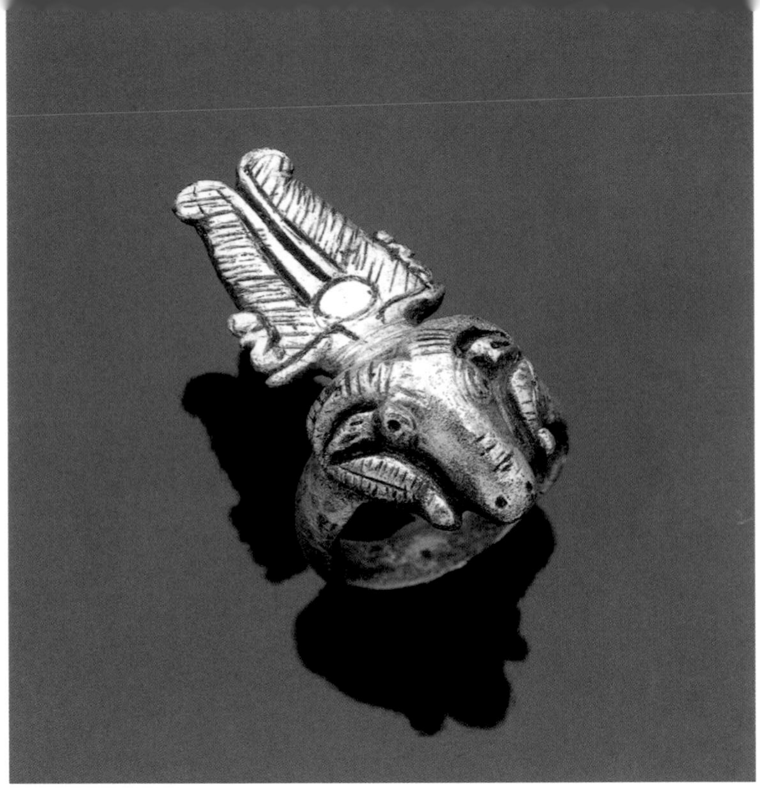

124 Meroitic Jewelry

Meroe West, tomb W179
Meroitic period, 1st to 2d
century A.D.
Museum of Fine Arts, Boston

A *Crowned Ram Ring*
Cast silver
H (bezel): 3.4 cm (1⅜ in.);
diam: 2 cm (¾ in.)
24.485

B *Bracelet*
Gold and carnelian
H: .9 cm (⅜ in.); L: 9.2 cm (3⅝ in.)
24.1091

The fortuitous collapse of a roof effectively sealed private tomb W179, in the western cemetery at Meroe, from looters. Because the number of unplundered tombs at this site is limited,[1] the field records and objects from W179 provide a rare opportunity to examine a complete assemblage of jewelry as it accompanied the deceased to the grave.[2] Numerous objects of adornment were found on the body, in wooden, bronze, and ivory boxes, and scattered on the floor.

The five rings in the cache were cast in silver.[3] One is a signet or seal, a ring form popular throughout the Meroitic period.[4] Another has a circular bezel with scored parallel lines. The remaining three tridimensional rings include two in the shape of rearing uraei (one with double feather crown, the other with inlays, now missing) and one in the form of a ram's head with an Amun crown flanked by small uraei.

The intaglio and uraei rings were found on the hands of the deceased,[5] but the crowned-ram ring was discovered next to a decayed ivory box on the floor of the burial chamber. The small, rectangular box, decorated with an incised sphinx, contained red, blue, green, and gilt glass beads of varying shapes and sizes; five pierced spiral shells; a green faience crocodile; three bronze ball beads; a silver barrel bead; thirty-five silver Hathor mask pendants; six silver uraei; six silver rams (unpierced); eleven silver cruciform pendants; two hollow gold uraei; and a small gold wire *wadjet* (sacred eye) pendant.

Ram-headed jewels were a prominent feature of Nubian adornment throughout the first millennium B.C. The necklace of three pendant ram heads with sun disk and uraeus worn by Napatan kings continued to be associated with royalty during the Meroitic period, although additional jewelry frequently accompanied it.[6]

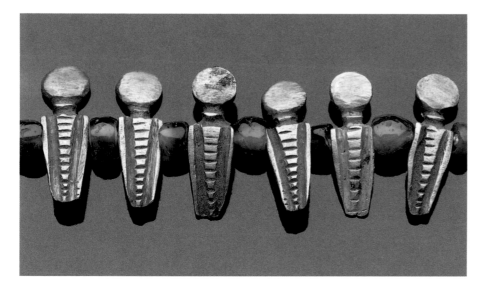

George A. Reisner also recovered ten bracelets from W179, divided and symmetrically placed on the wrists of the deceased. Each bracelet, composed of multiple repeating amuletic elements of gold occasionally interspersed with carnelian or glass ball beads, was delicate, finely crafted, and originally strung with linen. There were no metal hoops or clasps for attachment, so that each unit was probably tied in place. The very small borings in many of the beads (around .5 millimeter) and the use of hollow, thin gold sheet for the amulets indicates a funerary purpose.[7]

One of the bracelets found in situ on the right wrist of the deceased consists of a string of twenty-one gold uraei beads alternately separated by twenty carnelian ball beads. The upreared cobras are surmounted by sun disks and detailed with chased horizontal striations along the midline. The uraeus was especially meaningful to the rulers of the 25th Dynasty and persisted as a popular amuletic form during the Meroitic period.[8] YM

BIBLIOGRAPHY 124A: Dows Dunham, *The Royal Cemeteries of Kush*, vol. 5, *The West and South Cemeteries at Meroe* (Boston: MFA, 1963), 177, fig. 130e. 124B: ibid., 184, 186, fig. 133.

NOTES
1. Another intact cache was recovered from Meroe W5; see Dows Dunham, *Two Royal Ladies of Meroe*, Communications to the Trustees 7 (Boston: MFA, 1924).
2. For a description of the burial goods and chamber, see Dunham, *The West and South Cemeteries*, 177–88.
3. Pamela Hatchfield, associate curator, Research Lab, Museum of Fine Arts, Boston, determined that the ram ring was cast in one piece, most likely using the lost-wax technique.
4. Sixty-two seal rings form a significant portion of the Ferlini Treasure. Five are cast silver; the remainder are gold. See Karl-Heinz Priese, *The Gold of Meroe* (New York: MMA; Mainz: Philipp von Zabern, 1993), 21. Of the nineteen silver rings found on the hands of King Aryesbekhe (Meroe North 16), eighteen were signets and one was of a seated ape in the round; see Dows Dunham, *The Royal Cemeteries of Kush*, vol. 4, *Royal Tombs at Meroe and Barkal* (Boston: MFA, 1957), 139, pl. LX, G.
5. In general, the signet and crowned-uraeus rings were worn on the left hand, while the uraeus and linear-patterned rings were associated with the right hand. The field records for W179 do not specify the fingers on which the rings were worn, only that the uncrowned-uraeus ring still had a finger bone through the hoop.

6. E.g., Queen Amanishakheto wears a long ball-bead necklace and broad collar in addition to the ram necklace; see Dows Dunham, *The Royal Cemeteries of Kush*, vol. 3, *Decorated Chapels of the Meroitic Pyramids at Meroe and Barkal* (Boston: MFA, 1952), pl. 16B.
7. Because elaborate metal terminals and decorated hoops are often found on Meroitic bracelets and necklaces, Dunham generalized that jewels from Meroitic burials were worn in life, as opposed to Napatan jewelry, which is largely funerary (see *Two Royal Ladies*, 15).
8. The use of multiple uraei in bracelets, necklaces, and within the sun disk itself is well attested. For an example of the latter, see the head ornament of Queen Amanishakheto in Steffen Wenig, *Africa in Antiquity: The Arts of Ancient Nubia and the Sudan*, exh. cat., vol. 2, *The Catalogue* (Brooklyn: Brooklyn Museum, 1978), nos. 164, 237.

125 Signet Rings

Meroitic period
Cast gold
Museum of Fine Arts, Boston

A *Signet Ring*
Meroe West, tomb W134
c. 10 B.C.–A.D. 114
H (bezel): .5 cm (¼ in.);
diam: 1.7 cm (⅝ in.)
24.571

B *Signet Ring*
Meroe West, tomb W106
c. A.D. 90–225
H (bezel): .5 cm (¼ in.);
diam: 1.9 cm (¾ in.)
24.568

C *Signet Ring*
Meroe West, tomb W333
c. 100 B.C.
H (bezel): .5 cm (¼ in.);
diam: 1.8 cm (¾ in.)
23.303

Finger rings of various shapes and materials were popular items of adornment in Nubia during the Meroitic period. They were often of the seal or signet type, although other forms, such as tridimensional uraeus rings,[1] also existed. Signet rings were cast in three-part molds and typically have round to ovoid bezels of varying heights. The bezel designs encompass geometric patterns, amuletic symbols, royal figures, and images of the gods in various forms.

The rings excavated by George A. Reisner from Meroitic contexts were crafted from carved stone, glass, bronze, iron, silver, and gold. Silver was sometimes gilded, and the hoops and bezels of bronze and iron rings were occasionally covered by thick gold sheet. Several gilded silver rings were enameled using a variety of techniques.[2]

While gold signet rings dominate the excavated finds, silver intaglios were also common. From one royal burial in the Northern Cemetery at Meroe,[3] nineteen silver rings, many of them signets, were left behind by plunderers. Several of the king's fingers wore more than one ring, a custom in parts of the Roman world and well documented on royal representations at Meroe. The practice of wearing multiple rings on several fingers might explain the range of ring sizes found in several tombs.[4]

Five signet rings were all that excavators found in the plundered burial of Meroe West 134. Located in the debris on the coffin bench were a gold signet with circular bezel featuring a seated figure and a standing Harpocrates, a gold signet with circular bezel depicting a ram-headed hawk on a bark, a silver signet with a round bezel featuring a hawk with outspread wings, a silver signet encased in gold sheet with an illegible oval

bezel, and a gold signet with circular bezel depicting a crowned hawk within a sun disk flanked by uraei.[8]

Common to the iconography of this ring group[9] is its falcon imagery. The gold signet ring (cat. no. 125A) with a crowned falcon head in profile, encircled and flanked by uraei, manages to incorporate powerful and enduring royal symbols in the smallest of spaces.

One finger ring, a signet (cat. no. 125B), was found in the chamber debris of Meroe West 106, a plundered late Meroitic burial.[10] On the bezel is an image of a vulture in profile, poised atop the tail of an upreared cobra. The body of the bird is highly textured, with striations along the wings and a punctate pattern along the back, chest, and legs. The cobra is also detailed with linework.

Vulture imagery appears on the bezels of four gold signet rings found by Giuseppe Ferlini and reputed to have come from the pyramid of Queen Amanishakheto (c. 20 B.C.). Two of the rings feature a seated, heraldic vulture while the others depict vultures consuming or carrying off the bodies of the enemy.[11] The inclusion of the uraeus on the late Meroitic signet ring represents an amalgam of two powerful Nilotic images.

Very little survived the plundering of Meroe West 333.[5] Reisner, however, recovered twelve finger rings and the fragments of several others. The diverse lot included four silver rings inset with glass intaglios, four iron rings encased in gold with glass bezel inlays, and one silver ring with a glass bezel set in a gold frame. Of three signet rings, one was bronze and two were gold.

Most outstanding in degree of preservation and craftsmanship is a gold signet ring (cat. no. 125C), which features four stylized lion heads facing inward. Centrally located on the flat bezel is a uraeus with sun disk, a Nubian royal emblem frequently found on jewelry.

The quadruple lion-head image is most likely of Nubian origin. A group of nine mica appliqués depicting four addorsed lion heads was excavated by Reisner from tumulus X at Kerma.[6] These ornaments, believed to have decorated a leather cap, demonstrate the early use of this multiple, which later became an aspect of the Meroitic god Apedemak.[7] YM

BIBLIOGRAPHY 125A: Dows Dunham, *The Royal Cemeteries of Kush*, vol. 5, *The West and South Cemeteries at Meroe* (Boston: MFA, 1963), 230, fig. 160 (4). 125B: ibid., 194, n. 12, fig. 141g. 125C: ibid., 260, fig. 169.

NOTES
1. There is a delicate gold wire uraeus ring from Meroe West 453 (MFA 23.305) and two silver rearing-cobra rings from Meroe West 179 (MFA 24.515, 22-2-590); see Dunham, *The West and South Cemeteries*, 155, 183, figs. 154h, 130e.
2. Recent study of Meroitic metalwork suggest that powdered glasses were occasionally fused into pockets created by the removal of metal (champlevé enameling); see Yvonne Markowitz and Peter Lacovara, *The Jewels of Ancient Nubia* (New York: Abbeville Press, forthcoming).
3. King Amanitarakade, pyramid N16, ruled around the middle of the first century A.D.; see Dows Dunham, *The Royal Cemeteries of Kush*, vol. 4, *Royal Tombs at Meroe and Barkal* (Boston: MFA, 1957), 137–41.
4. It has been suggested that rings of small size were childhood keepsakes. It is also possible that they were worn on the fifth finger or between the second and the third joint.
5. Dunham, *The West and South Cemeteries*, 260, pl. 169.
6. George A. Reisner, *The Excavations at Kerma*, pts. 4–5, Harvard African Studies 6 (Cambridge: Peabody Museum, Harvard University, 1923), 278, pl. 56.
7. Louis Zabkar, *Apedemak, Lion God of Meroe* (Warminster: Aris and Phillips, 1975), 47–51.
8. Dunham, *The West and South Cemeteries*, 230, 231.
9. There is some evidence that themes are repeated in Meroitic burials in which multiple rings were deposited. For example, in Meroe West 5 three of the four metal rings have rectangular bezels with alternating registers of seated lions and crocodiles (see ibid., 122, fig. 92h, j, k).
10. Ibid., 194, fig. 141g.
11. Karl-Heinz Priese, *The Gold of Meroe* (New York: MMA; Mainz: Philipp von Zabern, 1993), 42, fig. 40b–c.

126 Decorated Cups and Vessels

Karanog
Meroitic period
Ceramic
The University of Pennsylvania
Museum of Archaeology
and Anthropology

A *Jar*
Grave 173
c. 100 B.C.–A.D. 300
30.5 x 5.1 (diam) cm (12 x 2 in.)
E8232

B *Jar*
Grave 546
c. 100 B.C.–A.D. 300
13 x 6.3 (diam) cm (5⅛ x 2½ in.)
E8196

C *Cup*
Grave 626
c. 100 B.C.–A.D. 300
H: 8.5 cm (3⅜ in.)
E8486

D *Jar*
Grave 739
c. 100 B.C.–A.D. 300
H: 29.5 cm (11⅝ in.)
E8751

E *Cup*
Grave 315
c. A.D. 100–300
8.3 x 8.7 (diam) cm (3¼ x 3½ in.)
E8476

F *Cup*
Grave 673
c. A.D. 100–300
8.5 x 9 (diam) cm (3⅜ x 3½ in.)
E8488

G *Cup*
Grave 626
c. A.D. 100–300
8.5 x 8.7 (diam) cm (3⅜ x 3⅜ in.)
E8486

H *Jar*
Grave 614
c. 100 B.C.–A.D. 300
H: 23.5 cm (9¼ in.)
E8313

The ancient Nubians of the Meroitic period were exceptionally gifted potters who created a wide range of vessel shapes and devised their own vibrant style of decoration. Meroitic vessels frequently mirror Greek and Roman forms, but, as W. Y. Adams has noted, their method of manufacture, including the use of the potter's wheel, updraft kiln, and fine residual clays,[1] can be traced back to Egypt. Similarly, certain motifs employed by Meroitic vase painters doubtless were inspired by earlier Egyptian and Greco-Roman motifs. The resulting vessels, however, are hardly derivative. Nubian potters and vase painters of the late Meroitic period produced admirably functional and decorative wares whose painted compositions are lively and whimsical.

The vessels shown here all come from the Meroitic cemetery at Karanog, although from different burials. Three of the cups display brown to reddish brown decoration on a buff-colored ground. The range of motifs is representative, with one showing a quite stylized and somewhat enigmatic design (cat. no. 126E), another displaying a more naturalistic vine and leaf pattern (cat. no. 126G), and the third bearing three playful quadrupeds, perhaps mice (cat. no. 126F).

The cup from grave 315 (cat. no. 126E) was part of the largely intact burial of a woman. Other items discovered in this burial include a bronze kohl stick, a wooden kohl container, six pottery vessels of various shapes, several beads, and a wickerwork box. The body of the deceased owner was wrapped in a cloth covering.[2]

The ovoid jar (cat. no. 126B) is quite similar in terms of its fabric and decoration to the cups. Sixteen stylized plant forms, in tones of red-brown, purple-brown, and brown, are arranged fairly evenly around its surface. It comes from a burial that contained several other pots and a wooden kohl stick, but the excavators recorded that all of the contents were discovered in a "robber's hole, not in the chamber proper."[3]

A second ovoid jar (cat. no. 126A) is much simpler in composition and shows two birds painted in black-brown and red-brown in a register band at the shoulder. The fabric is red-brown, with buff, yellow, and purple-brown decoration. A similar fabric and color scheme appear in the well-formed jar with single handle (cat. no. 126H). The decoration is a pleasing mixture of stylized designs, naturalistic motifs, and geometric patterns. Also included is a black handmade cup (cat. no. 126C). The excavators stated that this pottery "belongs, on the whole, to the poorer tombs."[4] The wheel-made jar (cat. no. 126D) displays an attractive decoration of alternating bands of red-brown and purple-brown. GS

BIBLIOGRAPHY 126A: Charles Leonard Woolley and David Randall-MacIver, *Karanog: The Romano-Nubian Cemetery* (Philadelphia: University Museum, University of Pennsylvania, 1910), vol. 1, 263, vol. 2, pl. 64. 126B: ibid., vol. 1, 262, vol. 2, pl. 58. 126C: ibid., vol. 1, 267, vol. 2, pl. 101. 126D: ibid., vol. 1, 275. 126E: ibid., vol. 1, 268, vol. 2, pl. 51. 126F: ibid., vol. 1, 268, vol. 2, pl. 81. 126G: ibid., vol. 1, 268, vol. 2, pl. 52. 126H: ibid., vol. 1, 265, vol. 2, pl. 48; Steffen Wenig, *Africa in Antiquity: The Arts of Ancient Nubia and the Sudan*, exh. cat., vol. 2, *The Catalogue* (Brooklyn: Brooklyn Museum, 1978), 294 (ill.), no. 244.

NOTES
1. See W. Y. Adams, in Wenig, *Africa in Antiquity*, vol. 2, 129.
2. Woolley and Randall-MacIver, *Karanog*, vol. 1, 172–73.
3. Ibid., 204–5.
4. Ibid., 52.

127 Metalwork

Karanog
Meroitic period, c. 100 B.C.–A.D. 300
The University of Pennsylvania
Museum of Archaeology
and Anthropology

A *Patera*
Grave 187
Bronze
L: 27.5 cm (10⅞ in.);
L (of handle): 10 cm (4 in.)
Bowl: 2.4 x 16.2 (diam) cm
(1 x 6⅜ in.)
E7146

B *Axe Head*
Grave 187
Iron
L (shaft to edge): 9.2 cm (3⅝ in.);
W (across blade): 6.2 cm (2½ in.)
E7299

C *Bowl*
Grave 331
Bronze
5.5 x 10.5 (diam) cm (2¼ x 4¼ in.)
E7131

A wide range of metal objects come from the Meroitic cemetery at Karanog. Braziers, bowls, offering dishes, and utilitarian implements are each represented. The *patera*, or offering dish, included here is a particularly sophisticated object. At the center of the dish a large, raised knob is decorated with concentric bands at different levels. The handle, made separately and attached with rivets, shows a human head and extended arms. It is reminiscent of mirror, cauldron, and similar handle ornaments from elsewhere in the Greco-Roman world. The head is upraised, and the eyes, nose, mouth, and long hair are carefully delineated. At the end of the handle, on the upper surface, is a second human head, also with a long hairstyle. These heads are quite similar to those on other objects found in Meroitic settings, including the masks on two pitchers (E7512, E7513) found at Karanog and in the collection of the University of Pennsylvania Museum of Archaeology and Anthropology.[1] The lower surface of the handle is also embellished with a plant motif.

Metal bowls are well represented at Karanog. This example shows a punched decoration of swags and ellipses as well as concentric circles on the base. The excavators believed it to have been manufactured locally.[2] The axe head, made of iron, comes from the same burial as the patera. GS

BIBLIOGRAPHY 127A: Charles Leonard Woolley and David Randall-MacIver, *Karanog: The Romano-Nubian Cemetery* (Philadelphia: University Museum, University of Pennsylvania, 1910), vol. 1, 61, 243, vol. 2, pl. 29. 127B: ibid., vol. 1, 243, vol. 2, pl. 35. 127C: ibid., vol. 1, 242, vol. 2, pl. 31.

NOTES
1. Steffen Wenig, *Africa in Antiquity: The Arts of Ancient Nubia and the Sudan,* exh. cat., vol. 2, *The Catalogue* (Brooklyn: Brooklyn Museum, 1978), 262, no. 199.
2. Woolley and Randall-MacIver, *Karanog*, vol. 1, 62; for a similar bowl, see Wenig, *Africa in Antiquity*, vol. 2, 262, no. 198.

128 Aryballoi (Oil Vessels)

Karanog
Meroitic period, c. 100 B.C.–A.D. 300
Glass, bronze
The University of Pennsylvania
Museum of Archaeology
and Anthropology

A *Aryballos*
 Grave 45
 H: 15.2 cm (6 in.)
 E7352
B *Aryballos*
 Grave 135
 H: 9.3 cm (3⅝ in.)
 E7347

The archaeologists of the University of Pennsylvania's expedition to Karanog discovered twenty-eight glass vessels, either intact or able to be reconstructed, and many additional fragments.[1] This suggests that glass, while almost certainly something of a luxury item for the ancient residents of the site, was not rare. All examples found sufficiently intact were of blown glass and consistent with blown-glass vessels from other parts of the Roman world at this time.[2]

The two examples shown here closely resemble the classic oil flask, or *aryballos*, more typically made of terra-cotta or metal. The excavators, however, identified them by the term *Delphinflasche* (dolphin flask).[3] The form in glass is known from at least the first century A.D., and stylistically these two examples should probably be dated to the first or second century A.D.[4] The glass in both vessels is thick, especially at the handles. The color is a standard pale green, typical of glass that does not contain other additives, such as manganese.

The larger example (cat. no. 128A) has three bronze attachments, which form a convenient handle and might have been added at a later date. Wheel-cut decoration in the form of straight lines, circles, and ellipses is arranged in a pleasing, balanced composition. The vessel was found in an undisturbed burial of a woman which also contained three metal bowls, a metal tripod and lock, two wood and ivory boxes, several beads,

and three pots.[5] The second example (cat. no. 128B) must have been from a fairly important burial, to judge from what remained of the superstructure, but it had been largely plundered, and only this glass vessel and three plain pots were recovered.[6] Similar vessels were found in Karanog graves 330 and 355.[7] GS

BIBLIOGRAPHY Charles Leonard Woolley and David Randall-MacIver, *Karanog: The Romano-Nubian Cemetery* (Philadelphia: University Museum, University of Pennsylvania, 1910), vol. 1, 72, 122–23, 136–37, vol. 2, pl. 38.

NOTES
1. Woolley and Randall-MacIver, *Karanog*, vol. 1, 72.
2. Ibid.
3. Ibid.
4. Axel von Saldern et al., *Gläser der Antike: Sammlung Erwin Oppenlander* (Mainz: Philipp von Zabern, 1974), 202–3, no. 565.
5. Woolley and Randall-MacIver, *Karanog*, vol. 1, 122–23.
6. Ibid., 136–37.
7. David O'Connor, *Ancient Nubia: Egypt's Rival in Africa*, exh. cat. (Philadelphia: University Museum, University of Pennsylvania, 1993), 154, nos. 132, 133.

129 Box

Karanog, grave 140
Meroitic period, c. 100 B.C.–A.D. 300
Wood, ivory, brass
22.7 x 20.2 x 26 cm (9 x 8 x 10¼ in.)
The University of Pennsylvania
Museum of Archaeology
and Anthropology, E7518

Wooden containers of various types were discovered in a number of the Meroitic graves at Karanog. Typically inlaid with ivory or bone, these containers could be rectangular, such as this example, or cylindrical. The cylindrical containers are smaller and are thought to have been used for powdered eye cosmetics such as kohl. Rectangular boxes, larger and more versatile, probably contained a range of objects, including jewelry, cosmetic implements, and other personal items.[1] Although much of its wood is modern, this box retains most of its original ivory inlays and metalwork. The inlays are arranged in cruciform, geometric, star, and plant motifs, and a particularly pleasing vine decorates the box lid. Brass fixtures include the handles on both the lid and body of the box, the decorative lock plate, the bands at the corners of the lid, and the corner bands and nails securing them to the body of the box.[2]

The box was discovered in the fill of the superstructure of a fairly substantial grave at Karanog that included a brick altar supporting a stone offering table (now in Cairo) and a painted stela. No other significant finds were reported, however, and the grave appears to have been thoroughly plundered in antiquity. The box apparently saw long service before being interred with its owner, as the metal fixtures were put in place to strengthen its corners and the ornamental lock plate covers the original keyhole. GS

BIBLIOGRAPHY Charles Leonard Woolley and David Randall-MacIver, *Karanog: The Romano-Nubian Cemetery* (Philadelphia: University Museum, University of Pennsylvania, 1910), vol. 1, 70, 136–37, 245, vol. 2, pl. 21.

NOTES
1. For kohl tubes and boxes, see Steffen Wenig, *Africa in Antiquity: The Arts of Ancient Nubia and the Sudan*, exh. cat., vol. 2, *The Catalogue* (Brooklyn: Brooklyn Museum, 1978), nos. 203–9; David O'Connor, *Ancient Nubia: Egypt's Rival in Africa*, exh. cat. (Philadelphia: University Museum, University of Pennsylvania, 1993), 152–53, nos. 123–27, pl. 17.
2. Woolley and Randall-MacIver, *Karanog*, vol. 1, 70.

Archaeological and Research Expeditions to Egypt and Nubia

Sponsored by North American Institutions

American Museum of Natural History

Archaeological Research at Hierakonpolis (Nekhen)
1967–94
DIRECTORS: Walter A. Fairservis (1967–70, 1978–82); Michael A. Hoffman, University of South Carolina (1982–90); Jay Mills, University of South Carolina, and Walter A. Fairservis, Vassar College (1990–94)

American Research Center in Egypt

Gebel Adda
1962–66
DIRECTOR: Nicholas B. Millet

Catalog of the Luxor Museum Project
1973–76
DIRECTOR: Bernard V. Bothmer

Remains of a Temple of Tutankhamen and Ay, Karnak
1977–78, 1985–86
DIRECTOR: Otto Schaden

Isis Temple Project
1978
DIRECTOR: Mark Lehner

Sphinx Project
1980–84
DIRECTORS: James P. Allen and Mark Lehner

Archaeological Survey of the Southern Fayyum
1980–86
DIRECTORS: Mary Ellen Lane and Robert J. Wenke, University of Washington

Archaeological Survey of the Western Desert of Egypt
1982–83
DIRECTOR: Alan H. Simmons

Giza Plateau Mapping Project
1983–90
DIRECTOR: Mark Lehner
See also Oriental Institute, University of Chicago

Royal Mummies of the Egyptian Museum
1985, 1987, 1992
DIRECTORS: James E. Harris and Fawzia Hussein

Watetkhethor Copying Project
1986
DIRECTOR: Ann Macy Roth

Urban Archaeology Project
1989–90
DIRECTOR: Michael Jones

A Catalog of the Masterpieces of the Graeco-Roman Museum in Alexandria
1991–present
DIRECTOR: Robert S. Bianchi

Theban Tomb Publications Project
1992–present
DIRECTOR: Peter Piccione

American Schools of Oriental Research

Wadi Abu Had-Wadi Dib, Eastern Desert Project
1995–
DIRECTOR: Ann Bomann

American University in Cairo

Old Kingdom Mastabas in the Great Western Cemetery of Giza Necropolis
1972–74
DIRECTOR: Kent R. Weeks

Theban Mapping Project: To Prepare a New Archaeological Map of the Theban Necropolis
1989–present
DIRECTOR: Kent R. Weeks
See also University of California, Berkeley

Boston University

The Predynastic Site of Hu
1991
DIRECTOR: Kathryn Bard

Brigham Young University

Egypt Archaeology—Fayyum
1980–present
DIRECTOR: C. Wilfred Griggs

Brooklyn College

Taposiris Magna
1975–76
DIRECTOR: Edward Ochsenschlager

The Brooklyn Museum

Excavations between Esna and Edfu at el-Mamariya, el-Adaima, Kom el-Ahmar, el-Qara, and el-Kilabiya (East)
1906–7
DIRECTOR: Henri de Morgan

Excavations between Esna and Gebel el-Silsila at el-Mamariya, el-Adaima, Kom el-Ahmar, Abu Zaidan, el-Masaid, and el-Sibaiya (East)
1907–8
DIRECTOR: Henri de Morgan

Expedition to the Precinct of the Goddess Mut (South Karnak)
1976–79
FIELD DIRECTOR: Richard A. Fazzini
1980–present (in association with the Detroit Institute of Arts)
PROJECT DIRECTOR AND CO–FIELD DIRECTOR: Richard A. Fazzini
CO–FIELD DIRECTOR: William H. Peck, Detroit Institute of Arts

The Brooklyn Museum Theban Expedition (Mut Expedition and Theban Royal Tomb Project)
1977–79
PROJECT DIRECTORS: Richard A. Fazzini and James B. Manning
FIELD DIRECTOR: John Romer

Beni Hasan Photographic Project
1994–present
DIRECTOR: Donald B. Spanel

Brown University
Hibis Temple, Kharga Oasis
1985–86
DIRECTOR: Eugene Cruz-Uribe

The Canadian Museum of Civilization (The National Museum of Man)
Canadian Prehistoric Expedition to Nubia at Kom Ombo
1962–63
DIRECTOR: Philip E. L. Smith

Claremont Graduate School (Institute for Antiquity and Christianity)
Excavations at Gebel et-Tarif
1975
DIRECTOR: James M. Robinson
ARCHAEOLOGICAL DIRECTOR: Torgny Save-Soderbergh, University of Uppsala

Columbia University
Nubian Expedition in Sudan
1961–62
DIRECTORS: Rhodes W. Fairbridge and Ralph S. Solecki

Cranbrook Institute of Science
Prehistoric Egyptian Socio-economic Structure Project
1987–89
DIRECTORS: Richard Redding and Robert J. Wenke, University of Washington

Detroit Institute of Arts
Expedition to the Precinct of the Goddess Mut (South Karnak)
See The Brooklyn Museum

Egypt Exploration Society/ Brown University
Epigraphic Recording at Semna East (Kumma) and Semna West
1962–64
DIRECTOR: Ricardo Caminos

Getty Conservation Institute/ Egyptian Antiquities Organization
Conservation of Wall Paintings of the Tomb of Nefertari
1986–92
DIRECTOR: Luis Monreal and Miguel Angel Corzo
FIELD DIRECTORS: Paolo Mora and Laura Mora

Harvard University
(*see also* Museum of Fine Arts, Boston)
Excavations at Marsa Matruh
1913–14, 1915
DIRECTOR: Oric Bates

Excavations at Gamai
1915
DIRECTORS: Oric Bates and Dows Dunham

Excavations at Serabit el-Khadem (Sinai)
1927, 1930
DIRECTOR: Kirsopp Lake

The Johns Hopkins University
First Cataract Epigraphic Survey
1964, 1967
DIRECTOR: Hans Goedicke

Excavations at Giza
1972, 1974
PROJECT DIRECTOR: Hans Goedicke

Tell el-Rataba Survey
1977–80
DIRECTOR: Hans Goedicke

The Johns Hopkins University Expedition to Thebes
1993–present
DIRECTOR: Betsy M. Bryan

The Metropolitan Museum of Art
Excavations at Lisht
1906–9, 1912–14, 1916–18, 1920–25, 1931–34
DIRECTORS: Albert M. Lythgoe, Arthur C. Mace, and Ambrose Lansing

Excavations at el-Kharga Oasis
1907–13, 1924–31
DIRECTORS: Albert M. Lythgoe, Herbert E. Winlock, H. G. Evelyn White, and Walter Hauser

Graphic Section of the Museum's Egyptian Expedition
1907–17, 1919–37 (Thebes, el-Kharga Oasis, Beni Hasan, Amarna, Maidum, Lisht, Wadi Natrun)
DIRECTOR: Norman de Garis Davies

Excavations at Wadi Natrun
1909–11, 1919–21
DIRECTORS: Walter J. Palmer-Jones and H. G. Evelyn White

Excavations at Thebes
1910–31, 1934–36
DIRECTORS: Herbert E. Winlock, Ambrose Lansing, and Arthur C. Mace

Excavations at Hierakonpolis
1934–35
DIRECTOR: Ambrose Lansing

Memphis
1971
DIRECTORS: Christine Lilyquist and Donald P. Hansen, New York University

Senenmut Tombs Project
1981–87
DIRECTOR: Peter F. Dorman

Lisht Project
1984–89, 1991–present
DIRECTOR: Dieter Arnold

Tomb of the Three Wives of Thutmosis III Project
1988–89
DIRECTOR: Christine Lilyquist

Excavations at Dahshur (Senwosret III)
1990–present
DIRECTOR: Dieter Arnold

**Museum of Fine Arts, Boston/
Harvard University**

Excavations at Giza
1905–10, 1912–16, 1923–37
DIRECTOR: George A. Reisner

Archeological Survey of Nubia
1906–11
DIRECTORS: George A. Reisner
(1906–8) and Cecil Firth
(1908–11)

Excavations at Zawiyet el-Aryan
1910–11
DIRECTOR: George A. Reisner

Excavations at Mesa'eed
1910, 1913
DIRECTOR: George A. Reisner

Excavations at Mesheikh
1912
DIRECTOR: George A. Reisner

Excavations at Naga el-Deir
1912, 1923–24
DIRECTOR: George A. Reisner

Excavations at Naga el-Hai
1913
DIRECTOR: George A. Reisner

Excavations at Kerma
1913–16
DIRECTOR: George A. Reisner

Excavations at Sheikh Farag
1913, 1923–24
DIRECTOR: George A. Reisner

Excavations at Deir el-Bersha
1915
DIRECTOR: George A. Reisner

*Excavations at Gebel Barkal
(el-Kurru)*
1916, 1918–20
DIRECTOR: George A. Reisner

Excavations at Nuri
1916–18, 1920
DIRECTOR: George A. Reisner

*Excavations at Begrawiya
(Meroe)*
1920–23
DIRECTOR: George A. Reisner

Excavations at Coptos
1923
DIRECTOR: George A. Reisner

Excavations at Kafr Ghattati
1924
DIRECTOR: George A. Reisner

Excavations at Kumma
1924
DIRECTOR: George A. Reisner

Excavations at Semna
1924, 1927–28
DIRECTOR: George A. Reisner

Excavations at Uronarti
1924, 1928–30
DIRECTOR: George A. Reisner

Excavations at Shalfak
1931
DIRECTOR: George A. Reisner

Excavations at Mirgissa
1931–32
DIRECTOR: George A. Reisner

Museum of Fine Arts, Boston

*Yale University/Museum of
Fine Arts, Boston, Giza Pyramids
Mastabas Project*
1970–present
DIRECTORS: Edward Brovarski
and William Kelly Simpson,
Yale University

*University of Pennsylvania
Museum/Yale University/
Museum of Fine Arts Giza
Mastabas Project*
1972–75, 1977, 1981–82
DIRECTOR: William Kelly Simpson

Deir el-Ballas Project
1980, 1982–83, 1985, 1986
DIRECTOR: Peter Lacovara

Excavations at Gebel Barkal
1986–89
DIRECTOR: Timothy Kendall

*Giza Pyramids Mastabas Project
(Western Cemetery)*
1989–90, 1994
DIRECTOR: Ann Macy Roth

*Museum of Fine Arts, Boston/
University of Pennsylvania
Museum/State University of
Leiden Expedition to Bersheh*
1989–present
DIRECTORS: Edward Brovarski,
Rita E. Freed, and David Silver-
man, University of Pennsylvania
Museum

Giza Mastabas Project
1993–present
DIRECTOR: Peter Der Manuelian

*Museum of Fine Arts, Boston/
University of Pennsylvania
Museum Expedition to Sakkara*
1993–present
DIRECTORS: Edward Brovarski,
Rita Freed, and David Silver-
man, University of Pennsylvania
Museum

New York University

Excavations at Mendes
1964–66, 1976–80
DIRECTOR: Bernard V. Bothmer
FIELD DIRECTORS: Donald P.
Hansen (1964–78) and Karen L.
Wilson (1979–80)

Memphis
1971
DIRECTORS: Donald P. Hansen
and Christine Lilyquist,
Metropolitan Museum of Art

Embalming House of the Apis Bulls
1982–88
DIRECTORS: John Dimick and
Bernard V. Bothmer
FIELD DIRECTORS: Michael Jones
and Angela Milward Jones

Northern Arizona University

Hibis Temple Project
1984–86, 1988, 1990, 1992–93,
1995
DIRECTOR: Eugene Cruz-Uribe

**The Oriental Institute,
University of Chicago**

*Epigraphic Survey of the
Oriental Institute of the
University of Chicago, Luxor*
1924–present
FIELD DIRECTORS:
Harold H. Nelson (1924–47),
Richard Parker (1948–49),
George Hughes (1949–58),
John A. Wilson (acting, 1958–59),
George Hughes (1959–64),
Charles Nims (1964–72),
Edward Wente (1972–73),
Kent R. Weeks (1973–76),
Charles Van Siclen, III
(acting, 1976–77),
Lanny Bell (1977–89) and
Peter F. Dorman (1989–present)

Architectural Survey of the Oriental Institute of the University of Chicago, Luxor
1926–32
FIELD DIRECTOR: Uvo Hölscher

Prehistoric Survey in Egypt and the Sudan
1926–38
DIRECTORS: Kenneth S. Sandford (1926–38) and William J. Arkell (1926–30)

Sakkara Expedition (Mastaba of Mereruka)
1931–37
FIELD DIRECTOR: Prentice Duell

Excavations at Qasr el-Wizz, Serra East, and the Qustul-Adindan Area
1961–64
DIRECTORS: George Hughes (1961), Herbert Ricke (1961), and Keith C. Seele (1962–64)

Excavations of Serra East and Dorgainarti
1963–64
DIRECTOR: James Knudsted

Qasr el-Wizz
1965
DIRECTOR: George T. Scanlon

Quseir el-Qadim Project
1978–86
DIRECTORS: Donald S. Whitcomb (1978–86) and Janet H. Johnson (1985–86)

Giza Plateau Mapping Project
1990–present
DIRECTOR: Mark Lehner
See also American Research Center in Egypt

Bir Umm Fawakhir Survey Project
1991–present
DIRECTOR: Carol Meyer

Luxor-Farshut Desert Road Survey
1992–present
FIELD DIRECTOR: John Darnell

Pacific Lutheran University
Valley of the Kings Project
1989, 1990, 1991
DIRECTOR: Donald Ryan

Valley of the Kings Preservation Project
1993
DIRECTOR: Donald Ryan

Royal Ontario Museum/ The Society for the Study of Egyptian Antiquities
Royal Ontario Museum Survey Expedition to Dongola Reach
1976–86
DIRECTORS: Nicholas B. Millet (1976–82) and Krzysztof Grzymski (1984–86)

Dakhleh Oasis Project: An Archaeological Study
1978–83, 1988–present
DIRECTOR: Anthony Mills

Royal Ontario Museum Expedition to Illahun
1988–present
DIRECTOR: Nicholas B. Millet

Southern Methodist University
Initial Survey of West Bank
1962
DIRECTOR: Fred Wendorf

Excavation at Ballana and Tushka
1963–65
DIRECTOR: Fred Wendorf

Excavations at Wadi Tushka
1966
DIRECTOR: Fred Wendorf

Survey of Aswan-Dishna Area
1967
DIRECTOR: Fred Wendorf

Survey of Dendera-Luxor Area
1968
DIRECTOR: Fred Wendorf

Excavations at Dishna and Mucadema
1968
DIRECTOR: Fred Wendorf

Excavations at Fayyum
1969
DIRECTOR: Fred Wendorf

Excavations at Bir Sahara and Bir Tarfawi
1972–74, 1985–89
DIRECTOR: Fred Wendorf

Combined Prehistoric Expedition
1972–74, 1986–present
DIRECTOR: Fred Wendorf

Excavations at Nabta
1975, 1977
DIRECTOR: Fred Wendorf

Excavations at Kharga Qasim
1976
DIRECTOR: Fred Wendorf

Excavations at Wadi Kubbaniya
1978, 1981–84
DIRECTOR: Fred Wendorf

Excavations at Bir Kiseiba and Bir Eyde Areas
1979, 1980
DIRECTOR: Fred Wendorf

Excavations at Nabta Playa and Isna Areas
1990–94
DIRECTOR: Fred Wendorf

Southwest Missouri State University
Archaeological Investigation of Pastoral Nomadism in Egypt
1982–86

Eastern Desert Project
1983–84, 1989
DIRECTOR: Juris Zarins

State University of New York at Binghampton/The Society for the Study of Egyptian Antiquities
Chapel of Osiris Heqa-Djet Project
1971–72
CODIRECTORS: Gerald Kadish, Donald B. Redford

Texas A & M University
Institute of Nautical Archaeology Red Sea Expedition
1994–present
DIRECTORS: Cheryl Haldane and Douglas Haldane

The Underwater Archaeological Survey between Sidi Abd al-Rahman and Ras Hawala
1995–
DIRECTOR: Douglas Haldane

University of Arizona
Western Valley of the Kings Project
1990–93
FIELD DIRECTOR: Otto Schaden

Amenmesse Project (KV-10)
1992–94
FIELD DIRECTOR: Otto Schaden

Valley of the Kings Motif Alignment Project
1992–present
FIELD DIRECTOR: Richard Wilkinson

University of California, Berkeley

Excavations near Coptos and Surafa
1899–1900
DIRECTOR: George A. Reisner

Expedition to Tebtunis
1899–1900
DIRECTORS: Bernard P. Grenfell and Arthur S. Hunt

Excavations at el-Ahaiwah
1900
DIRECTOR: George A. Reisner

Excavations at Deir el-Ballas
1900–1901
DIRECTOR: George A. Reisner

Excavations at Naga el-Deir
1901–4
DIRECTOR: George A. Reisner

Excavations at Giza
1903–5
DIRECTOR: George A. Reisner

Sociological Analysis of Village at Deir el-Medina
1975–76
DIRECTOR: Cathleen A. Keller

Theban Mapping Project: To Prepare a New Archaeological Map of the Theban Necropolis
1980–88
DIRECTOR: Kent R. Weeks
See also The American University in Cairo

Seila (Faiyum) Project
1981
DIRECTOR: Leonard Lesko

Craftsmen of Deir el-Medina Project
1986–88
DIRECTOR: Cathleen A. Keller

Tell el-Muqdam Leontopolis Project
1992–present
DIRECTORS: Carol Redmount and Renee Friedman

University of California, Los Angeles

Excavations at Askut
1962–64
DIRECTOR: Alexander Badawy

Excavations at Dabinarti
1963–64
DIRECTOR: Jay Ruby

UCLA Expedition to Giza: Tombs of Iteti, Sekhemankhptah, and Kaemnofert
1973
DIRECTOR: Alexander Badawy

UCLA Expedition to Giza and Saqqara: Tombs of Nyhetepptah and Ankhmahor
1974
DIRECTOR: Alexander Badawy

UCLA Expedition to Saqqara: Tomb of Kagemni
1975–78
DIRECTOR: Alexander Badawy

UCLA Expedition to Saqqara: Tombs of Meriteti and Watetkhethor
1978–79
DIRECTOR: Alexander Badawy

UCLA/Christ College Cambridge Theban Tombs Expedition (TT 253, 254, 294)
1988
DIRECTOR: Nigel P. Strudwick

UCLA/Universität Göttingen Ma'abda Project
1990
DIRECTORS: Antonio Loprieno and Ursula Rößler Köller, Universität Göttingen

UCLA/Deutsches Archäologisches Institut Dra' Abu el-Naga Project
1994–present
DIRECTOR: Daniel C. Polz
FIELD DIRECTOR: Stuart T. Smith

University of Chicago

(*see also* The Oriental Institute, University of Chicago)
Photographic Survey of Nubia (Aswan to Meroe)
1905–7
DIRECTOR: James H. Breasted

University of Colorado

Nubian Expedition
1962–66
DIRECTORS: Gordon W. Hewes (1962–63, 1964–66), Joe Ben Wheat, and Henry Irwin (1963–64)

University of Delaware

Red Sea Roman Ports Survey
1984–85
DIRECTOR: Steven E. Sidebotham

Red Sea Project, Myos Hormos Project
1986–88
DIRECTOR: Steven E. Sidebotham

Abu Sha'ar Roman/Byzantine Fort Red Sea Project
1988–present
DIRECTOR: Steven E. Sidebotham

Excavations at Bernice on the Red Sea Coast (in conjunction with Leiden University)
1994
DIRECTOR: Steven E. Sidebotham

University of Illinois

Wadi Feiran Project
1982–86
DIRECTOR: James L. Phillips

Ecological Survey of the Egyptian Eastern Desert
1987–89
DIRECTORS: Douglas Brewer and Steven Goodman, University of Michigan

Early Pharaonic Socioeconomic Structure of the Nile Delta
1989–94
DIRECTORS: Douglas J. Brewer and Robert J. Wenke, University of Washington

University of Kentucky

Egypt Exploration Society Archaeological Investigations at Qasr Ibrim
1972, 1974, 1976, 1978, 1980, 1982, 1984
DIRECTOR: William Y. Adams

University of Memphis (Memphis State University)

Amarna Project
1983–86
DIRECTORS: William Murnane and Charles Van Siclen, III

Amarna Boundary Stele Project
1988–91
DIRECTORS: William Murnane
and Charles Van Siclen, III

*Great Hypostyle Hall Project
Joint Centre franco-égyptien
d'étude des temples de Karnak
and the Institute of Egyptian Art
and Archaeology, University of
Memphis*
1991–present
DIRECTOR: William Murnane

University of Miami

*Trans-Sinai Roman Road
Between Clysma (Suez) and
Aqaba*
1992–94
DIRECTOR: David F. Graf

University of Michigan, Ann Arbor

*Excavations at Karanis
(Kom Aushim)*
1924–35
DIRECTORS: J. L. Starkey
(1924–26) and Enoch E.
Peterson (1926–35)

*Excavations at Dimai
(Soknopaiou Nesos)*
1931–32
DIRECTOR: Arthur E. R. Boak

*Excavations at Terenouthis
(Kom Abu Billo)*
1934–35
DIRECTOR: Enoch E. Peterson

*Cemetery Populations of Gebel
Adda*
1965
DIRECTOR: James E. Harris

*Royal Mummies of the Egyptian
Museum*
1966–68, 1970–71, 1982–83,
1985, 1987, 1992
DIRECTOR: James E. Harris

*Skeletal Material from Giza
Necropolis*
1968
DIRECTOR: James E. Harris

*Mummies of the Nobles in the
Valley of the Kings*
1970
DIRECTOR: James E. Harris

*Mummies in the Tomb of
Amenhotep II*
1974
DIRECTOR: James E. Harris

*Mummies of the Old Kingdom
Nobles at Aswan*
1974
DIRECTOR: James E. Harris

Mummy of Tutankhamun
1978
DIRECTOR: James E. Harris

*Greek-Roman Mummies of the
Alexandria Museum*
1982–83
DIRECTOR: James E. Harris

*Ecological Survey of the
Egyptian Eastern Desert*
1987–89
DIRECTORS: Steven Goodman
and Douglas Brewer, University
of Illinois at Champaign-Urbana

*University of Michigan/
University of Asyut Joint Project
at Coptos and the Eastern Desert*
1989–94
DIRECTORS: Sharon Herbert and
Henry Wright

University of Minnesota

Western Valley of the Kings Project
1972
DIRECTOR: Otto Schaden
See also University of Arizona

Excavations at Akhmim
1980–1983
DIRECTOR: Sheila McNally

Naukratis Project
1980–86
DIRECTORS: William D. E.
Coulson and Albert Leonard Jr.

University of Pennsylvania Museum of Archaeology and Anthropology

*Excavations at Areika, Aniba,
Karanog, Shablul, and Buhen*
1907–11
DIRECTOR: David Randall-
MacIver

Excavations at Giza
1915
DIRECTOR: Clarence S. Fisher

Excavations at Dendera
1915–18
DIRECTOR: Clarence S. Fisher

Excavations at Memphis
1915–19, 1921–23
DIRECTOR: Clarence S. Fisher

*Excavations at Dra Abu
el-Naga, Thebes*
1921–23
DIRECTOR: Clarence S. Fisher

Excavations at Maidum
1929–32
DIRECTOR: Alan Rowe

*University of Pennsylvania
Museum/Egyptian Antiquities
Organization Excavations at
Memphis*
1955, 1956
DIRECTOR: Rudolf Anthes

*University of Pennsylvania
Museum/Yale University
Expedition to Nubia*
1960–63
DIRECTOR: William Kelly
Simpson, Yale University

Expedition to Dra Abu el-Naga
1967
DIRECTOR: Lanny Bell

*University of Pennsylvania
Museum/Yale University Abydos
Expedition*
1967–present
DIRECTORS: David O'Connor
and William Kelly Simpson,
Yale University
FIELD DIRECTORS: David Silver-
man (1978, Ramesses II Portal
Epigraphy), Janet Richards
(1986, Abydos North Cemetery
Project), Matthew Adams (1991,
Abydos Settlement Site: Kom el-
Sultan), Stephen Harvey (1993,
Almose Complex Project) and
Josef Wegner (1994, Senwosret
III Mortuary Temple)

Museum Excavations at Malqata
1971–77
DIRECTORS: David O'Connor
and Barry Kemp, Cambridge
University

*University of Pennsylvania/Yale
University/Museum of Fine Arts,
Boston, Giza Mastabas Project*
1972–75, 1977, 1981–82
DIRECTOR: William Kelly Simpson

Archaeological Survey of Abydos
1982–86
DIRECTOR: David O'Connor
FIELD DIRECTOR: Diana Craig
Patch (1982–83)

*The University of Pennsylvania
Late Bronze Age Project at
Marsa Matruh*
1985–90, 1995–96
DIRECTOR: Donald White

*Archaeological Survey of Marsa
Matruh (Western Egypt)*
1986–93
DIRECTOR: Donald White

*Agricultural Scenes in the
Private Tombs at Thebes*
1989–90
DIRECTOR: Patricia A. Bochi

*Museum of Fine Arts,
Boston/University of Pennsylva-
nia Museum/State University of
Leiden Expedition to Bersheh*
1989–92
DIRECTORS: David Silverman;
Edward Brovarski, Museum of
Fine Arts, Boston; Rita E. Freed,
Museum of Fine Arts, Boston;
and Harco Willems, State Uni-
versity of Leiden

*Museum of Fine Arts, Boston/
University of Pennsylvania
Museum Expedition to Sakkara*
1993–94
DIRECTORS: David Silverman;
Edward Brovarski, Museum of
Fine Arts, Boston; and Rita Freed,
Museum of Fine Arts, Boston

See also University of Toronto

University of South Carolina
*Archaeological Research at
Hierakonpolis (Nekhen)*
1994–present
DIRECTOR: Jay Mills
See also American Museum of
Natural History

Excavations at HK64
1986–94
DIRECTOR: Renee Friedman

University of Toledo
*Topographical and Petrological
Survey of Ancient Egyptian
Quarries*
1989–present
DIRECTOR: James A. Harrell

University of Toronto
*University of Toronto/University
of Pennsylvania Akhenaten
Temple Project*
1965–present
DIRECTORS: Ray Winfield Smith
(1965–71) and Donald B.
Redford (1972–present)

*The Akhenaten Temple Project
(Field Operations)*
1976–present
DIRECTOR: Donald B. Redford

East Karnak Excavations
1976–present
FIELD DIRECTOR: Donald B.
Redford

Wadi Tumilat Project
1978–85
DIRECTOR: John Holladay

Epigraphic Tomb Survey
1988–present
FIELD DIRECTOR: Susan Redford

*Mendes Expedition
(Tell el-Rub'a)*
1990–present
FIELD DIRECTOR: Donald B.
Redford

*Tel Kedwa Excavations (Joint
Sinai Expedition with the Egyptian Antiquities Organization)*
1993–present
DIRECTOR: Donald B. Redford

University of Washington
Old Kingdom Delta Project
1984–88
DIRECTORS: Robert J. Wenke
and Richard Redding

*Prehistoric Egyptian Socio-
economic Structure Project*
1987–89
DIRECTORS: Robert J. Wenke
and Richard Redding, Cranbrook Institute of Science

*Early Pharaonic Socioeconomic
Structure of the Nile Delta*
1989–present
DIRECTORS: Robert J. Wenke;
Douglas J. Brewer, University of
Illinois at Champaign; and
Donald B. Redford, University
of Toronto

Mendes Archaeological Project
1989–present
DIRECTORS: Robert J. Wenke
and Douglas Brewer

Vassar College
*Archaeological Research at
Hierakonpolis (Nekhen)*
1990–94
DIRECTOR: Walter A. Fairservis
See also American Museum of
Natural History

Yale University
*University of Pennsylvania
Museum/Yale University
Expedition to Nubia*
1960–63
DIRECTOR: William Kelly Simpson

*Yale University Prehistoric
Expedition to Egypt and Nubia*
1962–64
DIRECTOR: Charles Reed

*University of Pennsylvania
Museum/Yale University
Abydos Expedition*
See University of Pennsylvania
Museum of Archaeology and
Anthropology

*University of Pennsylvania/Yale
University/Museum of Fine Arts,
Boston, Giza Mastabas Project*
See University of Pennsylvania
Museum of Archaeology and
Anthropology

*Yale University/Museum of
Fine Arts, Boston, Giza
Pyramids Mastabas Project*
See Museum of Fine Arts,
Boston

Selected Bibliography

ALDRED, CYRIL. *Jewels of the Pharaohs*. London: Thames and Hudson, 1971.

———. *Akhenaten and Nefertiti*. Exhibition catalogue. Brooklyn: Brooklyn Museum; New York: Viking Press, 1973.

ARNOLD, DIETER. *The South Cemeteries of Lisht*. Vol. 1, *The Pyramid of Senwosret I*. The Metropolitan Museum of Art Egyptian Expedition 22. New York: Metropolitan Museum of Art, 1989.

———. *The South Cemeteries of Lisht*. Vol. 3, *The Pyramid Complex of Senwosret I*. The Metropolitan Museum of Art Egyptian Expedition 25. New York: Metropolitan Museum of Art, 1992.

BAINES, JOHN, and JAROMÍR MÁLEK. *Atlas of Ancient Egypt*. New York: Facts on File, 1980.

BOAK, ARTHUR E. R., ed. *Karanis: The Temples, Coin Hoards, Botanical and Zoölogical Reports, Seasons 1924–31*. University of Michigan Studies, Humanistic Series 30. Ann Arbor: University of Michigan Press, 1933.

BOTHMER, BERNARD V. *Egyptian Sculpture of the Late Period, 700 B.C.–A.D. 100*. Exhibition catalogue. Brooklyn: Brooklyn Museum, 1960.

BREASTED, CHARLES. *Pioneer to the Past: The Story of James Henry Breasted, Archaeologist*. Chicago: University of Chicago Press, 1943.

BROOKLYN MUSEUM. *Africa in Antiquity: The Arts of Ancient Nubia and the Sudan*. 2 vols. Exhibition catalogue. Brooklyn: Brooklyn Museum, 1978.

———. *Cleopatra's Egypt: Age of the Ptolemies*. Exhibition catalogue. Brooklyn: Brooklyn Museum, 1988.

CARROTT, RICHARD G. *The Egyptian Revival: Its Sources, Monuments, and Meaning*. Berkeley: University of California Press, 1978.

COONEY, JOHN D. *Egyptian Art in the Brooklyn Museum Collection*. Brooklyn: Brooklyn Museum, 1952.

D'AURIA, SUE, PETER LACOVARA, and CATHARINE H. ROEHRIG, eds. *Mummies and Magic: The Funerary Arts of Ancient Egypt*. Exhibition catalogue. Boston: Museum of Fine Arts, 1988.

DAVIS, THEODORE M. *The Tomb of Thutmosis IV*. Westminster, England, 1904.

DAWSON, WARREN R., and ERIC P. UPHILL. *Who Was Who in Egyptology*. 2d rev. ed. London: Egypt Exploration Society, 1972.

DORMAN, PETER F. *The Tombs of Senenmut: The Architecture and Decoration of Tombs 71 and 353*. The Metropolitan Museum of Art Egyptian Expedition 24. New York: Metropolitan Museum of Art, 1991.

DUNHAM, DOWS. *Two Royal Ladies of Meroe*. Communications to the Trustees 7. Boston: Museum of Fine Arts, 1924.

———. *The Royal Cemeteries of Kush*. 5 vols. Cambridge: Harvard University Press, 1950–63.

———. *The Egyptian Department and Its Excavations*. Boston: Museum of Fine Arts, 1958.

———. *The Barkal Temples*. Boston: Museum of Fine Arts, 1970.

———. *Excavations at Kerma, Part VI*. Boston: Museum of Fine Arts, 1982.

ELSASSER, ALBERT B. *Treasures of the Lowie Museum*. Exhibition catalogue. Berkeley: Robert H. Lowie Museum of Anthropology, University of California, 1968.

ELSASSER, ALBERT B., and VERA-MAE FREDRICKSON. *Ancient Egypt: An Exhibition at the Robert H. Lowie Museum of Anthropology of the University of California, Berkeley*. Exhibition catalogue. Berkeley: Robert H. Lowie Museum of Anthropology, University of California, 1966.

EMERY, W. B. *Archaic Egypt*. Harmondsworth: Penguin Books, 1961.

Expedition: The University Museum Magazine of Archaeology/Anthropology, University of Pennsylvania 21 (Winter 1979). Special issue: *The University Museum in Egypt.*

FAZZINI, RICHARD A. *Images for Eternity: Egyptian Art from Berkeley and Brooklyn.* Exhibition catalogue. San Francisco: Fine Arts Museums of San Francisco; Brooklyn: Brooklyn Museum, 1975.

FAZZINI, RICHARD A., ROBERT S. BIANCHI, JAMES F. ROMANO, and DONALD B. SPANEL. *Ancient Egyptian Art in the Brooklyn Museum.* Brooklyn: Brooklyn Museum; New York: Thames and Hudson, 1989.

FREED, RITA E. *Ramesses the Great: His Life and World.* Memphis: City of Memphis, 1987.

FRIEDMAN, FLORENCE D. *Beyond the Pharaohs: Egypt and the Copts in the 2nd to 7th centuries* A.D. Exhibition catalogue. Providence: Rhode Island School of Design, 1989.

GAZDA, ELAINE K. *Guardians of the Nile: Sculptures from Karanis in the Fayoum (c. 250 B.C.–A.D. 450).* Exhibition catalogue. Ann Arbor: Kelsey Museum of Archaeology, University of Michigan, 1978.

————, ed. *Karanis, an Egyptian Town in Roman Times: Discoveries of the University of Michigan Expedition to Egypt (1924–1935).* Exhibition catalogue. Ann Arbor: Kelsey Museum of Archaeology, University of Michigan, 1983.

HAYES, WILLIAM C. *Ostraka and Name Stones from the Tomb of Sen-Mut (No. 71) at Thebes.* New York: Metropolitan Museum of Art, 1942.

————. *The Scepter of Egypt.* 2 vols. New York: Metropolitan Museum of Art, 1953–59.

HAYNES, JOYCE L. *Nubia: Ancient Kingdoms of Africa.* Boston: Museum of Fine Arts, 1992.

HOFFMAN, MICHAEL A. *Egypt before the Pharaohs: The Prehistoric Foundations of Egyptian Civilization.* Rev. ed. Austin: University of Texas Press, 1991.

HÖLSCHER, UVO. *The Excavation of Medinet Habu.* 5 vols. Oriental Institute Publications 21, 41, 54, 55, 66. Chicago: University of Chicago Press, 1934–54.

J. PAUL GETTY MUSEUM. *In the Tomb of Nefertari: Conservation of Wall Paintings.* Exhibition catalogue. Malibu, Calif.: J. Paul Getty Museum; Marina del Rey, Calif.: Getty Conservation Institute, 1992.

JAMES, T. G. H. *Corpus of Hieroglyphic Inscriptions in the Brooklyn Museum.* Vol. 1. Wilbour Monographs 6. Brooklyn: Brooklyn Museum, 1974.

————, ed. *Excavating in Egypt: The Egypt Exploration Society, 1882–1982.* Chicago: University of Chicago Press, 1982.

KARIG, JOACHIM S., and KARL-THEODOR ZAUZICH. *Ägyptische Kunst aus dem Brooklyn Museum.* Exhibition catalogue. Berlin: Ägyptisches Museum, Staatliche Museen, 1978.

KOZLOFF, ARIELLE P., and BETSY BRYAN. *Egypt's Dazzling Sun: Amenhotep III and His World.* Exhibition catalogue. Cleveland: Cleveland Museum of Art, 1992.

LACOVARA, PETER, ed. *Ancient Egyptian Ceramics: Colloquium on Ancient Egyptian Ceramics II: Non-Typological Approaches to Ceramic Material.* Boston: Museum of Fine Arts, 1982.

LEE, CHRISTOPHER C. . . . *The Grand Piano Came by Camel: Arthur C. Mace, the Neglected Egyptologist.* Edinburgh: Mainstream Publishing, 1992.

LICHTHEIM, MIRIAM. *Ancient Egyptian Literature.* 3 vols. Berkeley and Los Angeles: University of California Press, 1973–80.

LUCAS, ALFRED. *Ancient Egyptian Materials and Industries.* 4th ed., rev. and enl. by J. R. Harris. London: Histories and Mysteries of Man, 1989.

LUTZ, HENRY FREDERICK. *Egyptian Tomb Steles and Offering Stones of the Museum of Anthropology and Ethnology of the University of California.* University of California Publications, Egyptian Archaeology 4. Leipzig: J. C. Hinrichs, 1927.

————. *Egyptian Statues and Statuettes in the Museum of Anthropology of the University of California.* University of California Publications, Egyptian Archaeology 5. Leipzig: J. C. Hinrichs, 1930.

METROPOLITAN MUSEUM OF ART. *Treasures of Tutankhamun.* Exhibition catalogue. New York: Metropolitan Museum of Art, 1976.

Metropolitan Museum of Art Bulletin 41 (Winter 1983–84). Special issue: *Egyptian Art.*

MUSEUM OF FINE ARTS, BOSTON. *Egypt's Golden Age: The Art of Living in the New Kingdom, 1558–1085 B.C.* Exhibition catalogue. Boston: Museum of Fine Arts, 1982.

NEEDLER, WINIFRED. *Predynastic and Archaic Egypt in the Brooklyn Museum.* Wilbour Monographs 9. Brooklyn: Brooklyn Museum, 1984.

O'CONNOR, DAVID. *Ancient Nubia: Egypt's Rival in Africa.* Exhibition catalogue. Philadelphia: University Museum, University of Pennsylvania, 1993.

PATCH, DIANA CRAIG. *Reflections of Greatness: Ancient Egypt at the Carnegie Museum of Natural History.* Pittsburgh: Carnegie Museum of Natural History, 1990.

PETRIE, W. M. FLINDERS. *The Royal Tombs of the Earliest Dynasties.* Part 2. London: Egypt Exploration Fund, 1901.

———. *Abydos.* Part 1. London: Egypt Exploration Fund, 1902.

———. *Seventy Years in Archaeology.* New York: Holt, 1932.

QUIBELL, J. E., and F. W. GREEN. *Hierakonpolis.* Part 2. London: Egyptian Research Account, 1902.

QUIBELL, J. E., and W. M. FLINDERS PETRIE. *Hierakonpolis.* Part 1. London: Egyptian Research Account, 1900.

RANDALL-MACIVER, DAVID, and CHARLES LEONARD WOOLLEY. *Buhen.* Philadelphia: University Museum, University of Pennsylvania, 1911.

REISNER, GEORGE A. *Excavations at Kerma, Parts I–III.* Harvard African Studies 5. Cambridge: Peabody Museum, Harvard University, 1923.

———. *Excavations at Kerma, Parts IV–V.* Harvard African Studies 6. Cambridge: Peabody Museum, Harvard University, 1923.

———. *Mycerinus: The Temples of the Third Pyramid at Giza.* Cambridge: Harvard University Press, 1931.

———. *A History of the Giza Necropolis.* 2 vols. Cambridge: Harvard University Press, 1942–55.

ROBERT H. LOWIE MUSEUM OF ANTHROPOLOGY. *Journey to the West: Death and the Afterlife in Ancient Egypt.* Exhibition catalogue. Berkeley: Robert H. Lowie Museum of Anthropology, University of California, 1979.

SALEH, MOHAMED, and HOURIG SOUROUZIAN. *Official Catalogue: The Egyptian Museum, Cairo.* Mainz: Philipp von Zabern, 1987.

SCHNEIDER, HANS. *Shabtis: An Introduction to the History of Ancient Egyptian Funerary Statuettes.* Vol. 1. Leiden: Rijksmuseum van Oudheden, 1977.

SCOTT, GERRY D., III. *Ancient Egyptian Art at Yale.* New Haven: Yale University Art Gallery, 1986.

SIMPSON, WILLIAM K., and WHITNEY M. DAVIS, eds. *Studies in Ancient Egypt, the Aegean, and the Sudan: Essays in Honor of Dows Dunham.* Boston: Museum of Fine Arts, 1981.

SMITH, WILLIAM S. *A History of Egyptian Painting and Sculpture in the Old Kingdom.* London: Oxford University Press, 1946.

———. *Ancient Egypt as Represented in the Museum of Fine Arts, Boston.* 6th ed., rev. Boston: Museum of Fine Arts, 1960.

———. *The Art and Architecture of Ancient Egypt.* 2d rev. ed. Baltimore and Harmondsworth: Penguin Books, 1981.

SPANEL, DONALD B. *Through Ancient Eyes: Egyptian Portraiture.* Exhibition catalogue. Birmingham, Ala.: Birmingham Museum of Art, 1988.

TRIGGER, BRUCE G., BARRY J. KEMP, DAVID O'CONNOR, and ALAN B. LLOYD. *Ancient Egypt: A Social History.* Cambridge: Cambridge University Press, 1983.

WILBOUR, CHARLES EDWIN. *Travels in Egypt (December 1880 to May 1891): Letters of Charles Edwin Wilbour.* Edited by Jean Capart. Brooklyn: Brooklyn Museum, 1936.

WILLIAMS, BRUCE B. *Excavations between Abu Simbel and the Sudan Frontier.* Part 5, C-Group, Pan Grave, and Kerma Remains at Adindan Cemeteries T, K, U, and J. Oriental Institute Nubian Expedition 5. Chicago: Oriental Institute, University of Chicago, 1983.

———. *Excavations between Abu Simbel and the Sudan Frontier.* Part 1, The A-Group Royal Cemetery at Qustul: Cemetery L. Oriental Institute Nubian Expedition 3. Chicago: Oriental Institute of the University of Chicago, 1986.

WILKINSON, CHARLES K., and MARSHA HILL. *Egyptian Wall Paintings: The Metropolitan Museum of Art's Collection of Facsimiles.* New York: Metropolitan Museum of Art, 1983.

WILSON, JOHN A. *Signs and Wonders upon Pharaoh: A History of American Egyptology.* Chicago: University of Chicago Press, 1964.

WINLOCK, HERBERT E. *Excavations at Deir el Bahri, 1911–1931.* New York: Macmillan, 1942.

WOOLLEY, CHARLES LEONARD, and DAVID RANDALL-MACIVER. *Karanog: The Romano-Nubian Cemetery.* 2 vols. Philadelphia: University Museum, University of Pennsylvania, 1910.

Acknowledgments

This exhibition and catalogue are the result of more than five years of planning by a host of individuals committed to the advancement of American Egyptology. At a 1989 meeting of the executive committee of the American Research Center in Egypt (ARCE), Bruce Ludwig, ARCE board member, active supporter of the Los Angeles County Museum of Art, and patron of American archaeological expeditions to Egypt, proposed an exhibition that would highlight the contributions of American institutions to the "discovery" of ancient Egypt. Recognizing that American Egyptology had never been the subject of an exhibition and that a wealth of excavated objects reside in American collections, the museum and ARCE, represented by Executive Director Terry Walz, agreed to organize the project jointly. With the collaboration of four primary consultants—David O'Connor (then president of ARCE), Gerry D. Scott, III, Terry Walz, and myself—planning of the exhibition rapidly moved forward.

Walz, assisted in New York by Catherine Clyne, Robert Arbuckle, Livia Alexander, and Amira Khattab, organized a 1992 planning conference sponsored by the National Endowment for the Humanities and has been a valuable consultant at all stages of the project. Cocurator Gerry D. Scott, III, of the San Antonio Museum of Art, conferred with me in considering objects from American collections of Egyptian art for inclusion in the exhibition, and he contributed an introductory essay and numerous object entries to the catalogue. David O'Connor, who recently moved from the University of Pennsylvania to become Lila Acheson Wallace Professor of Art at the Institute of Fine Arts, New York University, was a valued adviser in the planning of the exhibition, and he authored an essay on New Kingdom archaeology for the companion volume to this catalogue. Peter Lacovara of the Museum of Fine Arts, Boston, provided research assistance throughout the project and offered much-needed support. Richard Fazzini of the Brooklyn Museum added invaluable curatorial advice, as did Dorothea Arnold, Metropolitan Museum of Art, New York, and Rita Freed, Museum of Fine Arts, Boston.

The crafting of a complex catalogue with twenty contributing authors demanded the attention of a team of able professionals. Mitch Tuchman, the museum's editor in chief, gave the green flag to this ambitious book project, supervised the editing, and arranged distribution plans. Suzanne Kotz worked as the primary editor, coaxing the diverse writing styles of the contributors into a consistent and accurate manuscript. Karen Jacobson edited portions of the catalogue, compiled the bibliography, and completed editing tasks through the production phase. With great style and determination, Pamela Patrusky designed the book under pressure of close deadlines. Photographer Peter Brenner traveled to Egypt in early 1995 to make the eloquent site photographs that grace many pages of the catalogue. In addition he photographed objects from the Oriental Institute of the University of Chicago. Cathryn Tagliani Croall of the Department of Ancient and Islamic Art took on the enormous task of entering editorial changes into the computer and provided general project assistance. Hours of time were contributed by department interns and volunteers Nicole Hansen, Meg Abraham, Doris Bryant, Carolyn Estill, Marjorie MacIntosh, and Romita Ray, and by Hélène Cooper, Carol Epstein, and Maggie Murray of the Ancient Art Council. Nancy Carcione, Jim Drobka, Carol Pelosi, and Matthew Stevens of the publications and graphics departments offered additional assistance.

All the catalogue authors are to be credited for their scholarship. Bruce G. Trigger and Gerry D. Scott, III, made original contributions to the study of American Egyptology in their essays. The authors of the catalogue entries, whose names are listed on the contents page, supplied valuable information regarding the objects under their care at their respective institutions, and some entries represent the culmination of longtime research, such as those by Yvonne Markowitz on ancient jewelry and Diana Wolfe Larkin's discussion of a monumental Egyptian gateway.

Photo archivists and researchers at a number of institutions provided valuable assistance with photographic materials. These include John Larson and Lisa Snider of the Oriental Institute, University of Chicago; Douglas Haller and Charles Kline, University of Pennsylvania Museum of Archaeology and Anthropology, Philadelphia; James P. Allen, Susan Allen, and Marsha Hill, Metropolitan Museum of Art, New York; Joan Knudson, Phoebe A. Hearst Museum of Anthropology, University of California, Berkeley; Peter Der Manuelian, Karen Otis, and Mary Sluskonis, Museum of Fine Arts, Boston; Karen Sinsheimer, Santa Barbara Museum of Art; and Patricia Svoboda and Linda Thrift, National Portrait Gallery, Washington, D.C. Carolyn Brown, Stephen White, and Michael Wilson generously lent photographs to the exhibition catalogue, and Egyptologists Matthew Adams and Timothy Kendall contributed personal photographs. Museum photographers Dean Brown, Brooklyn Museum; Gene Prince, Hearst Museum; and John Woolf, Museum of Fine Arts, Boston, made an extra effort to enhance object photography from their institutions. Other individuals coordinated object photography and loan documents, including Sylvia Smith Duggan, Janice Klein, Robin Meador-Woodruff, Guillermo Ovalle, and Ray Tindel. Curators assisting with loan requests include James P. Allen, Betsy Bryan, Joan Knudson, Peter Lacovara, Kurt Luckner, Susan Matheson, William Peck, James Richardson III, and Donald B. Spanel.

Conservation projects were undertaken by several institutions to prepare objects for extended travel. At the Museum of Fine Arts, Boston, Arthur Beale supervised the conservation of the Coptos temple gateway, assisted by Jean-Louis Lachevre and AQW Architecture. Kenneth S. Moser and Ellen Pearlstein supervised conservation of objects at the Brooklyn Museum; Joan Gardner conserved an object from the Carnegie Museum of Natural History, Pittsburgh; and Tamsen Fuller and Rosie Saraga of Northwest Objects Conservation prepared loan objects from both the University of Pennsylvania Museum and the Hearst Museum. In addition, Madeleine Fang of the Hearst Museum completed conservation treatments for the exhibition.

At the Los Angeles County Museum of Art, a number of individuals contributed directly to the success of the exhibition: Ronald Bratton, chief deputy director; Arthur Owens, assistant director, operations, and members of his staff, including Lawrence Waung, Mee Mee Leong, Tim Anderson, and Jeff Haskin; Ann Roland, Mark Mitchell, and Deanna Navarette of the business office; Leslie Bowman, John Passi, Beverley Sabo, and Cecily MacInnes of the exhibitions department; Stephanie Barron, coordinator of curatorial affairs; Pieter Meyers, Victoria Blyth-Hill, John Twilly, Steve Colton, Maureen Russell, John Hirx, and Don Menveg of the conservation department. The development department helped to build the essential financial base for the project, and Melody Kanschat, Tom Jacobson, Stephanie Dyas, Dana Hutt, Greg Murphy, and Talbot Wells assisted at various stages. The media and public affairs department, headed by Barbara Pflaumer, with support from Sarah Gaddis and Janine Vigus, coordinated the public information programs. Deborah Barlow, John Barone, and Anne Diederick assisted with library research requests. Jane Burrell wrote the exhibition brochure and, assisted by Jenny Siegenthaler and Elizabeth Waters, coordinated the education programs for the exhibition. Exhibition travel and registration were overseen by Renée Montgomery and Tamra Yost. Bernard Kester devised elegant installation plans for the exhibition at several stages, including preliminary designs for grant-writing purposes, and supervised the final installation.

Two additional venues have expanded the reach of this important exhibition. Sidney Goldstein, associate director of the Saint Louis Art Museum, embraced the project from its early planning phase, and Theodore Celenko, curator of African art at the Indianapolis Museum of Art, has been equally enthusiastic.

We are thankful for the generous support of the May Department Stores Company, Gily AG of Switzerland, the National Endowment for the Arts, and the National Endowment for the Humanities. In addition, Bruce Ludwig and Pamela and Benson Harer Jr. contributed funding for initial research leading to the exhibition and catalogue.

NANCY THOMAS
Curator, Ancient and Islamic Art

Lenders to the Exhibition

The Brooklyn Museum

Carnegie Museum of Natural History, Pittsburgh

Detroit Institute of the Arts

Field Museum of Natural History, Chicago

Johns Hopkins University Archaeological Collection, Baltimore

Kelsey Museum of Archaeology, the University of Michigan, Ann Arbor

The Metropolitan Museum of Art, New York

Museum of Fine Arts, Boston

The Oriental Institute, the University of Chicago

Peabody Museum of Natural History, Yale University, New Haven

Phoebe A. Hearst Museum of Anthropology, University of California, Berkeley

Special Collections Library, the University of Michigan, Ann Arbor

The Toledo Museum of Art

The University of Pennsylvania Museum of Archaeology

and Anthropology, Philadelphia

Index

Numbers in *italics* refer to pages with illustrations.

Photo Credits

The works of art in this volume are subject to claims of copyright in the United States of America and throughout the world. None may be reproduced in any form without the written permission of the owners.

Unless an acknowledgment appears below, the photographs in this volume have been provided by the owners of the works of art or by the Los Angeles County Museum of Art. We are grateful to all those who supplied photographs for this book.

The Academy of Motion Picture
    Arts and Sciences: figs. 1, 3.

Matthew Adams: pp. 11, 117, 157.

The American Research Center
    in Egypt: fig. 41.

Peter Brenner: pp. 4, 12, 14;
    fig. 39; pp. 77, 173, 256, 276.

The Brooklyn Museum:
    figs. 15, 16, 18, 19, 31, 32.

Carolyn Brown © 1988: p. 15.

The Church of Jesus Christ of
    Latter-day Saints, Historical
    Department: fig. 2.

Dementi-Foster Studios,
    Richmond: fig. 7.

Egypt Exploration Fund, Archive
    Photo (from Edouard
    Naville, *Bubastis* [London,
    1891], pl. 5): p. 97.

The Field Museum, Chicago:
    cat. no. 7 (neg. nos. A95210
    [front], A95211 [back]).

Tamsen Fuller: p. 118.

Raymond Johnson: p. 168
    (drawing).

Kelsey Museum Archives:
    fig. 40; pp. 223, 229.

Timothy Kendall: pp. 17
    (three images), 203.

David Kiphuth: p. 88 (drawing).

Diana Wolfe Larkin and John
    Williamson: p. 218 (drawing).

Aaron M. Levin: cat. no. 2.

Manuscripts Print Collection,
    Special Collections Depart-
    ment, University of Virginia
    Library: fig. 12.

Yvonne Markowitz: pp. 112,
    241 (drawings).

The Maryland Historical
    Society: fig. 14.

The Metropolitan Museum
    of Art, Department of
    Egyptian Art: p. 36.

The Metropolitan Museum
    of Art Egyptian Expedition:
    p. 13; figs. 10, 33–37;
    pp. 149, 150.

The Museum of the City of
    New York, Gift of Astor
    Lenox and Tilden Founda-
    tion: fig. 6.

The Museum of the City of New
    York, Print Archives: fig. 5.

Museum of Fine Arts,
    Boston: figs. 22–25, 30;
    pp. 137, 161, 164, 221.

New Haven Colony Historical
    Society: fig. 8.

The Oriental Institute of the
    University of Chicago:
    figs. 9, 21, 38; pp. 114
    (drawing), 205.

Phoebe A. Hearst Museum of
    Anthropology, University of
    California, Berkeley: fig. 29;
    pp. 129, 138.

The Redwood Library and
    Athenaeum: fig. 20.

Peggy Tenison: pp. 80, 81;
    cat. no. 52.

Nancy Thomas: pp. 2, 3, 16, 89.

The United States Department
    of the Treasury, Historical
    Resource Center, Bureau of
    Engraving and Printing: fig. 4.

The United States Naval
    Academy: fig. 17.

The University of Pennsylvania
    Museum of Archaeology
    and Anthropology,
    Philadelphia: fig. 26
    (neg. no. G5-35515),
    fig. 27 (neg. no. G3-38942),
    fig. 28 (neg. no. S4-138640);
    pp. 157 (drawing), 187
    (neg. no. T4-556).

Michael Wilson: fig. 13.

EDITORS
Suzanne Kotz and
Karen Jacobson

DESIGNER
Pamela Patrusky

PHOTOGRAPHIC SUPERVISION
Peter Brenner

PRODUCTION ASSISTANCE
Theresa Velázquez

MAPS
Anne Gauldin,
Gauldin/Farrington Design